I0029161

Sociology
of Race and
Ethnicity

Bodies out of Place

Sociology of Race and Ethnicity

SERIES EDITORS

David L. Brunsma
David G. Embrick

SERIES ADVISORY BOARD

Margaret Abraham
Elijah Anderson
Eduardo Bonilla-Silva
Philomena Essed
James Fenelon
Evelyn Nakano Glenn
Tanya Golash-Boza
David Theo Goldberg
Patricia Hill Collins
José Itzigsohn
Amanda Lewis
Michael Omi
Victor Rios
Mary Romero

Bodies out of Place

Theorizing Anti-blackness in U.S. Society

Barbara Harris Combs

The University of Georgia Press

ATHENS

Sociology of Race and
Ethnicity web page

© 2022 by the University of Georgia Press
Athens, Georgia 30602
www.ugapress.org
All rights reserved

Set in 10.5/13.5 Garamond Premier Pro Regular
by Kaelin Chappell Broaddus

Most University of Georgia Press titles are
available from popular e-book vendors.

Printed digitally

Library of Congress Cataloging-in-Publication Data

Names: Combs, Barbara (Barbara Harris), author.
Title: Bodies out of place : theorizing anti-blackness
    in U.S. society / Barbara Harris Combs.
Description: Athens : The University of Georgia Press,
    [2022] | Series: Sociology of race and ethnicity |
    Includes bibliographical references and index.
Identifiers: LCCN 2021058919 | ISBN 9780820362366
    (hardback) | ISBN 9780820362359 (paperback)
    | ISBN 9780820362373 (ebook)
Subjects: LCSH: African Americans—Social conditions.
    | African Americans—Violence against. | Racism—
    United States. | Human body (Philosophy) | Place
    (Philosophy) | United States—Race relations.
Classification: LCC E185.86 .C5819 2022 | DDC
    305.896/073—dc23/eng/20220222
LC record available at https://lccn.loc.gov/2021058919

To Darrell and our wonderful children—
Breann, Jason, and Nia, the baby we lost.
Nia, thank you for teaching me the invaluable
lesson that purpose (the meaning of your name)
never dies.

CONTENTS

ACKNOWLEDGMENTS

I reflect on all the people who somehow contributed to this book. First, I give all glory and praise to my Lord and Savior Jesus Christ. He put a song in my heart and gave me the courage to sing it. God also put a number of people in my path who have helped me to get here. Ironically, some of them are not even known to me. I am profoundly grateful to the anonymous reviewers of this book. Their comments reflect countless hours of sacrifice and commitment. Even if the academy does not recognize the import of that labor, I do. I commit to helping others do the same. Someday I hope to publicly recognize them and their sacrifice. I am awestruck by their willingness to share their time and intellect. This work is immeasurably improved because of them.

I am an exhorter. I love lifting other people up. It is part of my nature. It is rewarding work, but it can also be exhausting and thankless, especially as exhorters are seldom likewise the beneficiaries of encouragement. That is probably why I am especially appreciative of other encouragers. As they say: "Game recognize game." I see you, Zandria Felice Robinson, and I am so pleased and honored to call you my friend. You are a beyond measure treasure, and, despite your own dazzlingly bright light and the warmth that emanates from it, you are always ready to lift others and let them shine without fear of it diminishing you. Thank you also to Kirsten Dellinger for your unwavering faith in me and ready willingness to share some the burdens of others, so they did not have to carry it alone. Thank you to my Sistah Scholar circle from the University of Mississippi—Deirdre Cooper Owens, Shennette Garrett-Scott, Jodi Skipper, and Mikki Harris. Thank you to my "Cos" (community of scholars) from Clark Atlanta University—Obie Clayton, Danille Taylor, Eve Graves, Maurita Poole, Corinne Warrener, Teri Platt, E. Ken Shell, Kenya Jones, and Leonissa Johnson. Everyone should have a group of cheerleaders like you in their lives. Other cheerleaders include my OpEd Project family (Katie Orenstein, Anya Tudisco, Njeri Mathis Rutledge, Mary Curtis, and too many others to name—you are so brilliant!), the Green Family (John, Eleanor, and Edith-Marie), Kirk and Willa Johnson, Leslie Hossfeld, Adia Harvey Wingfield., J Shim, and Anthony James Williams. Thank you all for providing me with roots and wings.

Thank you to Joe Feagin for sitting with me one evening at the annual American Sociological Association meeting while I was fretting over a review and helping me to see the gift in it. Thank you also to our dear friend Carly Jennings for encouraging me to show it to you. That encounter made a huge difference in my life, and I will be forever grateful. Shout out to my Racial Democracy Crime and Justice Network family, including my mentors, Charis Kubrin and Delores Jones-Brown, and my 2016 Summer Research Institute cohort members—Annika Anderson, Jamien Cunningham, Mimi Kim, Vanessa Panfil, Gabriella Sanchez, Mercedes Valadez, and Robert Vargas. I especially thank Waverly Duck, who despite the fact that he knew little more about me than that, like him, I was a member of the RDCJN, gave me copies of his own book proposals to help me in crafting my own. Even now, I am amazed by that gift.

Thank you to the Faculty Resource Network at NYU for their support and to my mentor, Jill Conte. I especially appreciate UNCF/Mellon Programs and the James Weldon Johnson Institute at Emory University for funding and otherwise supporting this work. I express my heartfelt appreciation and admiration to both Cynthia Neal Spence and Andra Gillespie, the respective directors of these organizations.

Finally, in the Hebrew, the name "David" means beloved. That seems particularly fitting. David Brunsma and David Embrick, thank you for shepherding me and always encouraging me to write the book I wanted and not the one I thought others would support. You are a beloved gift to me, to the academy, to our discipline, and to the world.

Bodies out of Place

INTRODUCTION

Yet do I marvel at this curious thing:
To make a poet black, and bid him sing!

—COUNTEE CULLEN, "Yet Do I Marvel"

This book developed out of a general inquiry born from two of my social identities. As a sociologist, I want to understand the social world—perhaps even contribute to making it better. As a Black woman who is married to a Black man and the mother of two Black children, I want to protect them from that world. Reasoned rational inquiry is the tool of the social scientist. In many ways, I use that tool as a Black woman as well to safely navigate diverse spaces and places, but in that capacity it is not the only tool in my kit. I am equipped with what W. E. B. Du Bois terms "second-sight."[1] This second-sight affords me a keen awareness of the social world, which is born of my twoness: I am Black and American, Black and female. My historical past and contemporary present suggest that I am at once hypervisible yet invisible, valuable as property yet presumed to be propertyless, to be used yet not useful. I am a proud Black woman in a world that values neither women nor Black people, and while, to quote Audre Lorde, "the master's tools will never dismantle the master's house [of racial oppression]," 450 years of Black survival have taught me how to use a few tools of my own.[2]

Some of my tools are visceral. In encounter after encounter, I hypothesize about people's responses and interactions with me and toward me. I know the felt experience of race and racial oppression, and my sense of self-preservation compels me to trust these instincts if I want to remain safe. But safety is not my only aim. So too is freedom.[3] Navigating the two states—safety and freedom—can result in a freedom amid constraint.

We live in what Simone Browne, author of *Dark Matters: On the Surveillance of Blackness*, terms a "racialized disciplinary society," where Black bodies are subject to constant surveillance and other schema whose aim is social control over the group. Browne argues that surveillance is structured by processes of racialization.[4] Reviewing *Dark Matters*, Megan Wood writes, "Racializing surveillance is Browne's term for the ways in which technologies, policies, and practices of surveillance are ordered by and reify boundaries, borders, and bodies along discriminatory and deleterious racial lines."[5] Though invisible, the racial lines created through these processes are real, and they influence human interactions and outcomes.

I am, at heart, a symbolic interactionist—someone who believes that we are social products and that patterned, organized interactions often emerge amid human actors based on their responses to symbolic identity markers. Black skin is one of those markers, and the reality is that the embodied experience of those who wear it is different than that of Whites. With this knowledge, I do not take mobility for granted. Safely navigating social spaces and physically moving from one location to another is something few Blacks in America have the luxury of taking for granted. Over the last few years, my husband and I have been compelled to have that conversation with our son and daughter on several occasions—too many occasions and too many victims as young as or younger than our own children. The assaults (some resulting in death) on Trayvon Martin, Jordan Davis, Tamir Rice, Oumou Kanoute, Martese Johnson, Dajeeria Becton, and countless others necessitated it.

Black Identity in a White World

My husband and I wanted our children to understand the centrality of race to their lives and the reality of racism. It may surprise non-Blacks to realize that race (or "the race card" as those deflecting their own personal responsibility and culpability in human exchanges often call it) is not the first factor many Blacks consider in dealing with the slights we face daily. Instead, unlike our paler brothers and sisters, we go through the extra effort of carefully weighing and considering other explanatory concepts, including what, if anything, we might have done to prompt an offense. It is an exercise emerging out of the deeply ingrained politics of respectability instilled in us. It is only after this process that we often settle on the historical reality—I know what this is; it is because I am Black.

In *Suspicion Nation*, author and attorney Lisa Bloom outlines how George Zimmerman coded Trayvon Martin's intersecting identities—male, Black, and young adult—to read him as suspicious and up to no good. Zimmerman then used this nebulous characterization to justify following Martin. "Suspicious" became code for Black.[6] Zimmerman's problematization of the teenage Martin had deadly consequences for the latter. My children wanted to know why Zimmerman thought Martin looked suspicious. In the case of Michael Dunn's second trial for shooting and killing 17-year-old Jordan Davis, my son, who was then around Davis's age, wondered why it was so hard to get a conviction and how someone could shoot repeatedly into a crowded vehicle and then just drive off.

There were countless other questions. As a family, we watched an episode of the sitcom *black-ish* together, which wrestled with the same queries. Soon the questions stopped, but our children never asked the most important question: "Could this happen to me?" I think our son knew the answer. So did we. Our daughter flirted with the fiction that this is something that happens to Black boys and men, but she was soon robbed of that confidence. Still, she was seven years younger than her brother, so we focused on him. We gave him tools to navigate exchanges with the police, and we warned him to make good choices about the people with whom he associated. When a high school administrator caught and punished two White friends for smoking weed, I had another version of the talk with our son. We talked about the dangers of drugs in general, but the real point I needed him to get was this: If he was ever the only Black kid riding in a car with the White kids, and they got pulled over by the police, officers might presume the marijuana belonged to him. As self-interested beings, many of his "friends" might corroborate the same. The "truth" would not matter. Only perception matters, and, as any good symbolic interactionist will tell you, perception is reality.

Abstract racial oppression was not difficult for my children to grasp, but the realization that it could happen to them was. I understood their reticence. After all, they live in a society that makes vehement ideological claims to color-blindness. But what people say and what they do are not always consistent. It was a sobering time, but it was also an illuminating one. I was teaching at the University of Mississippi—an institution steeped in its own entrenched history of racial oppression—and I was desperately trying to make sense of the racism I saw all around me. I relied on the tools I had honed as a social scientist, and I began to take "field notes" about my observations. I would reflect on them later. Soon I was building a theory. One by one, the tenets of the theory I advance in this book unfolded.

I term my framework Bodies out of Place (BOP). I first used it in an article, "Black (and Brown) Bodies out of Place: Towards a Theoretical Examination of Systematic Voter Suppression in the United States," which appeared in the journal *Critical Sociology*.[7] The article scrutinized the rise of voter identification laws and attacks against the Voting Rights Act as examples of political violence meant to frustrate Black progress and push Black (and brown) bodies back into a position

of subservience to Whites.[8] Political violence has always been a useful tool in oppression, but it is certainly not the only tool. Soon I began to see the utility of my
theory for understanding other forms of violence against Black bodies and how
the aim of each form of violence was the social control, sanction, and subjugation
of the group.[9]

I am a product of two Black parents raised under Jim Crow, the name given
to the set of laws that enforced legal segregation. This gripping system simultaneously forced them to be strong and robbed them of strength. Their lives and sacrifice compel me to tell this story. In many ways, I feel called to do so. A smile breaks
out over my face as I recall that my deceased father's childhood name for me was
Bop-de-Bop. There it was, BOP. Five decades before I began to write about it, my
father called me by the name of the theory I advance. This is his story too.

Toward the tail end of the Great Migration, my parents moved from Alabama
to Ohio. They sought better opportunities. They believed life—for them and their
children—would be better in the next place. But, like in the old places they fled,
in the new places to which they migrated their Black bodies remained subject to
continued surveillance and threat of violent attack. Jim Crow–like attitudes did
not know or respect state boundaries. This realization is, perhaps, not surprising,
especially to those who recognize, as Du Bois did, that blackness is devalued across
the globe.[10]

Some 50 years apart, my parents and I came to the same discovery. Despite
Black gains, the new social structure looks and operates a lot like the old one.
Blacks today can attain heights not permitted under the old system with this one
exception: Blacks belong in subservient positions to Whites in America.[11] White
supremacy is about maintaining a social order with Whites on top, and the regulation or control of bodies is key to that. In this stratification system, Black bodies
are on the bottom.[12] This hierarchy is totalitarian in nature; it undergirds and preserves White supremacy, and it is so deeply ingrained in society that even subordinated groups can be complicit in maintaining and defending this order.

Jim Crow 2.0

Today's Jim Crow–like attitudes are embodied in fixed ideas about where Blacks
belong, when, with whom, and in what position. These ideas communicate "a hierarchical racial order that legitimates anti-Black racism. Any Black person outside his or her societally designated "place" is presumed to be a malevolent actor
and must be pushed back into position. I call this the pushback, and violence—in
the various forms it takes—is used to accomplish it. It is an attempt to police, preserve, and maintain distinct White physical and social space. The idea of distinct

Black and White space evokes Jim Crow. Although most prominent in the South, Jim Crow existed in the North and West too.[13] Jim Crow mandated separation in every part of life, including housing, education, theaters, restaurants, public parks, and more. The separate facilities, which the U.S. Supreme Court affirmed in its 1896 decision in *Plessy v. Ferguson*, were always inferior and helped institutionalize the total subservience of Black life.[14]

Today's policing of Black bodies extends to a scrutiny of the most mundane daily activities. The continuing nature of the attacks has the aim and sometimes the effect of constraining Black mobility and attainment on both an agentic and structural level. What looks like choice must be scrutinized. For example, homophily (i.e., a preference for sameness, often expressed by the notion that birds of a feather flock together) does play a role in the choices people make. However, given the impact various organizational policies and practices, including mortgage redlining, blockbusting, steering, exclusionary zoning, and predatory policing, have had on Black lives, it stretches the imagination to view all the housing and employment choices Black people make today as purely voluntary. Additionally, gains in school integration achieved post–civil rights movement have stagnated.[15] As a result, balkanization occurs consciously and subconsciously. It happens under actual and perceived threat of physical force, and under socioeconomic or other social and psychological pulls, to Black communities, schools, houses of worship, and other social groupings. This contributes to and reinforces ingrained Jim Crow–like attitudes that there are distinct White and Black spaces.[16]

I believe that to understand continuing violence against Black bodies, physical and social place have to be a central part of the analysis. My inquiry is both visceral and cerebral. Chiefly, I ask what role does the desire to maintain a place-based social structure (as a physical and social construct) play in the continuing violence perpetrated against Black bodies?[17] In the soul-stirring ballad "What Are You Gonna Tell Her?," performed by Mickey Guyton, the listener is reminded of the difficulty of explaining something that you yourself do not understand.[18] Before I could have a meaningful conversation with my children about the roots of continuing racism in society, I had to make sense of it for myself. Now I have the same conversation with the readers of this book.

Conclusion

I approach this book as if I am having a conversation with a friend, actually a conversation with all my friends. My friends come from a variety of backgrounds. That has always been the case. My close circle is less racially diverse than it was for the first three decades of my life, but in a host of other respects it still has quite a bit of variety. When I was in college, I remember inviting people in my friend group to a party. I had been involved in student government, the Black student association, programs for peace and justice, the newspaper, and the thespian society. I invited all my friends. It was just before the Christmas break, so we had ample reason to celebrate. The party was an unqualified disaster. Every group had a different interpretation of the word "party." Some of my friends thought it meant music and dancing, so they began to move all of the furniture in the apartment to make room for dancing. Some brought Christmas ornaments to decorate the tree, and there was also popcorn for stringing. Some of my other friends thought "party" meant food, so they ate the popcorn and irritated the group that was trying to string it. Some of my friends thought "party" meant liquor, so they opened my cabinets to find some to put in the hot apple cider and cinnamon sticks heating on the stove. Some of my friends thought "party" meant poetry reading, and while they were sharing their latest creations or spouting off someone else's, another group was in a corner laughing at them. I have never forgotten that experience. There have been many times when I tried to understand it. I guess I have always been a social scientist.

Despite that disastrous party experience, I write this book to all my friends. I even write to the ones I have never met. The stakes are too high and time too short for me to have polite conversations with each individually. Having said that, sometimes in this book I am speaking directly to a particular set of friends. Sometimes I am speaking *about* a particular set of friends. Such shifts will be readily discernible for the careful reader (friend), but I feel compelled to caution everyone else.

PART I

Connecting the Dots

CHAPTER 1

Testify

and when we speak we are afraid
our words will not be heard
nor welcomed
but when we are silent
we are still afraid

So it is better to speak.

—AUDRE LORDE, "A Litany for Survival"

A letter from Frederick Douglass to Ida B. Wells appears as the preface to Wells's seminal *The Red Record: Tabulated Statistics and Alleged Causes of Lynching in the United States*. Douglass writes, "You give us what you know and testify from actual knowledge. You have dealt with the facts with cool, painstaking fidelity, and left those naked and uncontradicted facts to speak for themselves."[1] In these pages, I attempt to do the same.

The central argument of this book and the theory I advance in it is that White people react with anti-Black violence—and then justify, excuse, and ignore that brutality—when they encounter perceived Black bodies "out of place." Black bodies are often identified as out of place when they are in physical and social spaces where White people believe Blacks do not normatively belong. It is an issue of boundaries or location or both. The dominant White racial group responds to out-of-place Black bodies with the "pushback," activity that takes the form of various attacks on Black bodies and their psyche. Pushback is a central component of anti-blackness, and it is a core dynamic in the related system of structural racism. Surveillance is the most common form of pushback, but the strike may also come via threatened or actual acts of physical, sociocultural, economic, political, and psychic violence on Blacks. This hegemonic White-sponsored violence seeks to constrain Black people's well-being and advancement by diminishing our agency, oppressing us structurally, and outright harming and killing us. Despite this, Black people continue to persistently and creatively resist constraint and to name the oppression and the oppressors. Black resistance, such as the declaration that Black lives matter, challenges and rejects White supremacist ideology. Denials of the existence of structural racism, rejection of the construct of White privilege, and a concomitant rise of overt anti-Black actions grew during the U.S. presidential administration of Donald Trump. These continue to reverberate. As award-winning writer Amanda Gorman implored in her Inauguration poem, "The Hill We Climb," "We must end this uncivil war."[2] To be clear, it will not end until structural racism does.

Why Focus on Bodies?

Racism as practice is often invisible, but it is performed on individuals and groups in society with harmful consequences that can be seen.[3] Howard Winant states it this way: "In its most advanced forms, indeed, it [racism as practice] has no perpetrators; it is a nearly invisible, taken-for granted, 'common-sense' feature of everyday life and global social structure."[4] Racial identity is about the body. In *Racial Formation in the United States*, scholars Michael Omi and Howard Winant define race as "a social construct which signifies and symbolizes social conflicts and interests by referring to different types of human bodies."[5] Examining the treatment of racialized bodies in society crystallizes the existence of a social system of advantage and disadvantage based on race.

We are embodied beings. Our bodies—individual and collective—shape and are shaped by society, and the form those bodies take is both highly politicized and socially regulated.[6] Not only can bodies be governed, many consent for their bodies to be governed. Critical social theorist Michel Foucault terms this biopolitics, the exertion of power over one's life.[7] It is important to recognize that though all bodies are subject to regulatory and disciplinary control, some are more imperiled than others.[8] Intersecting vulnerabilities are connected to particular embodiments, especially as it relates to matters like race, gender, class, age, sexuality, size, and physical ability. These variations are used to create strata and, in the process, hierarchies of human difference. The classifications then get mapped onto subaltern bodies and are used to subject them to discrimination. Therefore, the bodily lens is fruitful, for it aids in the recognition that perception matters and these perceptions have a profound impact on how people act, interact, and react to others. A lens on the body is useful for studying both the structural objectification of the body as a fleshy thing and the lived experience of the social body as mediated through the personal and institutional experiences of individuals and groups in society.

A bodily focus is also attentive to place, a central concept in this analysis. Racial enclosures and racial enclosure policies—like the plantation, segregation, the ghetto, and prison—provide a place-based mechanism for regulation of the body.[9] In *Regulating Bodies: Essays in Medical Sociology*, Bryan Turner describes modern society's movement toward a "somatic society...structured around regulating bodies." In the process Turner outlines, the body is the central site on which political and cultural power gets enacted. A bodily focus also recognizes the agency of bodies. The body is not just stripped of power. The body *is* power: it is "simultaneously [a site of] constraint and resistance." Not only are bodies regulated, says Turner, but so too are " spaces between bodies [and] the interfaces between bodies, societies and cultures.... The somatic society is...crucially, perhaps critically, structured around regulating bodies."[10] Control of bodies is accomplished through policies and practices administered by legal, religious, educational, familial, medical, and other institutions, often through the actions of their individual members. So a focus on the body permits analysis of both the individual and population level. It also incorporates the institutional level—public and private.

Consistent with the focus I propose, throughout this book I use the term or phrase "Black bodies" (or "the Black body"). The term is not meant to objectify or debase. Instead, I use it to foreground that the epidermal trace of Black skin is what marks the Black body as other. This feature triggers actions (motivated by ignorance of the other) manifested in hatred, fear, and loathing. As cultural historian Harvey Young explains in *Embodying Black Experience: Stillness, Critical Memory, and the Black Body*, "It is the black body and not a particular, flesh-and-blood body that is the target of a racializing projection."[11]

The Black Body as Other

The Black body is presumed as other. As such, it is believed to be inferior. This presumption privileges whiteness. I argue that the disciplining of Black bodies—in schools, policing, and public or private space—is tolerated as a necessary means to instill this hierarchy into the subjugated. In *Black Bodies, White Gazes: The Continuing Significance of Race*, philosopher George Yancy explains: "The Black body [has been treated] as an entity that is to be feared, disciplined, and relegated to those marginalized, imprisoned and segregated spaces that restrict Black bodies from 'disturbing' the tranquility of white life, white comfort, white embodiment, and white being." This categorization is central to White supremacy. Yancy continues:

> The history of the Black body in North America is fundamentally linked to the history of whiteness, primarily as whiteness is expressed in the form of fear, hatred, sadism, brutality, terror, avoidance, desire, denial, solipsism, madness, policing, politics, and the projection and production of white fantasies. From the perspective of whiteness, the Black body *is* criminality itself. It *is* the monstrous; it is that which is to be feared and yet desired, sought out in forbidden white sexual adventures and fantasies; it is constructed as a source of white despair and anguish, an anomaly of nature, the essence of vulgarity and immorality. The Black body is deemed the quintessential object of the ethnographic gaze.[12]

What Yancy describes is an anti-blackness so ingrained that even the blind can see it. In his book *Blinded by Sight: Seeing Race through the Eyes of the Blind*, Osagie Obasogie asks: How do blind people understand race? Obasogie conducted over 100 interviews with people of various ages and backgrounds, all of whom had been blind since birth. The sociologically trained bioethicist asked questions like "How do you define race?" and "What is your earliest memory of race?" and "How would your family respond if you dated someone of another race?" To his surprise, Obasogie discovered that "blind people understand and experience race like everyone else—visually." Obasogie's findings suggest that, much like sighted people, blind people often use visual markers like skin color and facial features they have never seen in order to describe race.[13] These cues are learned. Both blind and sighted people are socialized to see race in ways that contribute to continuing racial inequality in society. Obasogie's interviews revealed that some parents and friends of the blind respondents reinforced social boundaries by outlining specific prohibitions against race mixing.[14] Obasogie's study suggests that race has less to do with what you see and more to do with what you are taught.

What Is Meant by the Term "Blackout"?

When hearing the term "blackout," readers will likely think of the failure of an electrical power supply. A secondary definition of "blackout" is a suppression of information. My use of the word is closer to this. Though not always recognized as citizens or even fully human beings, Black bodies have had a physical presence on the American landscape for over 450 years. The contemporary pattern I outline is one in which Black bodies are welcome in physical and social space but only under certain conditions. These caveats on acceptance effectively foster, maintain, and promote continuing racial segregation and a racialized hierarchy amid the illusion of a purportedly open, post-racial society. "Blackout" describes a provisional and limited acceptance that rejects, denies, or ignores the continuing existence of a long-established White supremacist racial order. Through these processes, blackout acts as a violent, insidious attack on Black humanity, well-being, and life. It is a complex social landscape where Black progress and Black presence is desired for either the purposes of maintaining the fiction of equality or the fiction of personal, organizational, or institutional progress, but too much Black presence or Black progress is subject to White pushback—an attempt to reinstate the Jim Crow order of the past.

The embodied experience of most Blacks in the United States is that of "other," a decided classification of marginality or not belonging. As outside of the polity, the person (or group) so categorized as other is treated and viewed as a lesser, inferior being. The hope is that the subjugated will adopt a similar view of themselves. If they do, it facilitates the control of such bodies. Foucault writes, "A body is docile that[it] may be subjected, used, transformed and improved."[15] "Blackout" describes a modern-day project aimed at the docility and social control of Black bodies. "The captive body," argues Black feminist scholar and literary critic Hortense Spillers, "is reduced to a thing."[16] In the process I outline and describe in this book as blackout, Black bodies are often welcome in physical and social White space. However, Black embodiment is not welcome. (I define "Black embodiment" here as perceived or intentional use of the body or flesh to convey certain cultural, ideological, or other messages about identity, consciousness, and belonging to the social group).

First, Black bodies are welcome in a space as long as there are not too many of them, such as to threaten and endanger the comfort of Whites or the perception of the physical/geographic/social area as White space. The second condition under which Black bodies are welcome is if the Black bodies do not disturb or challenge the normative sensibilities or practices of the space. Social scientists Glenn E. Bracey II and Wendy Leo Moore cogently describe this process in their article "Race Tests: Racial Boundary Maintenance in White Evangelical Churches." Bracey and Moore write, "White actors in white social spaces initiate utility-based race tests to determine whether people of color are willing to serve the interests of whites in the space, or execute exclusionary race tests to coerce people of color into leaving the space.... Although the [institutional] norms [in white social spaces] are white, they are rarely marked as such. Consequently, racially biased institutional norms are wrongly defined as race neutral and merely characteristic of the institution itself (e.g., 'the *appropriate* way to act in church'), masking inherent institutional racism."[17] People of color who do not challenge White norms are usually welcome (subject to the caveats above) in White space. While the visual landscape might be slightly modified through the presence of Black bodies, the workings of institutional White space are not. This affords Whites the psychological and tactical advantage of looking like they have changed without actually having changed at all. The third condition under which Black bodies are welcome in physical/geographic/social space is if the Black bodies are performing stereotypical positions at stereotypical times. These three qualifications produce a form of racial enclosure—a geographic or social isolation with inequitable distribution of power and resources—that contributes to (if it does not produce) poverty. Sociologist and theorist Loïc Wacquant terms such structures "institutional encasement[s] founded on spatial confinement."[18] Under these conditions, the distinction between Black and White bodies ostensibly shrinks, but the disparity in outcomes between Blacks and Whites festers and grows.

The following example should aid in understanding the practice I describe as blackout and its consequences. Approximately 13.4% of the U.S. population identifies as Black, but a 2019 survey by Coqual (formerly the Center for Talent Innovation) found Black professionals make up only 3.2% of all executive or senior leadership roles and less than 1% of all Fortune 500 CEO positions.[19] This disproportionate representation has psychic consequences. A 2021 LinkedIn survey found 81% of Black professionals say seeing someone Black in leadership would make their workplace feel more inclusive.[20] Instead, Black and brown bodies get scripted into subordinate positions. For systemic change to occur, Black and brown faces need to be in decision-making places at the table. As long as individuals, companies, organizations, and institutions can point to that 3.2% of Blacks in leadership positions, the fiction that there are no barriers persists. Instead, the narrative becomes: "If X or Y [individuals] have made it, others just need to work harder in order to succeed on that level." This false narrative asserts that it is not systemic oppression but your own failings that have prevented you from rising higher.

Blackout as an operational practice is less overt than the anti-Black racism primarily performed in periods past, but it is a related enterprise, still rooted in White supremacy.[21] Black culture may still be consumed by Whites, but it is viewed as other culture—it may be commodified, it may be exoticized, but it is always inferior. Brandi Thompson Summers offers an example of this in her theorization of a practice she terms "black aesthetic emplacement." In *Black in Place: The Spatial Aesthetics of Race in a Post-Chocolate City*, Summers maintains that a Black aesthetic neither wants nor needs the presence of Black bodies.[22] The consumption of blackness is invited, but Black people are not. Summers uses the transformation of H Street, a once predominantly Black section in Washington, D.C., to illustrate how Black aesthetic emplacement operates.[23] She describes a form of Black appropriation in which blackness is sanitized and then used for capital. What remains is a representation of blackness devoid of Black people.[24] It is a form of what I term blackout.

Somebody Ought to Testify

The word "testify" comes from the Latin *testificari*; the root is *testis*, witness. The English definition of the term means to make a solemn declaration under oath for the purpose of establishing a fact. A secondary definition of "testify" is to make a statement based on personal knowledge or belief: to bear witness to or serve as evidence or proof.[25] The final definition of "testify" is to express personal conviction. This writing serves all those purposes. I bear witness to the pervasive and continuing nature of racial oppression in society. I reach these conclusions based on personal knowledge and the application of inductive and deductive analytical processes. In these pages, I share my personal conviction and beliefs, and I offer insights into how continuing violence against Black bodies persists today and is rationalized.

There has been a great deal of discussion about race and racism in society. However, this focus ignores the reality that anti-blackness is the true evil that must be eradicated. The global racial structure posits Whites on top, Blacks at the bottom, and everyone else somewhere in between. In the resulting struggle to jockey for a better position, those along the strata recognize Black as disfavored. Consequently, the kind of prejudice directed toward Black bodies is different than that leveled against any other group. To clarify, anti-blackness is not limited to overt racism. It is often embedded in policies, institutions, and ideologies. Those ideas and beliefs, whether expressed or not, and those actions, intentional or unintentional, that have the effect of minimizing, ignoring, rejecting, marginalizing, denying, or devaluing Black life are forms of anti-blackness. This denial rejects the legitimacy of Black perspectives and acts as a dehumanization and negation of Black persons' humanity.

As I testify, I am especially indebted to journalist and civil and human rights pioneer Ida B. Wells-Barnett (hereafter referred to as "Wells"). An anti-lynching activist and women's suffragist, Wells wrote about and legally challenged the rising Jim Crow laws that proliferated at the end of the period known as Reconstruction.[26] Wells was a seer. She saw beyond the veneers articulated to justify lynching and other personal affronts against the Black body and psyche.[27] Wells knew that lynching was an attempt to subjugate Black people.[28] She told anyone who would listen, and she presented them with cold, hard facts to make her case. In *The Red Record*, Wells wrote: "During the slave regime, the Southern white man owned the Negro body and soul. It was to his interest to dwarf the soul and preserve the body."[29] In *Southern Horrors*, Wells wrote, "Somebody must show that the Afro-American race is more sinned against than sinning, and it is seems to have fallen upon me to do so."[30] In an 1892 column in the *Memphis Free Speech* newspaper, of which Wells was a part owner, she wrote, "Neither character nor standing avails the Negro if he dares to protect himself against the white man or becomes his rival."[31] In *Lynch Law in Georgia*, Wells wrote, "The purpose of this pamphlet is to give the public the facts [about lynching and its pretexts], in the belief that there is still a sense of justice in the American people, and that it will yet assert itself in condemnation of outlawry and in defense of oppressed and persecuted humanity."[32] I share a similar belief and a need to put these insights on the record.

Wells knew that White supremacy rested on maintaining the fiction of Black inferiority and criminality. She discovered that the real transgressions for which Blacks in post-Reconstruction America were being punished were 1) in the case of men, having the audacity to become the White man's rival—in business or for the affections of a White woman, and 2) asserting his or her humanity and thereby claiming equality to Whites. To assume such a position or place in society drew White ire and elicited sanction.[33] Lynching was one of several expressive acts of violence meant to push Black bodies back into their place—a position of subservience to Whites. The violent performance of public lynching allowed the actors (racist agents) and the viewing community to share and reinforce a stratified racial imaginary with Blacks on the bottom.[34] I situate my work as a continuation of Wells's.

I had been laboring slowly over this book for five years, but after the confluence of three events it began to flow. The coronavirus pandemic, a painful personal assault on my character, and becoming caregiver for my mother (diagnosed with Alzheimer's) reminded me of my mortality, and they made me realize the importance of bearing witness. I want to leave something behind that makes the world a better place. I was reminded that social science testimony can make a difference and be persuasive in helping others see what is plain to some but hidden to others.[35] This was certainly the case in the 1954 landmark decision of *Brown v. Board of Education of Topeka, Kansas*.[36] *Brown* was the first recorded time that the U.S. Supreme Court was persuaded by social scientific data.[37] *Brown* overturned the longstanding *Plessy* doctrine of separate but equal. *Plessy* had institutionalized and constitutionally protected restrictive Jim Crow practices and separate accommodations based on race in nearly every facet of life. *Brown* may have ostensibly reversed *Plessy*, but Jim Crow would not "go gentle into that good night," to use the words of Dylan Thomas.[38] As in the past, each hard-fought Black gain was met with White pushback. The southern Massive Resistance Movement is one example.[39]

Throughout this book, I highlight the pattern of pushback against Black advancement. But as Newton's third law of motion says: for every action there is an equal and opposite reaction. Backlash in the form of the pushback can have a boomerang effect. Black agency and resistance has always been present, but sometimes others find incentive to join or support the fight. In *From Jim Crow to Civil Rights*, constitutional scholar Michael Klarman argues that televised broadcasts of southerners' massive resistance campaigns of terror and violence against peaceful Black protesters created a climate for social change.[40] Part of that social change led to the 2008 election of America's first Black president, Barack Hussein Obama. Many heralded the election of Obama as a sign that America was now a post-racial society. They were wrong.

The period since Obama was first elected president has been particularly dangerous. Practices of virulent racial entrenchment manifested in post-Obama expressions of anti-blackness can be seen in discursive, legal, interactional, and extralegal contexts. This became even more evident after the January 6, 2021, siege at the Capitol showcased emboldened citizens, a number carrying or wearing anti-Black and antisemitic iconography, ready to overthrow the government. These acts threaten the very essence of our democracy.[41] So at this moment fraught with precarity, I have decided to speak, or at least to let this book speak for me. Because to remain silent is to be complicit in the continuing oppression inequitably visited upon Black bodies. It is also to remain complicit in my own death—demise by what psychologist Chester Pierce has called a "death by a thousand cuts."[42] Each aggression (macro or micro) and other invalidation produces a cut. Soon they number in the hundreds, and before long you have death by a thousand cuts. I have suffered these cuts, and I refuse to remain silent any longer, for, as Zora Neale Hurston wrote in *Dust Tracks on a Road*, "There is no agony like bearing an untold story inside you."[43]

Violence

Anti-Black violence takes many forms. The World Health Organization (WHO) defines violence as "the intentional use of physical force or power, threatened or actual, against oneself, another person, or against a group or community, that either results in or has a high likelihood of resulting in injury, death, psychological harm, maldevelopment or deprivation."[44] This understanding of violence is much broader than just the use of physical force. It includes the use of threatened or actual power. The WHO definition embraces sociologist Pierre Bourdieu's concept of symbolic violence, which occurs when those with symbolic capital use that power to unconsciously coerce less powerful groups to subordinate their norms to those in power.[45] Symbolic violence is the process by which the dominant group wields its power in ways that reinforce the idea that their norms, tastes, and preferences are superior and all other standards and beings inferior. Johann Galtung's notion of structural violence, harms that result from social injustice as a form of force, is also included.[46] Inspired in part by the WHO "World Report," epidemiologist Seema Patrikar asserts, "An analytical framework or typology is needed to separate the strands of this intricate tapestry [of violence] so that the nature of the problem—and the action required to deal with it—become clearer."[47]

Violence can be seen as legitimate or illegitimate. For example, self-defense can often be understood, but other forms of violence must be rationalized and excused in order to be justified. Creating sociological frames helps people to make sense of details and justify their behavior or response to things.[48] In his 1974 classic *Frame Analysis*, Erving Goffman wrote, "A central component of any dominant racial ideology is its frames or *set paths* for interpreting information."[49] These ideologies are applied by individual actors and social systems and used to justify the oppression of people of color. This justification is a form of racism, which David Wellman defines as "culturally sanctioned beliefs which, regardless of the intentions involved, defend the advantages whites have because of the subordinated positions of racial minorities."[50] Once the culturally sanctioned racist ideology or belief is ingrained, oppression gets actualized through various attacks—emotional, psychological, verbal, cultural, physical, political, economic, et cetera.

Anti-Black violence in the form of racism is not an individual or group level process, it is both. Wellman's definition tethers, connects, and inextricably loops racism performed at the micro (individual, interpsychic, or familial), meso (organizations or groups of people), and macro (larger systems like law, institutions, or policy) levels. Racial discrimination is not just the result of racist choices by individuals.[51] Individual actors are part of a system designed to oppress people. While I foreground this nexus, I do not seek to reduce racism to individual-level prejudices manifested through thoughts, attitudes, and behaviors, nor do I focus on systemic racism. Instead, I want to highlight the interconnected loop between the two. As one of the essays in *Readings for Diversity and Social Justice* suggests, "Racism is in the set of institutional, cultural and interpersonal patterns and practices that create advantages for the people legally defined and socially constructed as 'white,' and the corollary disadvantages . . . for people not considered white."[52]

Research Questions and Rationale

Three principal research questions guide this project.

1. What can expectations about bodies, space, place, and belonging tell us about the ways anti-blackness operates and is perpetuated?
2. What historical, social, and political processes and practices influence the perception of being a body out of place (i.e., how does race interact with other identities)?
3. Where and how does racism appear in American culture and shape the ways we interact with one another (or fail to interact)?

Classification animates my research questions. Classification is one of six major cognitive acts.[53] It is a means of "lumping and splitting" and carving reality up into "islands of meaning."[54] The designation of belonging in or to a certain space is accomplished through classification. Some historical classification systems have divided the world into two: human versus subhuman, civilized versus uncivilized, nature versus reason, and public versus private. These distinctions rely on reductionist binaries. Across time, they have been assigned not only to things but also to bodies, thereby sometimes sorting people into a non-person status.[55]

Like people, places get classified and assigned to groups. This process makes place a particularly useful lens through which to see and understand continuing patterns of racial inequality.[56] The inquiry can help us interrogate why, despite the end to legal segregation, de facto segregation remains entrenched. I argue that one way this occurs is through the expectation that certain positions (social, political, geographic) are reserved for specific types of racialized (and gendered) bodies. Therefore, my inquiry is attentive to place—both as a geographic location and as a social position.

Sociologist Nirmal Puwar has investigated space and politics relating to bodies, class, and gender.[57] Puwar argues that bodies are not neutral; instead, they are raced, classed, and gendered sites. In "The Racialised Somatic Norm and the Senior Service," she writes, "One of the central ways in which institutionalized racism is perpetuated is through the designation of the somatic norm."[58] The somatic norm naturalizes certain bodies. Everyone else is the lesser other. Built on the racial contract and the sexual contract, the somatic norm contributes to the inequalities it perpetuates.[59] The White male body remains the unmarked somatic norm.[60] Further, it is subject to multiple advantages.[61] I build upon the work of Puwar, but my examination is keenly interested in movement to and through physical and social space.

Critical race and gender scholar Sherene Razack cautions, "To interrogate bodies travelling in spaces is to engage in a complex historical mapping . . . [and] tracking of multiple systems of domination."[62] These insights and others lead me to believe that interrogating physical, geographic space or symbolic (sociopolitical) place can be useful in understanding continuing racialized oppression.[63] Puwar argues that "social spaces are not blank" and open for anyone to occupy.[64] Thus, I sought to better understand Black life as what Susan Hanson calls a "daily mobility project."[65] I also explored how ideas about who belongs and does not belong in certain spaces influences how African Americans live their lives and where they go and do not go. To do so, I investigated interactions and experiences in sites of commerce, recreation, residency, transportation, work, and school, for example, and, because no group is homogeneous, I paid careful attention to intersectional identities.[66]

My Call to Action

Most of my friends and colleagues know about my research interests, and many of them send me stories from across the globe detailing instances of racialized violence. To get through the day, I have become somewhat desensitized to these stories. Consistent with critical race theory, I believe that racism is endemic in society.[67] Therefore, while I was disheartened, I was not surprised when a number of pernicious and often insidious racial incidents happened, even in the midst of a spring and summer when a global pandemic threatened the world. Some of the violent acts resulted in death.[68] However, none struck me more than an incident involving an Oklahoma delivery driver named Travis Miller Sr.[69] His story stirred raw emotions in me. I believe this is because he reminded me of so many of my male students. He could have been any one of them. Miller had a large frame, but he seemed eminently approachable and caring. Despite his girth, his countenance read more like a teddy bear than a threat or menace. Several stories I learned in the late spring and early summer of 2020 angered or incensed me, but Travis Miller Sr.'s story made me want to cry.

On May 11, 2020, 43-year-old Miller, an African American man, and a co-worker (also African American) were completing their last appliance delivery of the day.[70] The delivery was to a client in a gated upper-class neighborhood in Oklahoma City.[71] The customer gave Miller the access code to enter, and, after completing his delivery, Miller looked for a safe area where he could turn his truck around without having to back into someone's yard or drive on grass. Before he could exit the neighborhood, a White resident of the community parked his vehicle so as to block Miller's egress, and then the resident peppered him with accusatory questions about why he was in the "private" subdivision and how he had gained access. Several minutes into the encounter, another neighbor (also White) joined the inquisition, and the first neighbor called the police to request assistance. Miller drove a marked company truck, and he was wearing a shirt that bore both his name and the employer's logo on it.[72] Still, the White male residents perceived him as a threat or interloper.

The encounter lasted almost 40 minutes. At some point, Miller went on Facebook Live, so he could have an account of the incident. You can hear Miller softly say, "You picked the wrong day. Move out the way." Those words pierced my psyche. I knew that this was not the first time Miller had confronted such an attitude. Later in the taped encounter (and in subsequent interviews), Miller confirmed the same.[73] Miller's frustration was as palpable as the White residents' indignation at his refusal to answer their questions. I was struck by the extra burden Miller endured in the course of simply trying to do his job. Miller called his boss to explain what he was facing and apologized for not handling the situation better. Miller told his employer that most days he could take it, but he was reeling from the recent loss of two relatives, so he did not have the same capacity to tolerate idiocy that he usually exhibited. I felt another pain in my chest. Miller was not the one who needed to apologize. Approximately six minutes into the Facebook Live video, Miller said, "If I go around him, I'm gonna have to go on someone's property, and I'm gon make a bad situation worse." It occurred to me that Miller went through multiple levels of analysis in a relatively short amount of time. Then I remembered what must have occurred to Miller: countless Black lives are inhumanely taken based on erroneous split-second decisions. A look or gesture perceived as errant is often coded as a furtive movement and used by state actors to justify the taking of a life. In the face of someone falsely imprisoning him, Miller carefully calculated every move he personally might take and the likelihood that move, though rightful, might be falsely construed and used against him. He chose not to get out. Instead, he remained in his company transport—a vehicle that his White false accusers effectively turned into a prison. About 24 minutes into the encounter, the homeowner Miller made the delivery to vouched for him and his coworker to the two residents who were detaining them. Instead of apologizing to Miller and his colleague, one of the residents said, "All you had to do was tell me where you were going." Miller rightly retorted, "I don't have to tell you anything."[74] The two exchanged a few more words. Then Miller asked the resident if the police were still coming. The resident stated that they were not. Both residents departed.

For Miller, the encounter did not end with the residents' departure. After their departure, Miller was still visibly shaken and nervous. I thought about all the things that must have been swirling through his head. When they called the police, the White residents put Travis Miller's life on the line. His livelihood was at risk too. He makes his living driving a truck. He did not need a blight on his record. Miller's colleague was also concerned. After a moment, the colleague asked, "Do you think they'll follow us?" Miller responded, "I don't know. That's why I'm waiting. I don't know if I should move just yet." The two men sat in silence. Then Miller wiped a tear from his eye.[75] Miller's agony was clear, and so was the callousness of the White residents who caused that pain. Incidents like this are far too common, and in the wake of the killing of Ahmaud Arbery—a young Black man shot and killed while jogging through a middle-class White neighborhood—they serve as a reminder that blackness is commonly equated with suspicion, and this suspicion is used to justify surveillance and judicial as well as extrajudicial action.

Miller did everything right, but, more importantly, he never should have been attacked in the first place. Every move he made was calculated to increase his chances of returning safely home to his family.[76] I thought about all the Travis Millers who never make it home to tell their stories, and I decided that I wanted my work to live to testify to the disproportionate and racially motivated violence Black bodies face every day. I want *this book* to offer insight to those who sincerely seek to understand the crisis and point to public policy recommendations for those who seek to change this violent racial system. I am incentivized to speak in the place of all those who have been denied an opportunity to testify.[77] As I testify, I am reminded of the rich legacy of people of color who have testified before me. Some are my contemporaries, and many are ancestors, but their voices remain. I join my voice with theirs in a resounding chorus of Amen!

A Moment in Time

According to Foucault, all periods of history have possessed certain underlying epistemological assumptions that determine what is acceptable and true.[78] Change requires an epistemic shift. From time to time, shifts do occur. This is a moment when the potential for radical democratic social change exists. We stand on a shifting fault line. The illusions of safety and equality are eroding. Amid enormous pressure, the fantasy of a post-racial U.S. society is imploding. Young people brutalized by a police officer at a pool party in McKinney, Texas, discovered that youth is not a safe, protected time. Walter Scott, an unarmed Black man shot in the back while fleeing officers, found that daylight provides no safe refuge against excessive police force. Eric Garner, Sandra Bland, Raynette Turner, George Floyd, and countless others found that police custody is not a safe state. For nine members of Emanuel African Methodist Episcopal Church in Charleston, South Carolina, murdered by a White supremacist on June 17, 2015, church was not a safe space, just as it was not in Birmingham, Alabama, in 1963. Mother Emanuel was the kind of reminder that comes along every generation or so to warn Blacks and others that there is no place Black bodies are safe.[79]

African Americans have long hoped and believed in the emancipatory power of visual evidence. This hope rises out of dust, as if it was willed there by the ancestors. As poet Maya Angelou warned and extolled: "You may write me down in history / With your bitter, twisted lies, / You may trod me in the very dirt / But still, like dust, I'll rise."[80] Today there is a wealth of video evidence that testifies to the injustices visited on certain types of bodies. It is an auspicious time, but we have been here before. Photography came to America around 1839–1840, and Frederick Douglass (1818–1895) believed it was a way for Black people to reclaim their image and tell their own story.[81] In his lifetime, Douglass sat for over 160 photos.[82] Each portrait stood as a testament to Black dignity and honor. Douglass never allowed himself to be debased in an image. He knew that representation could then be used to paint a false narrative about himself and his people. Celeste-Marie Bernier, coauthor of a book about the abolitionist, told the online platform *Artsy*, "For Douglass, photography was the lifeblood of being able to be seen and not caricatured, to be represented and not grotesque, to be seen as fully human and not as an object or chattel to be bought and sold."[83] W. E. B. Du Bois saw a similar potential in documentary evidence when he curated a series of photos for the American Negro Exhibit at the 1900 Paris Exposition.[84] The award-winning exhibit that offered a visual and written representation of Black people included hundreds of images of "Negroes and Negro life." According to scholar Shawn Michelle Smith, "[Du Bois] believed that a clear revelation of the facts of African American life and culture would challenge the claims of biological race scientists influential at the time, which proposed that African Americans were inherently inferior to Anglo-Americans."[85] Du Bois sought to depict the progress and dignity of the race.

Ida B. Wells painted images with her words. Her writings and speeches depicted vivid accounts of lynchings. Wells was also attentive to data, and in 1895 she published her groundbreaking findings in *The Red Record: Tabulated Statistics and Alleged Causes of Lynching in the United States, 1892–1894*. She pioneered what some now call "data journalism" and used her new methodology to let the facts she detailed testify to the nature of vigilante lynching and reveal the pretexts that justified it. Wells's investigation revealed that numerous rape claims leveled against

Black men were sheer fabrication, pretext to justify violence against Black bodies. Wells helped willing readers see that fears about political and economic competition with Blacks provided the real root cause of the violence against Blacks.[86] In a May 21, 1892, column, Wells boldly asserted, "Nobody in this section of the country believes the old thread bare lie that Negro men rape white women."[87] In the 1996 book *Race, Rape, and Lynching*, author Sandra Gunning affirms Wells's conclusions. The false stereotype of Black males as sexual beasts intent on raping White women worked to legitimate White supremacy. In fact, the desire to lynch was so strong that alleged attacks on White women were concocted to justify the "blood lust" of White men. Gunning demonstrates how turn-of-the-century American literature often obscured White male drunkenness, savagery, and bestial behavior at lynchings and instead framed them as a tale of "black rape and white victimhood."[88] Her accounts of Wells note that White men saw raping Black women as something they were entitled to do, while using lynching as a warning to White women to not have consensual romantic or erotic relations with Black men.

Almost one hundred years after publication of *The Red Record*, Black America again held fast to the promise that documentary evidence would help the world see and then want to atone for the perils long visited on Blacks in this country. Video footage of Rodney King being brutally beaten by four White police officers was recorded and viewed across the globe in 1991, but a year later those hopes were again dashed when all four officers were acquitted.[89] Today we stand at another such precipice. Four years after Sandra Bland's death in police custody was ruled a suicide, which many have disputed, a recording by Bland of part of her exchange with Trooper Brian Encinia surfaced in 2019.[90] Together with her video blog, *Sandy Speaks*, these items testify from the grave. Finally, seventeen-year-old Darnella Frazier recorded the May 25, 2020, police killing of George Floyd, and she both witnessed and testified to the atrocity. Frazier's video recording sparked a global outcry. This is the moment in which I write.

Audience and Organization of Book

This book is for anyone who genuinely wants to understand the root causes of continuing racial violence in contemporary U.S. society. It is also for those who acutely feel and bear the pain of this violence—sometimes in silence and sometimes shouting. They deserve affirmation and to know that they are not alone in the way they see the world; they are not wrong, pessimistic, or anti-American for seeing it this way. In *The Racial Contract*, philosopher Charles Mills observed, "All whites are beneficiaries of the [racial] Contract, though some whites are not signatories to it."[91] Therefore, another audience for this book is those Whites who are ready to acknowledge that they are either racist or beneficiaries of racism. It is for those complicit through their action or inaction, including silence. And it is for those who can only muster the courage to admit that some of their actions might indeed be racist even if they cannot yet admit that they are.

In many ways, Travis Miller Sr. inspired this work. Every decision that he made was calculated toward one end: he wanted to get home to the safety and security of his family. He wanted to live to bear witness, to testify. Miller's story is woven throughout this narrative. You can even see it reflected in the organization of this book, which has three parts. Part I contains a short introduction and three chapters. This chapter, "Testify," outlines the purpose and the organization of the book. I serve as a witness, and, as James Baldwin noted, "Part of my responsibility—as a witness—[is] . . . to write the story . . . to get it out."[92] This chapter makes the case for why this is necessary. In chapter 2, "This I Believe," I introduce Bodies out of Place (BOP) as a sociological theory of oppression through which violence against certain bodies can be interpreted and understood, and I outline the tenets of the theory. The chapter explains the merit of foregrounding place in our inquiry and highlights how underexplored cognitive aspects of place (both as a geographical and social construct) can prove helpful in interrogating and challenging dominant narratives. Chapter 3, "The Pushback," provides an abbreviated timeline of African/Black presence in America, and it details acts of White resistance to Black advancement.[93] I do this for several reasons. First, I want to highlight agency and dignity in the Black community. Second, I want to demonstrate that the promise of Reconstruction has yet to be fulfilled. Third, the chapter serves to counter the prominent progress narrative that argues "but things are so much better than they used to be." This progress tale is particularly insidious. It denies consistent and organized White resistance to Black gains. It masks the actuality that while anti-Black racism may take a different form(s) than it has in the past, this does not mean that things are better, especially for large segments of the Black community. Finally, in outlining this history, the chapter underscores both the individual and structural nature of the pushback. It serves to disabuse people of the fiction that the larger society has made considerable efforts toward eradicating racism, and it is a call to arms to do something now to achieve that end.

Part 2 of the book contains five chapters, and each is dedicated to one of the five frames I identify as commonly used justifications to rationalize broad forms of violence against Black bodies, whether political, sociocultural, emotional (psychological), or physical. The BOP frames I outline are culturally determined definitions of reality that allow people to make sense of things.[94] Like sociologist Joe Feagin's "white racial frame," which extends his earlier systemic racism framework,

I proffer BOP frames as analytical tools useful for explicating "the nature of the problem [White supremacy as manifested through anti-blackness] and the action required to deal with it."[95] Chapter 4, "The Historical Fear Factor," examines a frame that operates through adopters justifying the use of violence as a preemptive act of self-defense against some perceived attack. Expectations of danger or harm generally rely on the use of historical stereotypes and tropes that paint the "other" as threatening. In chapter 5, "Presumed Criminal," the typological frame views Black bodies as suspicious until proven otherwise and properly subject to constant and heightened surveillance. The presumption of malevolence makes it acceptable to call in state actors—like police—for routine acts like shopping, walking, and driving. The chapter argues that once the presumption of criminality is invoked, any resistance to authority only heightens the assumption of criminality and is used to rationalize and justify carceral response. In chapter 6, "Massah Has Spoken," the frame is built on the presumption of White moral superiority, which undergirded biological racism, and it suggests that any White person (or his or her assignee or designee, whether White or otherwise) has the right to be sole arbiter of what is proper, reasonable, and necessary in a given circumstance. It is an extension of the concept of whiteness as property right. Marked with the legal standard of a "reasonable man or woman," the actor/opposer/overseer has the right to issue commands to the body he or she perceives as out of place and the expectation that the orders will be complied with fully and in the manner and with the speed desired. Failure to do so legitimately subjects the dominated body to violence. This chapter also highlights how the activities of individual actors often contribute to state-sponsored violence against Black bodies. Chapter 7, "*You* Don't Belong *Here*," describes a frame that relies on fixed ideas about where certain people belong, when they belong in those spaces, and with whom they belong. The chapter demonstrates how this ideology promotes the aims and objectives of White supremacy. Part 2 concludes with chapter 8, "It's All White Space." The frame described in this chapter largely depends on social control actualized through the use (and control) of place as a form of power. As sociologist Eduardo Bonilla-Silva describes, "All domination is ultimately maintained through social control strategies."[96] "It's All White Space" recognizes that White space is amorphous, shifting, and ever expanding. White space is more than a geographic designation. Bracey and Moore write, "The concept 'white institutional space' elucidates how institutions . . . become normatively white in policy and practice by explicitly accounting for the intersecting mechanisms—structure, culture, ideology, and discourse— that justify and reproduce white privilege, power, and accumulation of resources in these institutions."[97] This frame is reflected in broad attempts to control the body of another or attempts to control geographic and social space. In either case, the goal is the same. It is an effort to maintain a social order that preserves White privilege. Shannon Sullivan's concept of "white ontological expansiveness" best summarizes this frame. White ontological expansiveness, says Sullivan, is the inclination for White people "to act and think as if all spaces—whether geographical, psychical, linguistic, economic, spiritual, bodily or otherwise—are or should be available to them to move in and out of as they wish."[98] Each of the five chapters in part 2 provides examples of how the frame operates. None of the frames are mutually exclusive.

Part 3 looks not only to the past but also to the future. Chapter 9, "The Weight," discusses the psychological toll, pain, and weight that purportedly out-of-place bodies bear. This load is especially heavy in light of the cognizance that you are perceived as a danger or a problem. This weight means that people of color (and other bodies that defy the somatic norm) often carry the additional burden of taking preemptive action to make others feel comfortable with their presence in a space. Chapter 10, "Sincere Ignorance and Conscientious Stupidity," explores the Martin Luther King Jr. quote, "Nothing in all the world is more dangerous than sincere ignorance and conscientious stupidity."[99] The quote is taken from a sermon titled "Love in Action" published in his 1963 book *Strength to Love*. My examination of the idea challenges readers to acknowledge that both sincere ignorance and conscientious stupidity are willful states of being created to make inaction more palatable and thereby appear harmless. The chapter offers a call to action consistent with Karl Marx's charge that it is not enough to simply understand the social world, the point is to change it.[100] Chapter 11, "Policy Matters," explores public recommendations for affecting change. The final chapter, "Tell The Story: Lest We Forget," adds a counter-narrative to the oft-propagated one of Black subjugation. This chapter tells the story of Black hope, Black pride, Black agency, and Black love, and it encourages others to speak truth to power and tell their stories—lest we forget.

Conclusion

In a 2008 interview, award-winning author Toni Morrison, whose accolades include the American Book Award and both the Nobel and Pulitzer Prize, told National Public Radio host Michel Martin, "Racism will disappear when it's . . . no longer profitable and no longer psychologically useful. When that happens, it'll be gone . . . but at the moment people make a lot of money off of it . . . and also it protects people from a certain kind of pain . . . if you take that away, they may have to face something really terrible: about themselves: misery, self-misery, and deep pain about who they are."[101] To rid society of anti-blackness, it is critical to unveil both the economic and psychological dividends it pays. In this book, I clarify and highlight the culpability of individual actors in maintaining racism and other forms of anti-blackness. To do so, I reject the popular "few bad apples" narrative and argue instead that individuals are not bad actors divorced from social systems but rather are embedded in them.[102] Such a framework allows me to demonstrate how anti-Black racism operates not on a continuum between structural and individual levels but on an interconnected loop.

CHAPTER 2

This I Believe

The New Social Order Is the Old Social Order

In a racist society, it is not enough to be non-racist,
we must be anti-racist.

—ANGELA DAVIS

No one taught me to walk, talk, or run, but I learned these things just the same. In fact, most of the lessons we learn are not taught in school. Instead, they are experienced in and through our observations and interactions with others in the social world. The same is the case with the racial order in society. Perhaps this is why philosopher Lewis R. Gordon observes, "Race theorists theorize in a racist world."[1] The first step to solving any social issue is to acknowledge that it exists. But the mounting attacks on critical race theory demonstrate, anti-Black racism in society is a problem that some acknowledge and even fewer see.

Bodies out of Place operates as both theory and method. As a theoretical framework, BOP acknowledges the existence of the problem, and as a method it offers an approach for analyzing what Émile Durkheim called "social facts," collective attitudes and beliefs emanating from society that act as a constraint on others.[2] It is an emancipatory approach with the twin aims of liberation and social justice. Those atop the social chain have little incentive to see inequity or disrupt the current social order. "The construction of knowledge is about power—not only to construct discourse but also to justify or leave untouched the material basis for the distribution of power," states Aída Hurtado.[3] In recognition of the need to disrupt this schema, BOP theory offers a data-gathering tool aimed at creating new knowledge. In this chapter, I set forth the theoretical and methodological underpinnings of my framework, define key terms, lay out the underlying beliefs and assumptions of BOP, and underscore the value of an embodied approach.

As method, BOP has several components. First, BOP embraces counterstorytelling as a tool to 1) resist dominant narratives, 2) make the lived experience of the marginalized visible, and 3) allow subjugated groups to tell their own stories about their own lives from their own perspective and interpret the same. Second, as method, BOP insists that researchers widen the sources of data they use to understand the social world. It encourages the use of literature, legal discourse, music, and photography, among other materials. Third, BOP as method requires something akin to what cultural theorist Stuart Hall calls "oppositional reading."[4] It is a process where the researcher is encouraged to generate new knowledge by rejecting the preferred reading and interpretation of events to instead create their own meaning. It offers a counter-story or counter-narrative telling of the events in order to explore and foreground alternative conclusions or perspectives on the encounter. The counter-narrative reading is attentive to context, especially place, language, and intersectionality. A counter-narrative account of incidents recognizes that oppressed people have profound insights into the workings of society—something Patricia Hill Collins calls learning from the outsider within—and our silence is sometimes complicity in our oppression (or the oppression of someone else).[5] So we must tell our story. Finally, a BOP methodologically based approach demands cultural sensitivity. This sensitivity is required in the interpretation of data. It assumes a holistic examination of human beings that is attentive to their physical, psychosocial, and emotional states.

At the center of BOP as theory and method is the recognition that any such examination must focus on marginalized bodies. It is "a theory in the flesh."[6] Cherríe Moraga and Gloria Anzaldúa, editors of the anthology *This Bridge Called My Back: Writings by Radical Women of Color*, write, "A theory in the flesh means one where the physical realities of our lives—our skin color, the land or concrete we grew up on, our sexual longings—all fuse to create a politic born of necessity. Here, we attempt to bridge the contradictions in our experience."[7] Therefore, any approach that purports to be BOP must center the voices of the disenfranchised, and it must be grounded in their cultural and historical experiences. It is what sociologist and education scholar Tamara Beauboeuf-Lafontant calls a "voice-centered framework."[8]

In the tradition set forth in *This Bridge Called My Back*, BOP relies on "flesh and blood experiences."[9] It is a liberatory process that seeks to challenge the understanding and interpretation of evidence. It appreciates the plasticity of facts and is free of a devotion to the guild. BOP is attentive to what subjugated parties have to say for and about themselves as well as how they interpret their experiences in what Lewis Gordon describes as "a racist world."[10]

Seeing Violence

The racist, White supremacist roots of violence against Black bodies often get obscured, especially amid misguiding discourse about how much better things are now. The routinized nature of violence also facilitates this. Routinized violence includes organized and patterned actions that provide little opportunity for onlookers to raise moral objections. Lynching spectacles—some participated in by thousands—are one historical example of routinized violence. The routinization of violence reduces the need for decision making and minimizes the chances that moral questions may arise. Lack of punishment for such acts only serves to further legitimize the violence. A December 2014 Vera Institute of Justice publication reported, "Attention is increasingly being paid to the . . . disproportionate involvement of young men of color in the criminal justice system as those responsible for crime. Still missing, however, is recognition that these young men [and women] are also disproportionately victims of crime and violence."[11] The routine nature of violence against Black bodies is so acceptable that few even query its origins, especially when Black actors perform it against other Blacks. Valerie Castile (the mother of Philando Castile who was killed by police in the course of a "routine" traffic stop) declared simply, "We [Black people] are being hunted."[12]

Dehumanization also facilitates continuing violence against Black bodies, and some intersectional Black bodies are most at risk. After the May 2020 police killing of George Floyd, Johnetta Bryant, mother of 12-year-old gospel singer Keedron Bryant, penned poignant lyrics that described being a young, Black, and male and simply wanting to live to grow up to be a man. Instead of enjoying a carefree youth, Keedron sang about feeling hunted like he was prey.[13] Bryant posted a video of her son singing the song, and it quickly went viral. Keedron Bryant sang with a conviction and confidence that pierced the soul. Despite his tender age and middle-class upbringing, it was clear that the fear and feeling of being despised and hunted as prey resonated with him. This is not surprising. In the wake of the killing of Trayvon Martin, professor and columnist Stacey Patton wrote in a November 26, 2014, opinion piece in the *Washington Post*, "In America, Black children don't get to be children." In her book *Pushout: The Criminalization of Black Girls in Schools*, social justice advocate and scholar Monique Morris reached similar conclusions about Black girls more specifically.[14] Scholar Philip Atiba Goff and his colleagues found that Black boys in society are perceived as 3–4.5 years older than their actual age, are more likely to have dogs used against them by police, and are generally viewed as less innocent than White boys.[15] The recent highly publicized rash of attacks on Black bodies for doing ordinary mundane things (like sleeping, driving, bird-watching, shopping, and walking) has brought some members of society to an inflection point. Much attention has been focused on police and other state-sanctioned violence against Black bodies, and that is important, but it belies the reality that Keedron Bryant so eloquently proclaims: "Every day, *we're* [emphasis added] being hunted as prey." And, more often than not, ordinary citizens, not the police, are the hunters.

Changing the reality of anti-blackness requires acknowledging it. Former NBA legend and author Kareem Abdul-Jabbar expressed similar sentiments in a *Los Angeles Times* opinion piece he authored, pondering how one can acknowledge what one cannot see. Abdul-Jabbar wrote, "But African-Americans have been living in a burning building for many years, choking on the smoke as the flames burn closer and closer. Racism in America is like dust in the air. It seems invisible—even if you're choking on it—until you let the sun in. Then you see its everywhere."[16] This book lets the sun in. This chapter outlines the framework I offer to engage in more rigorous and interdisciplinary analysis of everyday incidents of violence perpetrated against Black bodies.

Key Definitions and Concepts

My theoretical framework, BOP, is, as its name suggests, attentive to bodies and place. The attention to place is critical because, as Katherine McKittrick states, "Black matters are spatial matters. And while we all produce, know, and negotiate space—albeit on different terms—geographies in the diaspora are accentuated by racist paradigms of the past and their ongoing hierarchical patterns."[17] The racist geographies and paradigms McKittrick discusses exist on the individual, institutional, national, and global levels.

Throughout this book, I challenge the reader to see the structural, systemic forces at play. While it is true that some incidents I interrogate in the book might be classified as interpersonal racism, nevertheless structural or systemic racism undergirds it, just as it does institutional racism, internalized racism, and implicit bias.[18] Consider internalized racism one of a number of possible responses to systemic oppression. Anti-racism trainer and consultant Donna K. Bivens writes, "As people of color are victimized by racism, we internalize it. That is, we develop ideas, beliefs, actions and behaviors that support or collude with racism. This internalized racism has its own systemic reality and its own negative consequences in the lives and communities of people of color."[19] As such, even internalized racism is rooted in systemic racism. Systemic racism is the host carrier through which all the other dimensions of racism thrive in our society.

Systemic racism is ingrained in society, and to the extent (if at all) it is hidden, it is hidden in plain sight. Black exclusion was built into most of the organizations and systems that came into being in North American society during the 17th and 18th century era of imperial settler colonialism. It was the order of things. Consider. Freedom itself was only for Whites.[20] After the founding of the United States, citizenship was for Whites. Landownership was only for White men. Voting was for White men.[21] After the Civil War and Reconstruction, Jim Crow laws maintained that separation. The institutional policies and practices of many current U.S. organizations were formed during this period or predate it. Colonial era education was built on exclusion. Numerous branches of the U.S. armed forces founded in 1775 were built on the same model. The same is the case for the American Medical Association (1847), Association of American Medical Colleges (1876), and the American Bar Association (1878). The exclusionary practices of these institutions are woven into the tapestry of not only the organizations but also their membership. Systemic racism is embedded through the formal and informal policies, practices, and cultural norms and expectations that sustain the racial advantages of White supremacy.

From 1619 to 1865—246 years—Black persons lived under the system of chattel slavery, and racial caste was inherent in the social institutions that formed then. The educational system, criminal justice system, religious orders, military, policing, and health care were all birthed during a time when the enslavement of Black bodies was legal. Even the family institution effectively excluded Blacks. Slavery forced separation—first from homelands and then from their kin in the new places—through forced sale. Exclusion was not only written into the law, it was also presumed and practiced, and those customs, orientations, epistemologies, and ways of being were framed and undergirded in the principle of Black elimination from the polity. Perhaps Martin Luther King Jr. said it best: "Our nation was born in genocide when it embraced the doctrine that the original American, the Indian, was an inferior race."[22] That has not altered. The end of slavery did not fundamentally change the social order. From 1877 to 1965, Black people lived under a new caste system known as Jim Crow. So for some 350 years, roughly 85% of their years in North America, Blacks have lived under these repressive systems. In the absence of one system, new exploitive ones formed.

In sum, racism was normalized into society's practices. It occurs in institutions like school and work. We see it in policies that punish hairstyles that are almost exclusively worn by racial and ethnic minorities. Historical practices have certainly resulted in continuing inequities. But not all acts of structural violence—increased risk of being harmed in a certain way due to one's position in a social structure—are historical. According to a 2018 MarketWatch report, the racist lending policy known as redlining continues to affect home values in major cities today.[23] New schemes reveal conscious and unconscious ways that blackness is devalued. After a discouraging first appraisal, a biracial Florida couple removed all traces of "blackness" from their home. The appraisal value increased by 40%.[24] A Black woman in Indianapolis also suspected that discrimination was a factor in her home's low valuation. She requested a second appraisal and asked a White friend to pose as the homeowner. The value of her Indianapolis home went up by $100,000.[25] These are but two illustrations of the practice.[26]

Home values are not the only contemporary example of structural violence. Consider how historical racial inequities in the placement of park and recreational facilities influence home values and quality of life today. A 2020 article in *National Geographic* remarkably reported that across more than 100 American cities, neighborhoods that were redlined in the 1930s are, on average, "about 4.7 degrees Fahrenheit hotter than un-redlined neighborhoods in the same city."[27] The largely Black and brown residents of these neighborhoods face heat stresses that their neighbors in non-redlined areas of the city do not. Other negative effects of redlining remain. A 1980s investigation into the Atlanta real estate market found that banks were more willing to lend to low-income White families than they were to middle- and upper-income Black families.[28] As a result of these and other systemic factors, Blacks and Whites today have inherited vastly different circumstances.

Systemic racism threatens the quality and longevity of Black lives. Indeed, Whites have a longer life expectancy than Blacks.[29] Economic circumstances, medical and behavioral issues, and geographic and environmental conditions all contribute to life expectancy. Each is influenced by historical inequality. The wealth gap is rooted in the denial of the opportunity for Blacks to make a wage, get an education, and own property. These denials (through law and structures like slavery and Jim Crow) consequently cut off the ability to accumulate and pass on wealth. They had other impacts too. According to a study by Princeton economist Michael Geruso, 70–80% of the life expectancy gap that persists between Blacks and Whites can be attributed to socioeconomic factors.[30] A 2020 Brookings Institution report asserts, "Its legacy [the legacy of inequality] is passed down generation-to-generation through unequal monetary inheritances which make up a great deal of current wealth."[31]

The single largest asset most people will own is a home, and a history of redlining, discriminatory lending, White flight, and outright discrimination have conspired to depress home values in majority-Black communities relative to those in White communities. These depressed home values have spiraling effects. They lead to a lower tax base, so schools receive less funding. Less funding means fewer kindergarten classrooms and overall resources for all students. This often leads to lower teacher salaries, higher teacher turnover, fewer resources, and more work (in terms of increased ratios of students per teacher). These factors can impact test scores, the number of AP classes offered, school ratings, graduation rates, and college readiness and completion.

Adverse geographic and environmental conditions—such as the likelihood of living near environmental hazards—is another factor that has a disproportionate impact on African Americans' quality of life and longevity.[32] According to a report by the Princeton Student Climate Initiative, people of color make up more than half of those who live near hazardous waste.[33] A 2017 article in the *New England Journal of Medicine* reported that Black Americans are three times as likely as their White counterparts to die from exposure to air pollutants.[34] These adverse environmental exposures did not happen by accident. Discrimination is the root. Behavioral practices (like propensity to eat red meat, smoke cigarettes, and not seek medical help) also influence life expectancy. However, it is important to understand that some behaviors are a response to racial and other stressors in society. These include economic insecurity and distrust of medical and other institutions leading to reticence to seek medical attention. All contribute to a pronounced Black and White infant mortality rate gap and maternal mortality gap. Here we see how gender and racial discrimination intersect to put Black female bodies at disproportionate risk compared to their White counterparts.[35] Gaps exist in the provision of mental health services too. In 2018, 8.7% of African Americans received mental health services compared to 18.6% of non-Hispanic White adults.[36] Each outcome is linked to not only a legacy of exclusion but also to current exclusionary practices.

The words "place" and "space" are often used interchangeably, but the concepts are both interdependent and overlapping. The locational certainty in geographic places often gets inscribed onto social place too. In *Space and Place: The Perspective of Experience*, geographer Yi-Fu Tuan writes, "Place is security, space is freedom."[37] Tuan suggests that space is like a border or boundary that makes place definite and concrete. The notion of place—either as a physical place or a social status (i.e., a metaphysical concept about fitting in, entitlement, or belonging to some nonphysical position or condition) is routinely applied to mark some bodies as out of place and then use that marked positionality to justify acts of violence against these out-of-place bodies. As geographer Katherine McKittrick notes in her book,

Demonic Grounds: Black Women and the Cartographies of Struggle, understanding racist paradigms requires attentiveness to history, time, place, and space.[38] Indeed, place-based attitudes facilitate White dominance in social relations. These attitudes incentivize Black bodies to stay in their perceived place.[39] This analysis is attentive to social and physical space. As space is carved and split, each incision is an attempt to impose a social structure. Illuminating this social order is a critical part of my analysis. According to Jamie Peck and Adam Tickell's article, "Neoliberalizing Space," "Social space provides an environmental framework for the behavior of the group."[40]

Violence is another key idea discussed in this book. The continuing violent assault against Black bodies I outline in this book has multiple modalities. Broadening the definition of violence has challenges (for example, almost anything can be considered a violation), but constraining it is also problematic. In "Two Concepts of Violence," Vittorio Bufacchi calls violence a violation of rights—human rights, personal rights (entailing the body or the dignity of a person), or the right to ourselves. Under this conceptualization, the harm caused by violence can be physical (actual or threatened) or psychological.[41] This is especially evident in the case of a violation of "human rights," which, according to Bufacchi, "include[s] any obstacle or impediment to the fulfillment of a basic need."[42] Adopting this definition of violence serves the critical objective of recognizing that violence has a psychological dimension, so that the victims of violence include broader categories than usually contemplated. It also allows me to highlight ways that the harm of violence is not fixed in time. Rob Nixon's *Slow Violence and Environmentalism of the Poor* makes a similar argument. Nixon remarks that some things, like climate change, are as acts of "slow violence." Nixon writes that slow violence is a "violence that occurs gradually and out of sight, a violence of delayed destruction that is dispersed across time and space, an attritional violence that is typically not viewed as violence at all . . . [and has] calamitous repercussions playing out across a range of temporal scales."[43] Slavery is an example of slow violence. The immediate effects of slavery are known (though often disputed), but its contemporary effects are disputed.[44] The harm of this kind of violence is unearthed in time and over time. It manifests in individuals and their communities, resulting in disparate outcomes and life chances for residents in communities where, for example, hazardous materials are dumped or run off.[45] Anti-blackness has immediate, intermediate, and long-term effects. In essence, it is an act of slow violence. Having established these key definitions and concepts, I move now to a discussion of theory.

The Emancipatory Power of Theory

Theory can make the invisible visible. Sociologist Gabriel Abend offers a detailed discussion of the ways people use the word "theory."[46] Abend outlines a number of distinct meanings for the term. Of significance for this discussion, theory provides: 1) a set of general related propositions that is an empirical work, 2) an explanation of a social phenomenon, 3) a hermeneutical task or way of making sense of a certain piece of the empirical world, and 4) an overall perspective from which one sees or interprets the world. Theory, Abend writes, can also refer to a theoretical framework, viewpoint, or perspective used to discuss ways that reality is socially constructed.[47] I adopt Abend's approach. I do so cognizant that some will argue that my BOP approach is not the correct way to do theory. To them, I offer the insights of Chicana cultural and feminist theorist Gloria Anzaldúa: "We need to give up the notion that there is a 'correct' way to write theory."[48] It is a constraining approach, and theory should liberate. BOP theory provides a way of making sense of the phenomena under examination by helping to uncover the hidden social processes that produce everyday forms of violence against Black bodies.

The Basics of BOP Theory

My engagement with other scholarship—including that of the humanities and legal, sociocultural, historical, and religious scholarship—as well as my life experiences have led me to several underlying assumptions about how society works. These form the tenets of my theory.[49] Many of these underlying assumptions are present (either in the foreground or the background) in the patterns and forms of anti-blackness that I outline in this book. A number of them are in the vein of critical race theory, which embraces storytelling.[50] Storytelling involves using narrative as a methodological tool to tell the experiences of people whose perspectives are not often told (or at least seldom told from their own vantage point).[51] Narrative bears a "relationship . . . explicit or implied, between past, present, and future."[52] It allows us to imagine a future that is free of oppression and to tell a counter-story about the past and the present that highlights the need for social change. In this respect, BOP offers a counter to the White racial frame's interpretation of existing racialized encounters.[53] My theory is also deeply indebted to Black feminist epistemology, which, as Nadia Brown writes, "is a useful tool for making new knowledge claims within an existing body of knowledge."[54]

Critical geographer James Blaut argues, "Racism-as-practice [discrimination] . . . has been supported by a historical sequence of different theories, each consistent with the intellectual environment of a given era."[55] Paraphrasing 1964 comments by Malcolm X about the adaptability of racism, noted American studies scholar George Lipsitz wrote:

> Racism . . . [is] like a Cadillac. [Malcolm X] explained that the General Motors Company brought out a new model of their car every year, that the 1960 version differed from the one produced in 1950, but both automobiles were still Cadillacs. Similarly . . . racism also changed its contours and dimensions . . . but it was still racism. He warned his audience against thinking that racism had ended because it looked different, while at the same time cautioning them that they could not defeat today's racism with yesterday's slogans and analyses.[56]

This new era requires new theories to expose continuing racism in society. I advance BOP as a sociological theory of oppression through which violence against certain bodies can be recognized, interpreted, and understood. The tenets—separately and together—express a kind of pedagogy of the oppressed, a theory and practice that attempts to help individuals question and challenge domination.

Bodies out of Place Framework and Tenets

Below, I list and briefly extrapolate on each of BOP's eight tenets.

1. BOP theory begins with the premise that racism is systemic and deeply ingrained in society.

This tenet offers a counter-narrative to the dominant view that racist acts are aberrant in society and violate the agreed-upon rules and expectations about how people are to be treated. The idea of racism as aberrant is supported by responses such as "It not a systemic problem, these are just a few bad apples" and "Yes, that was a racist act, but she is not a racist." These responses may be quickly followed by some assertion that the person cannot possibly be a racist because some of their best friends are Black. An example of the "few bad apples" response includes comments by Robert O'Brien, then U.S. national security advisor. In the wake of protracted unrest and protest over the police killing of George Floyd, O'Brien told CNN News, "No, I don't think there's systemic racism [in policing]. I think 99.9% of our law enforcement officers are great Americans." Without even considering the possibility of systemic racism, O'Brien quickly retorted that there were just "a few bad apples."[57] Even this framing is problematic since a "few bad apples" can spoil a bushel.

The prevalence of color-blind frames makes it easier for growing numbers to believe that racist acts are isolated incidents performed by a few bad actors. The acknowledgement of a few isolated bad actors becomes a trope, which Whites and others adopting the White racial frame rely on to appear reasonable about their ability to acknowledge continuing racial oppression in society without acknowledging its systemic nature or their part in its persistence.

2. BOP theory recognizes that physical integration is often falsely equated with social integration.

Americans are obsessed with image. During the Cold War, communist powers directed propaganda campaigns to point out American hypocrisy. They pointed out that the United States was quick to attack the purported civil rights violations of communist nations across the globe, all while trampling on the civil rights of its own Black citizens. The United States began its own propaganda campaigns to highlight Black progress. However, it was the appearance of equality that was desired; actual equality was not. "Our [U.S.] national greatness," writes Jon Meacham, author of *The Soul of America: The Battle for Our Better Angels*, "has been built on implicit and explicit apartheid."[58]

For the United States and for individual American people, image is more important than reality. I am always amused when the obligatory Black friend appears in almost every Hallmark movie. The visual reinforces the notion of equality and that all Whites have Black friends. However, according to 2020 Census estimates, Whites comprise 76.3% of the U.S. population while Blacks make up approximately 13.4% of the population. Based on these numbers, every Black person in America would need to have approximately six White friends in order to give any credence to the "some of my best friends are Black" mantra. There simply are not enough Blacks to go around. In reality, a 2013 study by the Public Religion Research Institute (PRRI) found that 75% of Whites have "entirely white" social networks, "with no minority presence."[59] In his research, scholar and public intellectual Bonilla-Silva found less than 10% of Whites report having Black friends.[60] If the popular claims to color-blindness and that "some of my best friends are Black" were truly widespread, we would expect more friendships between and across racial groups.[61] These assertions present a false, feel-good image of our society, and they ignore the reality that many people harbor lingering hatred for the other.

In 2013, an interracial couple featured in a Cheerios advertisement spurred widespread public backlash. A headline in the *New York Times* read, "Vitriol Online for Cheerios Ad with Interracial Family."[62] The ad featured a White mother and an adorable but ethnically ambiguous-looking young girl. In the next scene, the child poured Cheerios over her father. The father was Black. Hate speech in the comments section of a YouTube version of the ad became so toxic that General Mills disabled the feature. Six months later, Cheerios came out with a second ad featuring the same family. It debuted in a coveted and expensive spot during the

Super Bowl. A spokesperson for General Mills said, "Like millions of Americans, we just fell in love with this family."[63] Perhaps General Mills executives did fall in love with the family, but perhaps they also fell in love with the image of looking enlightened.[64]

Most organizations benefit from presenting themselves as diverse, open places. Advertisements for many companies, schools, and organizations are replete with images of diverse people. A few years ago, several colleges drew heat for photo-shopping Black faces into their brochures. National Public Radio's *Weekend Edition Sunday* noted in 2013 that schools were marketing diversity and "selling an image."[65] Even when the images are genuine, the people often inhabit the same public space, but they do not share intimate or personal social space.[66] This physical proximity is often falsely equated with social inclusion or parity. The image is supposed to convey a harmonious blending of the races. It embraces the rhetoric of Dr. King's words but not the spirit. King's view was not a romanticized one but an idealized beloved community where there was genuine sharing of rights, resources, and responsibilities.[67]

3. BOP theory posits that Whites have a possessive investment in whiteness and that their claims of color-blindness serve three purposes: denying their White privilege, denying the existence of racism, and circumventing their complicity in continuing racism.

As a group, poorer Whites have always had more in common with African Americans than Whites. When enslaved Africans were brought to this country, some Whites were already in a similar (but not permanent) condition called indentured servitude. After emancipation, many Blacks were caught in the oppressive system of sharecropping. There were White sharecroppers too. Each knew the pain and desperation of this financially exploitative system. In the early 20th century, White immigrants faced hostility. They too were the recipient of violence at the hands of the Klan and other groups. Yet, despite these similarities, poor Whites (immigrants and native) have generally shunned alliances with Blacks. Instead, they have embraced the notion of White superiority that undergirds White supremacy. Citing W. E. B. Du Bois's insights in *Black Reconstruction in America*, David Roediger, author of *The Wages of Whiteness*, writes, "Du Bois regards the decision of workers to define themselves by their whiteness as understandable in terms of short-term advantages." According to Roediger, when Whites, particularly White immigrants, received lower wages, they were compensated in other ways. This compensation, "in part ... [included] a public and psychological wage," and, "[the] pleasures of whiteness could function as a wage for white workers."[68] All Whites might not receive the same benefits, but inside a strict Black-White binary, Whites were given public deference denied Blacks. They might have been poor or looked down on, but at least they were not Black.

Anti-blackness is an intractable global ideology of White supremacy.[69] In the "Western European tradition," Roediger states, there is a tendency "of associating blackness with evil."[70] He observes a need to recognize "how inextricable these beliefs in racial inferiority and superiority have become to our institutions."[71] Because of this inextricability, Lipsitz writes, "Those of us who are 'white' can only become part of the solution if we recognize the degree to which we are already part of the problem—not because of our race but because of our possessive investment in it."[72] It is hard if not impossible to recognize the privileges of White racial identity while simultaneously denying the significance of race. The use of color-blind frames common today is the product of a tacit agreement to perceive the social world in a way that denies the widespread existence of racism and racists. It is part of a possessive investment that views whiteness as both rightness and moral superiority.

4. BOP theory identifies symbiotic macro and micro connections to racism: Racism is sustained on a micro level, but it operates on a macro level. It is also sustained on a macro level, and it operates on micro level.

In *Why Are They Angry with Us? Essays on Race*, university social work administrator Larry Davis reflects on his profession. Davis opines that it is easy for practitioners to focus on the lives of clients and their immediate needs (micro), while losing the bigger picture (macro). Davis encourages an epistemic shift. He suggests that service providers who want to build resiliency in clients must ask, "Why do people need to be resilient in the first place?"[73] After all, you cannot change outcomes without understanding how they have come about. This symbiotic approach is consistent with a social ecological framework.[74] I use the example of violence to help understand the symbiotic nature of the macro-micro relationship. To understand the violence Black bodies face and how it came about, we have to take into consideration both the macro level (large-scale social processes) and micro level (small group or intimate face-to-face interactions). The symbiotic approach avoids the pitfalls of a "which came first" analysis. I argue that they coexist.

5. BOP theory asserts that context matters, and it is that context, not what people say, that is most instructive in determining beliefs and attitudes. In appreciation of this environmental contextual approach, BOP recognizes a phenomenon where bodies may not be out of place per se but are seen or perceived as out of place in relation to other bodies.

There was a protracted period in U.S. history when Black bodies were out of place per se, but racism is an adaptable and changing beast. These changes include ideological and legal shifts that purport to accept racial and ethnic minorities but support "law and order" policies (including immigration policies) that justify subjecting certain bodies to heightened surveillance, suspicion, confinement, dispossession, displacement, bias, and other violent attacks while other bodies are presumed to belong. Sociocultural and historical context must help inform analysis. When time is involved, it is important to understand that this context may be shifting. The result is a more nuanced form of resistance to Black progress that professes to accept Black bodies but still seeks the subjugation of such bodies, especially relative to Whites. The case of Abigail Fisher illustrates the value of context in BOP analysis. Fisher was not accepted to the University of Texas at Austin, and she filed a lawsuit claiming that the school's admissions policy, which considered race as a factor, violated her equal protection rights. Fisher claimed that less-qualified minority students had been admitted while she was denied admission. She sought to end racial preferences in admissions.

The University of Texas at Austin is the state's flagship institution. The case went all the way to the U.S. Supreme Court. During the oral arguments, Justice Antonin Scalia suggested that Black students might be ill-prepared for schools like UT. Scalia declared, "There are those who contend that it does not benefit African-Americans to get them into the University of Texas, where they do not do well, as opposed to having them go to a less advanced school, a slower track school where they do well. . . . I'm just not impressed by the fact that the University of Texas may have fewer [black students] . . . Maybe it ought to have fewer. And maybe . . . when you take more, the number of blacks, really competent blacks admitted to lesser schools, turns out to be less."[75]

Justice Scalia's comments imply that UT is no place for Black students. His discourse is tinged with notions of biological racism, a largely debunked school of thought that suggests race is biological and that these biological differences resulted in Blacks being more violent or aggressive than others. His words support the belief that inherent differences in intelligence exist between Blacks and Whites.[76] Scalia's comments incensed and offended Black college students and others across the nation.[77] They also revealed a widely held but seldom voiced belief system about the abilities of Black students. By a margin of just one vote, the U.S. Supreme Court ruled that the university's policy, which considered race among a number of other factors, was constitutional.

After the Supreme Court ruling, Black Twitter dubbed Amy Fisher #Becky-WithTheBadGrades.[78] While Fisher's grades were not "bad" (she had a 3.59 grade point average), both her grade point average and her entrance exam scores fell below the median for the accepted class. It was reported, "UT has an admissions policy called the Top 10% Plan, which grants automatic acceptance to students within the top 10% of their graduating class. . . . The "Becky" tweets center on the assumption that if Fisher's grades . . . fell within the top 10% of her class, she would have automatically been admitted to UT."[79] Fisher presumed that the Black students admitted to UT were there because they had taken her rightful place at the institution.[80] In what would be former president Lyndon Baines Johnson's final speech he said, "So let no one delude themselves that our work is done. By unconcern, by neglect, by complacent beliefs that our labors in the fields of civil rights are completed." The speech was delivered at a December 1972 symposium on civil rights sponsored by the LBJ Library. Johnson insisted that the symposium not focus on any accomplishments of his administration but on the future and the progress that yet needed to be made. The former president lamented that he had not been able to do more during his six years in office to bring about equality. He unequivocally stated that the Black problem was ultimately about the inequity of being a Black man or woman in a White society. Johnson continued, "To be black or brown in a white society is not to stand on level and equal ground."[81] A native of Texas, Johnson came to this settled conclusion late in his life and political career. Johnson's epiphany reflects a mentality that that blues singer Big Bill Broonzy noted in his song "Black, Brown, and White": "They says if you's white, be all right. If you was brown, stick around. But as you black, oh brother, get back, get back, get back."[82] This case is further outlined in tenet 6 below.

6. Perceived out-of-place bodies evoke a response; such responses cumulatively work to affirm and reinstate the old Jim Crow social order.

BOP theory is relational and intersectional. (See tenet 8 for more discussion on intersectionality.) Bodies need not be out of place per se; instead, the body is often perceived as having taken the rightful place of the opposer (or a member of the opposer's in-group) who is somehow seen as more deserving of the position. The position might be a job, a spot in college, or a home in a nice neighborhood, but it might also be a relationship (e.g., "what is he doing with her?"), or it might even be a moral stance. The feeling that something is wrong or out of place is so offensive to the opposer that he or she feels compelled to respond. The response comes in the form of pushback, a type of status degradation ceremony that is a tool used to restore social and moral order (or at least discredit the social actor who dares violate the normative expectations about his or her position in society).

Performative practices bind communities. According to anthropologist Rita Laura Segato, even when performed by an individual, the act of violence still has an expressive dimension.[83] This is especially the case where the aggressors and community share the social imaginary of gender.[84] Segato's contribution in the edited volume *Terrorizing Women: Feminicide in the Américas*, distills the ways femicide, a gender-based violence, operates as a communicative system. Though she is discussing the unsolved murder of hundreds of women in Ciudad Juárez, Mexico, Segato argues that all violence has an expressive dimension.[85] "In a regime of sovereignty," Segato writes, "some are destined for death so the sovereign power can leave its mark on their bodies. In this sense, the death of those chosen to represent the drama of domination is an expressive death, not a utilitarian death." The violence signals a performance of the status order. She describes the killings as the actions of a parallel "second state." In this way, Segato frames the violent actions as "rituals cementing the unity of secret societies and totalitarian regimes." But despite her reference to a "second state," Segato terms these state crimes without "efficient legal categories and procedures" to end the violence. The violation of women's bodies is a vehicle to communicate sovereignty, discretionary power, and territorial control.[86] I extend Segato's concept to race. Rather than out of sight on the outskirts of a city, the performative practices I examine are conducted in public. They are apt to occur in schoolyard, on the street, on public transportation, or within a religious, political, professional, or other organization. The examination highlights the inextricable linkage between micro and macro in the performance and maintenance of oppression.

It is the existence of the pushback rather than its severity that matters most. Pushback responses may range from the benign to the ultraviolent. They act as a rebuke and repudiation of the perceived out-of-place act and actor. Whether the response is on the mild end of the continuum (e.g., amusement at the perceived displacement) or the severe end (e.g., violence up to and including murder), the objective is to push the "offender" back into place and to signal to others that such actions will not be tolerated. Let me again use the example noted in the previous tenet. While Fisher might not have been successful in gaining admission to UT Austin, the next African American student might think, why should I even apply to UT Austin? I know that I will not be welcomed there. Or, if I apply there and get in, people will think I only got in because I am Black. Finally, because the margin on the case's decision was so slight, the next attempt to challenge an admissions policy that considers race might be successful.[87]

In many ways, Fisher's response was that of a spoiled child wanting her way. She attended a well-funded school in a nearly all-White suburb. Based on a legacy of unearned White privilege, her family was well poised to provide her access to SAT preparatory courses on tests normed for White success. Finally, the university system had a transfer policy that would have allowed Fisher to transfer to UT Austin after one year of good grades at another UT campus. Instead of pursuing the transfer route, Fisher felt that some Black student had gotten her spot, and she wanted it back. She wanted it then, and she wanted it known to the world. No one suggested that Fisher should have worked harder in school. No one used language like Justice Scalia advanced regarding Black students, like, when you consider other factors, sometimes the "number of . . . really competent" Whites admitted turns out to be fewer.

7. White logic (i.e., Whites' racial common sense) is used to justify the pushback response (or failure to respond or intervene). This includes the use of language that sounds race-neutral but is laden with race-based ideologies.

Violence is a critical way that systems of domination work. Physical violence may be used, but cultural violence or symbolic violence or both are the weapons of choice more often than not. Symbolic violence is the tendency of the dominant or ruling social class to use its symbols and logics to debase the other. The success of these pushback mechanisms relies on White logics that label the perceived out-of-place actor as a wrongdoer and decide what punishment is appropriate.

Power includes the ability to have the symbols you support, label, or identify recognized and legitimated by other people, but it is also the ability to name. This naming power is critical because to name something is to frame it. Like a picture frame, what is cut out of the picture (or foregrounded) controls the message that is received.

Contemporary racism has a new discourse but old objectives. The new language avoids offensive words that have come to be associated with and signal old racist ideals. Instead, in contemporary society, opposers use "seemingly race-neutral language, which is laden with race-based attitudes."[88] Anders Walker outlines this process. According to Walker, the post-Brown southern strategy for maintaining social segregation and White supremacy relied on a shift to the use of seemingly neutral terms like "moral character" and "illegitimacy" that were imbued with racial meaning. Claiming Blacks were unfit on some purportedly race-neutral basis served as the proxy means to racially discriminate against groups. Walker writes, "By focusing on illegitimacy rates among African Americans that had been artificially increased by covert legislative means, segregationists achieved two important political goals. Not only did they develop a new mechanism for furthering racial discrimination based on facially neutral language, but by substituting the quality of blackness for the characteristic of immorality, they transformed blacks from victims of wrong, to the agents of it. Segregationists, in other words, developed a language that enabled them to disguise racial discrimination as moral reform."[89] Naming (i.e., framing) power includes the ability to label an act, and the power to have that label be viewed as accurate. As Bonilla-Silva has outlined in his body of work, once the body is labeled deviant, color-blind logics are evoked to justify and legitimate the response or outcome. These logics include meritocracy, minimization, naturalization (explaining race-based outcomes as part of the natural order of things), and cultural racism (using culturally based arguments to explain the standing of minorities in society)[90]

8. BOP theory is necessarily intersectional in its nature and applicable across multiple social structures.

Intersectional identities become more salient for those who fail to stay in their perceived place. The host of other identities and behaviors—class, gender, sexual orientation, religion, age, region, religion, dress, tone of voice, eye contact (or lack thereof), educational attainment, career, familial status, et cetera—are drawn on as a basis to further validate the presumption of one's place. Every attribute or move is subject to scrutiny and used to condemn the Black body that seeks to freely claim or traverse space. The freedom that I speak of is the exertive free use of space in a way that violates the stereotypical expectations of access and belonging there. It is an assertion of some of the basic civil and political rights enumerated in the Universal Declaration of Human Rights, including the rights to live in freedom and safety, be protected by laws, own property, and move to a different place. The ability to traverse space is the ultimate freedom of movement.

Identities are layered and complex, and tenet 8 brings the complexities of intersectional subjectivities into the analysis of whether a body is deemed out of place. This tenet also recognizes that not all Black bodies are viewed and treated equally. The treatment to which people are subjected is based on a host of factors that influence their relative social status. It also recognizes the inherent difficulty of bifurcating an individual's identity. Poet Audre Lorde cogently speaks to this issue: "As a forty-nine-year-old Black lesbian feminist socialist mother of two, including one boy, and a member of an interracial couple, I usually find myself as part of some group defined as other . . . I find I am constantly being encouraged to pluck out some one aspect of myself and present this as the meaningful whole, eclipsing or denying the other parts of self."[91] Lorde rejected this. Not to reject this can be akin to a denial of self. It too violates a fundamental civil and political right: the right to live in freedom and safety.

In recognition that different identities subject individuals to multiple forms of oppression, feminist legal scholar Kimberlé Crenshaw and others offer intersectionality as a prism for understanding oppression inside what Patricia Hill Collins calls the "matrix of domination."[92] Inside this system, power is relational, and multiple identities subject the individual to multiple (and varied) oppressions. Race matters, but so do other identities. For example, the oft-used White racial frame includes biases and prejudices against racial minorities, but it also places masculine privilege at its center.[93] Intersectional analysis is attentive to matters of gender, race, place, and other things, and this is imperative inside the BOP framework.

Koritha Mitchell explains, "In the United States, the success of marginalized groups inspires aggression as often as praise.... Because the purpose of violence is to mark who belongs and who does not, it is best understood as a severe form of *know-your-place-aggression*. Violence is a way of reminding targets of their 'proper place,' a way of insisting that certain people should not feel secure in claiming space."[94] Mitchell's insights disinter the essence of BOP theory. Perceived out-of-place bodies evoke a response; that response is an attempt to put them back in their place, a place of both separation and subservience. This tactical response is reminiscent of the slave codes, Black Codes, and various Jim Crow or Jim Crow–like laws and policing, including restrictive covenants, racial zoning, mortgage and insurance redlining, and broken windows policing.

Intersectionality offers a lens through which to see and combat prevailing cultural attacks. The knowledge and logics of oppressed people are often discounted. White logic is the default logic in society, and the acceptance of White logics is a form of cultural violence.[95] The ready acceptance of such logics acts as an attack on the psyche, but it reverberates through acts of political and economic violence. Galtung defines cultural violence as "those aspects of culture, the symbolic sphere of our existence—exemplified by religion and ideology, language and art, empirical science and formal science, logic, mathematics—that can be used to justify or legitimize direct or structural violence."[96] BOP is a framework for those who no longer want to remain quiet in the wake of these ongoing attacks.

Conclusion

Anti-Black sentiments in America may seem less overt and vocal than in the past, but they persist in nuanced, complex, and multilayered ways, which is part of what can make them so difficult to see. History, however, tells us that the current attack is not substantially different from the past. Whites were more vocal and overt about racism once slavery ended because they feared the freedom of Black people. Similarly, the advances made by the Black freedom struggle—then and now—may make some Whites feel all that more eager to display anti-Black racism. Seeing this truth is a beginning, not an end. In the pages of this book, I identify the attack. I speak to those who already recognize the reality of continuing racism and anti-blackness in society, and I speak to those who are willing to consider the possibility. NFL football player and activist Malcolm Jenkins said, "We for a long time have tried to put reconciliation before truth but when you do that, you don't really see what is really oppressing people and really what the problems are."[97] To paraphrase Jenkins, we need truth before we can have reconciliation. That truth is also a necessary prerequisite to understanding, contrition, and full reparation.

CHAPTER 3

The Pushback

> Our [Black] history is not a history of never having.
> It is a history of things being taken away.
>
> —PAULA GIDDINGS

Award-winning Du Boisian and social movements scholar Aldon Morris asserts that organizing, creativity, culture, leadership, and institutional capacity are all inherent within the Black community in spite of— or perhaps because of—a history of oppression.[1] Morris's *The Scholar Denied: W. E. B. Du Bois and the Birth of Modern Sociology* shifts the understanding of the founding of U.S. sociology away from its purported origins at the University of Chicago to the groundbreaking work Du Bois conducted much earlier in the social laboratory he led at Atlanta University, a historically Black college founded in 1865.[2] Elected the 2021 president of the American Sociological Association, Morris argues that denials of Du Bois's scholarship have impoverished sociology. Similar denials—through erasure, fabrication, and half-truths—have deprived the world of a fuller understanding of the Black experience in America. Acclaimed author and scholar Saidiya Hartman says that Black identity has been forged by the twin processes of terror and resistance.[3] Each hard-fought Black gain has been met with White pushback. This pattern of resistance and then pushback is reflected in the Paula Giddings quote that serves as the epigraph for this chapter: "Our [Black] history is not a history of never having. It is a history of things being taken away."[4] This chapter recounts that history.

The Permanent Evil of Violence

The author bell hooks argues that "there is no life to be found in violence." Perhaps that is its aim. White pushback is a form of violence, and it has dual aims. Its first goal is to frustrate, retard, and deny Black progress. The second and ultimate aim of the pushback is to repudiate Black advances and thereby restore and legitimate a hierarchy with Whites on top. The pushback is both an offensive and defensive maneuver that seeks to naturalize the White supremacist social order. We live in what Judith Butler describes as a "racially saturated field of visibility."[5] Inside the racially saturated field, only a limited range of social meanings are ascribed to certain bodies. Other social meanings are cut off. The bodies of Rodney King and Trayvon Martin became saturated with but one identity, the dangerous criminal who must be put down. This incentivizes—through violence and the threat of violence—Black bodies to stay in their place. The effect is to maintain a system of Black subordination and White dominance, especially in social relations. This is achieved while also denying Black bodies control over the places to which they are relegated, which are often owned or administered by Whites.

To illustrate the historical pattern of pushback that I outline, I engage in an exercise in what some scholars call writing across time.[6] The importance of time is revealed in statements like "equality is an idea whose time has come" or requests to "go slow" when enacting social change. Like place, time is complex. In many ways, the idea of being out of place is consonant with the idea of being out of time. It is an extension of my idea that, in this current era, Black bodies are not unwelcome per se. Even perceived dirty, aberrant things belong in certain times and places. Valerie Castile, mother of Philando Castile, sums up this concept best. Regarding the police killing of her son, Castile said, "[To them] he was black in the wrong time and place."[7] In his short 32 years on this earth, Philando Castile had been stopped by police at least 49 times.[8] A similar "wrong time and place" phenomenon can be observed when analyzing a number of the interactions described in this chapter. While border-crossing patterns that collapse, expand, or contract racial boundaries are sometimes present, what anthropologist Mary Douglas calls "border aversive emotions" (like fear and disdain) exist.[9] As Black bodies move through space, so too does the geography of dissent against them. This opposition is especially triggered if Blacks appear to be "moving on up" like the characters George and Weezy in the 1970s television program *The Jeffersons*.[10]

Historians will likely find this account lacking. However, it is not written for historians. I write this chapter with the knowledge that few people actually recall history, and even larger numbers were educated through the use of textbooks purposefully infused with White supremacist politics and thought. Historian Elizabeth Gillespie McRae describes this campaign in her book *Massive Resistance: White Women and the Politics of White Supremacy*. McRae outlines how White women affiliated with segregationist women's groups worked through their local Citizens' Councils and parent-teacher associations to carefully and intentionally recommend the censure of certain materials.[11] The groups championed the adoption of textbooks and curricula bathed in Lost Cause attitudes.[12] These ideas were passed on to generations of children to come. It is this telling of history that must be countered. I also write this account because ignorance of history still persists. A study by the Woodrow Wilson National Fellowship Foundation found that only 27% of U.S. citizens under the age of 45 exhibit even a basic knowledge of American history, and only about four out of ten Americans demonstrated passing knowledge of basic American history.[13]

History is more than just people, places, and dates. History reveals the character of a society. After all, the history of spaces, Foucault observes, is "the history of powers."[14] Society consists of a number of spaces, and this abbreviated history is attentive to all of them, but I especially want to highlight the importance of social space. Social space is relational space. It affords a place for the exchange of ideas, the development or maintenance of friendships, and the selling or trade of goods and services. In essence, the free use of social space is essential for a free and open society. The June 2020 forceful removal of peaceful protesters from Lafayette Square in Washington, D.C., accomplished by agents of the state, is a clear indication that not everyone in U.S. society is entitled to the free use of social space. This chapter tells the story of how we, as a country, got there.

The Pushback as Degradation Ceremony

The pushback functions as what Harold Garfinkel terms a degradation ceremony.[15] Degradation ceremonies serve to lower an individual's or group's status. As a public ritual, it reinforces the prevailing community standards (as set forth by the dominant group) about what behavior is appropriate, labels an individual as deviant, punishes the deviant actor, and acts as a warning to others who might contemplate similar acts that they do so at their own peril. In Garfinkel's framework, someone denounces an action by a perpetrator before a group (witnesses). The denouncer proclaims (to witnesses) that the activity by the perpetrator is a violation of the norms and/or values of the community. The denouncer and the witness are framed as righteous, good, upstanding members of the community, and the perpetrator is an outsider whose actions are inexcusable. Therefore, the perpetrator is branded a deviant only free to participate in the community in a limited fashion, if at all.[16] Slavery was a form of total degradation. All subsequent efforts to push back against Black advancement are a modification of this system of total degradation. The aim is the curtailment of Black liberty so as to limit participation in the larger society to where, how, and when the denouncers see fit.

Slavery

The first Africans were brought to the North American British colonial territory that would become the United States of America in August 1619; however, the Spanish and later the French brought Africans with them to North America a full century earlier.[17] Captured Africans were transported to Point Comfort, in the colony of Virginia.[18] They arrived via an English privateer ship, and, upon arrival, the captain traded the Africans to the colonists in exchange for food. Historian James Horn describes the exchange in his book *1619: Jamestown and the Forging of American Democracy*. Horn reveals a public performance, which allowed the Africans to be bought "at the best and easiest rate they could."[19] This open trade of people for victuals cemented the Africans' debased status before the community and each other. On the following day, a second ship carrying captive Africans arrived. Soon after, slavery began to grow throughout the territory.

Africans did not accept their plight without protest. White settlers feared African rebellion. This resulted in some colonies passing a series of restrictive laws known as slave codes.[20] With each rebellion, slave codes grew stricter, "further abridging the already limited rights and privileges this oppressed people might hope to enjoy."[21] Slave codes offered a form of institutionalized social control over Africans' bodies, which, ironically, were not considered human bodies at all but humanoid "property."[22] Subject to the force of law, these restrictions and denials cemented the Africans' juridical status as nonbeings.

Slave labor was integral to the survival of colonial society. That dependence, however, did not engender more humane treatment. Historian Edmund S. Morgan's book *American Slavery, American Freedom* and his influential article "The Labor Problem at Jamestown, 1607–1618" counter a popular narrative that paints the first African Americans (and their ancestors) as unintelligent and lazy.[23] Morgan's archival evidence suggests that it was the unwillingness of colonists at Jamestown, the first permanent English settlement in America, to do basic labor that made them dependent on Black Africans for their very survival.[24]

The year 1642 marked an important time in the Virginia colony. The status conversion of Africans from servants to enslaved people was almost complete, and law was an early tool used to cement the transformation. It codified and sanctioned the performance of rituals to degrade and demean Africans that had earlier occurred by custom. The 1642 Virginia colony fugitive slave law became a model for how to perform the degradation of Black bodies, including a stipulation that after a second runaway attempt, an enslaved person could be branded on the cheek with the letter R.[25]

From the 1660s through early part of the next decade, Virginia and Maryland led all the colonies in drafting a series of restrictive laws against their African population.[26] Assaults on Africans, including sexual assaults against African women, were neither punished nor deemed a crime.[27] These sexual assaults challenged the landscape of blackness since subsequently born mixed-race children served as a visual reminder that the strict racial binary was in jeopardy. In response, stricter colonial decrees were instated to preserve the privileges of whiteness. These laws codified the idea that enslavement was for life and transferred to children through the mother.[28] This legal doctrine was known a "partus sequitur ventrem," Latin for "that which follows from the womb." It clarified that slavery was a caste system and that children took the social status of their mother. Therefore, regardless of paternity, any child born to an enslaved woman was born into slavery.[29]

Slave patrols, created for the dual purposes of maintaining slavery and policing slave insurrection, became another part of the visual landscape and tool in the degradation and subjugation of Black bodies. The groups were precursors to the modern police.[30] Patrols made sure that enslaved people were where and with whom they were supposed to be.[31] However, White males could freely traverse space. The groups never patrolled or enforced any action against White men who forced themselves on Black women.

Patrols comprised a cross section of White citizens across all social classes.[32] The public nature of the patrols served as a visible reminder of defined social norms and a willingness to maintain social order by any means, including violence up to death. But it also marked a tension. Keeping enslaved people in line was a matter of pride, but it was also a community imperative. This system established whiteness as a cartel (i.e., a cooperative collective endeavor between parties for the purpose of supporting a mutual interest), not merely a function of individual acts of anti-Black racism.

Revolt

Revolts did take place. By 1711, the colony of New York erected a city-run slave market.[33] Enslaved people in the most densely populated part of the city lived in close proximity to their owners and to each other. This environment allowed for communication and planning. Approximately a year after the slave market was built, the enslaved revolted. It became known as the New York City Slave Revolt of 1712. Outnumbered and surrounded, the rebels faced certain capture. Six committed suicide rather than be taken back into slavery. Most of the remaining 21 were executed, some beaten, hanged, and then burned to death.[34] The colonial governor of New York estimated that nine White colonists were killed during the incident and another six wounded.[35] As news of the revolt spread, restrictions on enslaved people grew tighter, and slave codes became harsher, but so did the will of some enslaved people to fight.[36]

The Stono Rebellion occurred on September 9, 1739, about 20 miles from Charleston, South Carolina. While the precise roots of the uprising are unclear, decades in advance of it, the enslaved used the language of the coming American Revolution and cried out for liberty. It was one of the first major revolts by enslaved people in the southernmost colonies and happened on a Sunday. In August that year, the colony had passed the Security Act of 1739, which required White men to carry firearms to church on Sundays. On Sundays, the enslaved men and women had fewer restrictions than on other days, and they were often unguarded. Several enslaved individuals met near the river to plan their escape. They decided to take munitions and guns from a local store, and they killed the two White storekeepers they encountered there. Armed and emboldened, some 20 enslaved people marched down King's Highway shouting "Liberty!" It is said they were headed to St. Augustine, Florida, where the Spanish were granting fugitives from slavery freedom and land. Ten miles into their trek, they were overtaken by Whites, but not before they had killed many White slaveowners along their way.[37] Approximately 25 Whites were killed in this uprising.[38] Historian Herbert Aptheker estimates that 35–50 Africans were slain.[39] Most of the enslaved persons were recaptured and either executed or sold.

The South Carolina colonial assembly passed the Negro Act of 1740 in direct response to the Stono Rebellion. The Negro Act prohibited enslaved persons from growing their own food, assembling in groups, earning their own money, and learning to read or write.[40] These laws codified longstanding customs. Slave owners were also expressly allowed to kill their chattel.[41] The Negro Act also changed the visual landscape of the area since it required a minimum of one White man for every ten Blacks on a plantation. The hypersurveillance of Blacks present today has roots in these practices, and the Negro Act offered a model for the later Black Codes.[42]

America's Battle for Freedom and Early Government

Racial hierarchies, writes Cameroonian philosopher and political theorist Achille Mbembe, "operate through a logic of enclosure."[43] There is a spatial and temporal logic to enclosure, and it operates as a kind of boundary work. Enclosure may be physical or mental. Applied to this context, the racial hierarchy Mbembe outlines disqualified Blacks from freedom at the same time that colonists sought this status for themselves. As war between England and the colonies loomed, the colonists wanted to preserve their strict racial boundaries. Not only did the American Revolution of 1776 not bring freedom to the country's enslaved persons, historian Gerald Horne asserts, a major reason for the Revolution itself was to preserve the financially profitable system of slavery.[44] Enslaved persons accounted for approximately 20% of the total population of the American colonies and in the southern territories as much as 40%.[45] In sum, American slavery was a racial caste system in which White supremacy was tied to the denial of Black rights.

The 1781 Articles of Confederation were silent on the issue of slavery. The Constitutional Convention of 1787 resolved that three out of every five enslaved persons would be counted for the purposes of determining congressional representation in the newly formed federal government. The three-fifths clause gave Whites in slave-owning states more representation than Whites in free states.[46] Black personhood was still denied, and subsequent federal actions like the Fugitive Slave Acts of 1793 and 1850 guaranteed the right of slaveowners to recover their human property and mandated that all Whites assist in the capture of runaway enslaved people.[47] Through these acts, Congress endorsed and condoned the continuing public performance of ritualistic barbarism inherent in the system of slavery.

Freedom Is a Constant Struggle

The very existence of "slave states" and "free states" contributed to the insecurity of Black existence. The meaning of Black freedom was inconsistent, and concern about all classes of Africans—slave, free, runaway—was present throughout the country. In *Becoming Free, Becoming Black: Race, Freedom and the Law in Cuba, Virginia, and Louisiana*, authors Alejandro de la Fuente and Ariela Gross highlight this precarity. Unless special permission was earned from the legislature, any enslaved person in Virginia who earned freedom would be forced to leave the area within six months. Free Blacks literally had no place in that society.[48] Similar regulations emerged in other places. In Louisiana, manumission was only allowed if a ticket to Liberia accompanied the petition.[49]

It was a precarious kind of freedom. For example, the courts willingly entertained and enforced proceedings against manumitted Blacks who remained in the area.[50] If manumitted slaves remained in the territory, they could be sold back into slavery. Manumission did not ensure the ability to pay for the basic needs of food and shelter, so some freed persons petitioned for re-enslavement.[51] Blackness was a disfavored, unprotected legal status. As a result of this stigma, some sought legal protection in the form of a "Not a Negro" certificate—a legal declaration of non-Negro status that enabled them to claim the privileges of whiteness.[52]

Amid all this precarity, physical boundaries offered little protection. "Free states" were not necessarily free. Cincinnati is nestled on the Ohio River. The river acted as a border between Kentucky, a slave state, and Ohio, a free state. During August 15–22, 1829, White mob violence drove more than half of Cincinnati's Black residents from the city. American abolitionist David Walker's *Appeal to the Colored Citizens of the World*, published later that year was a call to self-defense."[53]

In 1820 there had been only 433 Black residents in Cincinnati. In 1829, approximately 10,000 Blacks lived in Ohio, and over 2,258 of them resided in Cincinnati.[54] From 1826 to 1829, Cincinnati's Black population increased by nearly 400%.[55] During the same period, the White population of Cincinnati remained relatively static. Further, half of all Cincinnati Blacks lived in an area called Bucktown, which, though segregated, was populated by Blacks and Whites. Poor Whites, largely immigrants, grew increasingly concerned about competition from Black laborers and a small number of Black-owned businesses there.[56] The Black and Irish in the city tended to live in residential clusters like Bucktown and "Little Africa," along or near the waterfront, where many of them worked.[57] Whites feared loss of social, political, and economic control. Ohio may have been a free state, but White Cincinnatians did not want the city to become a Black space.

The White community devised a twofold attack aimed at limiting Black growth and removing Blacks from some parts of the city. First, White residents petitioned the city government to enforce an 1807 law that had required Black residents to pay a $500 bond as proof of their good character.[58] The group used pretense in making this request. They alleged the area where many Negroes lived was a fire hazard.[59] On June 30, 1829, the local newspaper, the *Cincinnati Daily Gazette*, printed a notice stating that Blacks had 30 days to pay the bond or be run out of the city. The Black community brought a lawsuit arguing that the laws curtailing Blacks were unconstitutional, but the Ohio Supreme Court upheld them.[60] During August 15–22, 1829, hundreds of Whites ran through the streets of Cincinnati attacking Black residents; they drove them—under threat of death—from their neighborhoods and out of town. Half of the Black population fled the city.

Whether through law, contract, custom, or restrictive policy or practice, U.S. society has understood and organized places (either cognitively or spatially) through the lens of race. White spaces were places of opportunity ripe for investment. Black bodies are marked as illegitimate trespassers in the White space. This spatial imaginary conceives people and identities in place. In "The Racialization of Space and Spatialization of Race," George Lipsitz states it this way: "Not all people who are white consciously embrace the white spatial imaginary, and not all whites profit equally from their whiteness, but all whites benefit from the association of whiteness with privilege and the neighborhood effects of spaces defined by their racial demography."[61] In the wake of the 1829 attack on Black Cincinnatians, the missing people and businesses testified to the Black community's collective loss. Among those Blacks who remained, memory of the attack lingered. This memory fueled them, and in 1841, when Whites made another attempt to expel Blacks from the city, the community was prepared. Black Cincinnatians fought back against the attacking White mob and successfully repelled several attacks.[62]

Every free person of color in Cincinnati was a challenge to the existing social order. The embers of the 1829 riot were stoked by the presence and activities of the Ohio chapter of the American Colonization Society (ACS). In existence from approximately 1816 through 1865, the society's official name was American Society for Colonizing the Free People of Color in the United States. The group formed as an alternative to emancipation. Its goal was to send free Blacks back to Africa.[63] This objective allowed the group to attract both proslavery and abolitionist supporters. To be clear, the ACS was about Black removal, not Black liberation. Henry Clay, a slaveholding congressman from Kentucky and former U.S. Speaker of the House advocated for colonization as a way to rid the country of free Blacks, which he described as "a useless and pernicious, if not dangerous portion of its population."[64] Others supported the ACS on purported "moral grounds."[65] Reverend Robert Finley, one of the founders of the group, thought the moral character of free Blacks was a threat to the well-being of Whites. An added benefit of emigration, Finley thought, was that the formerly enslaved persons could bring Christianity to Africa.[66] Some ACS members feared that free Blacks would incite rebellion.

Slave rebellions continued during this period. The Haitian Revolution (1791–1804) had led to the end of slavery and French rule in that country. It was a time of global challenges to the institution of slavery. Black voices were some of the most resolute in their condemnation of both the system of slavery and slaveholders. In his *Appeal*, Walker warned the nation that what happened in Haiti could happen elsewhere.[67] Nat Turner's slave rebellion happened two years later in Southampton County, Virginia.

It is said to have been the bloodiest slave revolt in American history. The local militia eventually crushed Turner's revolt and killed some 120 Blacks.[68] Turner escaped and was able to evade capture for nearly two months, but ultimately he was captured, tried, and publicly hanged in Jerusalem, the county seat. The public spectacle was meant to dissuade other Blacks from similar acts and to reinforce the legitimacy of the system of slavery.

Abolitionists including Frederick Douglass began speaking up more forcefully against slavery.[69] The preceding year, Sojourner Truth joined the Northampton (Massachusetts) Association of Education and Industry, and through it she continued her human rights campaign. Their accounts stood as a compelling counter-narrative to the records that paint slavery as a benevolent system and enslaved people as content.

While Douglass, Truth, and others were calling for the abolition of slavery, U.S. Secretary of State John C. Calhoun sought to justify slavery and frame it as good for Black people. He used pseudoscience to do so. Calhoun insisted that 1840 census data, which included responses to a new question about the presence of persons then termed "insane and idiots," revealed higher rates of the "insane" or "idiots" among the "colored" population than Whites, and he said this was "proof of the necessity of slavery.[70] Calhoun claimed, "The African is incapable of self-care and sinks into lunacy under the burden of freedom. It is a mercy to give him the guardianship and protection from mental death."[71] Calhoun and others sought to plant the seed that Blacks were "unfit for freedom."[72] De la Fuente and Gross argue that census and other racial classification systems gave blackness a negative and pejorative juridical meaning.[73]

War Is in the Air

The 1850 Compromise helped delay the start of the impending clash over the continuation of slavery in the nation, which ultimately led to the Civil War. Unlike the Slave Act of 1793, the 1850 Compromise, which included the Fugitive Slave Act of 1850, required that "runaways" be returned to their masters, even if that runaway was in a free state. It offered a pecuniary incentive to treat any Black person as a runaway and implied that a Black person's immutable place was in bondage, not in freedom. A provision of the 1850 Compromise made the federal government responsible for searching for and returning escaped enslaved persons. But it did not stop enslaved people from running away. Between 1850 and 1860, Harriet Tubman, a celebrated conductor on the Underground Railroad, led over 300 enslaved persons to freedom.[74]

Despite the protections the institution afforded whiteness, some enslaved and free Africans turned to the legal system for redress of their grievances. Few of those actions were successful, but they demonstrate the undaunted will and courage of Blacks to fight against oppression and for their own liberation. Dred and Harriet Scott, a married Black couple, illustrate this idea. In 1846, the Scotts filed a petition for their freedom in circuit court in St. Louis.[75] Dred Scott was enslaved in Alabama; later, the family who owned Scott moved to Missouri and took all their property, including enslaved persons, with them. A few years later, Scott's original master (Peter Blow) died. Scott was sold and then taken to live and work in at least two areas where slavery was prohibited. Dred Scott married Harriet (also enslaved), and they had children together. Eventually, the couple's owner sent his family and property (including enslaved persons) back to St. Louis. In St. Louis, the Scotts filed freedom suits under the doctrine "once free, always free." This principle suggested if you were an enslaved person held in a free territory, then you should be free.

The Scott case was the subject of multiple appeals, but on March 6, 1857, the U.S. Supreme Court finally handed down its ruling in *Dred Scott v. Sandford*.[76] The ruling itself was an attack on Black humanity and dignity. The court stated that Blacks had no rights in federal court. Next, the court said that states no longer had to honor the "once free, always free doctrine." Finally, the court held that Congress never should have prevented slavery in the Wisconsin Territory or any territory. On the issue of whether African Americans were citizens of the United States and thereby able to file suit in federal court, Chief Justice Roger Taney notoriously wrote, "[Negroes] had for more than a century before been regarded as beings of an inferior order, and altogether unfit to associate with the white race, either in social or political relations; and *so far inferior that they had no rights which the white man was bound to respect*; and that the Negro must justly and lawfully be reduced to slavery *for his benefit*. He was bought and sold and treated as an ordinary article of merchandise and traffic whenever profit could be made by it."[77] The decision framed Blacks as aliens in a country they had helped to build. Taney noted that Blacks could not be citizens because citizenship was just for White people. You cannot be more out of place than that. The 7–2 Supreme Court decision connected citizenship and rights to race.

Civil War Era

Parties on both sides thought the Civil War would be short lived. The July 21, 1861, Battle of Bull Run in Virginia was the first major battle of the war, and it was a stunning Union defeat. It soon became clear that the Civil War would be a protracted fight. Battles waged on and off the literal battlefield. These included a battle in Memphis, Tennessee, between May 1 and May 3, 1863 that became known as the Memphis Massacre.[78] White civilians and police in this mid-South city killed 46 African Americans and injured many more, burning 90 houses, 12 schools, and 4 churches. The entire country was a powder keg.

Tensions in New York predated the famous 1863 draft riots there, with conflicts largely along race and class lines. Working-class New Yorkers became angry about a proposed federal draft law.[79] Commentator and author John Strausbaugh remarks, "When Lincoln issued his Preliminary Emancipation Proclamation in September 1862, New Yorkers launched protests, while soldiers or officers in New

York units deserted or resigned their commissions, declaring that they'd fight to preserve the Union but not to free the slaves."[80] The conscription law contained a provision that a draftee could buy his way out of service for $300, which was the approximate equivalent of a man's entire annual wage in 1863.[81] Effectively, the draft only applied to the poor and working class; those of means could buy their way out (or hire a substitute) if drafted. In the period between the Emancipation Proclamation and the start of the New York draft riots, those feelings continued to simmer. It came to a head with five days of rioting; hundreds of people were killed.

While White rioters had numerous targets for their frustration, the riots quickly proved to be about White racial animosity and hatred for Blacks. Thousands of White workers, including a number of Irish American immigrants, publicly attacked Blacks.[82] It was a degradation ceremony of unprecedented spectacle. They destroyed businesses, assaulted business owners, and beat and killed people—mostly Blacks. They also attacked military and government buildings as well as any police who tried to intervene. Abolitionists and White women married to Blacks were also targets. The rioters even set fire to an orphanage that housed 200 Black children.[83] White dockworkers were the most virulent.

The published death toll from the riots was 119, but some say as many as 1,200 Blacks were beaten or lynched.[84] Federal troops were brought in to restore order.

The NAACP has defined lynching as an extrajudicial killing performed by three or more people whose stated purpose is to uphold justice or tradition.[85] Lynching was a performative ritual. The violent, orgiastic ceremony not only degraded Blacks but also fostered bonding among Whites. In their article "Practicing What They Preach? Lynching and Religion in the American South, 1890–1929," Amy Kate Bailey and Karen E. Snedker, demonstrate that while the religious landscape in the American South had some variation, including communities that embraced social activism, they were still not willing to directly stand up against the prevailing racial order.[86] After the New York riots, many Blacks left Manhattan and settled in the borough of Brooklyn.

After the Emancipation Proclamation, Black soldiers began officially enlisting in the Union army, but their status as soldiers did not protect them from Civil War atrocities. One of the worst was the April 12, 1864, Fort Pillow Massacre. Surrounded, Union troops were attempting to surrender. These Union troops included approximately 300 African American soldiers at Fort Pillow. However, instead of taking them as prisoners of war, the Confederate army brutally murdered the Black soldiers.[87] This happened despite the fact that, a year earlier, the Confederate States had passed a law that stated that Negro soldiers captured while fighting against the Confederacy would be turned over to the state and tried according to state law.[88] The murder of the Black soldiers signaled that they did not deserve to be treated as equals with Whites, if they were even human at all.

Contraband camps, the name given to settlements that housed escaped enslaved persons as "contraband of war," were another active form of Black resistance to White Civil War insurgency.[89] The camps also signaled that, at best, Black freedom would likely be a liminal state. International law recognized the "legitimate right to confiscate as 'contraband of war' property used by the enemy against you."[90] Union major general Benjamin Butler reasoned that because the Confederate army used enslaved persons in the construction of their military defenses, enslaved persons qualified as contraband. Women and children were not included in this rationale, but eventually they were permitted in the camps too.[91] Approximately half a million formerly enslaved persons walked off the plantation and effectively emancipated themselves.[92] A number made their way to contraband camps, but the contraband rationale shrouded Blacks with a continuing type of property status and subordinate treatment. Those Blacks who resided in the contraband camps received a wage for their services to the Union, but they were paid less than White workers performing comparable services and usually paid late. Black women were even more vulnerable. They were subject to multiple abuses in the camps. For these reasons, author Chandra Manning writes, "the camps made for 'troubled refuge.'"[93]

The war officially ended on May 13, 1865, but the imprint of the racial caste system of slavery that the war was fought to protect would continue. This was true in the short and long term. In Texas, formerly enslaved people liberated on January 1, 1863, by way of the Emancipation Proclamation did not learn about their "free" status until June 19, 1865 (Juneteenth). According to Jon Meacham, "Slavery had been conquered but racism lived on across America."[94]

Mbembe writes, "To endure [such] a form of domination must not only inscribe itself on the bodies of its subjects but also leave its imprint on the spaces they inhabit as indelible traces on the imaginary."[95]

Reconstruction and Beyond

The end of the Civil War and the advent of Reconstruction saw advances for African Americans but also gave rise to concerted and organized pushback against Black advancement. Black Codes and subsequent Jim Crow regulations were a principal vehicle for that pushback. Black Codes became best known immediately after the Civil War, but they existed prior to it in both the North and the South. The regulations represented a form of social control of Black life and an effort to curtail Blacks' social and geographic mobility. Movement was heavily regulated.

Arrests for loitering and vagrancy were regularly made and used to force Blacks into labor conditions said to be worse than slavery.[96]

Vagrancy laws made it a crime to be unemployed. The heart of a vagrancy designation was this: failure of a Black man to be bound to a White person through a labor contract was criminalized. For example, in late 1865, a Mississippi law required Blacks (many of whom could not read) to enter into a written work contract by January of the coming year. These contracts contained significant penalties for those who left before the end of the term. Those who violated their "labor contracts" could face charges and fines that might subject the person to convict leasing, a system of peonage that Douglas Blackmon aptly labels "slavery by another name."[97] A South Carolina law dictated that Blacks could only be employed as farmers or servants if they paid an annual tax between $10 and $100. Attempts to search for gainful employment or receive an education were effectively thwarted.

Vagrancy and loitering laws criminalized Black life, especially Black mobility; vagrancy made it a crime for a person to wander from place to place without visible means of support. The objective was to tie Blacks to the South and force them into the cheap labor jobs (or worse) available there. Geographer Ruth Wilson Gilmore describes this this conundrum. Vagrancy, Gilmore argues, was a law against moving, and loitering was a law against standing still. Therefore, no matter what Black people did, they were criminalized.[98] Citing Gilmore, Lipsitz writes, "Under this system there were only two things that could get blacks arrested in the postbellum South: moving or standing still."[99]

The Freedmen's Bureau (1865–1872) created to aid Blacks in the transition from slavery to freedom had been short lived. On December 24, 1865, less than a year after the Freedmen's Bureau formed, the domestic terrorist group known as the Ku Klux Klan (KKK) was founded in Pulaski, Tennessee. By 1870, the KKK was in almost every southern state.[100] By 1873, southern Whites were loudly calling for "redemption" and the open return of White supremacy. By 1877, Reconstruction came to an end.[101]

Regarding this period, Du Bois wrote, "The slave went free; stood a brief moment in the sun; then moved back again toward slavery."[102] Former U.S. congressman Thomas E. Miller, a free-born Black and trained attorney, put it this way, "We were eight years in power. We had built school houses, established charitable institutions, built and maintained the penitentiary system, provided for the education of the deaf, and dumb, rebuilt the jails, and court houses, rebuilt the bridges, and reestablished the ferries. In short, we had reconstructed the state."[103] This pushback signaled that the country Blacks had sacrificed to build and then rebuilt was for White enjoyment and advantage.

Despite advances, attacks on Blacks were quite common during Reconstruction. As the 1868 presidential election drew closer, White southern Democrats and others became increasingly fearful about the Black male vote. To combat this, they devised tactics to suppress the Black vote. One very effective tactic was mass violence, and attacks in the Deep South were particularly virulent. The Opelousas Massacre (St. Landry Parish, Louisiana) began on September 28, 1868. In yet another degradation ceremony, a group of Whites executed 27 Black prisoners in cold blood. They also attacked other African Americans in the vicinity, killing between 200 and 300 people.[104] On October 25, 1870, in Eutaw, Alabama, Ku Klux Klan members attacked a Republican rally held by 2,000 Black citizens, killing four people and wounding 54. It became known as the Eutaw Riot.[105] Racially motivated political violence continued in other parts of the country, but it seemed especially heinous in the South.[106] By 1872, Red Shirts, members of an armed paramilitary White supremacist group, were guarding polling places in the South, especially the Carolinas. Their presence and actions made the declaration: a Black man's place is not on the ballot or even in the voting booth.[107]

The violence was meant to enforce a physical and social separation between Black and White life. Nearly two decades later, a young Ida B. Wells bravely spoke out against the widespread lynching of Black bodies.[108] Wells analyzed lynching and public transportation segregation as stemming from the perception of Black bodies being physically and socially out of place.[109] In her 1884 suit against the Chesapeake, Ohio, and Southwestern Railroad Company, Wells demonstrated how transportation was an important means Whites used to maintain separation.[110] Years later, Black plaintiffs challenged the constitutionality of the Louisiana Separate Car Act of 1890.[111] On June 7, 1892, one of the plaintiffs, a Black man named Homer Plessy, boarded a Whites-only section of the train.[112] Plessy was arrested after he refused to leave the first-class train. The case went to the U.S. Supreme Court.

Deciding against Plessy and the other Black plaintiffs, the court reasoned that the law was not discriminatory because, while it banned Blacks in the cars reserved for Whites, it also banned Whites from the Black cars. The decision made no mention of the fact that the White cars were well appointed and clean, while the Black cars were filled with dirt and soot and sometimes had animals in them.[113] The 1896 *Plessy* ruling reiterated that Blacks belonged in separate, distinct, and inferior spaces from Whites, although the doctrine upheld was labeled "separate but equal."[114] The court stated that separate but equal facilities did not violate the Fourteenth Amendment.[115] In the wake of *Plessy*, locales reacted with their own purportedly "separate but equal" restrictions.[116] Wells said she was not surprised by the decision.[117]

Despite the exposure Wells and others brought, public lynching continued, with increasingly larger public audiences. The large gatherings offer evidence that these heinous actions were the will of the community. Church Sunday school classes convened to witness and support lynching. Body parts of lynched Black people were put on display. Photographs of lynching were circulated as postcards. The violent acts served as a reminder of the fragility of life and thereby reinforced the virtues of silence. Whites who spoke out risked being lynched themselves.[118] Hearing no dissent, the judgments performed and meted out were reinforced as acceptable, even when they were particularly monstrous.

The February 1, 1893, lynching of Henry Smith in Paris, Texas, provides an example of the monstrosity of lynching spectacles.[119] Smith had been suspected of killing a White girl. He fled and was caught. His captors paraded him through the town. An enormous wooden stage was erected and placed in the center of town.[120] A White mob stripped Smith naked and beat him. Smith was tormented (for about an hour) with hot irons. Then he was doused with lamp fuel and set ablaze.[121] Even those who chose not to view the spectacle would find it difficult to ignore the cries that must have come from his tortured body or avoid the smell of Smith's burning flesh. According to the Equal Justice Initiative, at least 10,000 people were present. Smith maintained his innocence until the end. His tormentors sold his body parts, and the crowd also took ashes and bones as souvenirs.[122]

Black Advancement in the Early 20th Century

At the turn of the century, W. E. B. Du Bois predicted that the color line would continue to plague the 20th century.[123] He was right. The first decade of the century included race riots in locales as varied as Brownsville, Texas (1906); Argenta, Arkansas, just outside Little Rock (1906); Atlanta (1906); and Springfield, Illinois (1908).[124] African Americans and like-minded Whites joined to fight racial inequality, and in 1909 the National Association for the Advancement of Colored People (NAACP) was founded. The organization used its signature magazine, *The Crisis*, to combat the stereotypical images of Blacks common in society and present more humane presentations of Black life and embodiment.[125]

In the midst of a Black cultural awakening and the emergence of what Alain Locke named the New Negro, Black excellence was something that particularly inspired White ire.[126] A Black man's place, some reasoned, was beneath a White man. On December 26, 1908, Jack Johnson, a Black boxer, challenged defending world champion Tommy Burns for the title. Unlike his predecessors, Burns agreed to fight a Black man for the title if the purse was right.[127] The fight was held in Sydney, Australia. Johnson knocked Burns to the floor within seconds, but Burns got up. Burns was ill equipped to fight Johnson, though. People in the crowd began to yell. They did not want to see a Black man win this coveted prize, especially if it meant knocking out a White man to claim it. The movie cameras stopped recording. Jack Johnson was declared the winner. He was the first Black man to ever fight for the heavyweight boxing title, and he won it.[128] The title of heavyweight champion was a prize, and the boxer who held it was considered "the emperor of masculinity."[129] Black men were perceived out of place in such a competition.

White egos were soothed by claiming that Johnson would have never have defeated the retired champion, Jim Jeffries. Jeffries, touted the "Great White Hope," was urged to come out of retirement and show Johnson the superiority of the White man. The match made international news. On July 4, 1910, Johnson defended his title against Jim Jeffries. The outdoor fight was in Reno, Nevada, before a crowd of over 20,000 spectators. The temperature was in excess of 100F; it was expected to reach 110. The widely anticipated match was billed "The Battle of the Century." It was supposed to show "that a white man was king of them all."[130] In the 15th round, Johnson repeatedly knocked Jeffries down. Jeffries had never been knocked down before. Rather than have "the nigger" knock him out, Jeffries's side called it quits. Johnson retained his title. Johnson's victory was a source of Black pride and White anger. Enraged Whites all across the country responded with riots targeting Black people and their enterprises. Some states passed laws making it illegal to show a film or distribute an account of a fight in which a Black fighter defeated a White one. According to legal scholar Barak Orbach, it was a direct attempt to ban public dissemination of any form of Black excellence or supremacy.[131] In *Embodying Black Experience*, Harvey Young describes the initial victory and the resulting pushback. Young writes, "Despite an earlier victory [by Johnson in the ring], the black body, once outside the ring, was brought back into the 'ring' and again staged for the amusement of a white audience. The act of lynching created a new spectacle that served to neutralize the exploits of the black body between ropes by featuring a body hanging from one. The return to the rope marked the beginning of a second performance, a replay of the first but with a different ending."[132] Lynching served to rewrite the narrative of Jeffries defeat. In response to Johnson's win, White-led mob riots broke out across the nation. Decades later, Hank Aaron faced similar vitriol in the 1970s as he chased and ultimately surpassed Babe Ruth's home run record.[133]

President Woodrow Wilson (1913–1921) engaged in several acts aimed at putting Black bodies back into their place, if not outright degrading them. Wilson resegregated the federal workforce.[134] He championed a House of Representatives bill making racial intermarriage a felony in the District of Columbia and actions by the postmaster general ordering the segregation of its Washington offices.[135] Other federal agencies followed suit.[136] Federal workplaces, restrooms, and lunchrooms were segregated.[137] President Wilson also famously invited guests—including Supreme Court justices and other high-ranking federal officials—to a private White House viewing of D. W. Griffith's atrociously racist film *The Birth of a Nation*.

The second decade of the 20th century ended with violent race riots across the nation from late winter through early autumn of 1919, a period that would become known as Red Summer. In these assaults by Whites against Black citizens, White rioters believed that they were continuing Wilson's call to make the world safe for democracy, a call issued with the announcement of the nation's entrance into World War I. When the war came to an end, White servicemen returned home to find that some of the jobs they had held had been filled by immigrants and southern Blacks who had migrated North for better opportunities. In lieu of a foreign enemy, they waged their war on domestic soil again. Many White men believed these jobs belonged to them. They turned their anger and fear over increased competition in the housing and labor markets into frenzied, violent mob attacks on Blacks.[138]

Black men had served their country and fought in World War I too. Author David Krugler suggests that having fought abroad for the cause of democracy, they demanded democracy at home. And they were willing to fight for it.[139] Harlem Renaissance poet Claude McKay chronicled this resolve in his 1919 poem "If We Must Die." The website Blackpast calls the poem "an anthem for resistance against the anti-black violence then sweeping the nation."[140]

Boundary-enforcing practices continued throughout the 1920s. The same year the nation passed the restrictive Immigration Act of 1924 (the Johnson-Reid Act), the State of Virginia passed the Racial Integrity Act.[141] The law became a model for other states.[142] Under it, anyone born after 1912 had to certify their racial identity with local officials. It acted as a prohibition on "race-mixing." The legal definition of White specified that not one drop of "Black blood" was permitted. It was an attempt to preserve racial purity by defining who counted as White and noting this on birth and marriage records.[143]

As Wells noted, racial purity had become a dog-whistle political messaging ploy to incite violence against Black bodies, and protection of White womanhood and virtue was one of the rallying cries. This was used to justify violent attacks against Blacks, including the Tulsa Race Massacre of 1921 and Florida's Rosewood Massacre of 1923.[144] The Greenwood District in Tulsa, known as Black Wall Street, featured over 300 Black-owned businesses. In the events of the massacre, it was decimated, and it never returned to that glory. On the 99th anniversary of the events, CNN reported: "In the span of just 24 hours, 35 square blocks were burned and over 1,200 houses destroyed . . . historians now believe as many as 300 people died." The Tulsa Race Massacre is believed to be one of the worst incidents of ra-cial violence in American history.[145]

Despite the threat of violence, African Americans continued to move in, through, and to formerly White spaces. The *Negro Motorist Green Book* was one effort by Black people for Black people to aid in this movement.[146] Published from 1936 through 1966, it offered a guide to navigating through Jim Crow Amer-ica by listing safe places for Black travelers to find the accommodations and ser-vices they needed. The introduction to the 1948 edition of the *Green Book*, like most of the editions, clarifies that the guide was written to protect both the phys-ical and mental well-being of Black travelers. It was also overtly optimistic: "There will be a day sometime in the near future when this guide will not have to be pub-lished. This is when we as a race will have equal opportunities and privileges in the United States. It will be a great day for us to suspend this publication for then we can go wherever we please, and without embarrassment. But until that time comes we shall continue to publish this information for your convenience each year."[147] The civil rights movement was coming, but battles like the one waged in the *Green Book* were already being fought.

The Civil Rights Movement and Its Precursor

On May 24, 1951, a mob of 4,000 or more angry Whites engaged in a public per-formance aimed at preventing a Black family from physically moving into an apart-ment in the town of Cicero, Illinois. The mob hurled all the family's possessions out of the third-floor apartment window, and they attacked the police who came to assist.[148] Journalist Isabel Wilkerson describes the riot in her award-winning book, *The Warmth of Other Suns: The Epic Story of America's Great Migration*. She writes, "The Cicero riot attracted worldwide attention. It was front-page news in Southeast Asia, made it into the *Pakistan Observer*, and was remarked upon in West Africa. A resident of Accra wrote . . . asking for 'an apology to the civilized world.'"[149] Cicero became a symbol of White northern hostility to the arrival of millions of African Americans during the Great Migration. Cicero police tried to assist the Black renters, but Arnold Hirsch and others identify hundreds of inci-dents throughout the nation in which police and other authorities supported such mobs and their efforts.[150]

With the failure of Reconstruction in mind, some viewed the civil rights move-ment of the 1950s and 1960s as a second Reconstruction. A number of civil rights were restored.[151] But some legal victories proved more difficult to enforce than others. On May 17, 1954, the U.S. Supreme Court handed down its unanimous decision in *Brown v. Board of Education of Topeka, Kansas*.[152] The *Brown* ruling banned segregation in schools and overturned *Plessy v. Ferguson*, thereby toppling the almost 100-year-old doctrine of separate but equal. A year later, the plaintiffs returned to for a second *Brown* ruling, and in this the court said that desegregation should happen with "all deliberate speed."[153] The Massive Resistance Movement insured that this speed would be a crawl.

In response to the court dictate in the first *Brown* decision, Tom P. Brady, a Mississippi circuit court judge and former professor of sociology at the University of Mississippi, delivered a fiery speech called "Black Monday."[154] Brady asserted that the aim of the *Brown* ruling was not school integration but "racial amalgamation."[155] The speech was later expanded into a book. Brady wrote, "You cannot place little white and negro children in a classroom and not have integration. They will sing together. They will dance together and play together. They will grow up together and sensitivity of the white children will be dulled. Constantly the Negro will be endeavoring to usurp every right and privilege which will lead to intermarriage." White purity, Brady suggested, was in danger of being defiled by Black bestiality. Brady continued, "The supercilious, glib, young negro . . . will perform an obscene act, or make an obscene remark, or a vile overture or assault upon some white girl."[156] In a ploy similar to how Blacks who fought back during Red Summer were decried as Bolsheviks, integration was said to be a communist plot.[157]

Resistance to *Brown* took many forms. In 1962, nationally syndicated columnist James Jackson Kilpatrick published *The Southern Case for School Segregation*.[158] Kilpatrick argued there were "moral signifiers" of the inferiority of Blacks. He cited marriage and illegitimacy rates as his proof and roundly ignored the influence of slavery and the "high rates of common law marriage" among Blacks, particularly in the South.[159] These findings were then used to justify further violence against Black bodies.[160] According to Anders Walker, "Perhaps the best example of how moral classification replaced overt references to color emerges in Louisiana in the form of statutes regulating welfare." Louisiana law denied public assistance on moral grounds to any mother with more than one illegitimate child. The approach shifted the ostensible grounds for the denial from racial discrimination to character, but, consistent with the assumptions of BOP, this was just a proxy for the real prohibited category—blackness.[161]

In the years after *Brown*, like the language of racism, the agents of anti-Black practices shifted. Within months of the first *Brown* decision, the first White Citizen's Council (WCC) formed.[162] Citizens' Councils were ostensibly a gentler form of the Ku Klux Klan, but, like the Klan, their objective was to maintain White supremacy. The groups claimed not to sanction violence, but they fostered a hostile climate and used means like economic and political violence to preserve the racial order.

Black migration continued. Many southern Blacks who left Mississippi during the Great Migration ended up in Memphis or Chicago. Their children born outside of the repressive southern system were often naïve or ignorant of southern ways. Adherence to the rigid southern caste system contained imperatives for public deference in the presence of Whites that they had not ingrained, and missteps could be deadly. Since any public disavowal of the established social order by one Black person could embolden others to do the same, infractions were strictly policed and punished. One of these punishments galvanized the modern civil rights movement.

In August 1955, 14-year-old Emmett Till was visiting relatives in Money, Mississippi. Till was from Chicago. Soon after his arrival, Emmett and some friends decided to go to a local White-owned store. The owner's wife accused young Emmett of whistling at her. On August 28, 1955, her husband and his half-brother abducted young Emmett from his relatives' home. They beat him, mutilated him, shot him in the head, and sank his body in the Tallahatchie River. His grotesquely mutilated body was a warning to past, present, and future generations of Blacks about the dangers of failing to adhere to the social norms that uphold White supremacy.

Despite this warning, Emmett's mother, Mamie Till, refused to be silent about the murder of her son. She talked to the press and insisted on an open-casket funeral. Mamie Till wanted the world to see what they had done to her baby. She refused to bow to White will and remain silent. Decades later, the images of Till's mutilated body in an open casket are still compelling. They are included in a *Time* magazine book of the most influential photos of all time.[163]

Mamie Till was one of a number of courageous Black women. The actions of seamstress and activist Rosa Parks are well known. On December 1, 1955, Parks refused to give up her seat to a White man on a segregated city bus in Montgomery, Alabama. Her gender offered her no protection. Parks's subsequent arrest was meant to be degrading, but it inspired the Montgomery Bus Boycott. For approximately a year, African American riders boycotted the city bus. Several Black plaintiffs filed suit challenging the constitutionality of the Alabama state law requiring segregation on buses.[164] The case was known as *Browder v. Gayle*; a three-judge U.S. District Court panel ruled 2–1 that pursuant to the court's holding in *Brown*, segregation on intrastate buses was unconstitutional.[165] Because the bus traveled on federal roads and not just state ones, the interstate commerce clause was applicable, and federal courts had the power to regulate travel. On November 13, 1956, the Supreme Court affirmed the district court's ruling.[166] The ruling incentivized the city to integrate its buses or face certain financial ruin. The strike was called off, and the buses were integrated. That same year, southern members of Congress drafted the Southern Manifesto. The manifesto repudiated the *Brown* decision and, in a show of defiance, encouraged southerners to exhaust all lawful means to avoid desegregation.[167]

The fight for voting rights mobilized many Black Americans. On August 22, 1964, tenant farmer and social and political activist Fannie Lou Hamer testified before the Credentials Committee at the Democratic National Convention in Atlantic City and outlined the beatings and terror she and her Black Mississippi community endured because they dared to try to exercise their constitutionally granted, hard-fought right to vote. An impromptu press conference by President Johnson interrupted her testimony in the afternoon, but networks broadcast it in its entirety on the evening news.[168]

On March 7, 1965, peaceful protesters participating in a voting rights march in Selma, Alabama, were attacked on the Edmund Pettus Bridge. As they approached the bridge, a crowd of about 100 White men and women lining the streets came into view. The crowd jeered at them, shouted obscenities, and waved Confederate flags, but the protesters continued to advance. At the bridge's apex, a sizeable force of armed police, many on horseback, came into view. Major John Cloud (the officer in charge), shouted: "This is an unlawful assembly!" He ordered the protesters to return to the church or to their homes. Instead, they knelt in prayer. Less than one minute later, Cloud gave police the order to advance. The assembly was subjected to tear gas, trampled and run over by horses, and beaten with clubs and bullwhips. With each attack, cheers went up from the onlooking crowd.[169] "Get 'em! Get the niggers!" one woman gleefully screamed.[170] News media recorded the encounter.

The televised public beating of the peaceful protesters was yet another in a long series of public degradation ceremonies meant to debase and dissuade Blacks from walking in their full humanity, as full citizens. But the marchers could not be stopped, only delayed. As John Lewis noted, "Nothing could stop the marching feet of a determined people."[171] After two failed attempts at the march, on March 25, 1965, the marchers completed a three-day trek to arrive at the state capitol in Montgomery and deliver their petition for fair treatment to Governor George Wallace. Wallace did not come out of his office, but the marchers' crusade led to the passage of the Voting Rights Act of 1965.[172]

Almost every Black advancement has been countered with organized efforts at White pushback, but these efforts have never silenced Black voices and actors. Black protest in the 1960s took many forms. Sometimes, Black anger and frustration at systemic denials of rights, resources, and recognition boiled. This was the case following Martin Luther King Jr.'s assassination on the balcony of the Lor-

raine Motel in Memphis on April 4, 1968. Sometimes righteous anger is all people understand. Two days after King's funeral, President Lyndon Baines Johnson
signed the Civil Rights Act (CRA) of 1968 into law. The CRA was meaningful,
but it also represented yet another piecemeal attempt to cobble together the rights
Blacks had too long been denied.

Enforcement of the CRA could have brought about neighborhood integration, countering inequities in public education. Title VIII of the 1968 CRA,
known as the Fair Housing Act, directly addressed the view that Blacks in White
neighborhoods were bodies out of place. Title VIII, which prohibited discrimination in the sale, rental, or financing of dwellings, had the potential to change the
visual and social landscape of the nation. Interdisciplinary scholar of American
and racial studies George Lipsitz, in his book *How Racism Takes Place*, describes
the spatial and social imaginaries that undergirded the American landscape.[173] The
federal government took a distinct interest in creating policy that supported the
continued maintenance of distinct Black and White spaces. Lipsitz explains that
during the peak of the civil rights movement's mobilization, "The FHA recommended a plan . . . that favored control by private homeowner associations over
recreation centers and park land in planned developments. The effect of this plan
was to promote segregation."[174]

In the decades since passage of the CRA, there have been some changes in
neighborhood segregation patterns, but, overall, both private control and government control seemed to promote segregation.[175] According to Harvard Law
School professor Joseph Singer, "Although the Fair Housing Act (FHA) requires
any government entity managing or receiving federal funds 'affirmatively to further fair housing,' . . . enforcement of this provision has been remarkably lax since
the passage of the FHA in 1968."[176] Title VIII enforcement has been uneven
at best. Efforts to strengthen it have been met with pushback. For example, an
Obama-era rule that required local governments to take steps "affirmatively furthering fair housing" were withdrawn under the Trump administration.[177]

As in the past, today's neighborhoods are not race-neutral sites. Instead, they
are places of expectation. These expectations are scripted in the people, landscape,
and activities imagined as belonging in the space. The product, Lipsitz states,
are separate Black and White spatial imaginaries. The White spatial imaginary
is a good place that is clean, pure, and homogeneous. It is free of noisome pesti-
lence, including morally corrupt items and pollutants.[178] Impurities are reserved
for others. Consistent with this pure, racially homogenous White spatial imaginary, George Zimmerman scripted a teenage Trayvon Martin as a dangerous outsider whose presence inside the borders of his gated community signaled ill will.

Zimmerman's lethal response to Martin's presence in the space was the most extreme form of pushback under examination. Martin's murder and the subsequent acquittal of his killer signaled that despite gains, including the election of a Black president, Black bodies are not free to occupy social space, especially if that movement violates the expectations of the White spatial imaginary.

The Present Moment

Violent White pushback against Black advancement has never ceased. Instead, it has had ebbs and flows. Since the first election (and then reelection) of Barack Obama as president of the United States, I have observed a shift in where public acts of cultural and political violence in the form of degradation ceremonies are commonly employed. The success of many status degradation ceremonies as "communicative work" performed to lower an individual or group's status in the social schema has been tied to the social imaginary. This sociopolitical imaginary is composed of perceptions about the acceptable social order and design of social life. In essence, it is a manifestation of the imagined hierarchical organization of society and the distribution of power in that society. Prior to Obama's election, no actual representation of a Black man or woman as leader of the United States existed, and the collective social imaginary precluded such a reality. Like Jack Johnson's win of the heavyweight title, Obama's election pierced the long-established vision of a social order with Whites atop. This piercing of the veil allowed those young and old alike a moment to reflect on—and even reject—the earlier schema.

In the years since the first election of Obama, there have been a number of significant political and social attacks on Black life and culture aimed at reinstituting the racist social imaginary of old. This requires that the newly established social identity be stripped and replaced with a lower identity. Total institutions (like prison and slavery) facilitate the imposition of a new, lower identity, as can the performance of exclusion from those in power. The election of Donald Trump, a man who has used his bully pulpit to make a host of offensive remarks against people representative of various forms of non-White embodiment signaled the tacit agreement of millions in U.S. society to restore a Jim Crow social order. Like Wilson, Trump used the power of the presidency to give his bigoted ideas legitimacy and a veneer of truth.

Some notable Trump-era attacks on civil and human rights include a Muslim immigration ban, a ban on transgender people in the military, rescinding of the Deferred Action for Childhood Arrivals (DACA) program, withdrawal from the UN Human Rights Council, cessation of the moratorium on federal death penalty executions, rollbacks on affirmative action, and a disavowal of the applicability of Title VII of the Civil Rights Act of 1964 to cases of discrimination based on sexual orientation. Time and space will not permit me to discuss each of Trump's incendiary actions, but I highlight one from the final months of his presidency to illustrate my point.[179]

In Trump's final days in office, the Biden Presidential Inauguration Committee hosted a nationwide Covid Memorial to remember and honor the lives of the nearly 400,000 Americans lost to the deadly virus. Four hundred lights, each representing 1,000 American lives lost to Covid-19, lined the 2,000-foot-long Lincoln Memorial Reflecting Pool. Speaking at the event, then-president-elect Joe Biden said, "To heal we must remember. And it's hard sometimes to remember. But that's how we heal."[180] We remember expressly so history does not repeat itself.

The day prior to the Covid Memorial ceremony was Martin Luther King Jr. Day 2021. No doubt not coincidentally, that is the day the Trump-appointed 1776 Commission released its report. The 1776 Commission had been formed as a partial rebuke—pushback—against the *New York Times* award-winning 1619 Project. The brainchild of journalist and 2017 MacArthur Fellow Nikole Hannah-Jones, the 1619 Project aimed to "reframe the country's history by placing the consequences of slavery and the contributions of Black Americans at the very center of our national narrative." Trump and others rejected this Black-centered frame as a false narrative. When he announced the 1776 Commission's formation, Trump shared his hopes that it would counter and reverse growing acceptance of the Black Lives Matter movement and repudiate and reject teachings about White privilege and critical theories for the study of race. Regarding the growing protests over inequality, Trump argued, "The left wing rioting and mayhem are the direct result of decades of left-wing indoctrination in our schools."[181] Trump called for a rejection of teachings that supported claims of systemic racism. He extolled the need for a more "patriotic education" curriculum in schools that was "pro-American" and insisted that the then-unwritten report be taught in the nation's schools to replace less-favored ideas he deemed unpatriotic.

The writers of the 1776 Commission report accepted their charge. The report is highly contemptuous in its effort to reframe U.S. history, especially as it relates to slavery. Devoid of footnotes, citations, or attributions of individual authorship, the report was published less than four months after it was commissioned and only a month after its members were announced.[182] The report equates progressivism with fascism and downplays the role of slavery in the country's founding. It treats slavery as a world problem and downplays the horrors of the system by insisting that its U.S. form was less repressive than in other places. The report also suggested that the U.S. Founders all abhorred slavery.

Critics argued that the 1776 Commission report, whose contributors included no professional U.S. historians, was overly simplistic and naive. James Grossman, the executive director of the American Historical Association, called the report "cynical politics." Grossman continued, "This report skillfully weaves together myths, distortions, deliberate silences, and both blatant and subtle misreading of the evidence."[183] The 1776 Commission's efforts to reframe history are not the first such effort, but they are a reminder of the inclination to whitewash the truth of America's racial past. In one of President Joe Biden's first actions in office, he removed the 1776 Commission report from official White House website. Its dangers, however, live on.

Conclusion

This chapter has demonstrated that violence—in various forms—has been used to reify geographic and social boundaries and cement the ongoing project of the re-racialization and re-subjugation of Black bodies. The first 250 years of African Americans' history were spent in enslavement. The next 100 years were spent under an oppressive system of racial apartheid and terror. Since approximately 1969, a somewhat milder but no less insidious form of racial oppression has been perpetrated. Less overt, eschewing or even condemning the use of racial epithets, it relies largely on using institutions like the criminal justice system to maintain social control, and it encourages individual actors to either become agents of the state or enlist state actors to police boundaries. It uses the "minimization of racism" frame that Bonilla-Silva warns against in *Racism without Racists*.[184] It says there are no racists but acknowledges occasional racist acts devoid of racial actors. But there are racists. There are racist actors and there are racist systems, and, while their structures may be obscured, they are not invisible. As basketball legend and author Kareem Abdul-Jabbar noted in an *LA Times* opinion piece he penned after the murder of George Floyd, "Racism in America is like dust in the air. It seems invisible—even if you're choking on it—until you let the sun in. Then you see it's everywhere. As long as we keep shining that light, we have a chance of cleaning it wherever it lands. But we have to stay vigilant, because it's always still in the air."[185]

Light exposes the patterns Koritha Mitchell described when she wrote, "Any progress by those who are not straight, white, and male is answered by a backlash of violence—both literal and symbolic, both physical and discursive—that essentially says, *know your place!*"[186] It reveals a discursive violence that scripts people into places. It is time we let in the light.

This concludes part 1. Part 2 identifies a typology of the various forms that the pushback takes. The boundaries of these typologies are porous. The encounters I examine represent only a few incidents in a sea of daily attacks against embodied

Black personhood, but these incidents reverberate widely. I consider the interactions I discuss to be what some call an "individuated multiplicity," a reflection of the embodied experiences of countless other Black men, women, boys, and girls. They represent the individual and the communal. Within the larger social landscape, they speak to the lived experience of Blacks.

PART II

BOP Frames

CHAPTER 4

The Historical Fear Factor

> A vast amount of the energy that goes into what we call the Negro problem is produced by the white man's profound desire not to be judged by those who are not white, not to be seen as he is, and at the same time a vast amount of white anguish is rooted in the white man's equally profound need to be seen as he is, to be released from the tyranny of the mirror.
>
> —JAMES BALDWIN, *The Fire Next Time*

A 2017 article in *Smithsonian* magazine noted, "[Fear] is a fundamental, deeply wired reaction, evolved over the history of biology, to protect organisms against perceived threat to their integrity or existence."[1] The perception of threat can trigger what is commonly known as the fight or flight response.[2] But while fear may be deeply wired, fear of the racial other is learned. "Fear," writes architecture and environment behavior scholar Kristen Day, "is a key mechanism for justifying and maintaining race privilege and exclusion."[3] In public and private space, who is feared and who is perceived as entitled to be in space is deeply intertwined with the history of segregation. Those who employ what I term the historical fear-factor frame rely on stereotypes, historical inaccuracies, and false perceptions in order to legitimate and substantiate their need to employ protectionist responses against a manufactured danger. They use these feelings to evoke notions of threat. Then, once raised, they construct a compelling need for action against the perceived bad actor. They justify that response by intimating that it is for the purported purpose of defense of others, self-defense, or self-preservation.

Fear of Blacks has been used to legitimate a number of responses to the mere presence of Blacks in a space. Examples include slave patrols, terroristic vigilante groups, and surveillance. This fear frames Blacks as outside the polity. Alejandro de la Fuente and Ariela Gross, authors of *Becoming Free, Becoming Black*, argue that the law, which disfavored Blacks, was used to effectively link blackness with degradation and frame citizenship as something inconsistent with the very status of being Black.[4] Fears of racial mixing stoked waves of White flight and disinvestment in areas; it also spawned the creation of private clubs and other segregated spaces.[5] As Whites fled newly desegregated public spaces, it created "a new division in which the public world was abandoned to blacks and a new private world created for whites."[6]

Fear

Aristotle said fear is caused by whatever we feel has the great power of destroying us.[7] The first election of Barack Obama as president of the United States stoked White fears that the race advantage Whites have long held was slipping. A team of psychologists warns, "People experience negative emotions when they believe their ethnic group's future is under threat through losing their cultural identity practices, or from becoming a minority."[8] Those who see racism as a zero-sum game are particularly susceptible to this threat.[9] A 2011 study revealed that a majority of Whites believe that prejudice against Whites is now a "bigger problem" than discrimination against Blacks and that Black progress has been made at their personal expense.[10] Amid the backdrop of this belief that Black progress is a zero-sum game won by Blacks at the personal expense of Whites, it is not unreasonable to believe that individuals and groups may respond to this threat by employing mechanisms to restore order. Ironically, one of the greatest threats the United States faces today is domestic terrorism. As during the period of Ida Wells's activism, Whites' real fear is a concern about the loss of social advantage and position in society. The rest is pretext. The real goal is the protection of White power and social dominance. Fear looks outward, not inward. It points at others and assigns blame. The forces of fear, Jon Meacham argues, have "kept equality at bay."[11]

Fear was a factor in the growth of the Klan in the 1920s. It is a likely factor in the growth of White nationalist groups today too. By 1924, the Klan was in every state in the Union, with an estimated two to six million members. Five factors contributed to the Klan's growth: 1) misrepresentations in the film *Birth of a Nation*, 2) fear of immigrants flooding in from a Europe decimated by war, 3) unease about crime, 4) worry about anarchists, and 5) anxiety about communism.[12] Fears of competition over limited resources (like jobs, money, or other opportunities) and fear of the other run through most of these causes. Whites, especially poorer Whites, feared the loss of their position of privilege over Blacks—a position Du Bois called the psychological wages of whiteness.[13] Fear is likely one reason some stood by while the Klan committed numerous extrajudicial acts.

Throughout American history, fear has been an intense motivator and uniting force. It can also divide individuals and groups. Meacham quotes Lawrence Dennis's 1936 book *The Coming American Fascism: The Crisis of Capitalism*: "The easiest way to unite and animate large numbers [of people] . . . is to exploit the dynamic forces of hatred and fear."[14] And today politicians afraid of losing power remain silent in the face of obvious human rights violations. Fear also blinds people and can make them subject to irrational thought. In *Ronald Reagan the Movie and Other Episodes of Political Demonology*, Michael Rogin outlines three distinct periods in U.S. history when fear reigned. The first pitted Whites against people of color and acutely demonstrates the blinding irrationality of fear.[15] Rogin states that counter-subversion is what unites anti-blackness, anticommunism, and Indigenous dispossession. Whites are encouraged to not think about who they are but instead to draw their identity from whom they are against.

In 1919, the Great Migration saw the movement of many southern Blacks to other parts of the country, especially northern cities. The physical presence of growing numbers of Blacks combined with the financial uncertainty of the postwar period stoked fear and anxiety among Whites. Whites feared economic competition and potential loss of social control. Racial tensions were increasing, and White-on-Black violence erupted across the land. Conservative estimates say hundreds of Blacks were killed. The period became known as Red Summer (discussed in chapter 3), an homage to its brutality and the Black blood that ran in the streets. Along with other groups, Blacks were also subject to political attack at that time. Acting in his capacity as a special assistant to the U.S. attorney general, a young J. Edgar Hoover collected information on Blacks whom he considered "political radicals."[16] Rogin argues that by labeling them subversives under Bolshevik influence, Hoover made "blacks the perpetrators rather than the victims of the outrages."[17]

A similar pattern is discernible today. As a result, while the historical fear-factor frame is used against Black bodies, it can seldom be credibly evoked by Black bodies—unless doing so against another Black person. Black fear of Whites is deemed irrational. Unfounded fears regarding Black embodiment place all Black bodies in danger, especially as this irrational apprehension increases the likelihood of an armed state response.[18] Many of these fears are rooted in stereotypes.

Stereotypes

During slavery, stereotypes regarding Blacks emerged as a means to justify the complete domination and exploitation of Blacks. After slavery, such stereotypes served a similar purpose. In her book *Clinging to Mammy: The Faithful Slave in Twentieth-Century America*, Micki McElya argues that loving (or hating) Mammy is one of the ways Whites made sense of shifting economic, social, cultural, and racial relations in society.[19] The Mammy myth is quite compelling for Whites. Mammy is the picture of a faithful and content slave; she is satisfied with her position and desires no higher station in life. These images matter.[20] They are an important way that racial stereotypes of early American history quickly became ingrained in society. This occurred through literature, education, religion, and other means.

Cultural iconography is one of the most insidious ways that negative stereotypes about Blacks were passed through society. Kevin Goings's *Mammy and Uncle Mose: Black Collectibles and American Stereotyping* discusses the vast body of everyday objects using the likeness of Blacks produced from 1880 through 1950. These included mass-produced lithographs, books, postcards (some with images of lynchings), consumer products, and household items (plates, cups, cookie jars, coin banks, etc.) that degraded Black bodies or reduced them to racial caricatures. The exaggerated features on the memorabilia offered supposed evidence of Black inferiority.[21] Black studies scholar and cultural critic Patricia Ann Turner's book *Ceramic Uncles and Celluloid Mammies: Black Images and Their Influence on Culture* illustrates how these popular culture images perpetuate anti-Black prejudice.[22] Black images commonly used in the mass production of consumer goods evoked notions of the plantation South. These items could them be found in homes, on store shelves, and in film and commercial advertisements. As material culture, they reveal a social reality some would like to hide. Whites were hungry for these representations of Blacks. David Pilgrim, author of *Understanding Jim Crow*, believes that racist memorabilia can also help Americans confront and understand racism.[23]

The enduring and profitable nature of these stereotypes is evidenced by the fact that it was not until February 2021 that Quaker Oats announced it would rename and rebrand its popular Aunt Jemima products. The company said it was doing so in an effort to retire the racist stereotype associated with it.[24] These historical images of Aunt Jemima and other visual stereotypes commodify Black bodies and dismiss their humanity, and they have served multiple purposes. Even today they evoke and leverage nostalgia that longs for a time when the position of Blacks in society was more fixed. They shape White attitudes toward African Americans and justify and validate their mistreatment.

Stereotypes offer a rationalization and justification for White fear. The body is seen and understood in social context, explains Mary Douglas: "The social body constrains the way the physical body is perceived. The physical experience of the body, always modified by the social categories through which it is known, sustains a particular view of society."[25] In the remainder of this chapter, I focus on stereotypes of Blacks to show how they are deployed today to script Black bodies into certain places and roles and justify ill treatment of them when they stray from those places. I am especially attentive to those in film, due to its popularity and wide reach but also due to the continuing impact and influence of D. W. Griffith's 1915 film *The Birth of a Nation*.

The Birth of a Nation created a template for Black characterization that would be relied on and duplicated for the next 100 or more years. Because Blacks and Whites still live largely segregated lives, the characterizations create or reinforce the worst views of Black people, and these ideas are embraced by the dominant society as true.[26] While the 1980s and 1990s brought a host of films developed by Black artists that challenged these stereotypes, Griffith's images universalized, reinforced, and commodified minstrelsy character types.[27]

Blacks have consistently challenged negative stereotypes of the group, especially through performing the rich oral traditions associated with African culture. These traditions, which Lawrence Levine describes in his book *Black Culture and Black Consciousness*, were a source of Black pride, unity, and connection to ancestors.[28] Even in the early 20th century, negative images of Blacks prevalent in film and other media did not go unopposed. Filmmaker Oscar Micheaux, a Black man from Illinois, contested Griffith's characterizations. Micheaux formed his own movie company, and in 1919 he became the first Black person to make a film.[29] Black studies scholar Cedric Robinson writes that Micheaux wanted to "use film differently" and create political critique of the limited representations of African Americans. According to Robinson, "Micheaux pushed race movies into explicit political critiques of the American national myth." Micheaux's film *Within Our Gates* offered a searing counter-narrative to the racist stereotypes of Blacks in *The Birth of a Nation*. The film's story line included a White mob attack, lynching of a Black family, and the attempted rape of a Black woman by a White man who later realizes that the very woman he chased (and who escaped his attack) is actually the mixed-race daughter born of his liaison with a Black woman. While false narratives in *The Birth of a Nation* were embraced, the White-led Chicago board of censors tried to block the showing of *Within Our Gates*. Micheaux's film was ultimately banned in the South, which deemed it too incendiary to show.[30]

Some Black stereotypes could elicit White fear.[31] All the stereotypes of Blacks supported White superiority. Film historian and author Donald Bogle has identified five Black stereotypes in film.[32] They include the Tom, the Coon (whose variations include pickaninny and Uncle Remus), the tragic mulatto, Mammy (including Aunt Jemima), and the Brutal Black Buck (whose variations include the Black Brute and the Black Buck).[33]

The Tom is a socially acceptable "good Negro." He is stoic and submissive. He is kind, and he never turns against Massah (regardless of how he is treated). The Coon figure is a source of amusement and humor. He is not clever and provides comic relief through buffoonery. For Bogle, the Coon was "the most blatantly degrading of all Black stereotypes . . . [presented as] those unreliable, crazy, lazy, subhuman creatures good for nothing more than eating watermelon, stealing chickens, shooting crap, or butchering the English language." Bogle describes the pickaninny as "a harmless, little screwball creation whose eyes popped, whose hair stood on end with the least excitement, and whose antics were pleasant and diverting."[34]

The final male stereotype prevalent in film is the Brutal Black Buck. There are two variations. One is the Black Brute, who is barbaric and out to raise havoc. His physical violence is said to be an outlet for his sexual repression. The Black Buck, by contrast, is presented as "oversexed and savage, violent and frenzied [with a] lust for white flesh."[35] These images gave credence to the fear that Black men sought sexual relations with White women and were prepared to take it by force. This stereotype also acted as a form of cultural violence and a continuing attack on Black womanhood and beauty through its assumptions that White womanhood was the ultimate standard of beauty.[36]

Meanwhile the prevalent stereotypes of Black women paint them as asexual or hypersexual. The Mammy character cares for others. That is her life. She is just a little ornery and is usually older, plump, and asexual. As noted, Aunt Jemima was a variation of Mammy. She is a good cook, religious, sweet, jolly, and good natured.[37] The tragic mulatto stereotype features a mixed-race female so torn asunder by her heritage and lack of belonging in either world that she is often despondent or suicidal. She is a visual reminder of sexual relations between Blacks and Whites. Despite the presence of this image, there is never a suggestion that White men raped Black women. Instead, the stereotype presumes that Black men physically abused White women. (As Wells noted decades earlier, if anyone was getting raped, it was Black women.)[38] The mulatto is tragic because she cannot reconcile these two warring sides. Mental instability is a part of this characterization. The instability is because of the volatility of the Black blood battling against the pure White blood. The tragic mulatto is beautiful and generally longs to pass as White, especially as White women are presented as pure and beautiful and objects of desire.

By contrast, the Jezebel stereotype was depicted as a hypersexual being. The Jezebel type varied little over time. According to Bogle, blaxploitation films of the 1970s would glamorize the ghetto. These films valorized Black male outlaw types like pimps and rebels while Black women were often depicted as whores. This was also a common characterization of some Black women during slavery. The Jezebel stereotype was used to rationalize nonconsensual or otherwise coerced sexual relations between White men and Black women. Black Jezebels were not only depicted in film but also in material culture. Black women's stereotypes include asexual and hypersexual presentations. African American men are presented as having predilections for violence and sex or buffoonery. As the contemporary examples I outline in the remainder of this chapter note, the representations of race reflected in material culture have a profound influence the way Black men and women are perceived today.

The Tragic Case of Jonathan Ferrell

Jonathan Ferrell was a 24-year-old Black man with his whole life ahead of him. Ferrell had recently moved from Florida to Charlotte, North Carolina, in order to be with his fiancée, who had a job there. He was working two jobs and trying to pay off his $15,000 college debt. Ferrell had played football at Florida A&M University, a historically Black college. On the evening of September 14, 2013, Ferrell lost control of his car and crashed on a dark stretch of road in North Carolina.[39] He was alone and in an unknown area. After kicking out the back window of his car, Ferrell walked to the nearest subdivision and knocked on the door of a home. It was approximately 2:30 a.m. in the morning. The White female homeowner heard banging and ran to open the door. She thought it was her husband and that he had forgotten his key. When she saw Ferrell standing in front of her, she quickly closed the door and called 911. What happened next is disputed.

In the 911 audio, you can hear the frantic voice of the female caller. The female homeowner tells the dispatcher she needs help and that someone is trying to break in through her front door. She specifically states that a Black man is at the door. The *Chicago Defender* reported four days later:

> On the 911 tape released by the city, the woman tells a dispatcher that she thought her husband had returned home around 2:30 a.m. But when she opened the door, a man tried to get in. Sobbing and trying to catch her breath, the woman asked the dispatcher: "Where are the cops?" The dispatcher tried to calm her down, repeating over and over that they were on the way. He also asked her to describe the man. She

told him he was black, about 210 pounds and wearing a green shirt. At one point, the woman told the dispatcher about her baby. "He's in his bed. I don't know what to do. I can't believe I opened the door . . . Please don't let him get my baby," she cried. When police arrived at the scene, she peeked out her window. And when the officers began looking for a man, the dispatcher assured the woman they weren't leaving.

Before police arrived, the 911 caller was frantic:

"There's a guy breaking in my front door—trying to kick it down," she told the operator. "Oh god. Oh my god." The woman . . . told the 911 operator that the stranger approached her front door and she opened it, thinking it was her husband coming home from work, and then slammed it shut when she saw the man. The opening of the door set off the alarm on her home, and the man began yelling for her to turn off the alarm, she told the operator. . . . "He's not in the house, he's in the front yard yelling," she told the operator. "I can't believe I opened the door. What the f**k is wrong with me. My husband has a gun and I can't find it." When police arrived at the woman's home, Ferrell began running toward one officer, according to the police account of the incident. "Oh my god. Where is he going? Why is he running? Why is he leaving?" the woman can be heard saying on the 911 call. "Oh my god." According to police, when Ferrell began running at the officer, one cop tried unsuccessfully to Taser him. When that failed, another officer fired his gun, shooting at Ferrell 12 times and hitting him 10 times.[40]

There is no physical evidence that Ferrell tried to break in or kick the homeowner's door down, and at trial the homeowner suggested she did not say so. The homeowner's fear was real. Some would even suggest it was rational, but the chain of events it set off are deeply rooted in stereotypical fears of Black males as sexual predators and criminals. Less than minute after police responded to the call, the unarmed Ferrell was dead.

During his trial for voluntary manslaughter, the shooter, Officer Kerrick, described his encounter with Ferrell. Kerrick repeatedly used language that painted Ferrell's behavior as animalistic. Like those Blacks killed in the violence that came to be known as Red Summer, Ferrell was painted as an aggressor, not a victim. Officer Kerrick described "grunting" sounds and said Ferrell "didn't care [that] the taser," which had been deployed by Kerrick's partner but misfired, "was on him." Kerrick continued, "He [Ferrell] had a very aggressive posture." Despite the initial distance between them, Kerrick indicated that he had felt threatened by Ferrell and feared for his life. Then, to solidify his own humanity and the bestiality of Ferrell, Kerrick stated, "I fired, and it didn't faze him [Ferrell] . . . my gun is not stopping him."[41] The Charlotte-Mecklenburg Police Department suspended Officer Kerrick, and the city quickly charged him with voluntary manslaughter.[42] According to prosecutors, "Kerrick ignored his police training and acted out of fear."[43]

Both the Ferrell family and the city eschewed claims of systemic racism. Counsel for Ferrell's family made it clear that they subscribed to the one bad apple sentiment. The family's lawyer said, "This is a bad cop in an otherwise respectable Police Department." Kerrick had only been on the force a short time. Before joining the police force, Kerrick had worked in animal control as a dogcatcher.[44] Kerrick funneled his perception of Ferrell's behavior through the lens of an animal control worker. To him, Ferrell was not someone in need. Instead, he was a beast. To the extent that Kerrick viewed Ferrell as a man, he viewed him as a Black Brute, who was to be feared —and put down. The term "brute" is not used much anymore, but new labels, such as "thug," have replaced it. "The accused," "the suspect," "the suspicious person": each is rooted in the demonization and criminalization of Black bodies.

Responses by the homeowner, 911 operator, and police provide an almost eidetic mirror of comments Negrophobic writer George T. Winston laid out in his 1901 *Annals of the American Academy of Political and Social Science* article, "The Relations of the Whites to the Negroes." Winston mused, "[W]hen a knock is heard at the door [a White woman] shudders with nameless horror. The black brute is lurking in the dark, a monstrous beast, crazed with lust. His ferocity is almost demoniacal. A mad bull or tiger could scarcely be more brutal. A whole community is frenzied with horror, with the blind and furious rage for vengeance."[45] Ferrell's bestiality was presumed before he even uttered a word or made a move. The defense of White womanhood exhibited here is no different from that at the height of the Jim Crow era when Black men were readily lynched under the pretext that they looked at, spoke to, whistled at, or raped a White woman.

At trial, Kerrick was merely repeating his earlier claims about Ferrell's aggressive stance. Throughout the proceedings, both the defense counsel and Kerrick referred to Ferrell as "the suspect." In a post–Willie Horton, "war on crime" society, the word "suspect" stands as proxy for "Black person."[46] Describing Ferrell's behavior as aggressive is also racialized discourse, which conjures up stereotypes of the Black Brute. As if one stereotype was not sufficient, concomitant with the use of the Black Brute imagery, Kerrick's counsel also painted Ferrell as some type of drug addict or fiend. At trial, the defense repeatedly stressed that Ferrell had a blood alcohol level of .06 (which is well under the legal limit) and that he had smoked marijuana earlier in the day.[47] Kerrick's defense counsel also highlighted testimony from Adam Neal, another officer at the scene. Officer Neal described

Ferrell as looking "like he was in a zombie state."[48] Neal did not draw his gun. He did not hear Kerrick direct *any* commands at Ferrell before or after Ferrell began running toward the officers.[49]

Almost all the stereotypes of Black men are employed here. Ferrell is either a dangerous Black man who is a criminal or sexual predator, or he is painted as some kind of simpleton not bright enough to know how to behave in a context where he is in distress or need. References to poor judgment and animal-like behavior by Ferrell are meant to evoke an image of him as an irrational, unhinged beast who failed to obey lawful commands and thus caused his own death. In closing arguments, Kerrick's counsel said, "Ladies and gentlemen, this case is not about race. It never was. This case is about choices. Jonathan Ferrell's bad choices forced officer Kerrick to make the ultimate choice." Witnesses suggested that Ferrell behaved aggressively when he knocked on the door for help. Defense lawyer Michael J. Greene even went so far as to argue that Ferrell brought on his own death by not "politely asking for help from either [the homeowner] or the police." All of these efforts are attempts to place the victim on trial, demonize him in death, and victimize his family anew.

The psychological projection of fear that Wells identified in her lynching examinations abounds in this case. A White female homeowner feared the Black Buck or Brute with his frenzied lust for White flesh. I do not suggest that when someone knocks on your door or bangs on it at two thirty in the morning it is not cause for concern. I, do, however, suggest that the police response it set in place increased the likelihood that Ferrell would end up as a victim of state violence. No one—not the homeowner, not the 911 operator, not the police officers who responded—saw Ferrell as someone in need of help. In fact, they did not see him as a person at all. He was subperson. No one considered that would-be rapists and burglars are unlikely to knock on your door and announce themselves, and they are less likely still to remain in the area for 10 minutes (all while your burglar alarm is blaring and you have announced that you have called the police). The stereotypical cloak of Coon would suggest that Ferrell was not bright enough to recognize all of these things and flee the area. It is only through deploying the offensive stereotype of the dim-witted Black Coon that all of the actors involved are able to dismiss what I argue is the most likely explanation of all—Ferrell was a person seeking assistance.

At no turn was Ferrell afforded the benefit of the doubt. Even in testimony after his death both the homeowner and the police clung to their assertions that he was an aggressive, menacing threat who acted unreasonably and never asked for help. The homeowner's own words seem to discredit her. When she asserts that she opened the door for him and quickly closed it, this implies there would not be time for Ferrell to ask her for help. When exactly was he supposed to ask for help? In the background of the 911 call, a man's voice can be heard saying "Hello?"[50] Perhaps that is when he asked for assistance. But even if Ferrell never overtly asked for help, no one stops to consider that perhaps he was dazed and affected by the accident. His blackness negates a presumption that he might be hurt. Like his forefathers who labored in the fields without wage or compassion, he is presumed to have super strength.

The police are supposed to be there to help you. Perhaps Jonathan Ferrell's action of moving toward the police officer, which Kerrick interpreted as aggression, was just the act of someone reaching out for help. Maybe Jonathan Ferrell was banging on the door because most people are asleep at 2:30 a.m., and he wanted to wake someone so that they could assist him. Other counter-narrative explanations abound, but they were all dismissed.

In a September 2013 article about the incident, the homeowner, like Kerrick's lawyer, asserted that this was not about race, but the words chosen to describe Ferrell are laden with racial connotations. A friend of the homeowner defended the woman's actions. The friend told the *Daily Mail*, "Ferrell wasn't acting like a helpless man but a ferocious threat."[51] That "ferocious threat" was put down—shot over and over.[52] Subhumans, like Ferrell was presumed to be, are not considered capable of rational thought. Charles Mills notes that the various implications regarding the denial of the equal intellect and cognizing ability of Blacks "invites the intervention of those who are [deemed] capable of culture ... [and] it precludes full membership [of Blacks] in the polity." In some cases, these historical denials included precluding Blacks from even testifying in court.[53] The recent rash of video-recorded police killings of unarmed Blacks acts as a continuation of that denial. Even with the video evidence, the dead are not able to sit in court and testify.

The Formula for Killing Black People (and Getting Away with It)

Kerrick's state trial on charges of voluntary manslaughter for the shooting death of Jonathan Ferrell resulted in a mistrial. The prosecution declined to refile the case. In many ways, the example of Darren Wilson, the officer who shot and killed 18-year-old Michael Brown on August 9, 2014, in Ferguson, Missouri (a suburb of St. Louis) provided the textbook example of how to take the life of an unarmed Black person and get away with it.[54] The playbook Kerrick's council used seemed to come from insights gained from the failure of the grand jury to return an indictment against Wilson. A *Time* magazine article, "All the Ways Darren Wilson Described Being Afraid of Michael Brown," lays out the framework in reporting on the case in November.[55]

In many ways, the killing of Brown stands as a modified modern-day lynching spectacle.[56] After Officer Wilson fatally shot Brown, the teen's bloodied body lay in public view on the street for nearly four hours. Blood could be seen streaming from underneath the sheet that partly covered Brown's body, and his feet were uncovered. Those in the area were forced to look on this gruesome scene. Witnesses alleged that when the officer fired the fatal shots Michael Brown had his hands up. The incident sparked months of civil unrest. Then, on November 24, 2014, St. Louis County prosecutor Bob McCulloch announced the grand jury's decision not to indict Wilson on any charges.

In his sworn grand jury testimony, Wilson described Brown's behavior as animalistic and aggressive. He said that Brown presented a threat and that he had fired—repeatedly—to stop the threat. By referencing continuing acts by Brown after Wilson's first shots, Wilson framed his own actions as reasonable and the actions of Brown as beastlike. Wilson asserted, "[Brown] was just staring at me, almost like to intimidate me or to overpower me." He continued, "When I grabbed him, the only way I can describe it is I felt like a five-year-old holding onto Hulk Hogan." Of course, unlike most five-year-olds, Darren Wilson was six foot four and weighed 210 pounds. Officer Wilson evoked an effective visual imagery that aroused both notions of fear and sympathy for his personal plight. It suggested, "I did not want to do it, but his actions made me do it." Wilson implored, "He looked up at me and had the most intense aggressive face. The only way I can describe it, it looks *like a demon*, that's how angry he looked."[57] These remarks robbed Brown of his personhood and humanity. Instead of being human, Brown was framed as a savage beast who was to be feared and had to be controlled. It was implied that this action was for the good of society. Brown was the "animalistic other" devoid of human form and unworthy of human courtesy.

The purported anger and demonic behavior of Brown are relied on to suggest the reasonableness of Wilson's response. Wilson asserts, "[Brown] turns, and when he looked at me, he made like a grunting, like aggravated sound . . . it looked like he was almost bulking up to run through the shots." Wilson fired repeatedly. He hit Brown several times in both his head and right arm. The officer described the frenzy one might feel when a wild animal was charging. Wilson claimed to witness one of the several shots he fired that hit Wilson. He asserted, "When it [the bullet} went into him, the demeanor on his face went blank, the aggression was gone, it was gone, I mean, I knew he stopped, the threat was stopped."[58] A message was also sent to the many witnesses to this modern-day lynching: behave, or you too will be put down in this way.

Darren Wilson's ability to successfully avoid an indictment for the killing of Brown, much less punishment, offers a model for those who seek impunity for acts of violence against Black bodies. There are variations of the model, but they all go something like this: Create an image of the other person as aggressor, but avoid racial designations. Instead, discuss seemingly race-neutral factors. It is safe to discuss how the person looked, but use descriptors about the person's size or demeanor, not "Black," because that would subject you to allegations of racism, and you want to deflect those. Discuss things that cannot be seen clearly in video: a look in the person's eye, a twitching finger. Describe something that cannot be clearly verified in audio. We saw this in the debate over whose voice was on the audio of the encounter between George Zimmerman and Trayvon Martin. Zimmerman said it was his voice, and the parents of Trayvon Martin said was their child's voice, but only one of the two people there was alive to testify. You might also talk about your feelings. The inference of reasonableness will be read in to any discussion of White feelings, especially when they involve fear of Black bodies.

Black people have long articulated the felt experience of racism. It is the feeling of going into a store and being followed because people presume you are there to steal. It is being in a space and being singled out as being too loud when others around you are engaging in the same behavior. It is experiences like those Brent Staples articulated in his 1986 article in *Harper's Magazine*, "Black Men and Public Space." It is the feeling of shame W. Kamau Bell outlined in describing being asked to leave a café because of the perception that he was bothering the nice table of White women dining there, one of whom included his wife.[59] It is the feeling that no place—north, south, east or west—is safe, because, as Marcus Hunter and Zandria Robinson note in *Chocolate Cities: The Map of Black American Life*, the entire United States is the American South.[60] Across the country, blackness is feared.

Every Day We're Being Hunted as Prey

Increasingly, White fear (really paranoia) is used to justify calls to police for ordinary activities performed by Blacks. These are non-criminal matters where police are called in to regulate behaviors. This is done with knowledge that in each encounter a potential exists for it to turn out deadly. Put another way, the potential for an armed response always exists when the police are engaged. Whether it is sleeping in the common area of a dormitory, picking up trash outside an apartment, presenting a coupon at a store, returning an item to a store, playing a round of golf, or a host of other mundane activities, Black bodies are subjected to scrutiny every day. Acts of symbolic (cultural) violence abound as well. Judgments about the hairstyles, clothing styles, vernacular language, music, and mannerisms often associated with Black life and culture are ingrained as legitimate bases for White fear.

When participants (many of them children) in an antiviolence march in North Charleston, South Carolina, stopped to buy drinks at a Murphy's gas station, the manager called the police and stated, "It's like a riot out there."[61] In Amherst, Massachusetts, a Black male University of Massachusetts employee was walking to work when someone called to report an "agitated" Black man walking on campus.[62] The man had worked at the institution for 14 years. Because of the report, he was questioned, and a building was locked down for 30 minutes. In Orange Village, Ohio, approximately 30–40 Black, female sorority sisters went to dinner at Bahama Breeze. They raised questions about the bill, and management called police.[63] In Birmingham, Alabama, a Hobby Lobby manager called the police on a Black man trying to make a return.[64]

The surveillance of Black bodies is both overt and covert. In May 2018, in Rialto, California, an older White female resident of a predominantly White neighborhood called the police after she observed two Black females and one Black male loading a car outside of her neighbor's house. One of the guests was the granddaughter of reggae legend Bob Marley.[65] The Black male noticed the neighbor watching, and he playfully told his companions, "She's watching us. She's probably going to call the police."[66] They laughed. Soon they were not laughing. The neighbor did call the police. Seven police cars responded. The police surrounded the group and told them to put their hands up.[67] An officer tried to probe the neighbor to better understand the basis for her call. The resident responded, "Well, I walked out here and uh, just to check the mail and I see these strange people coming and going back and forth. You know with luggage, and I didn't recognize them."[68] The officer's follow-up question is as insightful as the woman's response is telling. The officer asked, "What made you think they were strange?" The woman replied that they had luggage in their hands and weren't really looking at her: "You know they just kind of avoided me and they didn't wave you know like neighbors do."[69]

Today a language has emerged to describe Black bodies without using racial terms that might subject the accuser to allegations of racism. In the above incident, "strange" was the resident's code word for "Black." Checking the mail was a pretext to get a closer look at the "strange" Black people she feared. It was a surveillance act intended to tell Black people, "Don't get comfortable in this space. I am watching you." In her comments to the police, the neighbor stated that the people were "coming and going back and forth." Part of what bothered the White woman was the "strange" people's free use of the space and willingness to come and go. The Black people moved as if they were entitled to be in the space. The comment "they weren't really looking at me" evidences her reliance on a Jim Crow–like White supremacist ideology that Black people need to show proper deference to Whites. The neighbor's statement that the group did not wave to her is part of the same mentality.

In these actions, I see an attempt to reinstate the Jim Crow order. The young Black trio was expected to show deference and wave, but the 911 caller herself could have waved. Hunter and Robinson's insights are again instructive here. They suggest that the entire United States is the American South. In the American South, waving is framed as southern hospitality and good manners. However, the propensity to wave to people as you pass by is often less about southern hospitality and more about letting the other know "I see you, and I have my eye on you." This concept is evident in multiple comments at a Rialto Police Department press conference. The police expressed gratitude for the neighbor's willingness to call and report "suspicious activity." What went unsaid is that the activity itself was not inherently suspicious, the Black actors were. The homeowner who rented to the trio expressed gratitude that her neighbor called police. She continued, "'I applaud her for that. I went over to her home after I got home from work and thanked her,' ... 'If the kids had simply smiled at [my neighbor] and waved back and acknowledged her and said, 'We're just Airbnb guests checking out,' none of this would have ever happened,' she said. 'But instead, they were rude, unkind, not polite.'"[70]

Calling the thirtysomething trio "kids" served to infantilize them. Jasmine Rand, counsel for the trio, aptly responded, "We don't want to live in an America where black people are forced to smile at white people to preserve their lives."[71]

The neighbor's full expectation was that the group would wave to her and make her feel comfortable in the space. This attitude is steeped in White supremacist ideology. The group was not supposed to feel comfortable in the space, certainly not comfortable enough to brazenly come and go back and forth. That kind of use of space violates the racial order and provokes the fear defense among Whites. The neighbor's watching eyes also acted as a social control message to the trio and other Black bodies who might consider home ownership or rentals in the area: "The next time you look for a place, look elsewhere. You are not welcome here." By calling the police, the neighbor-actor sought to give this edict the force and color of law. In this respect, the historical fear frame often overlaps with the frame *You Don't Belong Here!*

Police questioned the trio for somewhere between 20 and 40 minutes.[72] The group explained they had rented the home through Airbnb, and they tried to show their documentation. During the course of the interrogation, additional armed officers arrived. After the police supervisor arrived on the scene, things got discernably worse. In a CNN interview that aired on the morning of May 12, 2018, one of the members of the group said, "At first we joked about the misunderstanding and took photos and videos along the way. About twenty minutes into this misunderstanding it escalated." One said, "We felt like we were going to be able to go, but the sergeant came, and . . . the mood and the energy changed completely."[73] The sergeant did not believe anything they said. He did not believe the Airbnb reservation they showed him. He did not believe the call they made to the landlord was real. He did not believe the pictures they showed him. The full spectacle was on display for everyone in the community to see. Their Black skin and age brought them under immediate and continuing suspicion.

As the group laid out their claim to the space, their pleas got filtered through historical stereotypes about Blacks. Their firmness was coded as rage. Black bodies are not permitted to display certain emotions, such as ire or outrage. Instead, gratitude (for being allowed to remain in the space) and deference are expected. Any other emotions are subject to severe sanction in the form of pushback. Here an additional pushback occurred in the form of a rebuke of the trio by the homeowner who rented them space. The *Los Angeles Sentinel* reported that the owner of the Airbnb location blamed the encounter on the guests' "lack of good nature."[74] The righteous indignation the Airbnb renters expressed was coded as belligerence, hostility, and aggression. By contrast, the caller's White privilege allowed her to invoke fear as dog whistle cover for the purposes of legitimating her concerns and the use of police force she sought. Her real goal was to contain the spread of Black bodies traversing her social and physical space.

Conclusion

The root cause of the fear of Black bodies is complex, but its effect is not: it is to maintain White supremacy. Perhaps that is its objective too. As this counternarrative reading demonstrates, White supremacy manifested as anti-blackness runs through all the encounters described in this chapter. Unfortunately, many remain blind to this because of what James Baldwin noted: "the white man's profound desire not to be judged by those who are not white." Baldwin described a burden created by White people that is Black people's to bear. Each day that burden threatens to drag one down a little bit more. The weight can be crippling. It is difficult to live in a world with deeply entrenched anti-Black sentiments, a world in which we pay our tormentors to stay in their Airbnb homes, pay them tuition, and purchase goods from them at a store and still are treated as subhuman. Supporting Black businesses and colleges offers some salve. But in the world of White supremacy, it takes a daily emotional and physical toll to behave in ways that do not make Whites uncomfortable. As in the case of the Rialto Airbnb rental, we are expected to smile and be polite even amid intense disrespect. We are expected to display deference and to hide the pain of being treating as second class. We must never engage in behavior that might make a White person feel uncomfortable. This toll will be discussed more in chapter 8.

CHAPTER 5

Presumed Criminal

> People in this country are triggered by race. Hell, *I'm*
> triggered. When I walk down the street, if I see a Black
> person—*and it's me in the mirror!*—I give it a second look
> 'cause I've been primed by this society to suspect Black
> people.
>
> —VAN JONES

In many ways, the presumption of criminality runs through all of the frames I offer as typologies of Bodies out of Place. The presumption is at the root of continuing surveillance strategies that seek to monitor Black bodies. In the presumed criminal frame, the presence of certain types of bodies in specified areas (or in relationship with certain people) is for the purpose of ill will or criminal intent. A presumption of guilt or anticipation of future crime shrouds Black bodies. With respect to social status or position, there is presumption that the position is not earned. In a May 6, 2020, opinion piece in the *New York Times*, "The Killing of Ahmaud Arbery," columnist Charles Blow wrote, "These men stalked Arbery, projecting onto him a criminality of which he was not guilty, then used self-defense as a justification to gun him down in an altercation that they provoked."[1]

Illegitimacy surrounds the presence of the bodies implicated in this frame. The presumption of criminality is not limited to matters related to the criminal justice system. Under the presumed criminal frame, a person may also be presumed incompetent or to have illegitimately obtained a credential or access to a space or position. Illegitimacy is heightened with respect to certain intersectional bodies. The Black man is a priori suspect.[2] To be young, Black, and male, all three, makes one more likely to be presumed criminal than other Black bodies, but the presumption exists for most (if not all) Black bodies. This presumption of criminality is what allowed the McMichaels to go uncharged in Arbery's shooting death for 74 days, and in the case of their codefendant Roddie Bryan even longer. As D. L. Hughley and Doug Moe write in their biting social commentary *How Not to Get Shot and Other Advice from White People*, "Blacks are presumed criminals, cops are presumed heroes."[3] Greg McMichael worked in law enforcement for more than 30 years.[4] His long tenure and his whiteness cloaked both him and his son with a presumption of innocence while Arbery was presumed to be a criminal.

Everyday Encounters

Heightened surveillance and scrutiny of Black bodies is a pattern that has been present since the slave patrols.[5] It endures in even the most mundane everyday activities. Critical theorist Philomena Essed has found that racial and ethnic minorities are subject to what she terms "everyday racism," through numerous day-to-day violations of their human dignity. The shift in understanding the meaning and experience of racism as something aberrant and infrequent to an everyday encounter is important. It takes the focus away from exceptional acts of racism and places it on the normal, daily practices in society that work to disadvantage individuals and groups.[6] BOP is useful to expose the quotidian nature of racism. Police violence against Black bodies is a pressing social issue, but so are the various forms of the violence that happen in everyday interactions between Blacks and the private citizens around them.

When private citizens report activities to police or other state actors, it heightens the likelihood that there will be a state response. Because U.S. police officers are armed, use of the police implies a need for an armed response. A 2016 report by the Center for Policing Equity found that while police deploy force in less than 2% of encounters, they are 3.6 times more likely to use force in encounters with Blacks than Whites, and the overall use of force against Blacks is 2.5 times higher. Similar patterns hold for other people of color, but they are most pronounced with Blacks.[7] The arrival of police in encounters with Blacks heightens the likelihood that the person engaging in the reported activity, no matter how routine, will be presumed criminal and treated as such.

Place—social and geographic—is central to this analysis. In his book *The New Black Middle Class and the Twenty First Century*, sociologist Bart Landry clarifies the importance of place in social scientific analysis involving Black Americans. Landry writes, "Place is always looming large in African American history, beginning with the forceful removal of Africans from a place of their own to a place of

chattel slavery, in the United States, the Caribbean, and South America."[8] Place
looms large in my analysis too. In the rest of this chapter, I interrogate cases of
everyday racism perpetrated against Blacks in various places engaged in routine,
everyday activities. My examination highlights how structures, policies, practices,
and norms in society (as performed by individuals, groups, and institutions) operate as anti-Black racism. As a weapon, anti-Black racism includes various forms
of violence used to dehumanize and systematically marginalize Black bodies. The
dual objectives of these actions are to push Black bodies back into place and,
through the use of spectacle and degradation, disincentivize other Black bodies
from trying to expand their positions in geographic or social space.[9]

Going Out with Friends

Few social activities are more routine than going out with friends, and relatively
few of them end with police involvement. This section investigates racialized encounters while out with friends that ended with the involvement of state actors.
The first examines a 2015 incident involving a college student outside a bar in
Charlottesville, Virginia, and the second interrogates a 2018 incident at a fitness
center in Sterling, Virginia, a suburb of Washington, D.C.

On March 18, 2015, Martese Johnson was a junior at the University of Virginia,
a public research institution in Charlottesville. That evening, the young Black
man went out with friends to an Irish bar near campus. It was March, and there
were numerous St. Patrick's Day celebrations going on all around. Three Virginia
Alcoholic Beverage Control (ABC) Authority agents, vested with full police powers, accused Johnson of presenting fraudulent credentials, and they denied him entry to a local bar. During a contested exchange, ABC officials slammed Johnson to
the ground and cuffed him. The officers' force produced a gash in Johnson's head
that required 10 stitches to close. Pictures of Johnson's bloodied face went viral.
Most of the accounts noted that during the assault, Johnson, an elected member
of his university's Honor Committee, screamed "But I go to UVA!"[9]

NBC News reported that the officers beat Johnson and kneed him in the back
and that, as Johnson lay face down, he screamed, "But I go to UVA You F***rs!
[*sic*]"[10] Johnson, a college student, was accused of presenting fake identification.
The officers' public response to this charge (which was later proven false) was fla-
grantly excessive. Johnson countered the officers' allegations, but, in the eyes of
the officers, his Black skin already branded him as a criminal bad actor with no legitimate rights in the space. Still, Johnson loudly shouted his declarative claim to
belonging for all to hear: "But I go to UVA!" Johnson also shouted his criticism of
the officers' actions. For his defiance, "Johnson was charged with two misdemean-

ors: obstruction of justice without force, and profane swearing and/or intoxication in public."[11] Both charges were eventually dropped.

Johnson described the encounter in an October 2015 *Vanity Fair* magazine article: "Officers asked me for identification ... I showed them my I.D., which they wrongly assumed was a fake I.D. After a brief interaction with these officers, I was slammed to the ground violently, detained with handcuffs and leg shackles, and arrested without justification ... blood flowed freely from my face and my friends and classmates surrounded the scene.... They watched helplessly as I yelled, "How did this happen? I go to U.Va.!" By both the standards of the larger society and according to the politics of Black middle-class respectability, Martese Johnson had done everything right. He had made good grades and earned admission to a selective institution. He expected UVA to offer protection from the police and the state-sanctioned violence inequitably visited on Black men, but racism is ubiquitous, as Johnson learned. "My lifelong vision of sanctuary in success was destroyed in seconds."[12] A Black male UVA alum echoed Johnson's sentiments: "It is a nauseating reminder that no amount of education, poise or good behavior can protect a black person in America."[13]

Johnson learned that no amount of hard work can insulate a Black man from systemic racism. His innocence shattered, Johnson was left with the realization that working hard does not protect you. It is not enough. Research supports this conclusion. A study revealed that people with White-sounding names receive substantially more job interview requests than their counterparts *with the same credentials* and non-White-sounding names.[14] Reports in 2019 noted statistical evidence of racism in unemployment.[15] The Economic Policy Institute reported:

> Black workers are twice as likely to be unemployed as white workers overall (6.4% vs. 3.1%). Even black workers with a college degree are more likely to be unemployed than similarly educated white workers (3.5% vs. 2.2%). When they are employed, black workers with a college or advanced degree are more likely than their white counterparts to be underemployed when it comes to their skill level—almost 40% are in a job that typically does not require a college degree, compared with 31% of white college grads. This relatively high black unemployment and skills-based underemployment suggests that racial discrimination remains a failure of an otherwise tight labor market.[16]

Whites continue to reap the fruits of systemic racism. This is the essence of White privilege. They are benefits for which they did not labor. Johnson's labor brought him to "Mr. Jefferson's University," but a presumption of criminality shrouded his presence there.

The area where Johnson was attacked is steeped in history, and the encounter should not be divorced from that context. When folded into the analysis, it tells a tale of the place and Johnson's perceived position in the space. To set that historical context, I begin with a discussion of a man who is arguably America's most notable Virginian, Thomas Jefferson.

Jefferson served as president of the United States from March 4, 1801, to March 4, 1809, and he was the main author of the Declaration of Independence. The Founder was born in 1743 on a plantation in Shadwell, Virginia, near present-day Charlottesville. Subsequent to his presidency, Jefferson founded UVA in 1819. Biographer John Boles calls Jefferson (who was a slaveholder and an ardent believer in American democracy), "the architect of American liberty." In addition to the institution Jefferson founded and the Declaration of Independence he drafted, the Virginia native was most proud of the Virginia Statute of Religious Freedom he crafted. The statute, a forerunner of the First Amendment, guaranteed freedom of religion to all groups. The preamble to the act supported the concept of religious and intellectual freedom and ensured that government and religion would remain separate.[17] This is the geographic and intellectual space in which Jefferson grew. In many ways, it was a space full of contradictions. For example, it is widely believed that Jefferson inserted the language "all men are created equal" in the Declaration he drafted, but this Enlightenment thinker held complex and contradictory views about the people he enslaved and the institution of slavery. Enslaved men and women were widely viewed as property, not people. Another Thomas Jefferson biographer, Jon Meacham, wrote, "Sex across the color line—sex between owner and property—was pervasive yet rarely directly addressed or alluded to." Thomas Jefferson had a decades long "relationship" with Sally Hemings, a slave who was both his wife's servant and her half-sister. Their liaison, which has been described as a contested consensual relationship, lasted 40 years and produced six children.[18]

Although Jefferson was an Enlightenment thinker, some of his ideas on race were less than enlightened. In *Notes on the State of Virginia*, published approximately 15 years before Jefferson first assumed the presidency, he wrote, "Deep rooted prejudices entertained by the whites; ten thousand recollections, by the blacks, of the injuries they have sustained; new provocations; *the real distinctions which nature has made* ... will divide us into parties, and produce convulsions which will probably never end but in the extermination of the one or the other race. To these objections, which are political, may be added others, which are physical and moral. ... Comparing them [Blacks] by their faculties of memory, reason, and imagination, it appears to me that in memory they are equal to the whites; *in reason much inferior*."[19] A well-read man who would serve as U.S. ambassador to France and hold a number of state and federal offices, including governor of Virginia, secretary of state, vice president, and president, Jefferson developed more parochial views than one might expect or hope.[20] On the treatment of Africans in the U.S. territories, Jefferson opined that "blacks on the continent of America" were treated better than Roman slaves in history had been treated.[21] Over two centuries after Jefferson was writing, Donald Trump's 1776 Commission used similar language to suggest that U.S. slavery was not as harsh as in other places and that the Founders did not hold hypocritical views on slavery.

In *Ebony and Ivy: Race, Slavery and the Troubled History of America's Universities*, Craig Steven Wilder notes, "Enslaved black people built Thomas Jefferson's intellectual monument: the University of Virginia."[22] According to historian Nancy MacLean, UVA scholars in the 20th century produced the ideological template for the South's post–*Brown v. Board of Education* Massive Resistance Movement against desegregation.[23] A deliberate response aimed at thwarting the *Brown* decision came out of UVA's Economics Department, an effort led by Nobel Prize–winning economist James Buchanan.[24] Marshall Steinbaum's review of Nancy MacLean's *Democracy in Chains* explains how these efforts furthered "the University of Virginia's status as a bastion of white supremacy and white-supremacist-validating scholarship."[25]

Today the institution that slavery built is still thriving. A 2020 *U.S. News and World Report* "Best Colleges" list ranks UVA, known by many insiders as "Mr. Jefferson's University," 28th overall in the nation. In past years, it has achieved similarly high standing and often ranks even higher for undergraduate teaching. Approximately 27% of applicants are accepted to the highly selective institution, which also boasts an endowment of $6.9 billion and a 93% graduation rate.[26] That history of exclusion, inclusion, and selectivity, is incarnate on the campus.

UVA is the flagship institution of Virginia, and it and the city of Charlottesville are both deeply mired in history. William B. Kurtz, managing director and digital historian at UVA's John L. Nau III Center for Civil War History, told a *UVA Today* writer, "More than 3,000 UVA alumni fought for the Confederacy, and approximately 90 percent of the student body enrolled [at UVA] in the fall of 1860 enlisted into Confederate military units by the end of 1861."[27] In contemporary memory, the city is where in 2017 Heather Heyer was killed when a White supremacist deliberately drove a car into her and a gathering of counter-protesters of which she was part.[28] The counter-protesters were assembled to demonstrate against Unite the Right, a neo-Nazi rally in the city.

When Donald Trump, the sitting U.S. president, was asked about the protests in Charlottesville, he famously responded that there were "very fine people on both sides."[29] President Trump said, "You had people in that group that were there to protest the taking down of, to them, a very, very important statue and the renaming of a park from Robert E. Lee to another name.... I'm not talking about the neo-Nazis and the White nationalists, because they should be condemned totally... [I]n the other group also, you had some fine people. But you also had troublemakers ... with the black outfits and ... baseball bats. You had a lot of bad people in the other group."[30] While Trump stated that neo-Nazis and White nationalists should be condemned, he did not say that *he* condemned them. The meaning of those remarks continues to baffle and confound. Heyer died, and 19 others were injured when the neo-Nazi intentionally drove his car into the counter-protesters.[31] Former KKK grand wizard David Duke spoke at the Unite the Right rally and said, "We are determined to take our country back. We are going to fulfill the promises of Donald Trump. That's what we believed in, that's why we voted for Donald Trump. Because he said he's going to take our country back. And that's what we gotta do."[32] This is the social and historical context around Martese Johnson and the Charlottesville police officers who enacted a spectacle that marked him as a criminal outsider.

The degradation ceremony is a communicative act done to lower the status of an individual. In order to be complete, it requires a public audience. After Johnson presented his identification to the officers, he stumbled over his zip code. His mother had recently moved, and he indicated he could not remember if his identification had the old or new zip code. It is plausible that the ABC officers actually thought his identification was fraudulent, but a fraudulent identification by a college student certainly does not warrant what happened next. I argue that after Johnson questioned the officers, they decided to put this young Black man in his place.[33]

The excessive nature of the officers' response is all about performance. The performance was both for the benefit of Johnson and any onlookers. An audience was crucial. The officers' denunciation of Johnson acted as a public spectacle designed to shroud the young Black man with the pretext of criminality and put him in his place. That place was a position of humble subservience to White officers. Johnson may have been a student in the venerated halls of the University of Virginia, but he should not have felt comfortable freely using all its space. The ABC officials justified their response by branding the young man as a malevolent actor who needed to be put down. The three White officers' excessive use of force (slamming him to the ground, placing him in handcuffs, and then putting shackles on his legs) was a total denunciation of Johnson's character, and the shackles connoted, re-envisioned, and reimagined servitude. He was the slave, and they were his masters. The performance acted as a denial of Johnson's humanity and entitlement to free use and enjoyment of the social space that is part of the extended university experience. In a post-*Brown* society, they were not be able to stop Johnson from attending the university, but their actions communicated other restraints on his movement indicative of a second-class citizenship.

The fact that everyone was watching the encounter meant that the image of a Black man shackled at the wrists and legs with three White men exerting control over him is seared in the memory of onlookers. This is what Rita Laura Segato argues. The public demonstration is an open secret meant to flaunt impunity. For the officers to publicly cross the line and get away with it is to establish the victim as having no rights the oppressor is bound to respect. The year was 2015. It was not 1619, but it might as well have been. Some of the onlookers video-recorded the encounter, and at this writing the attack has been viewed over five million times. These images hold extra import when we consider the incident's location on the outskirts of a campus designed by Jefferson and near his Monticello plantation and attendant slave quarters. It implies that a Black man's place is on the plantation, not lording over it. During the exchange, Johnson repeatedly cried out. He tried to communicate that he was not an interloper but someone who belonged in the space. Over and over he cried out, "But I go to UVA!" It was a statement and a plea. The ABC officers did not believe him, did not hear him, or did not care. However, because the charges levied against the student included "profane swearing in public," we know his assertions that the officers were "fucking racists" were heard. "How does this happen?" Johnson asked later. Even though Johnson was ultimately vindicated and charges were dropped, the public humiliation he suffered is a message to Johnson and other Black bodies in the social space (or observing the video) that they are not welcome there. You may enter it, but you will always be presumed criminal, no matter how "good" you act.

In July 2018, a Fox News affiliate in Washington, D.C., reported on "a basketball game gone wrong."[34] The exchange involved a mixed-race group of men in a pickup basketball game at an LA Fitness gym in Sterling, Virginia. After a six foot five Black man used a basketball move known as a pick, the White man on whom he set the pick fell to the floor. No fouls were called. The White man was not injured, but he was angry, so angry that he went to the receptionist and asked her to call the police. The receptionist obliged and reported that a member had been assaulted. When police arrived, they interviewed patrons and quickly surmised that it was not a police matter. Someone in the gym posted the exchange on social media. Soon after the police departed, all the parties continued to play.

Basketball is a contact sport. I argue that the act of calling the police was a not-so-veiled effort by the White player to tell the Black player (and other Black players watching) "You don't guard me." In the future, each time they play, the memory of this encounter will linger and consciously or subconsciously influence the assertiveness used in the game. In this case the criminality of the Black player was presumed and supported by the receptionist who called to report the "assault." While the responding officers used sound judgment in their determination that this was not a police matter, the public spectacle of being questioned by police in front of witnesses accomplished its intended purpose. Basketball may be a contact sport, but in the game of life and in basketball, a Black man has no business blocking a White man. That was the public lesson the White player wished to convey.

Providing Services and Seeking Services

Gas stations and supermarkets are transitory places. People come and go, but some people are discouraged from full use of the space. Charitable acts by a Black woman named Erika Martin and her family in one of such transitory place brought them all under suspicion and prompted a call to the police. The incident occurred in Mountain View, California. According to 2019 census data, less than 2% of the population of Mountain View identifies as Black alone. Martin pulled up to a Safeway supermarket parking lot. She was looking for a homeless man who frequented the area. She wanted to give him some food. Her son, sisters, and their young children were with her. The sisters gave toiletries to two other homeless men in the area. They chatted with the men. The children went in to the store to ask for one of the freshly baked cookies the bakery regularly disseminated to kids. After a bakery counter attendant told them "We don't have any more cookies to give to you," they returned to the car.[35] Soon after, a Safeway employee came outside, peered at the vehicle, and quickly went back into the store. An employee called police and reported a theft in progress.

Two police cars responded to the call. They surrounded the vehicle and questioned the family. Martin and her family cooperated, but the encounter left them all shaken. Martin was told that police were called out in response to a report of stealing. The description of the person who was stealing did not match her and bore only a vague resemblance to her sister. Martin told CNN, "My son was crying so much, he was so scared because he thought he did something wrong. He thought the police were going to arrest him for looking behind the [cookie] counter.... To see my child in so much fear broke my heart."[36]

As with the other encounters discussed in this chapter, there are multiple audiences that need to be considered. We have Martin, her family, the homeless in the area, and the general audience. Here the intersectional lens matters. The public rousting of a Black family, one clad in a religious T-shirt, signaled to Black onlookers that none of us are safe from the presumption of criminality. In this case the presumed criminal frame overlapped with the frame *You* Don't Belong *Here!* I argue that that the real intent was to discourage Martin and her family from congregating in the space and inviting homeless patrons and others down on their luck to linger there. The store was willing to engage in transactions with them for financial gain but nothing more. Handouts would not be tolerated.

Consistent with Jim Crow prohibitions against the public gathering of Blacks, the sheer presence of a group in excess of three threatened to turn the perception of the area into Black space. The public rousting by police is etched in Martin's memory and her sisters', but it is also seared in the minds of their young children, the next generation of Black Americans who, because of this incident, may now be less inclined to keep claiming space. As in the basketball game incident, even though the police did not arrest the Black patrons, a public marking or staining has taken place, and presence in the space has been delimited. Such a public denunciation germinates a societally reinforced seed in the minds of all, in this case including children and onlookers. In a society where people think and understand in terms of strict binaries, even Martin's child presumed that if the police are good, then that must mean that he is bad. Further, the homeless men and women were made to know that if a charitable Black woman traveling with family and clad in a "Jesus" T-shirt was not safe in the space, they certainly were not.

Other Mundane Encounters

Age offers no shelter from the presumption of Black criminality. A septuagenarian went into a bank in Victoria Park, Florida, to cash a $140 check.[37] A bank teller and manager thought the check was fraudulent. They detained the woman and called the police. During the ordeal, the bank refused to return her identification or the check. She was released some three hours later. Calls to the check writer verified its authenticity. Ultimately the bank cashed the check, but they failed to apologize.

When a middle-aged Black female special education teacher named Madonna Wilburn presented a digitally downloaded coupon at a Dollar General in Buffalo, New York, the White male store manager, Ken Dudek, accused her of fraud. Dudek ranted, "You people always want discounts.' . . . 'I hate people like you,'" Although Dudek denied it, "people like you" was code for Black people. In a tense exchange, Dudek told Wilburn that she was just trying to "take advantage of the system," and he called police. Wilburn told *BuzzFeed News* she began recording the exchange in order to protect herself. The manager's diatribe included a barrage of insults and orders for Wilburn to "shut up." Wilburn said she "didn't know how it was going to end."[38] Social media quickly dubbed the manager "Coupon Ken."

Dudek used both the presumed criminal and Massah Has Spoken frames. He fashioned himself the arbiter of right and Wilburn as the criminal bad actor. He charged and convicted her as a criminal bad actor in a vocal public performance meant to silence her and shame her into quiet subservience. Her silence would then be used to reinforce her guilt, but her continued questioning of his public degrading of her character would have the same effect. Then she would be branded the angry Black woman or welfare queen or some other variation of those. The manager's mere accusation of wrongdoing by Wilburn is meant to publicly cement the idea that Wilburn and "people like her" are criminal bad actors. Exactly who constitutes "people like you" is unspoken, but it is understood. Black people are criminal actors trying to get undue discounts and cheat good law-abiding White people like Dudek.

At every turn, the criminality of Black males as young as children is presumed. A White woman named Teresa Klein claimed that while in a crowded bodega in Flatbush, Brooklyn, a nine-year-old Black boy improperly touched her behind.[39] Klein followed the boy, his mother, and sister to the street, where she confronted them. On a call to police, Klein could be heard saying, "I was just sexually assaulted by a child. . . . The son grabbed my ass and she [the mother] decided to yell at me."[40] The boy denied any inappropriate behavior, but Klein insisted it happened.

A number of people recorded the exchange. In video Klein emphatically stated, "I want the cops here right now!" As onlookers grew, Klein mocked deriders, and she stated, "White lady calling the cops on a black kid. Yeah! I get it." With exaggerated gestures, Klein yelled, "I was essentially just assaulted by a child!" By now, both the little boy and his sister were hysterical, in tears. One of them can be heard yelling "Mommy?" After video of the encounter was posted to social media, public contempt for Klein grew. Klein stood by her account of events, and the boy's mother insisted it never happened. Days later, Klein return to the bodega to make a purchase. Upon her return, residents and local media persuaded her to watch surveillance video of the alleged assault.[41] *NBC News 4* reported, "The footage clearly shows the boy's hands were in plain sight, and it is his bookbag that grazed her."[42]

Even after Klein viewed the video and was aware of the grave mistake she committed, she expressed an insincere apology to the boy and painted herself as a victim. Making full use of her public platform, Klein insisted that since the video was posted, she could no longer walk the streets of Flatbush, and she wanted to pursue criminal charges against the mother of the boy she falsely accused. Rather than turn her inquiry inward, Klein turned it outward and doubled down with the allegation that the boy's mother threatened her. She then insisted on publicly communicating her message that Black people are criminals—in the hope that others would adopt the view and she (and all of White womanhood) would be vindicated. To accomplish this end, Klein pivoted and alleged that she called 911 because the boy's mother was "very aggressive."[43] By this time, Klein, who was dubbed by social media as Cornerstore Caroline, knew her error but was still intent on finding a criminal bad actor, so she made the child's mother the bad actor. If she could discredit the mother's reputation, a seed of doubt would be planted about the child. As with the doctrine of partus sequitur ventrem in slavery that established that a child's legal status flowed from the mother, if the mother could be painted as deviant, that status would flow to her child. Given the history that includes false accusations against boys of color, ranging from the Scottsboro Boys to Emmett Till to the Central Park Five, Klein's performance was maleficent—seemingly intent on inflicting harm.

On the other side of the country, a Black male entrepreneur named Viktor Stevenson opened a gourmet lemonade stand in the gentrifying Mission District of San Francisco. Early one morning, he went to his business and started to open the door. His keys were in his hand. A White woman passing by accused him of trying to break in, and she called police. Four officers reported to the scene.[44] Throughout the exchange, one of the officers kept his hand on his gun.[45] On public display for all to see, Stevenson was forced to assume the role and public image of criminal. In full view of other business owners in the area and his potential patrons, he was compelled to explain his presence in the space and prove his ownership interest. Before Stevenson was cleared, he was asked to go through several public performances. Police had Stevenson remove his arm from his pocket, show his key, demonstrate his ability to get in and out the establishment, show his identification, and wait while the officers ran him through their computer system.[46]

Zayd Atkinson, a student at Naropa University in Boulder, Colorado, was taking a break from picking up trash in front of the apartment complex where he lived and worked. Had Atkinson been hunched over and engaged in this stereotypical labor in the space, he might not have come under scrutiny, but he had decided to rest. Atkinson had a plastic trash picker in his hand. An officer approached him and told Atkinson that the townhouse complex was private property and that he needed him to prove he belonged in the space. During the exchange, the officer pointed his gun at Atkinson and told him to put down his weapon (the trash picker). A White resident yelled through a window and vouched for Atkinson. The resident told the officer Atkinson was just picking up trash. When Atkinson refused to put down the trash grabber, the officer called for backup and reported that the suspect was "uncooperative and unwilling to put down a blunt object."[47] Nine officers responded.[48]

In Upper Arlington, Ohio, a suburb of upscale homes outside Columbus and near the main campus of The Ohio State University, a 12-year-old Black boy was on the first day of his paper route. Police were called because a resident deemed the child's behavior "suspicious." The youth's mother posted on Facebook: "First day of paper route and we are pulled over by police. Sad I can't even teach my son the value of working without someone whispering and looking at us out the side of their eye perhaps because we DON'T 'look like a person that belongs in their neighborhood.' . . . My apologies Upper Arlington for bringing my 12 year old African American son into your neighborhood to deliver the paper and make a few dollars on the side . . . NO HARM INTENDED [frowning face]. I will make sure my boss changes his route."[49] The young man's mother added that she was feeling disappointed.

"Suspicious" is code for the socially prohibited category Black. In Upper Arlington, Ohio, the public arrival of police produced one desired effect—the removal of a Black body from the space. However, it also produced a counter-response in that the child's mother publicly identified and denounced the actions as racist. She removed her child from the space so that she could try to shield the 12-year-old from as much of the pain of racism as she could for as long as she could.

In the instances outlined above, and countless other instances that I do not have time or space to record, Black men working were presumed to have gained illegitimate access to a space or be in a space for some criminal purpose.[50] Their activity was not suspicious. Their very bodies were, and those who sought to push them out of the space used language ostensibly neutral but laden with race-based connotations.

Shopping

Shopping is another routine activity that many people engage in without even a second thought, but shopping while Black comes with attendant risks.[51] In Brentwood, Missouri, three male Black teens went shopping for their prom. They had money and did not engage in any inherently suspicious behavior. Everywhere they went, a store employee shadowed. It should have been a fun time for them, but the constant surveillance robbed them of some of that joy. Then an elderly White female shopper called them bums. The teens made their purchases and left. Someone called the police. After the young men exited the mall, police stopped and detained them on suspicion of shoplifting. The police quickly determined they had not stolen anything and let them go. Their experience, however, is not so easily released. One of the teens told a news outlet about his experience in the store: "I was nervous the whole time. Every time we move, they move. When we looked up, they looked up."[52] Their youth and Black skin had branded the teens before they even entered the store. Even after their vindication, the teens' comments reveal that they still carry the psychological weight of the accusation.

Late one evening, Darren Martin, a former aide in the Obama administration, started moving things into his new apartment in a gentrifying area on the Upper West Side of Manhattan. Mindful of the fact that it was evening, Martin tried to be quiet. In the midst of one of his trips back and forth to the apartment, Martin was confronted by police. A resident had accused him of burglarizing an apartment. The caller told police Martin was brandishing a large weapon.[53] Police responded to a report of an armed robbery.[54]

Martin said he considered the call a "symbolic" act. In my estimation, the call said "We are watching you. You do not belong, and we are not waiting for you to step out of line. Your mere presence suggests you are out of line and out of place." The neighbor made an a priori determination that Martin's presence in the space suggested criminal activity. The neighbor did not apologize for the call. The former Obama aide noted that his skin color and his presence in a "gentrifying neighborhood" were factors that led to the police being called. Martin stated that while the police were doing their job, a call to police alleging a home invasion in progress with a "possible weapon" involved increases the likelihood that police are "going to come in full force."[55] Perhaps that was the caller's intent.

Like all the incidents described, Martin did nothing wrong. However, like the other incidents discussed, it is his dignity that was on trial. Martin poignantly stated, "There are fewer moments less dignifying than [being] at the scene when the police and witnesses assess you to determine if you committed this crime or perceived crime—when you know you didn't."[56] This modified version of a perp walk is a status degradation ceremony intended to demean and lower the status of the person in the eyes of others.[57] Martin's comments indicate that despite his innocence, the act of being made to defend his presence and actions was debasing. Like Travis Miller, Martin's aim was just to make it home safely. Even at his own doorstep, Martin was not safe.

In "The Rhetoric of Antiblack Racism," philosopher and social critic Erik Garrett condenses advice he received for successfully navigating space outside of his or other Black-majority neighborhoods. Garrett writes, "You are taught don't shop with your hands in your pockets for fear that one's body is mistaken for a shoplifter; don't run through an affluent neighborhood for fear of being mistaken for the body of a thief, and don't behave 'ambiguously' with a White spouse or partner for fear of being mistaken as a rapist."[58] These activities limit free will, but they increase the chances of arriving home safely. More importantly, they make others feel comfortable with the presence of Black bodies in the geographic and/or social space by attempting to disabuse others of the presumption that one is a criminal.

The cost, however, may be the loss of dignity that Martin discusses. That may also the intent of the public accusation.

Conclusion

Daily life requires mobility to and through spaces, but this chapter evidences that a presumption of criminality shrouds Black bodies in many public spaces and attempts to control Black movement and full free use of space. This presumption comes through most cogently in the case of Teresa Klein. In a dense urban space, Klein felt something brush up against her body, and she immediately presumed a nearby nine-year-old Black boy had groped her. Klein was so intent on Black blame (and her own faultlessness) that when faced with video evidence of her grave error in judgment, she easily and quickly shifted her narrative to place culpability for the encounter on another Black actor. Klein's ready ability to denounce the mother's defense of her own child against the wrongful attack of a strange woman is as troubling as it is telling. It shows a deeply entrenched belief system that supports and presumes the criminality of Blacks, especially Black male criminality, and an unwillingness to take personal responsibility.

Klein relied on historical notions of White female virtue, Black male bestiality, and Black female aggression in order to absolve herself from personal blame. Then, in order to make her absolution (and the denunciation of the Black actor) complete, Klein publicly invoked another stereotype of Blacks. This time, Klein evoked the trope of Black women's anger and aggression in painting herself as victim. The mother's righteous defense of her son, whom Klein had already publicly vilified and reduced to tears, was demonized if not criminalized.

Like other victims of video-recorded attacks, this young Black boy was traumatized during the original encounter and then forced to relive the pain of the event. In this way, video evidence is incredibly complex. Video-recorded racialized incidents both inform and revictimize. The victims are also subjected to scrutiny and attack. The video evidence can shift the gaze and incite and excite those who seek to dehumanize the individual or group the attack is levied against. In this way, video evidence becomes like lynching postcards of the past—another trophy collected at the expense of the victimized.

After Klein's attack on the character of the child and then his mother, the local community held a rally in support of them. The child's mother described the encounter as the day her child lost his innocence. She said she had since had two talks with her nine-year-old son and his younger sister who was also present and traumatized by Klein's accusations. One talk was about what racism is and one talk was about what constitutes "sexual assault," of which the boy was accused.

The children's innocence was not lost. It was taken. New York Assembly member Rodneyse Bichotte said, "I cannot imagine how traumatized this young boy is. Innocent, coming home from school, and having to live this, having to live 1955." A rally attendee who identified herself as a teacher and antiracism activist said, "We put a bunch of people in a melting pot without a proper understanding or ways to relate to each other, we get anti-black rhetoric or behavior projected onto us and our children."[59] This inability of many Whites to relate to Blacks as equals may be why Bart Landry notes that many upper-middle-class Blacks who have the financial ability to live almost anywhere they please are no longer interested in integration.[60]

The public rebuke and accusation against a child for an uncorroborated act and persistence in maintaining this claim despite his tears and denial is more than malice. It is criminal, and it evidences a pattern one team of researchers has called the "dehumanization of Black children."[61] The "presumed criminal" label is most often, but not exclusively, evoked against Black men and boys. It is generally invoked through some type of public performance. Whether targeting an individual or a group, it creates a cognitive dissonance that is carried around as extra weight. No one should have to bear this weight but especially not a child.

CHAPTER 6

Massah Has Spoken

> Racial caste systems do not require racial hostility or overt
> bigotry to thrive. They need only racial indifference.
>
> —MICHELLE ALEXANDER

            In slavery, the master's orders were not to be questioned or countermanded. They were to be obeyed without delay. Failure to do so had consequences, some as dire as death. The reasonableness of any request by the master (or his designate) was assumed, so to question such a directive would be presumed insubordinate if not downright mutinous. Vestiges of that system remain. I see it running through the encounter between Ahmaud Arbery and the residents of Satilla Shores, Georgia, who chased and ultimately killed the unarmed Black jogger. This mentality is especially salient in the 911 audio featured in an *ABC News Nightline* segment on the Arbery case. Greg McMichael can be heard ordering Arbery to stop running away from him: "Stop right there [expletive]! Stop! Hey!"[1] When Arbery chose instead to keep running, to contravene the orders of angry White men chasing him through the public streets, it raised those men's ire and revealed a still-present mentality that Black bodies are bound to obey the orders of Whites—or risk the consequences.

            To recap, Arbery was being chased through the public street by two or more armed White men in a truck. A separate White man pursued him from another direction. As Arbery ran through the neighborhood, the men tried to cut him off—more than once, and, in the chase, Arbery's pursuers (residents of the neighborhood) become so disoriented that they did not even know where they were. Ironically, the fact that Arbery had the nerve to disobey the orders of armed White men in a truck chasing him through the streets was later used by some to justify the actions that followed. Alan Tucker, the attorney who leaked video of the shooting, told *Inside Edition*: "The video speaks for itself . . . What happened, happened. I don't have an excuse for it. I can't explain. Other than, we always say, 'What if he had just froze and hadn't done anything, he wouldn't have gotten shot.'"[2] In Tucker's world, Arbery would still be alive today if he had just obeyed the orders of the White men illegally pursuing him and stopped. Tucker lives in a fantasy world. That is why counter-narrative perspectives are so important. They help us to point out the fallacies in certain logics and connect these to continuing examples. For example, Philando Castile and Daunte Wright froze, did nothing, and got shot anyway. Some might say you are "damned if you do obey orders, and you are damned if you don't." How did we get here?

The Advent of Cultural Racism

In 1992, James Blaut argued that there have been three distinct eras of racist theory and control in society. According to Blaut, "The dominant racist theory of the early 19th century was a biblical argument, grounded in religion; the dominant racist theory of the period from about 1850 to 1950 was a biological argument, grounded in natural science; the racist theory of today is mainly a historical argument grounded in the idea of . . . culture."[3] The cultural racism era relies on the use of symbolic violence through suggestions that minorities are backward and less culturally evolved than Whites. Instead of the former disfavored language of a superior White race (which evokes politically disfavored notions of the Aryan race, Hitler, and eugenics), there is instead the suggestion of a superior culture with superior ways of knowing and doing things.

The shift Blaut outlines from biological racism to cultural racism highlights the import of the concerns Bonilla-Silva and Zuberi raise in their edited volume *White Logic, White Methods: Racism and Methodology*, about the influence living under a regime governed exclusively by White racial logic has on the life chances of those subjugated. They warn, "Sociology has been—and still is—a White-led and White-dominated field and, therefore, it should not surprise anyone that the logic of analysis and methods used to investigate racial matters reflect this social fact."[4] For the authors, "White logic" refers to the ways social science's thinking, knowing, and reasoning are oriented in White supremacist ideologies. These comprise a cultural attack. The belief in a culturally superior worldview allows those who adopt this ideological stance to see themselves as humanitarian saviors bearing the burden of redeeming society from its impending fall. All others are viewed as infantile children who would fail without their guidance and direction.

The Massah Has Spoken framework is best understood as a form of symbolic violence and a way of seeing the validity of Blaut's insights on cultural racism. In this vein, the commands issued to Ahmaud Arbery can be seen as building on the notion of superior White intellect and reason (especially Eurocentric thinking). This superior reason gives the person issuing the command (or his or her designee) the right to direct purportedly less intelligent non-Europeans as to what to do, how to do it, and when and where. After all, the edicts are framed as culturally superior logic issued for the good of the subjected individual, so the subjugated would do well to listen to and obey White commands. Under this logic, obeying such commands is part of the price of the ticket for permission to live in the society. Failure to heed the commands is a justification for removal from the society or relegation to its margins. As in the historical case of the overseer, these commands may also be issued by others at the behest of White dominants.[5] All that matters is that when Massah speaks, you better obey.

Failure to comply with White commands is commonly used to justify violent police response. It was the offense used often in Ferguson, Missouri, to stop, detain, arrest, convict, and fine Black youths. We are told that if Rodney King in Los Angeles had just complied with police orders, he would not have been beaten. We are told the 2020 shooting and paralysis of Jacob Blake in Kenosha, Wisconsin, is justified because a police officer told him to stop walking and pulled on his shirt. We are told that Sandra Bland invited her own arrest and death, and had she just put out her cigarette when the officer told her to do so, talked to him with respect, or stopped recording the exchange when he asked her to, she would still be alive. In 2013, two years prior to Bland's death, 34-year-old Miriam Carey was fatally shot after she refused orders to stop her car. Many of the facts in this case are disputed, but there is relative agreement that Carey drove into a restricted area near the White House, made a U-turn, and drove away without stopping.[6] Secret Service and Capitol police followed her. Carey did not stop. On several occasions, the officers shouted commands for her to get out of the vehicle. Carey ignored them all. The standoff ended after police who surrounded the vehicle fired between 16 and 24 shots inside.[7] Carey was shot five times. Her one-year-old child, who was in the car with her, was unharmed. The Secret Service has been criticized for their extreme response to what was essentially a traffic incident, especially in light of the information regarding dozens of incidents in which intruders actually breached the White House and were not harmed.[8]

Even when we comply, we are still at risk. A Bastrop County, Texas, sheriff's deputy responding to a report of a domestic dispute said he ordered Yvette Smith to come out of a house. When Smith came through the doorway, deputy Daniel

Willis shot her two times, killing her. According to the *Guardian*, "Willis, who is white, saw Smith, a black 47-year-old former caretaker, and ordered her to come outside. As she opened the door he shouted 'police!' then fired within about three seconds. She died in the hospital after being shot twice by the deputy, who was using his personal AR-15 SEMi-automatic rifle." The sheriff's office fired Willis, who had only been on the force about a year. Murder charges were later filed against the officer, but the first case ended in a mistrial, and Willis was cleared of murder by a judge in a retrial. Prior to delivering his ruling on the case, the judge fixed the blame on the two Black men whose fighting necessitated the 911 call.[9] Willis's defense counsel, Robert McCabe, was more explicit. McCabe said, "Daniel Willis was not driving around looking for trouble. This is two men fighting with weapons in a violent encounter when 911 was called. Had they not acted like fools, Daniel Willis would not have been called." The judge opined that the former officer, who lied about giving the order for Smith to put her hands up, acted within the "objectively reasonable" standard for the use of lethal force.[10]

After pulling Philando Castile over on a traffic stop, Minnesota police officer Jeronimo Yanez asked for his license and registration. While trying to comply, Castille disclosed to the officer that he had a firearm. Castile was licensed to carry the weapon. The officer told him not to reach for the gun. Castile clarified that he was reaching for the requested license and registration.[11] When Castile moved to comply with Officer Yanez's request that he produce his license and registration, Yanez shot him seven times and killed him.[12] Castile's fiancée streamed the aftermath of his shooting on Facebook Live. Officer Yanez was charged with second-degree manslaughter and two counts of dangerous discharge of a firearm in the death of Castile, but, as in the case of the officer charged with the death of Yvette Smith, Yanez was acquitted.[13] Countless other examples abound.

The Massah Has Spoken frame is an expression of anti-blackness in the form of cultural racism. The advent of cultural racism, which Blaut outlines, privileges White logics and rejects the reasonableness of all other explanations for phenomena, especially those put forward by subjugated persons. This discussion makes it easier (for those who wish) to see the historical parallels and paradigms still in place today. It is a reincarnation of a kind, benevolent master who issues orders and exerts control over you out of singular concern for your best interest. After all, as a non-European you do not know better. It is in this light that I read the comments expressed by attorney Alan Tucker at the opening of this chapter. Tucker suggests that if Arbery had just obeyed his pursuers' commands to stop running, he would still be alive today. White logic eschews the presence or reality of systemic racism, and it asserts that individual racism is rare and committed by only a few bad actors. In his 1992 article, "The Theory of Cultural Racism," Blaut predicted and identified this paradox: "Today . . . We have racism but few racists."[14]

The Moynihan Report

In many ways, the Moynihan Report planted the seed for the widespread cultural racism present today. Assistant U.S. secretary of labor Daniel Patrick Moynihan was one of the drafters of signature antipoverty programs for the nation under President Lyndon Baines Johnson. In 1965, Moynihan prepared a report about the state of Blacks in America. His 76-page report, "The Negro Family: The Case for National Action" (sometimes called the Moynihan Report) was written for internal circulation only, but soon it was widely shared and praised.[15]

Initial responses to the Moynihan Report were so widely heralded that subsequent criticism of the report took Moynihan by surprise. Black leaders, intellectuals, and liberal Whites alike decried the report.[16] They took exception to what appeared to be Moynihan's central point: "At the heart of the deterioration of the fabric of Negro society," Moynihan wrote, "is the deterioration of the Negro family. *It* is the fundamental source of the weakness of the Negro community at the present time approaching breakdown."[17] In an article in *The Nation*, Harvard psychologist William Ryan called Moynihan out for what he termed his "implicit point that the Negroes tolerate promiscuity, illegitimacy, one-parent families, welfare dependency, and everything else that is supposed to follow." Professor Ryan called the report a form of intellectual "savage discovery."[18] The Moynihan Report argued that the Black family structure in America would damage any government efforts for Blacks to receive full racial equality.

Moynihan did not conduct any original research. Instead, he synthesized the work of others (including the works of leading African American men) and interpreted it through his own (White) ideological and philosophical lens. From this, he concluded that the Black family structure represented a "tangle of pathology."[19] The seminal policy recommendation, if it could be called that, was Moynihan's expression of a need for full male employment and a livable wage guarantee for Black men. There was no discussion of a livable wage for Black women. Moynihan also suggested that Black men should be encouraged to join the military where they could learn values. The unstated inference was that Black men either lacked values or their values were substandard. In the military, Moynihan reasoned, they might stabilize their homes and learn the missing value of "discipline" they lacked.[20] Moynihan called the Black family a matriarchy and blamed Black poverty not on racism but on Black mothers doting on their sons. Moynihan demonized the heroic work of Black women relegated to domestic centrality by the twin evils of racism and sexism and called it "a tangle of pathology."

Legacy

Efforts to resist the Supreme Court dictate in *Brown* set the stage for the Moynihan Report's lasting impact. After the Brown ruling toppled legal segregation, southerners looked for ways to frustrate school integration, which they equated with wider social integration and amalgamation of the races. They mounted a cultural attack on Black life and culture and looked for ways to manipulate social science data to support their allegations of Black inferiority. Anders Walker writes, "Not only did segregationists find a new vocabulary for referring to race following *Brown* . . . they were [also] able to clothe that vocabulary in a garment of fact. Social science, in other words, become an important tool that segregationists manipulated to promote racist ends."[21]

This tangle of pathology began with Black women. Representations of deviant Black mothering still stand at the center of the U.S. racial imaginary. The Moynihan Report's condemnation of the Black family was especially critical of Black women. Inside this cultural attack, poor Black women were subjected to the most pernicious treatment. In *Killing the Black Body: Race, Reproduction and the Meaning of Liberty*, race, gender, and law scholar Dorothy Roberts outlines the stigmatization and devaluation of poor Black mothers. Roberts writes, "For three centuries, Black mothers have been thought to pass down to their offspring the traits that marked them as inferior to any white person. Along with this biological impairment, it is believed that Black mothers transfer a deviant lifestyle to their children that dooms each succeeding generation to a life of poverty, delinquency, and despair. A persistent objective of American social policy has been to monitor and restrain this corrupting tendency of Black motherhood."[22] Roberts highlights the cultural and legal ways U.S. society has levied attacks on the Black female body. She also connects contemporary government restrictions placed on welfare recipients to practices born under the system of chattel slavery that attempted to operate as a form of total regulation over Black women's bodies.

Counter-challenges to the findings in the Moynihan Report also persisted, including some by members of the emerging Black sociology movement. Scholars like Joyce Ladner of Howard University called for the "death of white sociology."[23] These scholars stressed that Moynihan's depiction of Black culture, life, and particularly the Black family structure as pathological falsely presumed the superiority of middle-class White norms and values. Further, the report's continuing references to higher incidences of female single-parent households in minority communities seemed to promote the worst racial stereotypes of Blacks, including inferences to domineering and/or promiscuous Black women and lazy, dominated Black men. It even seemed to favor taking jobs away from Black women and giving them to Black men so that the proper place of Black men could be restored; the proper place of Black women would be implied as behind Black men. And since Black men were behind White men, and White women above Black women, Black women were once again relegated to the bottom. It is reminiscent of Ida Wells's findings. Her investigations connected anti-miscegenation laws to regulations keeping Black women from entering the "ladies' car" on trains. By denying Black women admission to the ladies' car, Black women were performatively and perennially marked with a stamp that said they were outside the cult of southern womanhood. Since they were not ladies, this constantly performed denial of access reinforced their otherness. The denial of the classification as a lady was then used to justify further indignities visited upon Black women. At the same time, White womanhood was policed even more vigilantly. The "cult of true womanhood" implied that it was not ladylike to be in the workforce; instead, there should be a man at home providing for a woman. Though not a direct reference to the Moynihan Report, one Black feminist anthology title communicated the perverse extent of Black female exclusion from society: *All the Women Are White, All the Blacks Are Men, But Some of Us Are Brave.*[24]

The dominant cultural ideas in place at the time of the Moynihan Report reinforced patriarchy and exclusion. These ideals included:

1. a belief in the superiority of middle-class American values;
2. a belief that cultural assimilation of racial and ethnic minorities into society was best; and
3. a belief that male-headed households were most favorable.

The Moynihan Report acknowledged that not all White children grow up in two-parent households, but it stated, "White children without fathers at least perceive all around them a pattern of men working. Negro children without fathers flounder and fail."[25] There was no discussion of the social practices and policies that created the structure under attack. The family structure that a legacy of racially discriminatory practices built was now being critiqued by the agents of the very structure that built it. The purported ill moral character it supposedly reflected was used as a basis for continuing discrimination.

English professor Stanley Fish's observations in his 1994 book demonstrate how complete and perverse the shift from biological racism to cultural racism has been. According to Fish, there has been a perversion of Dr. King's words and wish for a society where his children "would be judged not by the color of their skin but by the content of their character." In this shift to cultural racism, it is ironically purported that Black bodies are no longer judged by the color of their skin but by the content of their character, and that character has been deemed deficient. Fish continues, "It's like alchemy or magic: now you see white supremacy, but, presto chango, it is given a new description, and now you see 'equality for everyone' with no change whatsoever in the practice or outcome."[26] The Moynihan Report managed to straddle two worlds. It was born out of structural inequities it failed to address, yet it remained committed to a fabled meritocracy. It acknowledged that nearly half of Black families were middle class, but it suggested that half were doomed. It acknowledged the strength and resiliency of Black women, but it called these pathological.

Now almost 50 years old, the Moynihan Report has been cited and revived in every decade since it original release. In the 1970s, Moynihan, then advisor to president-elect Richard M. Nixon, advised Nixon to carry out a policy of "benign neglect" in discussions of matters of race.[27] In the 1980s, conservatives used the report to rationalize a failure to enact racially progressive policies. Citing Moynihan, President Ronald Reagan argued that racial inequality was because of liberal welfare policies. Though more Whites than Blacks were on welfare, President Reagan successfully mounted a campaign that racialized welfare and promulgated the idea of Black women as "welfare queens" living off the government and the sweat of hardworking Americans.[28]

In 1995, former U.S. secretary of education William Bennett said, "The most serious problems afflicting our society today are manifestly moral, behavioral, and spiritual, and therefore remarkably resistant to government cures."[29] Soon after those comments, Congress abolished Aid to Families with Dependent Children (AFDC) and replaced it with Temporary Aid to Families with Dependent Children.[30] The Personal Responsibility Act of 1996, written by Republicans but supported and signed into law by Bill Clinton, imposed especially cruel conditions on women on welfare. These conditions only served to increase the number of children in poverty.[31] In the 1990s, William Julius Wilson used insights from the Moynihan Report to support theses he advanced about the Black underclass in several of his books. The Moynihan Report's life would seem to know no end, and its supposed "science" bolstered a cultural assault on Black life that is still being waged today.[32]

Ladner's 1973 edited volume *The Death of White Sociology* challenged the propensity in mainstream sociology to treat Black lives as social problems.[33] It offered a critique of the study of Black life by others, arguing instead that Black people were best equipped to study, interpret, and critique Black life. Ladner's project

sought movement toward a definition and theory of Black sociology. Later, sociologists Earl Wright II and Thomas Calhoun took up that challenge. Like Ladner, Wright and Calhoun maintain that Black sociology should "focus primarily
on Black Americans while producing definitions, concepts, and theories unique
to that particular group."[34] Second-wave feminists—Black and White alike—also
challenged the patriarchal norms present throughout the report. Not surprisingly, then and now, Black feminists offered some of the most eloquent and insightful critiques of the Moynihan Report. Internal inconsistencies in the report
facilitated a series of contentious assumptions about race, gender and the role of
government.[35]

I foreground the Moynihan Report in order to showcase the ways it reflects a
long-standing belief that success in the United States requires a certain set of cultural values missing in the African American community. The report's longevity
also evidences a widely held belief in the cultural superiority of White males and
the prevailing supremacy of White logics. The idea of the morally and/or intellectually bereft "Negro" invokes historical notions that Blacks need to be under
the care or charge of morally and intellectually superior Whites who know what
is best for them. As such, the argument goes, it is best for society and the Negro if
Whites lead and Blacks obey. This is the foundation for the Massah Has Spoken
Framework.

Massah Has Spoken Framework in Operation

When the Massah Has Spoken frame is used, it relies heavily on this paternalis-
tic premise that Massah knows best. While it may be used in conjunction with
other epistemological frames, at the heart of this BOP typology is the belief that
any direction given by this person (no matter how it is communicated) should be
obeyed without question. This is because it should be assumed that the request or
order (no matter how communicated) is given at the behest of a benevolent master type who knows what is best. Therefore, even a command made by an ordinary citizen should be heeded, and the failure to do so justifies any response by the
bidder. The balance of this chapter is devoted to analyzing three examples of this
framework. The first involves the killing of Jordan Davis, which many refer to as
the "loud music case." The second case study involves the killing of Trayvon Martin, and the third, discussed at the beginning of this chapter, is the case of Ahmaud
Arbery. There have been countless incidents that fit this framework and included
state actors such as police, but, for purposes of this initial discussion, I restrict the
analysis to ones involving private citizens.

On Friday, November 23, 2012, 17-year-old Jordan Davis and three teenage friends went out. It was the day after Thanksgiving. All were Black and lived in Jacksonville, Florida. Michael Dunn, a 45-year-old White man and his girlfriend were in town for the wedding of Dunn's son. Around 7:30 p.m., both groups stopped at a local gas station. The youth arrived first. The teen driver left the car running and went in to the gas station. The other teen boys remained in the car and listened to hip hop music. Dunn and his girlfriend pulled into the space next to the boys' vehicle. Dunn's girlfriend went into the gas station to make a purchase. By all accounts, neither the Davis group nor Dunn intended to remain in the parking lot long.

Dunn described the music as "very loud." According to Dunn's then-fiancée, Rhonda Rouer, when they pulled up beside the car, Dunn said, "I hate that thug music."[36] "Thug" was Dunn's code for "Black," and Dunn intended for those young Black boys to comply by his standard of what was appropriate or inappropriate in the space. By all accounts, Dunn asked the young people to turn the music down. The teens complied with the request, but eventually one of them turned the music back up. There was an exchange of words. A witness said he heard Dunn tell the teens, "You aren't going to talk to me like that!"[37]

This was not a case of a neighbor who had blared music for hours. It was a minor and temporary inconvenience, which is why I submit that it was not the music that troubled Dunn. It was the teens' failure to adhere to his command to turn down the music that seemed to incense Dunn, who, by any reasonable estimation, would have only been forced to endure the noise for a few minutes. In his mind, these Black male teens had no legitimate authority to contravene any order he gave. Dunn removed a gun from his glove compartment and shot repeatedly into the occupied vehicle. Dunn wounded several of the teens, and he killed Jordan Davis. When Dunn's girlfriend came out of the gas station, she got into the vehicle, and they drove back to their hotel where they reportedly drank the wine that she purchased. The next day, they drove back to their home in the Satellite Beach area of Florida, some 300 miles away.

On the evening of the incident, Dunn never called the police. Reports indicate that he was only located after a "witness gave police the tag number from a Volkswagen sedan that left the scene . . . after the shooting."[38] Dunn was not charged for the November 23 shooting until four days later. Dunn would later claim the teens had a weapon and threatened him. He could not explain why he did not call the police. He could not explain why he drove off. In my counter-narrative reading of the encounter, I suggest that what really angered Dunn was the teens' failure to obey his orders and the fact that they did not speak to him with deference. Recall the witness's comment that Dunn told the teens, "*You* aren't going to talk to *me* like that!"[39]

White supremacy also has a gender hierarchy built into it. As a White male, Dunn was socially conditioned to expect full subservience from Black bodies. Additional status factors contributed to this expectation. By virtue of their age and race, Dunn felt the teens owed him unearned, unconditional deference and respect. I submit that through the lens of history and culture, this is the only reasonable way to interpret Dunn's remark, "You aren't going to talk to me like that."[40] Dunn asserted full ownership over and right to regulate the organization or businesses space, the public space of the parking lot, the private space of the teen's vehicle, and even the bodies of the Black teens he demanded turn down the music. Then, amid questions from his girlfriend, Dunn ordered her to get in the car, and he sped away. All of it was his to regulate, and he expected to do so with full impunity from prosecution. After all, Massah can do whatever he wants to his "property," and no one has a right to complain. Massah had spoken, and he fully expected the teens to comply.

On February 26, 2012, George Zimmerman, a neighborhood watch volunteer in his Sanford, Florida, neighborhood, called 911 to make a "suspicious person report." That "suspicious person" was 17-year-old Trayvon Martin, whom Zimmerman killed in an encounter soon after the call.[41] By now, this case is well known. I focus instead on an aspect of the frame Massah Has Spoken that this case typifies.

Sociologists believe that all criminal behavior is deviant, but not all deviant (non-normative) behavior is criminal. In the discussion of culture outlined earlier in this chapter, I focused on how cultural expectations of the dominant class, including ways of thinking, dressing, and behaving, are not only normative but also seen as right and reasonable. All other forms of knowing are rejected. Therefore, actions contrary to those are considered not only deviant but also criminal. Here, I identify elements from Zimmerman's 911 call that underscore how Martin's noncompliance with Zimmerman's cultural expectations about how the teen should behave reinforced Zimmerman's certitude that Martin was a malevolent bad actor.

In the early evening hours, Zimmerman saw a young Black person walking through his gated, predominantly White neighborhood, and he decided to follow the young person. During the course of that pursuit, he called 911. Early in the call, Zimmerman stated, "Hey, we've had some break-ins in my neighborhood, and there's a real suspicious guy, uh . . . [this] guy looks like he's up to no good, or he's on drugs or something. It's raining and he's just walking around, looking about." At one point, Zimmerman told the 911 operator, "He was just staring . . . Now he's just staring at me."[42] Each comment Zimmerman made seemed to increase his certitude that Trayvon Martin was a bad actor. Narrating the teenager's every move, Zimmerman told the 911 operator, "He's got his hand in his waistband. And he's a black male." Next, Zimmerman indicated something was wrong with Martin.

"Yup," Zimmerman said, "he's coming to check me out, he's got something in his hands, I don't know what his deal is."[43] At no point did it occur to Zimmerman that he himself had something in his hands or that his own behavior might be perceived as suspicious. Martin had just turned 17. In essence, a grown man (Zimmerman) with a somewhat large build, was following a child around. It seems rational that Martin might conclude that Zimmerman was stalking and hunting him. From a disinterested viewpoint one might easily think that Zimmerman intended to do the child harm and that Martin had the right to defend himself against such a clear and present danger.

Zimmerman had made prior calls to police to report other suspicious persons in his neighborhood. The calls almost exclusively involved young Black men.[44] Martin's dress, his seemingly aimless stroll, his glances at Zimmerman, and his failure to speak were all classified as suspicious. You must greet Massah, but Massah need not greet you. Zimmerman even coded Martin's act of running away as criminal. After Zimmerman shot Martin, police officers heard Zimmerman's account, and they released him. Presumably, no attempt was made to filter the exchange through a lens other than the one Zimmerman proffered. Even more egregious is the fact that the legal system failed to detain Zimmerman or bring charges against him until there was mounting public pressure to do so.

When Zimmerman was finally brought to trial, he was acquitted. Koritha Mitchell wrote, "Zimmerman (and everyone watching) received confirmation that he had accurately interpreted the messages he had always received about the nation's values."[45] The jury verdict did not mean that Zimmerman was innocent, but it did say he was not guilty of the charges. Jurors accepted Zimmerman's claims of self-defense as a justification for his actions. Author Lisa Bloom uncovered that the jurors had sympathy for Zimmerman.[46] Her discussion of the jury's sympathy for Zimmerman provides more evidence of the legitimacy of this frame.[47]

Both the prosecution and the defense asserted that race had nothing to do with this incident. A six-member jury, which included five White people, agreed. Cultural racism relies on cultural distinctions (not biological ones) to mark the superiority of one group and inferiority of another. In this way, racism is obscured as the focus is on distinctions other than race; it fails to acknowledge that many cultural distinctions are rooted in racial group practices. The prosecution and jurors were blinded by outmoded ideas about what racism looks and feels like and how it operates. This case reflects a narrower application of the Massah Has Spoken framework, which points to an inclination by police and others to accept without question or investigation the assertions of some members of society to the detriment of others. By contrast, the Arbery case reflects a classic application of the Massah Has Spoken frame.

As I envision the assailants pulling up beside Arbery in their pickup truck, guns in hand, and ordering him to stop running, a scene from the past plays out in my head. The audio of that scene goes like this: "Boy. I told you to stop running. Don't make me have to get out of this truck and run after you. If I do, I'm gonna have to kill you." Basics of the Arbery encounter, which happened in the Satilla Shores community in Brunswick, Georgia, are outlined at the beginning of this chapter.[48] Massah's property includes not only the plantation but also all the property on it, including Black bodies.

Enlightenment philosopher Jeremy Bentham described property as the basis of expectation.[49] Legal scholar Cheryl Harris further explicated this notion in her now classic 1993 *Harvard Law Review Journal* article "Whiteness as Property."[50] Following the period of slavery and White conquest, White identity emerged as a type of status property and the basis of racialized privilege. Those who occupied this status (whiteness) received public and private benefits that the law protected. Among other things, Harris describes whiteness as a right of disposition, which includes the ability to buy and sell.[51] Here that right also includes final disposition of Arbery's life. Arbery had the nerve to disobey the orders of armed White men in a truck (McMichael and his son Travis) chasing him through the streets, and his failure to obey was later used by some to explain the violent response of Bryan and the McMichaels.

I argue that this frame reveals another intangible White property right: that whiteness is often viewed as a possessive investment in rightness. This can be seen in Harris's articulation of how the settled expectations of Whites (i.e., belief that someone—especially a subordinated being—will or should do something) has been recognized by the law. It is another unearned privilege and benefit of White supremacy. According to the initial report from the Glynn County (Georgia) Police Department, "[Greg] McMichael stated they [he and his son] saw the unidentified male and shouted *Stop, stop, we want to talk to you.* McMichael stated they pulled up beside the male and shouted stop again at which time Travis exited the truck with the shotgun. McMichael stated the unidentified male began to violently attack Travis and the two men then started fighting over the shotgun at which point Travis fired a shot and then a second later there was a second shot. McMichael stated the male fell face down on the pavement with his hand under his body. McMichael stated he rolled the man over to see if the male had a weapon."[52] The police report is clear. Two or more White men riding in a truck with weapons were chasing a Black man down a street in South Georgia. They shouted at the Black man to stop running, and when the Black man did not comply with their requests, one of them exited the vehicle, shotgun in hand. The Black man ended up dead. Fourteen different officers were called to the scene, and all of them saw the killing as reasonable.[53] I again remind the reader that no charges were filed until mounting public pressure forced the issue.[54] After all, the McMichaels told him to stop, and he did not stop.

Conclusion

In 2006, comedian Michael Richards (who portrayed Kramer on the popular TV sitcom *Seinfeld*) was performing at the Laugh Factory in Los Angeles. While on stage, Richards verbally attacked a group of Black patrons he thought were heckling him. Again we see a convenient venue for dishing out public humiliation, but the element of power is also highlighted in this example. Richards had a microphone to amplify his venomous words. According to *Vibe* magazine, "Mr. Richards misinterpreted what they said as heckling, and went off on a racial tirade." The three-minute attack also included a perverse lynching reference. Richards said, "Fifty years ago we'd have you upside down with a f***ing fork up your ass. You can talk, you can talk, you're brave now motherf**ker! Throw his ass out. He's a n*gger! He's a n*gger! He's a n*gger! A n*gger, look, there's a n*gger!" One of the Black men he targeted responded, "That's un-f***ing called for, ain't necessary." Richards retorted, "That's what happens when you interrupt a white man, don't you know?"[55] Some patrons got up and left. In *Black Bodies, White Gazes,* George Yancy describes Richards's repeated shouting of the disfavored pejorative term as "a communicative act" that "positioned those whites in attendance as racists as well."[56] Part of Richards's assault on the Black patrons was recorded.

The Richards exchange exposes how the mentality that Black people are supposed to stay in their place—a position of relative subservience to Whites—continues to undergird society. Richards uses the guise that the Black patrons are engaging in inappropriate behavior that operates outside the culturally accepted norms of society as a cover for his act of repudiation and attempt to push them back into place. Even if the Black patrons were heckling Richards during the show, it is certainly not the first or last time a comedian has been heckled. Richards intended to make the express point that these paying patrons—these Black bodies—had no right to speak when he was speaking. Richards's public rebuke was also a threat. It unveiled intimate knowledge of the actual horrors of a less widely known lynching ritual. As Michael Hatt, an author in the edited volume *Performing the Body/Performing the Text*, writes:

> Lynching was a long and complex ritual of torture and extreme violence. There would be a procession as the terrified victim was dragged from his place of capture to the site of execution; the body would then be mutilated and stabbed with knives, corkscrews,

forks, or other weapons; eyes would then be gouged or burned out; parts of the body would be severed; and the victim could be burnt with hot irons all over the body and in the mouth and throat. After this appalling violation of the body, the victim would be burned alive, although hanging and shooting were also used as forms of execution. After death, the body might be mutilated further or riddled with bullets and pieces of the charred flesh would be kept as souvenirs. These were often given to children as mementoes, as were ears, or fingers, or toes, or pieces of charcoal from the pyre.[57]

Certainly not every lynching was as grotesque as this, but Richards seemed to have knowledge of the most heinous version of this form of social control of Blacks.

The fork reference was a veiled lynching threat, and it was only veiled because of most people's ignorance about the horrors of lynching. The reference raises the question of whether such mementos were passed down in Richards's family. Regardless, his public tirade against the Black patrons was a degradation ceremony meant to silence and socially sanction Black bodies who dared to interrupt a White man.[58] The examples of Richards, Dunn, and the McMichaels illustrate the point that, even today, White women and men (and their designates) expect their orders to be obeyed, especially when they issue them to Black bodies. Failure to obey has dire consequences for the Black body (individually and collectively) and the Black psyche.

The essence of the Massah Has Spoken framework is a cultural argument that legitimates and rationalizes attacks against Black bodies, up to and including death. The presumed superiority of White culture and inferiority of Black culture undergirds it all. The expectation now, as in slavery, is that Black bodies should obey directions issued to them and do so without delay or question. This framework maintains White superiority and reminds us that White male dominance is at the center of this order.

CHAPTER 7

You Don't Belong *Here*!

What does it feel like to be a problem?

—W. E. B. DU BOIS

Throughout this book, I have sought to illustrate how the concept of place is useful for understanding and exposing contemporary ways that racism operates. The example of ESPN sports broadcaster Rachel Nichols's comments about her Black female coworker Maria Taylor help illustrate the utility of this approach. In 2020, during the height of the pandemic and racial and social unrest in the world, Nichols was caught on an open mic saying, "I wish Maria Taylor all the success in the world—she covers football; she covers basketball. If you need to *give* her more things to do because you are feeling pressure about your crappy longtime record on diversity—which, by the way, I know personally from the female side of it—like, go for it. Just find it somewhere else. You are not going to find it from me or *taking my thing away*."[1] Nichols's comments illustrate a lack of appreciation that Maria Taylor had *earned* a position at ESPN, and they illustrate an underlying belief that Nichols has a superior and possessive interest in hosting the NBA finals. Nichols framed her lament at being asked to take a secondary role to Taylor using positional language. She asserted that the dominant role was her "thing," perceiving this as her rightful place.[2] I argue that to the extent that this perception arises by contract, it is the racial contract in society that governs. According to this contract, Nichols's superiority is assumed and implied by her White birthright. Even in a world where White men occupy most positions of authority, White women are above Black women. Therefore, for a host of unspoken reasons, Nichols vehemently asserted that she did not belong in a subservient role to Taylor and could not envision a world in which such a placement would be valid.

W. E. B. Du Bois rhetorically asked, "What does it feel like to be a problem"?
And the question is still trenchant: where do you go when you are perceived to
be the problem? Black skin is a symbolic marker. As a Black person, you carry it
with you everywhere. In some ways, platitudes—"go where you are celebrated, not
where you are tolerated," "it's their loss," and "you are better off without them"—
are helpful, but they require an individual to first acknowledge the condition of
being undesired. A cognitive shift can only occur on recognition of this status of
being objectionable. Then individuals can assert that if you view my presence in
this physical or social space as a problem, that is your problem. Still, the revolutionary act of claiming a sense of belonging in space begins with responses to the
spoken or unspoken assertion "*You* don't belong *here.*"

Those who invoke the *You* Don't Belong *Here!* frame rely heavily on context, so
it has fewer absolutes than the other frames. Blacks have been a part of the American landscape for hundreds of years. Black bodies are not per se presumed not to
belong. Instead, what is desired is a blackout. Blackout denies that the presence of
Black bodies in social or physical space is freely available by virtue of a shared humanity with Whites. It also rejects the idea that Black presence in physical or social space has been hard-fought and earned by Blacks. Instead, the idea of blackout
says that you should be glad we let you have a seat at the table, and you should be
grateful for any seat you get. Now to remain in this space, you better be quiet and
not make any waves. The concept of blackout suggests that the presence of Black
bodies should not change the way White space operates or how White people
operate in it. Claims of color-blindness only reinforce whiteness as the presumed
norm. Defiant Black bodies do not belong. They must be pushed back (into a position of subservience) or pushed out of the space. Compliance is required in order to remain in the space. In the Arbery case discussed in the preceding chapter, the presumption that Arbery did not belong in the space surrounding his own
neighborhood outside Brunswick, Georgia (for anything other than illegitimate
purposes) is evidenced in the assumptions not only of his killers but of the police
who reported to the scene. It is also illustrated in District Attorney Barnhill's initial letter to the Glynn County Police Department stating that no charges should
be filed because the men were in "hot pursuit" of a burglary suspect, with "solid,
firsthand probable cause."[3]

Spaces are gendered, racialized, and classed sites of power.[4] Black bodies in
"White spaces" are often perceived as out of place. My theorization builds on this
idea. In "A Jim Crow State of Mind: The Racialization of Space in the McKinney,
Texas Pool Party Incident," I write, "Carceral functions maintain both places and
the liminal spaces that preserve them. Surveillance of the area and the people produces two kinds of bodies, one normal and the other abnormal. Normal bodies

are free to traverse spaces. Abnormal bodies are marked as the other and subjected to heightened surveillance."[5] Marking an individual as the interloper or the other requires action. This deed may occur on a continuum from mild (amusement) to violence up to and including death. The marking of an individual as an outsider in a space is an act of violence, something Koritha Mitchell says "is a performance of the denial of citizenship."[6]

The Link between Performative Violence and Maintenance of White Space

By "performative violence" I mean a type of violent act (as broadly defined in this book) meant to convey the message "you don't belong here." The mutilated bodies of hundreds of missing young women who migrated to the transit city of Juárez, Mexico, a border town across from El Paso, Texas, were often left in visible spots on the margins of the city.[7] This public aspect of the violent performance signals that the purpose has not only been to cause death but also to flaunt the oppressors' impunity from prosecution for the killing. This kind of performative violence not only signals that the victims were out of place but also performs the impunity of the oppressors. It is similar to a degradation ceremony, but it need not take place in front of a group. In such cases there is a primary target being told "You are out of place," but there may also be ancillary recipients of this message. Therefore, no buy in or accord is required from onlookers. As Michael Hatt noted, "Lynchings nearly always involved authority, either by the presence of leading citizens such as doctors and judges, or by the very fact that the authorities [saw what happened but did nothing]."[8] Mere presence in the space might reasonably be viewed as assent to the dehumanization. First, silence is often perceived as accord. Second, the intent of the message is to plant a seed of doubt or dissonance in and on the victim of the attack. This is often for the purpose of having the recipient withdraw from the space, but it might also be for the purpose of discouraging full use of the space or enforcing established norms regarding dress, voice, physical location, et cetera. Therefore, whether public or not, this violent pushback may also inspire others to engage in a type of frontier defense work aimed at safeguarding a community perceived to be under threat.[9] This is especially possible when actors retell their exploits to others.

The frontier defense mentality encourages and enables Whites (and those non-Whites who adopt this frame) to engage in boundary work to help colonize contested space. Most of the range of responses to the pushback a recipient might choose—removing himself or herself from the space, shrinking in the space, or fighting back—either reinforce "White space" or might be rebuffed by the actor. Possible rebuffs include claims that the victim was: 1) "too sensitive," 2) "violent or overreacted," 3) "playing the race card," or 4) somehow undeserving or otherwise illegitimate (e.g., asserting that the person only gained access because of a preferential program). Additionally, the actor might employ personal defenses, such as assertions that the actor 1) "was just having a bad day," 2) "did not mean it, " or 3) was just "following established protocols."

The claim "you don't belong here" can happen anywhere, but Black and brown bodies are especially vulnerable to it in elite institutional White space. All Black bodies are subject to such attacks. South Carolina's Tim Scott is one of the few African American members of the U.S. Senate. All members of Congress are given a lapel pin, so they can be easily identified. According to *Roll Call*, a Washington, D.C., newspaper and website published when Congress is in session, the "traditional lapel pin serves as more than just a form of identification; [it is a] unique symbol of a common bond."[10] It is a symbol of belonging in the space. In an interview, Senator Scott described a time early in his term when despite wearing his pin—a sign of belonging in the space—some staff viewed him as an interloper as he walked the halls of Congress. When he showed his Senate pin, someone thought it was a fake.[11]

Elite space is a social construction. For example, in numerous contexts, a top-ranked regional or local school or business might be seen as more coveted than a more highly ranked national space. This provincialism is a form of territoriality. The feeling is especially fierce in a society where there is a perception that advancement is possible but opportunities for advancement are limited. As in the zero-sum game, there is a prevailing belief that gains by another are at your expense. Restricting access to a space becomes a way of cutting off others' access to a resource viewed as limited. Opportunity is only available to some. A few examples illustrate this point. The visiting mother of a Colorado State University student called the police on a group of Native American high school students who were part of a college tour because she said they "looked like they didn't belong there."[12] In another instance, a Texas A&M University student told a group of minority high school students "go back where you came from."[13] These examples illustrate the frame *You* Don't Belong *Here*!

Perceived Out-of-Place Bodies

Out-of-place bodies occupy a tenuous space. Whites imagine Black bodies as being in need of their guidance, and they cling tightly to this fiction. This idea can be used by Whites on two opposite ends of the spectrum. It can justify both the savior complex and the infantilization of Black bodies and minds. Those with the savior complex believe Blacks can be redeemed or brought into the polity but that redemption is only possible with their help.[14] The concept of infantilization is elucidated in the work of Frantz Fanon. In this process, Black bodies are imagined to be much more junior than they are. Infantilization is a denial of the knowledge, experience, age, or maturity of the individual. Because of this presumption, perceived out-of-place bodies live with the burden of doubt and are seldom seen as having the competency needed for a position or station.[15] Any mistake made is amplified. Under hypersurveillance, two or three sitting together are seen as a gang. Under this schema, it is inconceivable that a Black man could become the duly elected leader of the United States. Hence, after the first election of Barack Obama was accomplished by a coalition of minority voters, widespread pushback occurred in the form of voter identification laws enacted across the country. These had the effect of limiting or constraining the Black vote.[16] Like earlier iterations of political violence against Black bodies—by the Ku Klux Klan and Citizens' Councils, and using tools and devices like all-White primaries, literacy tests, poll taxes, and gerrymandering—the rise of voter identification laws represented an effort to strengthen the power of the White vote by diluting the Black vote and denying Black voters. Black (and brown) voters were deemed out of place. The infantilization of Black bodies suggested that they were incapable of making such important determinations. In matters great and small, Black bodies are routinely subjected to obstacles and treatment that scream: "*You* don't belong *here*!"

Eating While Black

In late July 2018, Oumou Kanoute was a rising sophomore at Smith College, a highly selective, private women's liberal arts college in Northampton, Massachusetts. Notable Smith alumnae include Gloria Steinem, Sylvia Path, Julia Child, Nancy Reagan, and Barbara Bush. Kanoute had just finished her first year at the college, and she was teaching chemistry in a summer program for high school students. On the afternoon of the incident, Kanoute went to pick up lunch at one of several designated residential halls. She was alone.

After entering the hall, Kanoute was told that lunch service would be closing soon. She spoke with a cafeteria employee she had worked with during the regular academic year (just a few months earlier) as part of her work study assignment. She took her lunch to a common room in the hall. As she lay stretched out on a couch in the common area, Kanoute continued to eat, while she looked at her phone. Soon, Kanoute noticed two campus employees walking back in forth in front of the room. They kept peeking into the space. A Smith College employee had called the police and reported a trespasser in the space. A partial transcript of that call follows:

DISPATCHER: Campus Police, recorded line.

CALLER: I was just walking through here in the front foyer of Tyler and we have a person sitting there laying down in the living room area over here. I didn't approach her or anything but um and he *seems to be out of place* . . . umm . . . I don't see anybody in the building at this point and uh I don't know what he's doing in there just lying on the couch.

DISPATCHER: Can I have your last name please? . . .

DISPATCHER: All right [Caller], I'll send someone over and check it out.

CALLER: Okay. I'll wait over here.[17]

The caller seems to vacillate about the gender of the "out of place" person.

The initial report misgendered Kanoute and reported a suspicious male in the common area. Kanoute wore a hat over her closely cropped hair, and her frame was not readily identifiable, especially as she reclined in the space. Even after it was determined that the "suspicious male" at the private women's college was, in fact, female, a presumption still existed that she did not belong in the space. The language in the police report shifted from suspicious person to suspicious activity.

When the police officers arrived, they asked Kanoute why she was in the space. They also spoke to the two employees who paced in front the common room. One was the male cafeteria employee who phoned in the report while the other was the female cafeteria employee who had worked with Kanoute. No charges were filed. After all, there was no suspicious person or activity; it was just a college student resting in a common area on the campus of her university. What activity could be less out of place?

Kanoute retold her account of the event to several local and national media outlets. In those interviews, Kanoute expressed extreme distress over the experience and called for action. Smith College commissioned an independent firm to investigate the incident, and, in the end, it determined that racism had not motivated the incident. Part of the executive summary of the report read, "The College . . . asked . . . for ways Smith could improve its policies and practices related to observations of people in locations that they were not expected on campus ('suspicious persons')."[18] This classification itself ("suspicious persons") suggests a cultural attack on non-normative bodies in the university space. Elaine Chun and Joe Feagin discuss this encounter in their book *Rethinking Diversity Frameworks in Higher Education.* The authors write, "[Kanoute] learned from other black students that such experiences were commonplace at the college, including sometimes for their visiting parents."[19] Jodi Shaw, a former student support worker at

Smith, believes the institution mishandled the initial encounter and follow-up. Shaw resigned. In her official letter of resignation she wrote, "I have no choice. The racially hostile environment that the college has subjected me to for the past two and a half years has left me physically and mentally debilitated. I can no longer work in this environment, nor can I remain silent about a matter so central to basic human dignity and freedom."[20]

An old American Express advertisement from the nineties touted, "Membership has its privileges." Unfortunately, not all members are treated equally. Kanoute was a member of the Smith College campus community, but she was on the fringe of that society as a first-generation, Black college student from an immigrant family. This kind of fringe identity must always be displayed and asserted in such a way as to make those who might question one's right to belong in the space feel comfortable. It is a tenuous form of belonging, a kind of boundary work that, at best, places a person on the periphery of the society. Still, Kanoute was a member, and as a member she was issued a membership card. It is akin to what Nicholas De Genova describes in his examination of activities to fortify the U.S.-Mexico border as a "spectacle of 'exclusion' that mystifies its own obscene secret: the permanent subordinate 'inclusion' of illegalized (predominantly Latin American) migration."[21] De Genova illuminates how being present in formerly forbidden spaces does not mean full inclusion in them.

According to the independent report, a Smith College identification card (OneCard) is issued to each member of the Smith College community. It grants access to various buildings and services. Kanoute was a Smith College student and worked for its summer programs. As a summer programs employee, Kanoute was given a key card that granted her access to certain buildings. She had legitimate access to spaces that all students would have access to—such as a residential hall or dining space—and limited access to spaces associated with her summer employment. To borrow from De Genova, Kanoute had a subordinate form of inclusion in the community. But the Black card trumps the OneCard, and any other kind of card, every time. It was presumed that Kanoute did not belong, even on the borders of the Smith College community. The assumption seemed to be that she had gained access in some illegitimate way.

Two Smith employees, one known to her, thought Kanoute seemed out of place. Kanoute described the whole encounter as "a crushing experience." She told a CBS news affiliate, "I shouldn't have to explain my existence and my being as a woman of color." Through painful tears, she said, "It's just not fair. It shouldn't happen to anyone at all. It still [crying] upsets me to talk about it because I don't even feel safe on my own campus. I'm away from home. I'm the first in my family to go to college. I'm doing this not only for me but for my family, for my ancestors." Kanoute continued, "I tried to shake it off because I didn't even want to speak up and speak out because I know not everyone is going to agree with what you have to say. Not everyone is going to agree with you."[22] She was right. Kanoute was criticized for leveling what some called unwarranted accusations of racial bias; these same critics downplayed her experience.[23] Her embodied experience and purported pain were rejected.

Perspective: From the Margins to the Center

I am not a sports fan. My father was not a fan, and neither I nor my children are particularly athletically gifted. My high school was best known for academics, not sports, and my college, Xavier University in Ohio, did not even have a football team at the time I attended. I would attend basketball games, but it was more of a social event than anything. It was not until I married and I would occasionally watch a sporting event with ardent fans that I understood the immense power of a change of perspective. I have heard someone fervently insist that a ball was in (or out), only to be silenced by a replay from another angle. I wonder the extent to which the Smith College Incident Report, which was prepared by privately retained legal counsel, considered how Kanoute's multiple statuses—Black, female, immigrant, youth, et cetera—contributed to various Smith employees' perception that she was an outsider or intruder in the space.

If the independent investigators had used insights from Black feminist theorists, they might have reached different conclusions. Kanoute might have also felt heard instead of just tolerated or placated. The insider-outsider framework popularized by Black feminists, including bell hooks, Patricia Hill Collins, and Audre Lorde and intersectionality theory are most instructive. Together, the insider-outsider framework and intersectionality theory demonstrate how the status of being on the margins affords insight into the mind of the oppressed and the mind of the oppressor. They provide broader perspective on White spaces and the ways in which Black and brown bodies are expected to navigate such space in order to avoid the peril of violence—mental, physical, or otherwise.

Feminist theorists of intersectionality note that multiple statuses of disadvantage have a multiplicative effect on the oppression one faces. The U.S. Human Rights Network acknowledged, "An individual's identity has many dimensions. These dimensions, race, gender, age, class, religion, national origin, sexuality, etc. do not exist in isolation . . . they work collectively to affect our experiences . . . in relation to inequality, injustice, exploitation, and oppression."[24] Because the case under examination involves a young, Black, female from an immigrant family, I believe intersectionality theory offers a useful lens for understanding her status as an outsider in the exclusive, elite, White space of Smith College.[25] She was an outsider within.

The Outsider Within

Kanoute's comments express a keen awareness that some perceived that she did not belong in the social space of Smith College. The young woman willingly inserted herself into this potentially hostile White space in order to earn an education and take advantage of the opportunities available to her through this network. Her hard work afforded her this chance. In a personal Facebook post, Kanoute wrote, "All I did was be Black. It's outrageous that some people question my being at Smith College, and my existence overall as a woman of color. No students of color should have to explain why they belong at prestigious white institutions. I worked my hardest to get into Smith, and I deserve to feel safe on my campus."[26] Kanoute's possessive declaration of ownership and belonging to Smith College is denoted in the simple use of the pronoun "my" in her description of the campus. She is both a member of the community and on its margins.

On growing up Black in her small Kentucky hometown, bell hooks writes, "Living as we did—on the edge—we developed a particular way of seeing reality. We looked both from the outside in and from the inside out. We focused our attention on the center as well as the margin. We understood both. This mode of seeing reminded us of the existence of the whole universe, a main body made up of both the margin and the center. Our survival depended on an ongoing public awareness of the separation between margin and center and an ongoing private acknowledgment that we were a necessary, vital part of that whole." hooks continues, "This sense . . . provided us an oppositional world view—a mode of seeing unknown to most of our oppressors—that sustained us, aided us in our struggle to transcend poverty and despair, strengthened our sense of self and our solidarity."[27] The struggle hooks outlines and the one Kanoute face are one and the same. As Patricia Hill Collins has asserted, the positionality of being an "outsider within" equips one with a keen insight, "a special standpoint on self, family, and society for Afro-American women."[28]

Smith College is an elite overwhelmingly White institutional space, and this reinforces a normative sensibility and expectation of whiteness. Campus demographics for 2019–2020 reveal that 32.6% of the student population were minority, including 18.2% classified as underrepresented minorities and 14% classified as international students; approximately 18% of Smith College students were first-generation college students, and 21.3% were Pell eligible. The acceptance rate at Smith College the year of the incident was 32.5%, and total annual tuition, room, and board was $72,070.[29] Of the approximately 2,500 students enrolled as of October 15, 2019, only 161 were classified as Black. The faculty/student ratio was 9:1, and approximately 84% of the full-time faculty at Smith College were classified as White.[30]

This picture of the Smith College population shows a space that is largely White and elite despite its diversity. Kanoute's intersectional identities—first-generation, Pell-eligible, Black, from an immigrant family—placed her on the margin. And, as hooks writes, "To be in the margin is to be part of the whole but outside the main body."[31] This information affords a richer understanding of the social context in which the incident happened. Additionally, the fact that it was summer—a time when only a small fraction of the 161 students who identified as Black were likely to have been on campus—may have also influenced college employees' perception that Kanoute was a suspicious person with no legitimate right to use of the space.

The inclusion of people of color in previously exclusive White institutions has resulted in physically integrated spaces devoid of full and equal social integration. The only way to be fully integrated into the space, it is evident, is to assimilate. This moves the discussion beyond Kanoute's race to her presentation of her race and self. By cropping her hair and wearing it in a short natural hairstyle and then covering it with a cap, Kanoute did not present the image expected or desired in the space. While less favored, certain assimilating Black bodies may be tolerated in the university or other space, but other types of Black bodies are discouraged. The result is a physically integrated space devoid of social or cultural integration. It is an emotionally fraught terrain that people of color must carefully navigate in order to share in the resources and rewards these institutions offer.

People of color often bear the burden of engaging in emotion work that is not equally distributed with their White counterparts. Louwanda Evans and Wendy Leo Moore write, "Elite educational and employment institutions represent the path to upward mobility. However, when these institutions are white institutional spaces, they require people of color to perform particular kinds of emotional labor as a requirement of their position in those institutions." The authors continue, "White institutional spaces, built on a history of exclusion, are embedded with white discourses and ideologies that subjugate the racialized experiences of people of color."[32] All of this screams, "*You* don't belong *here!*"

The Continuing Significance of Race

As in the past, contemporary acts of violence against people of color take many forms. They may be physical, emotional, psychological, economic, or political.

Whatever form they take, the contemporary attacks on Black bodies have deep historical roots.[33] While some find it easy to discuss historical acts of racism, there appears to be a tacit conspiracy of denial and deflection that surrounds calling out racism and racist actors in the present. A great deal of this denial and deflection is accomplished through the use color-blind ideological frames.[34] Bonilla-Silva's color-blind frames are discussed in greater detail earlier in this book, but the predominant color-blind frames seek to either minimize or naturalize racist actions. Here the activity Kanoute identified as racially motivated was first minimized and then dismissed. Dismissal is cruel, but minimization is also harmful. The frames exempt Whites from personal responsibility for inequality and justify their own unwillingness to support policies to correct these patterns. Color-blind frames effectively absolve Whites from what James Baldwin called "the tyranny of the mirror." They render it unnecessary to consider the legacy of racism, the history of settler colonialism, White supremacy, or their own White privilege. The racism of the past was more overt. Contemporary forms of racism, however, subtly avoid overt racist discourse. This language appears nonracial.[35] Color-blindness operates as a false perspective, and those who look through this lens not only view African Americans as having a problem but also view African Americans as a problem. This reality makes the words of W. E. B. Du Bois ever more prescient.

Breaking the Silence

When color-blind frames are not employed, people are often silent on matters of race, but it is time to break the silence. The silence reflects a gap in knowledge. Caroline Criado Perez, author of *Invisible Women: Data Bias in a World Designed for Men*, reminds us that there are silences everywhere where the voices of others are left out. Perez quotes Simone de Beauvoir: "Representation of the world, like the world itself, is the work of men; they describe it from their own point of view, which they confuse with the absolute truth."[36] A male perspective should not be discounted; however, it should not be the only perspective considered, nor should it be, as Beauvoir writes, confused with the absolute truth.

While many deny contemporary biases against Black persons, blackness has been problematized in ways that have been used to justify preemptive assaults by police, other state actors, and everyday citizens alike. When Lolade Siyonbola was a graduate student at Yale University, she was interrogated by police after a White female graduate student called and reported that someone who did not belong was napping in a common room reserved for students. Police questioned Siyonbola, who is Black, for about 15 minutes. During the exchange, she was forced to show police her room key and identification so they could begin the process of verifying that she had a legitimate right to be in the space. Siyonbola videotaped the exchange. Police questioned her, and she peppered questions back at them. Siyonbola demanded answers about her accuser and the police presence. According to a news report, Siyonbola told police, "I deserve to be here. I paid tuition like everybody else. I am not going to justify my existence here. It's not even a conversation." In the end, Siyonbola was forced to suffer the indignity of the attack and comply with police orders.[37] But, first, Siyonbola, like Kanoute, made her claim of belonging and stood up and told the world about how she was treated and the racist roots of the treatment.

A *New York Times* article by Mihir Zaveri outlines other examples of this frame:

> When a black man staying in a Doubletree hotel in Portland, Ore., called his mother from the lobby, he was told by a white security guard that he was trespassing and was escorted out of the building by the police ... he has become part of the continuing documentation, through cellphone videos and social media, of black people being confronted by white authority figures or bystanders while going about their everyday lives ... The incident was one of numerous widely publicized confrontations this year in which people have called the police on black people for innocuous activities. In October, the police were called on a black man who was babysitting two white children. A white apartment complex manager in Memphis was fired after she called the police on a black man wearing socks in the pool on the Fourth of July.[38]

These examples are not isolated. Instead, they are quite mundane. The encounters do not often get recorded in books. Their harm often goes ignored also because the recipients of these attacks often shrug them off—at least in the presence of their oppressors—choosing instead to save their strength for battles to come or, as in the case of Travis Miller Sr., to make it home safely that night. I write about these encounters so they stand as a documentary proxy for a host of other daily affronts against Black and brown bodies treated as subhuman through either the essentialization of their blackness or denial of their humanity. Both are affronts.

Look, a Negro!

Fanon famously opened chapter 5 of *Black Skin, White Masks* with these words: "Look, a Negro!"[39] In some translations, the chapter is titled "The Fact of Blackness," and in others it is titled "The Lived Experience of the Black Man." While the chapter is about identity construction, it also acknowledges the constant surveillance that is both the "fact of blackness" and "the lived experience" of Black people. Neither age nor gender nor social status can exempt Black people from this experience.

I am reminded of the 2009 exchange when a person called 911 suspecting that two gentlemen might be breaking into a home in Harvard Square. At the time, it was not known that the one of the men was renowned Harvard University professor Henry Louis Gates Jr. and that the home was his own. Gates had just arrived back in town, and the front door of his university rental home was stuck. In order to get in, he and his driver applied force to the door. By the time police arrived, Gates was already inside. Police knocked and asked the professor to show his identification. Gates presented the requested credentials, but after a protracted exchange, one of the officers, Jim Crowley, proceeded to arrest Gates for disorderly conduct in his own home.

New York Times columnist Maureen Dowd wrote about the incident:

> No matter how odd or confrontational Henry Louis Gates Jr. was that afternoon, he should not have been arrested once Sergeant Crowley ascertained that the Harvard professor was in his own home.... From Shakespeare to Hitchcock, mistaken identity makes for a powerful narrative. A police officer who's proud of his reputation for getting along with black officers, and for teaching cadets to avoid racial profiling, feels maligned to be cast as a racist white Boston cop. A famous professor who studies identity and summers in Martha's Vineyard feels maligned to be cast as a Black burglar with backpack and crowbar.[40]

Harvard University convened an independent panel of experts in matters of race, policing, and law to investigate the incident. The committee was called the Cambridge Review Committee. The findings section of their report stated, "The Committee believes that Professor Gates, like Sergeant Crowley, missed opportunities to de-escalate the encounter. Professor Gates could have tried to understand the situation from the point of view of a police officer responding to a 911 call about a break-in in progress, and could have spoken respectfully to Sergeant Crowley and accommodated his request to step outside at the beginning of their encounter."[41] In a rationale similar to the sentiments Maureen Dowd expressed, the Cambridge Review Committee pointed to missed opportunities on the part of both men to de-escalate the encounter. But it is police, not private citizens, who are under an obligation to de-escalate. The committee's comments echo Trump's "fine people on both sides." In essence, Crowley's request that Gates come outside was a request that Gates participate in his own dehumanization. In the full display of all his neighbors, Gates would have looked like a criminal on a perp walk. I interpret the committee's view of the reasonableness of such a request as devoid of the insights experts on matters of race, policing, and law should possess. The officer's un-lawful request that Gates come outside echoes Justice Taney's remarks in the *Dred Scott* decision: the Black man has "no rights which the white man was bound to respect."[42]

My Positionality

Black survival in a White world necessitates the ability to see yourself as you are and as the White world sees you. The same is true for all subjugated bodies. In *The Souls of Black Folk*, Du Bois writes that the "American Negro" is equipped with a sort "double consciousness" that can lead to second-sight.[43] It is a description and embodied experience of looking at oneself through the eyes of others. Explor-ing this concept, Elizabeth Hordge-Freeman and Gladys L. Mitchell-Walthour ar-gue that when this unique positionality (i.e., double consciousness, also known by other names) is stimulated and directed, it "can ultimately give way to heightened awareness and discovery, what he [Du Bois] refers to as 'second-sight.'"[44] Femi-nist theorists also embrace the concept. In feminist applications, Du Bois's dou-ble consciousness takes on variant labels and iterations, including "situated knowl-edge," standpoint theory, and "insider-outsider" status.[45] Whatever the label, each appreciates that "situated and embodied knowledge" can be found in the "vantage points of the subjugated."[46] In "Situated Knowledges: The Science Question in Feminism and the Privilege of Partial Perspective," Donna Haraway writes, "'Sub-jugated' standpoints are *preferred* because they seem to promise more adequate sustained, objective, transforming accounts of the world."[47]

To change the inequities inherent in the current system, it is essential to seek, listen to, and implement knowledge from subjugated persons. Charles Hale makes a similar argument in the introduction to his edited volume *Engaging Con-tradictions: Theory, Politics, and Methods of Activist Scholarship*.[48] Hale offers a way to shift from reproducing existing frameworks that do little to change the con-dition of people inside or outside the ivory tower. Hale's collection encourages a focus away from asking for White generosity or acceptance and toward an indict-ment of White myopia, a narrowness that precludes society from deriving wisdom from the enhanced objectivity offered by viewing the world with the knowledge of those who have to confront its exclusions.

No understanding of power relations can be complete without incorporating the voices of the marginalized. This is not to say that only the voices of the mar-ginalized should be considered. Rather, it is a recognition that the historical so-ciopolitical position marginalized groups occupy affords them a certain epistemic outlook, which is born out of shared political struggle. This position results in a way of thinking (or, as some feminist scholars say, a standpoint) where epistemic knowledge about the nature of power relations can emerge. These insights afford people in marginalized groups the ability to see from the vantage point of both the oppressor and the oppressed. And, as bell hooks asserted, to understood both.[49]

Conclusion

My positionality as a Black woman matters. As a Black feminist scholar, I join other Black feminist scholars with the aim of ending gender-based violence and other forms of oppression, especially anti-Black racism.[50] This identity is how I experience a world replete with social, political, and economic structures accentuated by racist and sexist paradigms. This vantage point is particularly useful for gaining insight into social interactions, especially those shaped by gender, race, and/or class power relations. Subjugated knowledge is useful not only for understanding continuing violence against Black (and brown) bodies but also for naming racist practices and developing antiracist policies. I proudly claim the epistemic privilege my identity as a Black woman affords me. I brandish this "second-sight" as a tool that can be wielded to not only survive in the social world but also to change it.

CHAPTER 8

It's All White Space

> As ontologically expansive, white people tend to act and
> think as if all spaces—whether geographical, psychical,
> linguistic, economic, spiritual, bodily or otherwise—
> are or should be available to them to move in and out of
> as they wish.
>
> —SHANNON SULLIVAN

A great deal of the history of Blacks and Whites in
this country has been marked by processes of segregation, exclusion, and flight.
This is notably discernible in a practice like gentrification. However, there have
also been distinct periods when space once abandoned through a cycle like gentrification or White flight has been the subject of reclamation. When you add to this
the practices of colonialism and imperialism, it is easy to arrive at the conclusion
that it is all White space, they just let others use it sometimes.

Space gets expanded and contracted for the purposes of White use, comfort,
ease, safety, and enjoyment. The analytical frame It's All White Space is reflected
in actions (including language) by framers used to justify or explain their actions
by invoking some type of superior ownership of an area or right to govern it. The
framer uses this authority to decide who has a legitimate right to be in the space
and what actions are appropriate or inappropriate in the space. The assertion of
a right to govern the space amounts to an occupation or control of space, and, as
in slavery, it may even extend to a right to govern, control, or otherwise occupy
the body of the subjugated. Those who invoke this frame deem themselves, those
in their group, or their designates the final arbiter of what is right and moral. To
the arbiters, failure to respect, respond to, or adhere to the framer's directives is

deemed a criminal act and justifies any physical or extrajudicial action that may follow.

In order to explicate this frame, I return to an earlier example. Consider the case of Ahmaud Arbery. We see the assertion of a right to govern the space echoed in several official documents, including the 911 transcript and the police report. In a 911 call made at 1:08 p.m., caller Greg McMichael said, "I'm out here at Satilla Shores. There's a Black male running down the street."[1] Together, the reference to Satilla Shores and a Black male were supposed to express a sense of incongruity. What was a Black man doing on the streets of this White middle-class neighborhood? The answer was clear. He had to be up to no good. The street is a public place, but Arbery's presence in the sphere was deemed improper. He had previously been seen entering a house under construction. Having built a number of homes and lived in neighborhoods under construction, I have often witnessed curious neighbors (and others) come on site and look in and around the property. I have even done this myself. Ahmaud Arbery's short visit to a home under construction was criminalized. He was assumed to be the person suspected of burglarizing the community months earlier, and his attackers followed him through the public street. Here we see an extension of the desire to feel safe by controlling the intimate and personal space to a desire to control public space. It is an example of what legal scholar Cheryl Harris describes as "whiteness as property right."

Harris argues that contemporary views of property emanate from the insights of English philosopher and jurist Jeremy Bentham and support and maintain both White privilege and White Supremacy. In Bentham's view, "Property is nothing but the basis of expectation consist[ing] in an established expectation in the persuasion of being able to draw such and such advantage from the thing being possessed." Applied to human chattel, Bentham's definition suggests an expectation to extract advantage from slavery and especially slaves. This expectation turned into actual "use and enjoyment."[2] Harris expands on Bentham's ideas and offers an analysis of whiteness operating in myriad ways. Harris situates whiteness as 1) a traditional form of property; 2) a defining aspect of social relations and entitlement; 3) a right protected by law that enforces an expectation of certain ends; and 4) the right to possession, use, and disposition of items. With Bentham's work as her starting point, Harris argues that whiteness has a tangible and intangible value. Along with this come certain intangible property rights like the "right to exclude" people from space, and I argue that another intangible White property right is the right to be believed. Expressed by a White person, it says, "Things are as I say they are. The world only reasonably gets interpreted how I see it, and all other perspectives are a lie." It is part of the reason counter-narrative readings such as this are so important. White readings of social contexts get elevated, and other interpretations are readily devalued and discredited. Harris unearths how whiteness obtained a privileged status in law and is protected in ways that non-propertied identities are not. This privilege is the cornerstone of White identity.[3] White people expect the protection of the state.

In *Revealing Whiteness: The Unconscious Habits of White Privilege*, philosophy professor Shannon Sullivan writes, "White people tend to act and think as if all spaces—whether geographical, psychical, linguistic, economic, spiritual, bodily or otherwise—are or should be available to them to move in and out of as they wish."[4] This chapter examines several instances of what Sullivan describes as "white ontological expansiveness." In *Good White People*, Sullivan writes, "The habit of white ontological expansiveness has allowed and continues to allow white people to destructively invade the spaces of nonwhite people."[5] By placing Harris's insights on whiteness as property in conversation with Sullivan's work on White ontological expansiveness, we can see that the latter is not a new proposition. It continues a historical conversation about borders, passing, and trespassing, which is essentially a conversation about entitlement to the use of space and the privileges of White status. The expansion that Sullivan has outlined fits squarely into one or more of the frames of whiteness as property that Harris traces back to the work of 18th-century thinkers like Jeremy Bentham.

My Body Is Yours to Regulate

On June 30, 2019, while on an American Airlines flight from Montego Bay, Jamaica, to Miami, Florida, Dr. Tisha Rowe was told that her body was not hers to regulate. The 37-year-old Black woman was traveling with her 8-year-old son. The weather was 94 degrees outside, and the doctor boarded the plane wearing a short strapless romper. While sitting in her seat preparing for takeoff, a Black male flight attendant requested that Rowe and her son deplane. When they exited the plane, they were met by a Black female flight attendant. The flight attendant asked Rowe if she had a jacket to cover herself. Rowe told the flight attendant she did not have a jacket. The American Airlines attendant told Rowe that if she did not cover up, she and her son would not be able to reboard the plane. Eventually, Rowe used an airline-issued blanket to cover her body, and she and her son walked the shameful perp walk back to their seats. As they walked, all the passengers' eyes seemed to focus on Rowe.

The objectification and dehumanization of Black men and women is facilitated by stereotypes. Black men (and women to a lesser extent) face the threat of being labeled and treated as criminals. Their criminality might be seen as either sexually deviant (evoking the imagined threat of rape) or it might be a general criminality (evoking the threat of being robbed or attacked). Black women face being labeled as sexually deviant, which could include the idea of being a Jezebel with an insatiable sexual appetite. A Black woman might also be seen as deviant if she is non-feminine. The idea of being non-feminine might include being seen an angry Black woman who is "too aggressive." She might be seen as non-feminine in being a strong matriarch, and this strength may be used against her. Her tears are not allowed, and they are rejected when they are seen. Another way Black women might be seen as non-feminine (and thereby deviant) entails a judged failure to dress or present their bodies in gender-conforming ways. Stereotypes are used to justify various forms of violence.

Rowe was sexualized. She was cast as the Jezebel stereotype (a hypersexualized, promiscuous Black woman), and, like Hester Prynne in *The Scarlet Letter*, she was publicly branded for all to see—including her young son. This is what Garfinkel refers to as a degradation ceremony, communicative work directed at "transforming an individual's total identity to one that is lower in the group scheme of social types."[6] The aim of her public dishonor was to evoke feelings of guilt, shame, or humiliation and to show all those watching what is and what is not acceptable. This overlaps with the Massah has Spoken frame. Although the flight stewards who rebuked Rowe were Black, they stood in an overseer capacity. As Rowe sat on the plane, she observed other women wearing much shorter outfits than her own; one even commented on the same. She believes she was targeted for her curvy figure and her race.[7]

Certain bodies—particularly Black bodies—are more subject to sanction than others. In 2017, the NAACP issued a travel advisory to its members. The organization claimed that American Airlines unfairly applied its dress policy. In the wake of Tisha Rowe's experience, several women of various races have reached out to her. Many of them admitted to wearing similar or more revealing attire than Rowe and not being confronted about it or made to cover up. They were not targeted. The dress policy of American Airlines does not contain any specifications; it only says that passengers must dress appropriately and not wear offensive clothing.

While Rowe's experience was not a case of physical violence, she did experience a psychological assault. This attack was made worse by the fact that the rebuke came in front of Rowe's son, who was made to witness the public denunciation of his mother and, in the process, encouraged to view his mother as a deviant, bad actor. Rowe's curvy body and fitted outfit were framed as inappropriate. This treatment perpetuates the idea that women are to blame for being verbally or physically assaulted. The suggestion is that, based on her dress, she was asking for it. In a subsequent interview, Rowe asserted, "Had they seen that same issue in a woman who was not a woman of color, they would not have felt empowered to take [her] off the plane."[8]

Not even fame can protect you from attack. Serena Williams is an exceptional tennis player who has faced significant health challenges, including blood clots. When Williams began playing in a fitted body suit that promoted circulation and thereby improved her health and performance, the French Tennis Federation president said, "It will no longer be accepted. One must respect the game and the place." Williams's frame, which is curvy, was hypersexualized in a way different body types, especially those more common to White and Asian women, are not. After the rebuke, Williams took to Instagram. She posted a picture of herself at the French Open (in the bodysuit) poised to serve. The caption read, "Catsuit anyone? For all the moms out there who had a tough recovery from pregnancy— here you go. If I can do it, so can you. Love you all." The preceding year, Williams had almost died giving birth to her daughter.[9]

Not only the world of tennis but also the larger society has a long history of scrutinizing Williams. She has been subject to "random drug testing" more than any other female player, and numerous individuals and journalists have scrutinized her looks and raised invasive questions about her sexuality. In a July 24, 2018, post, Williams wrote, "It's that time of the day to get 'randomly' drug tested and only test Serena. Out of all the players it's been proven I'm the one getting tested the most. Discrimination? I think so. At least I'll be keeping the sport clean. #Stay-Positive."[10] To practice her craft, Serena Williams must willingly submit herself to "random" testing that does not appear random but targeted.

My Hair Is Yours to Regulate

Whenever the state acts, it is vulnerable to the allegation that it is violating a particular individual or a group's right to equal protection under law. Three separate standards of review are used to determine whether or not the government's actions on a matter are constitutional: rational basis, intermediate scrutiny, and strict scrutiny. The first asks: "Is there a rational basis for the governmental action?" The more rigorous intermediate scrutiny requires a legitimate reason for the government's action. Strict scrutiny requires a compelling reason for the governmental action and that means chosen to effectuate a regulation's purpose be narrowly drawn.[11] The standard of review that is applicable depends on the nature of the government regulation. In recent years, there has been an increase in rules and regulations policing appearance, and the standards they impose disproportionately disadvantage non-Eurocentric persons. Some of the regulations are instituted by private corporations and some by state actors (like public schools and cities).

It stretches the imagination to believe that local, state, or federal government have a compelling interest in hair, but in 2012 the Transportation Security Administration (TSA) conducted a pat down of singer-songwriter Solange Knowles's Afro to see if she was carrying anything dangerous in her hair.[12] The hairstyles that came under TSA scrutiny were almost exclusively worn by those of African descent. After court challenges that the policy was racially discriminatory, it was determined that while a compelling need existed for the government regulation existed, it was not sufficiently narrowly drawn to stand.

The regulation of Black bodies does not exempt young children, and failure to comply with this racialized standard of beauty or appropriateness can have serious consequences. An 11-year-old Black girl was kicked off her cheerleading team because she wore her hair in a natural style, and a Colorado cheerleader was allegedly removed as team captain (and then kicked off her squad) after she acquired demerits because her natural hair would not fit in the team-sanctioned ponytail style.[13] An 11-year old Black girl attending a private Roman Catholic school in New Orleans was sent home because her extensions were considered inappropriate under the dress code.[14] While the policing of hairstyles under this frame is usually reserved for Black girls and women, it is not exclusive to them. In Houston, a high school senior was suspended because the length of his dreadlocks (which he wore as part of his faith and refused to cut for the same reasons) violated the school's dress code. The student was told that unless he cut his locks, he would not be able to attend graduation.[15] Finally, a 6-year-old in Florida was not admitted to his school because his locks went below his ears. These regulations police Black bodies, critique Black bodies, and mark them as deficient, especially if they fall short of Eurocentric standards of beauty or do not match White views of how White property should be maintained and presented.

My Malicious Intent Is Yours to Determine

A Black female political candidate, her mother, and her child were canvassing in a neighborhood in Dane County, Wisconsin.[16] A resident called police and said he thought they were doing a drug buy at a local drug house. In Milwaukee, a young Black man went to his car to get change for the meter, and a White woman who appeared near him in age (or a little older) told him to get away from the car, called the police, and reported that the Black man was stealing a car. She yelled, "Hey, he's breaking in[to] that car. Dude, what are you doing? Is that your car?" Before giving him an opportunity to respond, the young woman was on the phone with 911. The accused man began recording the encounter and remained until police arrived. He proved to police it was his vehicle. Only then did the woman leave.[17] She did not apologize. In Oakland, a Black firefighter was conducting an inspection in a neighborhood. He was in uniform, and his truck was nearby. A resident video-taped and questioned him, then called police. When asked about it, the resident said he thought the man looked "suspicious."[18]

The Street and Public Space Is Mine to Regulate

In an incident many refer to as "BBQ Becky," a young White woman named Jen-nifer Schulte approached a group of Black picnickers and told them they were vi-olating the law by having a charcoal barbeque in an area of a public park in Oak-land, not designated for charcoal barbeque pits. Schulte was not a park employee but a citizen who decided the public space the group was using was hers to reg-ulate, control, police, and enforce. She relied on a local code stating that no fire shall be started unless in designated area. One newspaper account stated, "Lake Merritt has six designated barbecue zones, three for charcoal grills and three for non-charcoal grills. The family were using the incorrect grill in the area; however it is not illegal to do so."[19]

Schulte, a White female chemical engineer, called the police and stayed next to the group for approximately two hours waiting for the police to respond. When the police arrived, Schulte accused the group of harassing her. The video evidence did not support this. In fact, most of the group's interaction with Schulte occurred after she snatched a group member's identification and refused to return it. Once the police arrived, Schulte broke down in tears. She tried to evoke the histori-cal trope of defense of White womanhood to heighten a feeling that she was in danger and needed police rescue and intervention. Police considered evaluating Schulte for a psychiatric hold, but it was determined she did not fit the criteria.[20] Her intent on regulating the public space was so fierce that she worked herself into a frenzy.

Historically, swimming pools—public and private—have been highly reg-ulated spaces. In the late 19th and early 20th century, thousands of municipal pools were built throughout the United States. According to Jeff Wilste's *Con-tested Waters: A Social History of Swimming Pools in America*, some public pools were "larger than football fields," with "sand beaches, concrete decks, and grassy lawns" attracting many for leisure. They were even built in poorer, working-class, immigrant White neighborhoods. However, most cities avoided building pools in Black neighborhoods, and they used mechanisms to keep Blacks out of the other public pools. Two main tools were used to maintain segregated pools: seg-regation by law and segregation through violence. In the latter case, no segregating laws were necessary. Police simply looked the other way while Whites physically attacked Black swimmers. Physical violence was used to preserve pools as White space and maintain the ingrained system of segregation.[21]

Post-integration, de facto restrictions on interracial mixing could always be justified by relying on racist tropes and insinuation that Blacks were dirtier than Whites and subject to diseases that could then be passed on to others through contact in the pool.[22] In his 1948 speech accepting the Dixiecrat nomination for president, Strom Thurmond pledged his allegiance to continued segregation. Thurmond said, "I want to tell you, ladies and gentlemen, that there's not enough troops in the army to force the Southern people to break down segregation and admit the Nigra' race into our theaters, into *our swimming pools* [emphasis added], into our homes, and into our churches." The speech, which built on sentiments Thurmond expressed earlier that year during a speech in Jackson, Mississippi, was a hit. The listening crowd gathered in Birmingham, Alabama, cheered.[23] When litigation in the late 1940s–1950s resulted in the forced desegregation of a number of municipal pools, Whites retreated into private clubs with pools of their own; others built personal pools expressly to avoid mixing with Blacks.[24] Gender segregation also existed in public pools.[25]

Today pools continue to be highly regulated social spaces. Pools are intimate spaces where people have the opportunity to come into physical contact with each other. They also provide a venue for voyeurism. Because of this potential to see, be seen, and mingle, pools have long been highly regulated spaces.

On July 4, 2018, Kevin Yates, a Black man in Memphis, Tennessee, took his family to his apartment complex pool. He was asked to leave the space purportedly because he was violating the "no socks" policy. Images uploaded in postings on the incident show others (all White) in the pool area with non-swimwear on or committing other infractions of the written rules. Images of Yates show him wearing clean white socks. The apartment manager, who was in the pool swimming, not on duty, asked Yates to leave. When Yates did not comply, she called the police.[26] Camry Porter, Yates's girlfriend, remarked that they were the only Black family by the pool. Porter assumed that race, not a simple pool infraction, was the reason they were told to leave. The infraction certainly did not warrant calling the police.

Yates and his girlfriend describe feeling like they were under surveillance the entire time they were at the pool. They asked the manager why they were told to leave the pool area but other people (White) who were committing infractions of the written rules were not. They offered examples, like those who had on hats and T-shirts in the pool. In a live video recording, the manager said, "Hats are allowed if they're not dunked in the water." That distinction was not listed on the pool rules sign. In an interview with CBS News, Porter stated, "It's 25, 30-plus white people out here and you haven't said anything. You're partying with them! But when we come, it's an issue."[27] The manager's real intent was to maintain the pool area as White space and avoid the potential for physical intimacy between Blacks and Whites. Porter and Yates indicated that this was their first trip to the complex pool, so the public rebuff they received will likely linger in their memory and influence their future behavior.

My Home Is White Space

An off-duty police officer named Amber Guyger mistakenly entered the wrong apartment in her Dallas, Texas, complex. She shot and killed Botham Jean, the resident and lawful resident of the space, whom she found there. During the recorded 911 call immediately afterward, Guyger told the operator she was an off-duty officer involved in a shooting. In the middle of the call, Guyger seemed to have an epiphany. She said, "I'm going to lose my job."[28] That is when her expanded notion of White space seemed to get triggered. Over and over again, she tried to assert her ownership of and right to control her victim's apartment as her own space. Before the end of the recorded call, Guyger stated "I thought it was my apartment" no fewer than 20 times. It was not her apartment. Instead, it was the victim's apartment. Jean was a 26-year-old Black male who lived in the building. Guyger was on the wrong floor.

In her trial for the murder of Jean, Guyger's testimony constantly evoked the notion of ownership of the space. In part this was accomplished through the use of possessive language to describe the apartment where she fatally shot Jean. Guyger said, "I heard moving around inside my apartment.... Loud shuffling, someone walking."[29] This language choice is a clear attempt to assert a superior possessory interest over the space and make her actions seem more reasonable. Additional possessory language tried to evoke the rationale of the castle doctrine. The castle doctrine originated in the 1600s. It states that an individual has a right to protect their own home, even with the use of deadly force. It offers a legal justification for self-defense and negates the duty to retreat. Stand your ground laws, such as the one that was at issue in the Martin case and allowed Zimmerman to go free, are a variation of this legal principle. But this was not Guyger's apartment. So the domain was not hers to protect, and the castle doctrine was not applicable. Instead, it was an act of White ontological expansiveness where Guyger sought to expand the doctrine to apply to her case and afford herself impunity in the killing of a Black man.

By arguing her own right to be in the space and protect her person and her property, Guyger sought to negate Jean's right to the same. Through her assertions,

Guyger's claims to space effectively painted herself as a victim and Jean as an assailant. Guyger used possessive language to expand her right and entitlement to Jean's apartment and her right to defend herself against a phantom assailant. The former officer described putting *her* key into the apartment door. Guyger's comments constantly deflected personal responsibility. For example, Guyger said, the key (not her actions) "forced the door open."[30] At her trial for the murder of Jean, Guyger told the jury, "I was scared to death. I thought I came home and . . . I knew someone was in there inside of *my* apartment, and I wanted to find that threat."[31] Guyger described pulling out her gun, entering the apartment, and pointing the gun at a silhouette of a figure moving around her living room.

According to her sworn court testimony, in the span of what Guyger described as about three seconds, Jean paced menacingly back and forth, advanced toward her, and shouted "'hey, hey, hey!' in an *aggressive voice* [emphasis added]." Guyger said she yelled, "Let me see your hands! Let me see your hands!" But she "couldn't see his hands," and this alarmed her. She said she fired her service weapon at the man inside her apartment. She killed him. Guyger's language choices attempt to evoke stereotypical fears about Black men and use those to infer the reasonableness of the threat that she must have felt she was under.

Her attorney's questions continued that theme of [home] ownership and reasonableness. At trial, her counsel asked her, "Do you know your, the length of your apartment from the front door to the back door where that figure was?" But it was not her apartment. By this time that is known to everyone. "I was focused on him," she continued. Guyger said "him." She did not call her victim by his name, nor did she call Jean "the suspect," but that is implied. Guyger is painted as a police officer in an encounter with an invader, burglar, or worse. In keeping with Harris's concept of whiteness as property, Guyger is entitled to the expectation of the use and enjoyment of space—all the space in the apartment complex. Guyger's White privilege is a tool to reinforce her reasonableness. If an off-duty Black police officer made such an error, it would be framed as incompetence. Defense counsel painted her mistake as reasonable and wanted jurors to conclude that any reasonable person would have acted the same way. After all, there was a man—a Black man—inside *her* apartment. While that part was unspoken, it loomed. To make Guyger sound reasonable, she had to expand her entitlement to the space. The defense team painted Jean as a threat and unreasonable in his actions. Such a strategy could only be effective with White defendants and Black victims. After all, whiteness is a property right.

I reviewed the full video recording of Guyger's courtroom testimony. When her counsel asked, "Why did you shoot him?" Guyger answered, "I was scared he was going to kill me." Her counsel continues, "When you fired that shot, where did you think you were?" Guyger quickly replied, "Inside *my* apartment. It wasn't until I got halfway into the apartment [that I realized otherwise]—until then I was focused on the threat.... As I got closer, I was confused.... Everything started to spin."[32] Over and over, her counsel tried to reinforce the idea of Guyger's entitlement to protect this space as her own.

This exchange follows her counsel's questions about lighting in the apartment:

> DEFENSE COUNSEL: Do you remember turning on the light?
>
> GUYGER: No. I have no idea at what point. I have so many thoughts racing through my head. I turned on the light. I have no idea when I turned that light on.
>
> DEFENSE COUNSEL: Did that happen after the shooting?
>
> GUYGER: Yes. It did.
>
> DEFENSE COUNSEL: Do you know that for a fact?
>
> GUYGER: Yes. I do.[33]

On the one hand, Guyger states that she was confused and had no idea what was going on or even where she was or how the lights got on. Then, because it served her best interest in appearing reasonable and not a negligent (or worse) bad actor, she said that she had absolute clarity that she did not turn the lights on until after the shooting. Had she said otherwise, it would have forced her to come face-to-face with her negligence in not recognizing the apartment was not her own.

The prosecution focused on a series of texts that Guyger sent to Rivera, her married partner and lover, just a minute before and then a minute after the encounter. At 10:02 p.m. Guyger texted Rivera, "I need you. Hurry." A minute later, with Jean dying on the floor, she texted Rivera, "I f—— up."[34] On cross examination, the prosecution uncovered that while Guyger had training in CPR and supplies in her bag that could stop bleeding, she did very limited (if any) CPR on Jean and did not apply anything to stop bleeding. The prosecution also revealed that Guyger's training as a police officer dictated that when faced with a scenario of a possible intruder in a home, she should have retreated and called for backup. Guyger should not have entered the home.

Even as he lay dying on the floor of his apartment, Guyger did not see Jean as human and worthy of dignity and courtesy. Jean died under the stigma of suspicion, and every subsequent claim that Guyger made asserting ownership over the apartment painted Jean as out of place. Wielding her White property right interest, Guyger fully expected to receive the protection of the law. A jury convicted Guyger of the murder of Jean, and she was sentenced to 10 years in prison.[35] In late April 2021, Guyger and her counsel asked the Fifth District Court of Appeals in

Dallas to overturn her conviction. CNN reported that Guyger's counsel argued that "there was insufficient evidence to convict her of murder."[36]

Conclusion

As the Guyger case and others discussed in this chapter demonstrate, White identity provides individuals with a series of rights that interact with race and reinforce racial hierarchies. At its essence, whiteness as a property right negates the ability for Whites to be property. Blacks, on the other hand, have historically been legally classified as property and treated as commodities. The notion of whiteness as property promotes White superiority and non-White subjugation in ever-expanding ways. A critical part of White ontological expansivenss is a reclamation of the elements of the wages of whiteness. Sometimes this has occurred through certain immigrant groups being assimilated into whiteness and thereby acquiring the privileges associated with this status in U.S. society. (Italians, Irish, Polish, and others were all once considered non-White).[37] Once claimed, this unearned preferential status of whiteness can be wielded to gain other things. The intangible elements of whiteness as property right allow White people and White logics to be elevated and believed over those of non-Whites.

PART III

Do You See What I See?

CHAPTER 9

The Weight

What happens to the dream deferred?

Does it dry up
like a raisin in the sun?

. . . .

Or does it explode?

—LANGSTON HUGHES

There is a heaviness that comes with being perceived
as a body out of place. Sometimes it makes you wanna holler because, as Langston
Hughes expresses, keeping it inside can cause deep personal harm. The pressure
has to go somewhere. If it does not, one may "explode."[1] It taxes an individual
physically and emotionally, and it creates a burden that other bodies do not have
to bear. The psychological weight imposed on certain bodies exacts a toll. This
chapter paints a broad picture of the continuing psychological assault and crushing weight out-of-place bodies endure. To demonstrate how the weight operates
in the daily lives of people of color and how insidious and invasive it is, I look at
a variety of contexts, including Black mobility—physical and mental—in relation
to education, housing, and other areas of life. I demonstrate the inescapability of
this weight brought on by anti-Black attacks on people of color enacted through
policies and practices that seek to surveil and control Black bodies (as well as physical attacks and the threat of the same). Finally, I discuss some of the varied responses by Blacks to this weight.

Stereotypes

Whites tend to deal with each other as individuals, but they deal with African Americans through the lens of debasing group stereotypes that Whites themselves created. Perhaps this is why critically acclaimed author, novelist, and essayist Toni Morrison said, "The function, the very serious function of racism is distraction. It keeps you from doing your work. It keeps you explaining over and over again your reason for being."[2] To understand fully the weight Black bodies carry it is necessary to briefly revisit a discussion of stereotypes, especially regarding Black women.

Three of the most pervasive stereotypes of Black women include the Mammy (Matriarch), Sapphire, and Jezebel. There are some overlaps among them, but these overlaps only serve to further essentialize Black womanhood. For example, Sapphire is bossy and headstrong. Laura Green writes, "Sapphire possesses the emotional make-up of the Mammy [large Black mother] and Aunt Jemima combined." Modern iterations of Sapphire generally include labels like "angry Black woman."[3] She is viewed as emotional (usually angry) and domineering. As discussed earlier, the Jezebel is another common stereotype. The Jezebel is "a hypersexual seductress [who] serve[s] to absolve white males of responsibility in the sexual abuse and rape of African-American women."[4]

Stereotypes represent cognitive structures. From a psychological perspective, cognitive structures are a type of human knowledge. They offer a schema for organizing experiences and making meaning of things. In short, stereotypes encompass "the perceiver's knowledge, beliefs, and expectations about human groups."[5] When Black bodies navigate space, especially White space, we are literally carrying these stereotypes with us and on us. In the words of ethnographer and sociologist Elijah Anderson,

> Whites and others often stigmatize anonymous black persons by associating them with the putative danger, crime, and poverty of the iconic ghetto, typically leaving blacks with much to prove before being able to establish trusting relations with them. Accordingly, the most easily tolerated black person in the white space is often one who is 'in his place'—that is, one who is working as a janitor or a service person or one who has been vouched for by white people in good standing. Such a person may be believed to be less likely to disturb the implicit racial order—whites as dominant and blacks as subordinate.[6]

The stereotypes are the assumption. So too is subordination.

The dominant cognitive schemas held by most Whites come from these representations, which means some version of the stereotypes listed above and else-where in this book are what they expect to meet when they come in contact with Blacks. This expectation causes a desire for consonance; therefore, Whites make every attempt to fit the behavior Blacks exhibit within their preconceived stereo-types. That is the weight that must be overcome.

Violence

This chapter explores the impact that violence—in all its many forms—has on Blacks' well-being. My examination relies on an ecological model of violence and recognizes that many factors—biological, social, cultural, economic and politi-cal—influence well-being and exposure to violence. In addition to physical force, the World Report on Violence and Health typology recognizes the use of threat-ened or actual power as a form of violence. This model recognizes various forms of violence, including 1) physical violence, which includes the use of force but can also include self-directed acts like suicide or self-abuse, 2) interpersonal violence (e.g., against a family member or community member), and 3) collective violence (e.g. sociocultural, political, or economic acts).[7]

Collective violence is "the instrumental use of violence by people who identify themselves as members of a group . . . against another group or set of individuals in order to achieve political, economic, or social gain."[8] Social violence is a form of cultural violence. According to Galtung, it is any aspect of a culture that can be used to legitimate violence (e.g., sagging pants equals criminality).[9] Economic violence takes advantage of the economically weak or disadvantaged. Political vio-lence has the aim of achieving one's political gains through hostility or aggression. We see political violence in cases like the contemporary attacks on voting rights. For purposes of this discussion, I recognize the others, but I concentrate on collec-tive violence.

Microaggressions

There is nothing truly micro about microaggressions. A team of researchers at the University of Mississippi noted, "The term *microaggressions* does not necessarily refer to incidents that are small, but to those that are commonplace—thus ulti-mately corrosive."[10] In their racial diary project about the experiences of under-graduates at the University of Mississippi, the authors use "microaggressions" as an umbrella term to include "microassaults (explicit putdowns), microinsults (un-conscious rudeness and insensitivity), and microinvalidations (unconscious negation or nullification)."[11] These commonplace microaggressions communicate that intersectional Black bodies are out of place and attempt to push people back into place—a position of subservience.

Simone Browne has traced the long history of policing Black bodies from the transatlantic slavery structure to contemporary surveillance technologies and practices.[12] Black bodies are both invisible and hypervisible. This duality has been marked throughout history. Browne engages in an exercise Collins terms "writing across time." Collins explains the importance of this in her book, *Fighting Words: Black Women and the Search for Justice.* Collins writes, "Although fostering dialogues among Black Women in the here and now is important, of greater significance is reconceptualizing Black women's intellectual work as engaging in dialogues across time."[13] Listening to those who have come before can help expose and confront lingering contemporary injustices.[14]

Browne's analysis looks across time and uncovers continuing patterns—including 19th-century lantern laws, branding, and modern TSA screening—designed to surveil, count, and control certain bodies. This conversation necessarily incorporates Fanon's psychological account of the colonized. Browne writes, "The embodied psychic effects of surveillance that Fanon described include nervous tensions, insomnia, fatigue, accidents, lightheadedness, and less control over reflexes . . . [and] nightmares," and Browne says this continues today.[15] Centuries later, the effects of our collective trauma as Black people linger. As a character in James McBride's novel *Deacon King Kong,* says, "Y'all [society/police] don't watch out for us. Y'all watch over us."[16] This "watching over" is indicative of the "white gaze" outlined by Fanon. This ever-present gaze problematizes the Black body.[17]

The counter-narrative telling of events embraced in this chapter is also an exercise in historiography. Historiography embraces changing interpretations of history. The Dunning school of thought, named after a prominent Columbia professor who taught about Reconstruction and trained other scholars, falsely asserted that 1) Reconstruction was the lowest point of American democracy; 2) that it was a period of mismanagement of government by incompetent Negros, "carpetbaggers" and northern "scalawags"; and 3) that President Andrew Johnson was thwarted by "Radical Republicans."[18] This fabricated view of Reconstruction makes it difficult for people to understand both the civil rights revolution of the 1950s and 1960s and the one that looms today. Black people will not be unburdened of the weight that shackles and binds us until the promise of Reconstruction is actually fulfilled, and we will not stop fighting until that is the case.

It's Open Season on Negroes . . . Again

Since Reconstruction ended, there have been moments of reprieve, but largely it has been "open season on Negroes." The phrase has deep historical roots. Soon after the first acquittal of young Emmett Till's accused killers, one Mississippi man declared, "There's open season on the Negroes now!"[19] The White power structure in Mississippi doubled down on the economic, social, physical, and psychological tools they employed to maintain the established order in that society. This social order "kept African Americans not only on the bottom but also largely devoid of hope."[20] Black and brown youth today are often stripped of their hope and stripped of a future.

The attack begins in the psyche. Black and brown parents know this too, and so we have "the talk" with our children. It is a conversation about racial justice— actually racial injustice, especially the dangers of the police. We offer our charges tools and advice that we hope will keep them safe. It is an adult conversation had with children. In essence, we rob our children of their innocence and childhood, so they can have a chance at a childhood. The talk is not a one-time occurrence. It is something you do as often as circumstances warrant. Black elders do this until we feel a sense of certainty that the concepts have been ingrained. Then, when racial injustice happens, our charges are better prepared to handle it without losing their minds.

In the introduction to this book, I share one version of the talk that my husband and I had with our children. Now I share another. Our daughter was about 8 years old and her brother around 15. We had moved to Mississippi, so I could take a teaching position at the University of Mississippi.[21] The State of Mississippi did not recognize our son's learning difference, so he was failing miserably in school there. My husband wanted me to be able to remain, so we starting exploring options. Eventually, my husband accepted a job in Cullman, Alabama—a former sundown town. Sundown towns were places Blacks could work (usually in low-wage jobs serving Whites), but it was said they had to be out of town by sundown or risk harm.[22] We explained this to the children. The plan was for my husband to move there and check things out. On our first family trip to the area, we stopped at the local Walmart. Periodically our daughter would say a number. When we returned to the car, she sighed and said "Nine." We asked her what she meant. Flustered, she declared, "Nine black people . . . including us, and some of them were working." Then she burst into tears and said "I don't want to live here! Can we please live some place where there are Black people?" We laughed because we did not know what else to do, but her pain was real, and it was not funny. We decided I would leave my job, and we would move back to the metro Atlanta area where our son could receive the academic support he needed to be successful and where our daughter's trauma would be lessened.

Not the Race Card, the Black Tax

The dominant U.S. ideology holds that American society is a meritocracy. Inside this meritocracy, those who work hard succeed. Americans seldom state the inverse proposition, but it is there by inference: if you do not succeed, it is because you did not work hard. This mind-set leads to violent economic and cultural attacks on Black citizens. It supports a false narrative that Black people are lazy, and that is why they do not have the same level of economic success as other groups.[23] When a suggestion is made that race is a factor in continuing social inequity, it is generally not long before someone else (usually from a position of relative privilege) suggests that Black people are always playing a purported "race card."

The race card idiom implies that race is being exploited for some unfair advantage. In my counter-narrative telling, I proffer instead that race—particularly for African Americans—means that you need to work twice as hard as others. And that is only to get half as far. Some have termed this "the Black tax." Thomas Shapiro's book, *The Hidden Cost of Being African American: How Wealth Perpetuates Inequality* explains that despite shrinking income gaps between Blacks and Whites, the lingering effects of centuries of discriminatory practices disadvantaging African Americans contribute to a persistent and wide contemporary wealth gap between the groups.[24] It is this wealth gap that fuels continuing inequality.

I offer a brief account of the widespread inequality in U.S. society. According to 2017 data, for every $100 of White wealth, Blacks have $5.04. According to the Census Bureau's Current Population Survey data from that same year, Black families earned just "$57.30 for every $100 in income earned by white families."[25] Yet Whites have a tendency to overestimate the progress that has been made toward economic parity.[26] It is easier to ignore than confront the fact that continuing racial disparities are not only a legacy of a system of previous racial exclusion but also continuing practices. As a result of a schema that primes Whites to see African Americans as criminals and makes them all too willing to punish the group for these perceived infractions, African Americans are incarcerated at more than five times the rate of Whites. The NAACP reported, "A Black person is five times more likely to be stopped [by police] without just cause than a white person. A Black man is twice as likely to be stopped without cause than a Black women." According to 2015 data from a report sponsored by the NAACP, African Americans and Latinx people made up 56% of all incarcerated people that year.[27] According to 2019 information from the Department of Health and Human Services,

10.1% of non-Hispanic Blacks were uninsured, compared to 6.3% of non-Hispanic Whites. Covid-19 has aggravated many of these disparities.[28] Stereotypes foster facile answers to this. Inequality, this cognitive schema says, is all rooted in the individual failings of people of color. It places that burden on the backs of the very people it seeks to subjugate and asks them to carry that weight. But working hard, in the belief that hard work alone is all that is needed for success, comes at a physical and psychological cost.

The "race card" is often posited as a tool Blacks use in speaking about racism or racial history for the purpose of gaining some unfair political, economic, or social advantage (unlike the one earned through the wages of whiteness). However, rather than being granted some unfair advantage by virtue of race, African Americans have been dealt an unfair hand while Whites have not only an ace in the hole but also one up their sleeve. Economist William Darity's conceptualization of stratification economics is instructive. Darity provides a compelling argument that "claims about the defectiveness of a group with outcast/caste status are an ideological mask that absolves the social system and privileged groups from criticism for their role in perpetuating the condition of the dispossessed." Since Darity's original formulation of the concept, stratification economics has grown in its adherents and recognition. As an economics of exclusion, Darity's framework holds certain views about the world, which are consistent with the BOP framework. These include a recognition that "there are material benefits that redound to dominant groups that motivate their efforts to maintain privilege . . . and discriminatory practices to preserve privilege are likely to persist rather than to fade out; [that] financial success does not mean individual group members will be isolated from discrimination . . . and [that] while there will be group members who engage in dysfunctional behavior, such behavior is not . . . a collective trait or characteristic of the group."[29]

In short, stratification economics recognizes that racism is endemic in society. It acknowledges Whites' desire to maintain White privilege. Finally, it offers a nod to intersectional analysis through its recognition that, to varying degrees, all group members suffer a weight under this reality.

How the Burden or Weight Operates

Many falsely presume that when something happens in a Black person's life, race is the first explanatory variable that person considers to make sense of the event. That is not the case. Like Henry Louis Gates Jr., Christian Cooper (discussed in this chapter), Tisha Rowe, and Travis Miller Sr., whose stories are interrogated in this book, most African Americans still ask themselves a litany of questions—

many interrogating their own personal behavior and responsibility in the situation—before concluding: I know what this is. This is because I am Black.

Internal interrogation is an additional weight that bodies perceived as out of place bear that other bodies do not. For Blacks, the internal interrogation can have roots in the politics of Black middle-class respectability. In an interview, Giddings explained, "Black people were emancipated during the Victorian era ... And the idea—the rights of first class citizenship, people feel it needs to be earned ... Get education, accumulate wealth, you know, become this kind of ... first-class citizen, as is defined by the society. Be progressive. There's really nobody more progressive than Black people in this period of time, because they really believe in progress. And they're very hopeful for progress."[30] Black people have been striving for this place of first-class citizenship ever since. As Giddings noted, emancipation came about during the Victorian period. This was an era replete with contradictions.[31]

Victorian society was organized by gender and class. Social class was ascribed into nearly every aspect of life. It dictated matters as varied as occupation, education, family structure, sexual behavior, politics, and leisure activities. Prevailing Victorian gender ideology suggested that men and women belonged to separate spheres. In middle-class Victorian society, the doctrine "associated women with the private or domestic sphere [and] men with the public sphere."[32] Respectable women were not in the public sphere. They were confined to the home.[33] Middle-class Victorian men worked in office environments. They did not do manual labor. And "middle-class women were not supposed to earn money."[34] Sex was said to be something men craved. Polite middle-class women of the Victorian era, by contrast, were said to tolerate sex only for the purposes of child bearing.

In the United States, there were Victorian ideals regarding gender, race, and class. Newly emancipated Black people were strivers who desperately sought to prove that they could be as civilized as Whites. Inside this intersectional structure, and through our exercise of writing across time, it becomes clearer that the place of Black women has forever been subjugated. Wells's biographer, Giddings, describes the tension Wells felt. Giddings said, "As I looked at her diary—she has fragments of a diary that are available—you begin to see what's really inside of her. She wants to transform a society that isn't treating her very well, actually. And she wants to transform herself. What's very interesting and comes out in the diary is that she has a lot of anger, and she knows it will destroy her if she can't get a hold of it. So she works very hard to transform that anger into something positive. And this kind of urgent activism that she has, I think comes as a result of that."[35] Women were not supposed to get angry. Anger was a luxury inconsistent with female identity. The need for activism was so urgent that it required Wells's anger to be transformed into something positive.

The very necessity Wells feels to transform her anger into more positive pursuits is itself mired in the politics of Black middle-class respectability. It is an idea that has been inscribed in us as the descendants of slaves in search of full physical, economic, political, psychological, and social freedom. James Baldwin said it this way: "History is not the past. It is the present. We carry our history with us. We are our history."[36] As such, the politics of Black middle-class respectability have been ingrained in Black Americans. The indoctrination happens through churches, but it also happens through other social institutions like schools, sports, and civic and fraternal organizations. It tells us to stand up straight, look people in the eye, pull up your pants, do not wear anything too revealing or tight, and do not talk back. It told Martese Johnson that he would be safe at the University of Virginia. It was wrong.

Because of this indoctrination, I argue, Blacks first go through an internal mental checklist when injustice happens: Is it my fault? What did I do? What didn't I do? What could I have done? What should I have done? Only after that mental exercise, and if the checklist comes back clean, do Blacks start to consider: this is because I am Black. Until then, the idea only exists as a seed. To let it grow is to let anger and rage grow, so many Black people push it down, sometimes out of sight but never out of mind. It would be foolish not to prepare for the certainty of anti-Black sentiments in a world that has already said you are subhuman. So we strengthen ourselves for the attack. We harden or close off a portion of our hearts and minds because that additional inquiry requires time, insight, emotional energy, and physical strength in order to endure.[37]

Mobility Matters:
Moving to and through Physical and Social Space

Movement is an inherently optimistic act. It says, if I am down, I do not intend to stay there. I will pick myself up, dust myself off, and try again. Movement says, I believe I am not done fighting. Movement says, I am hopeful things will be better in this next place. But it is also important to recognize that movement can be motivated by trauma. People carry trauma wherever they go. Because dark skin has been weaponized, it gets read as a threat. Many people do not have to think about when, where, and how they enter, but Black bodies know the peril inherent in movement through social and physical, geographical space, and it is something that must be carefully considered.

Daily Mobility

Travel can be fraught with danger, especially in unknown territories. Sandra Bland was driving from Illinois to her new job at Prairie View A&M University when she was pulled over by a state trooper in Waller County, Texas, ostensibly for failure to signal a lane change.[38] Bland was only minutes away from her destination. When Jonathan Ferrell, discussed in chapter 4, was killed by police, he had only recently relocated to North Carolina. Travel presents potential for danger to the psyche too. Some historical accounts of such indignities are well known, others are not. President Lyndon Baines Johnson expressed surprise after he gained firsthand knowledge about the indignities and dangers Blacks faced in interstate travel.[39] Renowned gospel singer Mahalia Jackson might have been thinking of some of those indignities when she sang at the August 28, 1963, March on Washington for Jobs and Freedom. Jackson's performance enthralled the crowd. Award-winning civil rights movement historian Taylor Branch wrote, "Her first notes were a cry from the deepest wellspring of culture . . . a spiritual born of the slave experience, but Jackson managed also to stir emotions irresistible to whites. People fumbled for handkerchiefs, and responsive cries chased the echoes of her *a cappella* voice through the cavernous outdoors."[40] After she finished, the crowd broke out in thunderous applause. The feeling she sang about, of Black people being "buked and scorned," still exists today.

Constraints still exist on Black mobility. Some of them are self-imposed, but this might often be for the singular purpose of remaining safe in an anti-Black world. Fifty-seven-year-old Christian Cooper loves bird-watching, but he has not always been free to enjoy that pastime in the way non-Black enthusiasts are. Cooper came to the attention of the world when a White woman named Amy Cooper (no relation) falsely accused him of threatening her in New York's Central Park. Christian Cooper was in the Ramble, a wooded area of the park popular with birders. Signage in the area clearly stated that dogs had to be leashed. When the two Coopers met, Amy Cooper's dog was unleashed, and Christian Cooper asked her to comply with posted park rules and leash the dog. Irritated by his rebuke, Amy Cooper began to move toward Christian Cooper, and he asked her to stop. That is when she lobbed her best weapon. Amy Cooper threatened to call police and tell them there was an African American man threatening her life.[41]

The *New York Times* reported that Christian Cooper said, "I am one of the few male African Americans who birds the Ramble regularly. And I have always been aware that if I am crawling around behind a shrub trying to catch a glimpse of that rare bird, holding a metal object in my hands, I will be perceived differently than a

White man if police come across the scene."[42] The incident took place around 8:10 a.m. on a weekday morning.[43] Christian Cooper told CBS News that he makes a conscious decision to wear round, "nerdy" glasses because he has surmised that people perceive a tall Black man more favorably if he is wearing them. Christian's sister, Melody Cooper, was with him during the encounter. Melody Cooper recorded and posted the incident. She told CBS News her rationale: "I was through with it. Through with the weaponization of white women's tears." The siblings told CBS News's Gayle King that decades after Emmett Till "many Black people in America still tiptoe through daily life."[44]

Christian Cooper is not alone in expressing concern for how others will treat him based on erroneous perceptions of him. William Underwood of Chicago shares the same fear. In a conversation on National Public Radio's *Morning Edition* with host Michel Martin, Underwood described his experiences. Martin asked Underwood how often he felt like he needed to prove he is not a "dangerous Black man." Underwood replied, "Every day. Every day. I get tired of it. It is very difficult because you just are constantly thinking about what you have to do next. How you move around and how you perceive yourself not to be dangerous when you are in public areas like transportation. I don't pull my phone out really quickly because people may think it's a gun or something, and I wish that wasn't the case. I wish people would see me as the person that I am. People don't see that. And [voice cracking] that's heartbreaking sometimes." Georgetown law professor Paul Butler was also a guest on Martin's show. Butler described what he called the experience of making others feel comfortable with his presence and blackness. Butler said, "When you're in an elevator or walking behind somebody and you feel like you have to perform to make them feel safe, it's like apologizing for your existence. So I am in an elevator with a white woman and I have to look down to make her feel comfortable. It's like 'excuse poor black me.' And you get angry and you get tired."[45] The anger Butler described is a wholly deserved, righteous anger, but that does not make the energy it requires any less draining. More upsetting still is that the anger Butler describes is pointed inward, not outward at the society that has oppressed him.

Academic Matters

Education is still the most certain route to upward economic mobility, especially for minorities, but in many respects school is not a safe space. There has been a plethora of well-publicized racial incidents at schools across the United States. According to the *Atlanta Journal Constitution*, students at a private school in Midtown Atlanta were suspended after a video showed them in the school bathroom conducting a mock lynching of an Ethiopian student.[46] During a class trip to the Bronx Zoo, a teacher reportedly asked four African American students to pose in front of the gorilla exhibit. Then, during a public slideshow of the trip, the words "Monkey See, Monkey Do" were placed in between slides showing the animals and the students. One of the advanced zoology students in the photo said when he saw the staged image of them, he felt humiliated. People discounted the students' pain and described the teacher who created the presentation as "a good man who made an honest mistake and intended no malice."[47] In Gwinnett County, Georgia, a Photoshopped image of Martin Luther King Jr. holding a tablet with a racial slur written on it appeared in the student yearbook circulated to students.[48] The school recalled the yearbooks.[49] A young Black woman in Spring Valley, Tennessee, was body-slammed to the floor by a White school resource officer after she refused to put away her phone.

Black students struggle over both social and physical space. It contributes to what William A. Smith calls racial battle fatigue.[50] The 2006 unrest in Jena, Louisiana, provides an illustrative example of this battle. Latent racial tensions in the town of Jena grew more pronounced after a Black high school student asked an administrator if the Black students were permitted to sit under a tree on the school's campus. Historically, only White students ever sat under its branches. The administrator told the Black student he could sit anywhere he wanted. The next day three nooses were swinging from the tree. The nooses were placed there by some White members of the school's rodeo team. Outraged over the not-so-veiled threat, some called for the students to be expelled. The White school superintendent, other administrators, and principal dismissed the student's actions as a "prank" and gave them in-school suspension.[51]

Unsatisfied with the school's disposition of the matter, Black students called for action. After word circulated that the Black students were planning a walkout and silent protest under the tree, the school called the police and the local district attorney to the scene. A divided school assembly (Blacks on one side of the auditorium and White students on the other side) was held. NPR reported that then–district attorney Reed Walters looked at the Black students and said: "I can be your friend or your worst enemy. With one stroke of a pen I can make your life disappear."[52]

The unrest continued. Months later, the school was torched. Fights broke out, including one in which a White student named Justin Barker was beaten by several Black students. Barker attended a party later that evening, but Walters charged the Black students with attempted murder. Sixteen-year-old Mychal Bell was the first student tried; Bell was convicted and faced up to 22 years in prison.[53]

Students of color at the University of Minnesota and their allies have been on the forefront of demands for social justice for several years, so it was not surprising that many student leaders sprang into action when George Floyd was killed in their city. Jael Karendi was student body president at the University of Minnesota. She is Black. Karendi was interviewed on CNN News regarding protest efforts for justice for George Floyd. The student body president said,

> We're . . . so used to . . . the idea that this is such a great place to live, but you know Governor Walz said something this morning and he stated all these points and that's really great for a white person. So while this is a reality, I think some Americans, or some Minnesotans who are white are coming to realize, this is a reality we have lived with, the passive/aggressive racism . . . and not feeling safe. This is a world we have to operate in, and sometimes you almost have to—you get so exhausted or you get so tired that you try to ignore it, but then things like the murder of George Floyd happen or the murder of Jamar Clark, or the murder of Philando Castile, and you can't ignore it anymore.[54]

Karendi's comments describe the duality that W. E. B. Du Bois called double-consciousness, and they evoke his notion that "strength alone" keeps the Black body "from being torn asunder."[55] But unlike what theories of biological racism would suggest, African Americans do not have superhuman strength. We do have great resolve, but this does not come without a cost.

Paradoxically, while Blacks endure many negative stereotypes and name calling, simply calling a White person out for acts of racism can force many of them to crumble. So as Black bodies navigate space, we often find new ways to call a spade a spade. The Twin Cities area (i.e., the major metropolitan area encompassing Minneapolis and St. Paul, Minnesota) is reported to have one of the worst educational achievement gaps in the nation. The Black unemployment and poverty rates there, respectively, are three and four times the national average for Whites. Samuel L. Myers Jr., professor and director of the Roy Wilkins Center of Human Relations and Social Justice at the University of Minnesota, has been fighting this persistent problem. Myers describes something he calls the "Minnesota Paradox." He said, "One of the worst sins you can commit in public life in Minnesota is to call somebody a racist. In Minnesota people instinctively say, 'I believe in equality. I believe in fairness. And [they say] they're outraged when they see racial disparities . . . [So] how do you understand racial discrimination when there are no racial discriminators?"[56] Like the paradox Blaut and Bonilla-Silva identify, how do you combat racism when there are no racists?[57]

One reason people of color subject themselves to potentially hostile White spaces is to improve their life chances. The social network available through membership in elite colleges, social clubs, and organizations has been known to open doors of opportunity. In "Fraternity Life at Predominantly White Universities," researcher Rashawn Ray writes, "Descriptive statistics on GLOs [White Greek letter organizations] show that 48% of U.S. presidents, 40% of U.S. Supreme Court justices, 42% of U.S. senators, 30% of U.S. congressmen/women, and 30% of Fortune 500 executives have been members."[58] A number of these networks are incubators for racist ideas. *Inside Higher Education* writer Scott Jaschik noted, "A number of students believe that the traditional fraternities and sororities serve as attractors, incubators, and protectors for students wedded to the symbols and beliefs of the South's racist past."[59]

Membership in professional associations like the American Medical Association (AMA) and American Bar Association (ABA) was historically closed to Blacks. To illustrate the extent and implications of this exclusion, I discuss the history of one of those professional associations. The AMA was founded in 1847. From its inception, the organization engaged in systematic practices aimed at not only excluding Black doctors from their ranks but also constraining their opportunities to even practice their craft. Medicine, it seemed, was the province of Whites. Black doctors were barred from the AMA's ranks, and state and local affiliates denied Black doctors access to professional support and advancement. When Black doctors were listed in directories, the AMA placed the designation "col." by their names. In an attempt to reduce the number of doctors, in 1910 the AMA recommended the closure of all Black medical schools except Howard University College of Medicine and Meharry Medical College. Along with other groups, the ABA and the American Psychiatric Association have a similar history of exclusion. This legacy directly influences the system of adjudication that today still argues that people receive equal justice under law but still disproportionately punishes African Americans and metes out harsher sentences for similarly situated Blacks than Whites. We still live with the implications of how the systems were restricted to Whites, and this has a disproportionate effect on people of color. For example, lifetime appointment to the federal judiciary or Supreme Court impacts us for generations to come. Only 1% of federal prosecutors are women of color.

If membership has its privileges, some chapters of one of the most powerful White Greek letter fraternities in the nation have expressed a strong will to keep African Americans out. In 2015, a video of the members of the University of Oklahoma chapter of the Sigma Alpha Epsilon (SAE) fraternity surfaced. They had just come from an event, and they were dressed in formal attire. Riding on a bus, the group raucously sang chorus after chorus of "there will never be a nigger at SAE." They bellowed, "You can hang him from a tree, but he'll never sign with me. There will never be a nigger at SAE."[60]

After the incident, one of my students asked to meet with me. He was a nice young man who happened to be the president of the SAE chapter at the predominantly White institution where I was teaching. He wanted to assure me that he was not racist, nor was his fraternity. I assured him that I still held him in high regard. He concluded the discussion by reminding me that he could not be a racist or he would have never taken three classes with me. I told him I never thought that about him, and then I told him he had only taken two classes with me. He insisted it was three classes. He named the classes. One of the classes he listed was one I had never taught in my career at the institution. I leaned forward, gently touched him on the hand, and said that this class was taught by the other Black woman in the department.

The greatest single asset most people will own in their lifetimes is a home. Unfortunately, continuing discrimination means home values in Black neighborhoods tend to fall well below values for the same type of home in a White neighborhood. Allen Tillery, a professor at Northwestern University, has talked about the "daily physical trauma" he felt in the 1970s while integrating his New Jersey neighborhood. According to Tillery, housing discrimination accomplished in the North everything Jim Crow accomplished in the South.[61] The potential daily physical trauma Tillery discusses can act as a constraint on mobility. We can use the example of housing preferences to unveil ways that color-blindness serves the economic and emotional interests of Whites. Using one of Bonilla-Silva's often-cited frames of color-blind racism, segregation (which helps to achieve heightened surveillance inside and outside the Black community) can then be discussed as a natural choice or preference rather than be framed as a consequence of continuing racial oppression in society.

Homophily, the tendency for people to be attracted to those similar to themselves, does play a role in the housing selection choices people make. Some find freedom living in segregated communities. As a result, for many, Black life has become more segregated today than it was in the 1950s and not as integrated as in the 1970s.[62] Segregation patterns are evident in education, housing, and employment.[63] This balkanization occurs consciously and subconsciously, under actual and perceived threat of physical force, and under a socioeconomic or social psychological pull to Black communities, schools, houses of worship, and other social groups. It also contributes to and reinforces ingrained Jim Crow–like attitudes that there are distinct White and Black places (to live, work, or attend school) and social spaces to occupy.[64] But, to be clear, the overarching reason for this balkanization is systemic racism in society.

Systemic racism can cause some to internalize their oppression. In an interview on NPR's *Going There*, an episode titled "Fear of Black Men," host Michel Mar-

tin played a clip from Leo Cunningham, a Black man and ordained minister re-
siding in Columbus, Ohio. Cunningham told Martin, "I have been in situations
where I'll maybe assess another Black man. It's a question of his age, how is he
dressed, the environment that we're in. And sometimes it's as simple as the proverbial head nod to make sure that we see each other. We respect each other, and
neither one of us is not only [not] a threat to each other, but we [also] agree we're
all in kind of the same common journey as Black men in America."[65] Cunningham
confessed that he has a process he uses to assess whether another Black man is a
threat. His comments acknowledge this entails a culturally sanctioned attack and
a form of self-hatred. It also has a classist component to it, disadvantaging those
African Americans who do not wear a suit to work, rendering them suspicious.
It reinforces Eurocentric cultural norms about what attire is professional and acceptable.[66] Cunningham sees other Black men through the same discriminatory
social lens applied against him. Cunningham corrected his lens, but it required
additional effort.[67] That is the weight.

Doyin Richards, a guest on the same episode of *Going There*, shared his personal experience with being feared. Richards said, "I was out with my oldest
daughter, who's four. We were in a shopping mall [parking] garage in Los Angeles . . . and there was a lady who was with her husband. And I could tell they were
just really nervous around me. And then we went to an ATM—I had to get some
money—and there's another couple and I heard the woman say 'Hurry up, let's
go, let's go.' Like I was going to rob them, and my daughter was all like 'What happened dad? What was that all about?' And I have to go into this conversation.
'Well honey, sometimes people look at the color of my skin and they think I am
a threat to them.'"[68] It is unfair for adult men and women of color to have to bear
the weight of other people's ignorance and irrational fear, but it is untenable for
children to have to do so. So many adult people of color carry the weight for their
children too. And it exacts a toll.

Excellence in sports places individuals under heightened public scrutiny. Serena Williams has already been discussed in chapter 8. Her acclaim did not exempt
her from scrutiny. Similarly, Colin Kaepernick has been criticized for using his position as a professional athlete to raise awareness about an important social issue—
the police killing of unarmed Blacks. Kaepernick's protest—taking a knee while
the national anthem is played before games—subjected him to severe critiques
and ultimately cost him his job. Laura Ingraham of Fox News has repeatedly criticized Lebron James for making social statements, more than once telling him to
"shut up and dribble." Plying your craft at the highest level gives you a voice and
a platform, but players of color are often criticized for speaking out on social justice issues that do not dovetail with the views of management, professional sports

leagues, or team owners. In *Soul on Ice*, Eldridge Cleaver writes, "What white America demands in her black champions is a brilliant powerful body and a dull, bestial mind—a tiger in the ring and a pussycat outside it."[69]

Some believe that highly paid athletes have no right to complain about racism in society. These critics falsely perceive that green is the only color that matters and that athletes do not have the knowledge to speak up on such issues. They could not be more wrong. Racism is endemic in society. The perception that the sports uniform acts as some kind of shield that protects athletes from the everyday problems of others is false. The problem with that view is that it ignores the reality that at some point people have to take the uniform off. Then they are just another Black man or woman on the street. Just ask retired tennis star James Blake, who was slammed to the ground by a plainclothes policeman outside a hotel in Midtown Manhattan.[70] Or ask Seahawks defensive end Michael Bennett. After the 2017 professional boxing match between Floyd Mayweather and Conor McGregor, the NFL player was attacked by Las Vegas police. After they heard gunfire discharged, Bennett and others in the vicinity ran from the shots. According to Bennett, police singled him out and ordered him to get on the ground.[71] Finally, you can feel the fallacy of the logic that Black athletes and cultural stars do not know the pain of racism when you watch NFL player Malcolm Jenkins's tearful Instagram post in response to comments by teammate Drew Brees. Brees continued the well-worn mantra that taking a knee during the national anthem is unpatriotic. Jenkins told Brees that his comments were "extremely self-centered," "offensive," hurtful, and not what he would expect from someone he considered a brother in arms.[72]

The logic that Black athletes do not feel discrimination also belies the fact that much of the burden and weight of racism that many people of color carry is not for themselves. Instead, those who are better able to withstand the pain carry it to shield those friends and family members who are younger or more financially, emotionally, or physically burdened from having to carry it.

Let It Go

The physical and emotional toll racism exacts requires self-care. Physical exercise has the twofold benefit of improving one's health and psyche, but Black bodies do not have the same freedom to move through space that other bodies do. Almost 500 miles away from Minneapolis, where George Floyd was killed, a Black man in Nashville named Shawn Dromgoole learned about the death. Dromgoole's fear had always been there, but the public killing of George Floyd brought it to the surface. The brazen daylight killing of Floyd amid witnesses and protests to "get off his neck" brought Dromgoole's feelings of being unsafe—even in his own neighborhood—to the surface. Dromgoole posted on social media, "Yesterday I wanted to walk around my neighborhood but the fear of not returning home to my family alive kept me on the front porch. Today I wanted to walk again and I could not make it off the porch. Then I called my mother ... and she said she would walk with [me]. I still kept my ID on me and my phone in my hand but I walked." The neighborhood where Dromgoole grew up was gentrifying. He had lived there most of his life, but now he felt increasingly unsafe. The 29-year-old said he posted his statement on Nextdoor to counter all the "suspicious Black man" postings he frequently saw there. These postings contributed to his fear. Dromgoole said he wanted to share "what was in his heart" with the larger community.[73]

Dozens of his neighbors responded to his post. Most were White. They apologized for their insensitivity and offered to walk with him. Later, Dromgoole and about 75 neighbors went on a walk.[74] His neighbors learned some of the burden of doubt his blackness carries, but they could not carry the burden or remove the doubt. The best thing they could do was to walk with him and vouch that he was not someone that people need to fear.

One day comedian Jay Pharoah was out for a run. He found himself surrounded by police with guns drawn. They yelled at him to get on the ground. One officer briefly placed his knee on Pharoah's neck. During the exchange, a handcuffed Pharoah told police they were making a huge mistake. He said, "Google right now Jay Pharoah." Soon after, Pharoah was released. Police said they detained him because he fit the vague description of a Black man in a gray T-shirt and gray sweats.[75] The comedian had been working out and listening to an app that told him when to run and when to stop. He was stopped (because the app told him to do so), and he was wearing headphones. Pharoah reflected on this in an interview. He was mindful that had he been running with his music blaring and unable to hear and obey the police officers' commands, things might have turned out very differently. Those insights likely came from reflection on the various versions of "the talk" he had heard over the course of his life.[76]

In York, Pennsylvania, police were called on a group of Black women playing golf who had been asked by management to leave the course because they were said to be playing too slowly.[77] As these examples illustrate, it is dangerous to run, walk, jog, and even play golf while Black. How do you relieve the stress of racial battle fatigue if a stress reliever as common as exercise brings you under suspicion?

We Were Not Meant to Survive

A famous Langston Hughes poem, "Harlem," asks what happens to a dream deferred? After offering a handful of possible answers, Hughes queries: *"Or does it explode?"*[78] This section considers that last possibility, and it recognizes the consequences of the realization that "we were not meant to survive."[79] I look at the concepts of *internal* explosion (turning our pain inward on ourselves) and *external* explosion (turning our pain outward on others).

While Whites have irrational fear of Black people, little attention or even acknowledgment is given to the existence of Black fear. To the extent that Black fear of Whites is expressed, it is often portrayed as irrational. Failure to discuss Black fear has several roots. The Black-White power dynamic is already disproportionately weighed in favor of Whites, so little interest is served by the oppressed acknowledging fear of the oppressor. Additionally, many Blacks prefer to be seen as victors, not victims. For example, when someone targeted Congresswoman Maxine Waters, a Democrat from California and one of the highest-ranking members of the House of Representatives, she retorted, "I ain't scared!"[80] But shouldn't she be entitled to fear? The benefit of suppressing your fear is that exposing it can leave you open to more danger. Fear can be exploited by those with hate in their heart, and it can be miscoded as a litany of things (including guilt, shame, and malice) and used against you to justify preemptive force—up to and including lethal force. Sometimes you harden your heart so you will not feel more hurt. But the hurt is still there, and it has to have someplace to go, so you may turn it outward and harm others. Some of us, certain that the blow is coming, strike first—on deserving and underserving and real and imagined foes.

Pain has to have somewhere to go. Some people turn that pain on themselves. For example, Sandra Bland purportedly took her own life. On July 13, 2015, at 8:58 p.m. jailers found her hanging in her cell. While many disbelieve this finding, suicide was listed as the cause of death.[81] The internal harm takes other forms too—like abuse of alcohol, sometimes drugs, and often food. These coping mechanisms are "killing us softly." But the dead are not the only victims of violence.[82]

George Floyd's six-year-old daughter Gianna Floyd sat atop a relative's shoulders and declared, "Daddy changed the world."[83] She is too young to understand all the events in her life her dad will miss, but she knows that his death changed something for people. Floyd's death touched many people. In full public display, he lay on the ground with the force of three grown men on him. It was the kind of public communicative act that I outline elsewhere in this book. Floyd mustered all his strength and uttered a few words. In the midst of a looming global pandemic that attacks the respiratory system, Floyd's words resonate with even broader universal appeal. He said, "I can't breathe." Still, what stirred many was Floyd's cries for "Mama." One woman in San Francisco carried a sign that read, "All mothers were summoned when George Floyd called out for his mama."[84] Floyd's cries are a haunting reminder of the countless Black men and women whose lives are taken.

Police officer Derek Chauvin was sentenced to 22.5 years in prison for the murder of Floyd, but this does not undo the loss.[85] The pain that others felt over his death is a reminder that the dead are not the only victims of violence.

Many understand that the family of a victim is harmed, but victimization often extends much wider than this. Darnella Frazier was a 17-year-old Black girl who used her cell phone to record the last 8 minutes and 48 seconds of George Floyd's life, and it still haunts her. At Chauvin's trial, prosecutors "emphasized that Chauvin was on Floyd's neck for 9 minutes and 29 seconds—an update on the initially reported" time. Frazier indicates that she video-recorded the exchange because in her neighborhood she sees encounters like this daily.[86] She had had enough. Frazier's attorneys note that she continues to suffer from the trauma of what she witnessed. As Frazier relayed her testimony on the witness stand during Chauvin's trial for the murder of Floyd, she was still visibly shaken. The general public came together and pledged over half a million dollars to support Frazier's total healing. But there are Darnella Fraziers in neighborhoods all across the country. I am also reminded of Rodney King, whom I am convinced never fully recovered from the trauma of the senseless beating he took at the hands of multiple Los Angeles police officers. King continued to suffer the lingering mental effects of that beating for the remainder of his life. Whenever video of Floyd's death or King's beating are replayed, their families and communities are revictimized. The power of the videos is that they testify to the inhumanity Blacks endure. And, with each telling, Black people are reminded of the inhumanity visited daily on Black bodies. The dead are not the only victims of violence.

In *Prayers for the People: Homicide and Humanity in the Crescent City*, Rebecca Carter describes how a group of women who have lost children to violence—some recently and some 20 or more years earlier—still grieve them and perform acts of commemoration to welcome their children back into the community.[87] The children are not physically present, but they are not absent. They were loved, and they are loved. The women perform a public grieving ritual that symbolizes that the children are missed, grieved, and still a part of the community. The dead are not the only victims of violence.

I briefly return now to the experience of Travis Miller Sr. being stopped after making a delivery in an exclusive Oklahoma City neighborhood. The stop was an act of racism as his race marked him as out of place in the upper-class White community. In Miller's case we see evidence of the weight of being viewed as an out-of-place body and the range of emotions this effects. Miller checked his anger, confusion, and exasperation, and he displayed strength. It was a quiet resolve that said "usually I might let you mess with me, but not today." He had the presence of mind to think through multiple scenarios about what might happen, and he had the determination to ride it out instead of trying to flee. It took courage, but courage does not come without cost.

Miller did not want to cry in front of his assailants, but later he said that after the incident he "just cried for hours." Miller knew that the exchange was about racial bias but said, "I kept telling myself . . . I gotta make it home to my family."[88] He is not alone in his desire to hold back tears. Speaking about the funeral of his friend, slain civil rights leader Martin Luther King Jr., James Baldwin said, "I did not want to weep for Martin. Tears seemed futile. But I may also have been afraid . . . that if I began to weep I would not be able to stop."[89]

Black resistance to anti-Black racism is ongoing. It existed in slavery and has persisted through each phase of U.S. history. The structural nature of slavery has made a foundational imprint on the U.S. social order, and that influence persists today.[90] As an institution, slavery sought to exert control over not only Black bodies but also the Black psyche. That order persists in some hearts and minds. In *Cabin Pressure: African American Pilots, Flight Attendants, and Emotional Labor*, sociologist Louwanda Evans crystallizes this resistance and ways in which the emotional labor, though exacting, can also liberate. Evans writes, "This invisible emotional labor provides black flight crew members with a way to resist racism without causing too much discomfort in others."[91] It also allows the Black flight crew members to keep their jobs without losing their minds or their dignity. Even though in the face of insults and racist attacks there were only a limited range of emotions that they might display, they found other ways to perform their resistance.

Race, emotions, and work are complicated. Through an intersectional lens, we learn that the emotional work of the Black crew members in Evans's study was borne unequally, based on race, class (i.e., occupation), and gender. Black pilots described patrons deplaning when they discovered the person flying the plane was Black, but they also discussed being uplifted by the pride that Black patrons expressed when they discovered the pilot was Black.[92] Rather than hide in the cockpit, the Black pilots would show themselves. Reciprocal encouragement was one of the forms of resistance they used. Evans describes numerous incidents where White patrons relegated Black female flight attendants to a condition of servitude. These included being expected to materialize when called. White patrons beckoned Black flight attendants with a finger snap or a pointed finger. They recalled incidents of being directed to stow the heavy luggage of White male and female patrons alike and a host of other expectations outside those imposed on White female flight attendants.[93] Often, the dehumanization White patrons and crew visited on Black crew members was public, but so too were the forms of Black resistance to their debasing. I cite one example here, the case of a White female patron seated in the very back of a plane who publicly beckoned the lone

Black flight member, who happened to be assigned to the front of the plane, to come to the back and assist her.

> [The] female passenger proclaimed that she wanted to speak with "the colored girl."
> ... The [Black] flight attendant engaged in active resistance to counter the represen-
> tations of her as "colored" and "girl": So I finished my service in the front [the flight
> attendant said] and I got my lipstick on, and I went to the back.... She [the White
> woman] sitting there with her arms folded, and I'm walking all the way back, saying,
> "Somebody wants to talk to the colored girl; who was it?" ... She raised her hand
> to say that she wanted to talk to the colored girl... So I look at her and I said, "Now
> ma'am, before we get to what your problem is, you tell me what color I am." I leaned
> close to her and said, "When I smile, I'm brown. When I'm pissed off, I'm brown.
> When I die, I'm gonna be brown. So you tell me what color I am."[94]

This is but one example of the myriad ways Black female flight attendants are reduced to "the help"—there to console, comfort, perform at the whim of White
patrons. As in this example, workers find creative ways to resist this oppression,
resistance that allows them to keep their sanity and dignity, but this is additional
work. Black flight and crew staff are not compensated for this emotional labor.

Conclusion

According to the Healthy People 2020 Report, social determinants of health are
"conditions in the environments in which people are born, live, learn, work, play,
worship, and age that affect a wide range of health functioning and quality-of-life
outcomes and risks."[95] Racism is a social determinant of health and a significant
mental health challenge. It affects people at the micro, macro, and meso levels.
Institutional racism reduces well-being by negatively impacting access to housing,
community, quality education, and employment opportunities.

As a psychosocial stressor, racism can lead to adverse changes in health, including altered behavioral patterns that increase health risk. Feagin writes that African
Americans who face public racism may engage in a variety of responses, including "withdrawal, resigned acceptance, verbal confrontation, or physical confrontation."[96] Each response comes at a cost, and that cost is unfairly borne by Black and
brown bodies who bear the extra burden of managing the racism and ignorance of
others.

There are a variety of reasons to try to manage the racism and ignorance of others. Some people want to make others feel comfortable. Some want to increase
their chances of getting home safely. Some have absorbed the dominant narratives
that suggest that if you work hard, no harm will come to you, and you will prosper.

So they put their heads down, and they work. In every case, shouldering that additional burden and the attendant generational trauma has deleterious impacts on Black bodies. Writing about the time he was assumed to be a vagrant (or worse) harassing a table of White women at a café in Berkeley, W. Kamau Bell writes, "I told my [wife and the other women] what [had] just happened. I wanted to run away. I was actually strangely embarrassed, as if I had done something wrong. (Through my reading I have learned that's one way oppression also works, from the inside.) I felt numb, like I was going to pass out.... We were bothered by the fact that we [were] standing in Berkeley, California, a city so allegedly liberal that even the most progress-y progressives make fun of it, and yet . . . where I as a black man was being told to "GIT!""[97] Bell's words highlight the endemic nature of racism. No place offers shelter from the onslaught of it. Amid a global pandemic disproportionately claiming the lives of Black and brown bodies, author and basketball legend Kareem Abdul-Jabbar writes, "The black community's main concern right now . . . [is] whether their sons, husbands, brothers and fathers will be murdered by cops or wannabe cops just for going on a walk, a jog, a drive . . . the racism virus infecting the country is more deadly than COVID-19." Abdul-Jabbar continues, "What you should see when you see black protesters in the age of Trump and coronavirus is people pushed to the edge, not because they want bars and nails salons open, but because they want to live. To breathe."[98] The weight of racism makes it extremely hard to breathe.

CHAPTER 10

Sincere Ignorance and Conscientious Stupidity

"Nothing in all the world is more dangerous than sincere ignorance and conscientious stupidity," Martin Luther King Jr. states in *Strength to Love*, a collection of sermons published the same year he delivered his "I Have a Dream" speech.[1] The sermons crystallize King's convictions on matters of civil rights and clearly evidence his belief that equality is at once a biblical and constitutional issue. The book makes the argument that overcoming the evils of the world first requires a profound internal struggle. It involves a reconciliation. Do our actions as individuals and as a society align with what we purport to be and think we are? In Jewish culture there is a concept called *tikkun olam*. It means to heal or mend the world. It is a Jewish value that calls the community—individually and as a group—to do its part to make a difference, right wrongs, and stand in the face of injustice anywhere. The concept of healing or mending connotes labor. It is an active and vigilant process that requires each of us to do the work of justice, love, and compassion. This chapter looks at what is preventing some from taking that look within and then committing to justice.

Many presume that an actual or at least implied social contract, such as the one Jean Jacques Rousseau outlined in his 1762 treatise *The Social Contract*, exists. Rousseau argued that the only way a society can be formed is by a covenant or social contract with which people enter into a form of association (government) that "will defend the person and goods of each member with the collective force of all, and under which each individual, while uniting himself with others, obeys no-one but himself, and remains as free as before."[2] But in the "long, honorable tradition of oppositional Black theory," Charles Mills argues that the social contract is not so simple. Mills concludes that the social contract by which society is bound has three parts: it is a political contract, it is a moral contract, and it is a racial contract. Race runs through them all, since, Mills concludes, "White supremacy is the unnamed political system that has made the modern world what it is today."[3]

The racial contract is constantly being rewritten and revised. In *The Mis-Education of the Negro*, published in 1933, historian Carter G. Woodson argued that the racial contract presumes what Mills calls an epistemology of ignorance on the part of most White beneficiaries.[4] Mills describes this "epistemology of ignorance" as an active production supported by racism and White privilege used to justify the oppression and domination of others.[5] Binary classifications like barbarian and savage, civilized and uncivilized, and White and non-White have been used to communicate one status as desirable and the other as substandard. Inside this duality, one group is designated "persons" and the other lesser or "subpersons." According to Mills, subpersons "are humanoid entities who because of racial phenotype/genealogy/culture, are not fully human and therefore have a different and inferior schedule of rights and liberties applying to them. In other words it is possible to get away with doing things to subpersons that one could not do to persons, because they do not have the same rights as persons."[6] Building on Mills's notion, ethnic studies scholar Reiland Rabaka writes, "White rights are intimately intertwined with the denial of black rights. Or, to put it another way, white personhood is inextricable from black subpersonhood."[7]

The proclamation of subpersonhood is sometimes spoken (or written) and sometimes unspoken. In either case, it creates cognitive dissonance in persons so declared as lesser. This leads to what James Baldwin said: "There are days . . . when you wonder what your role is in this country and what your future is in it. How precisely you're going to reconcile yourself to your situation here and how you are going to communicate to the vast, heedless, unthinking, cruel white majority that you are here." Baldwin continued, "I am terrified at the moral apathy—the dearth of the heart—which is happening in my country. These [White] people have deluded themselves for so long that *they really don't think I'm human.*[8] The social contract may take personhood for granted, but the racial contract does not. Because this very proposition is diametrically opposed to U.S. ideology, acknowledging the truth of this counter-narrative requires a long look in the mirror.[9]

The Man in the Mirror

In *The Fire Next Time*, Baldwin describes what he called "the tyranny of the mirror."[10] Baldwin argues that among Whites, this tyranny manifests in an inability of White Americans to see themselves as anything but innocent, especially with respect to potential offenses against Blacks. White racial ignorance benefits Whites at the expense of all others, especially Blacks. Ali Meghji's article "Activating Controlling Images in the Racialized Interaction Order" is instructive in exposing patterns of White passivity and disregard for Whites' (individual and collective) role in continuing racial oppression.[11] Meghji outlines ways Whites actively deploy purported racial ignorance for their benefit and rely on "practical knowledge of white ignorance to activate controlling images in their interactions with black professionals." Meghji explains that "this white ignorance allows for white people to find creative ways to irrationally deploy controlling images" that then justify the exploitation of the other.[12]

Controlling images facilitate and rationalize subjugation. A 2019 survey estimated that U.S. adults (ages 18+) average over 12 hours of media time per day.[13] That amounts to half a day, and more than 75% of an adult's waking hours are spent engaged with media. Continuing segregation patterns mean most Whites spend far more time with controlling media images of Black people than they spend with actual Black people.[14] Images in film and news of Black men as criminals become "controlling images" manipulated to explain higher incarceration rates of Black men. These exclude structural explanations for the phenomena and become part of a disinformation campaign targeted against Black people. Similarly, "Black women have been assaulted with a variety of negative images," asserts sociologist Cheryl Gilkes.[15] American literary historian Trudier Harris identified a plethora of popular negative media representations of the Black woman, which have become controlling images in U.S. society. Harris writes, "[The Black woman is] called Matriarch, Emasculator and Hot Momma. Sometimes Sister, Pretty Baby, Auntie, Mammy and Girl. Called Unwed Mother, Welfare Recipient and Inner City Consumer. The Black American Woman has had to admit that while nobody knew the troubles she saw, everybody, his brother and his dog, felt qualified to explain her, even to herself." It is what Collins has described as "the objectification of Black women as the other."[16] These representations trace from slavery and weave through the Moynihan Report to the present, stopping at every decade along the way. They deny the very personhood of "Mammy," the "bad Black woman," and every other iteration of Black womanhood.[17]

Common contemporary controlling images of the Black female paint her as hypersexual, angry, or sassy. I am reminded of a story Brittney Cooper relays in her autobiography, *Eloquent Rage: A Black Feminist Discovers Her Superpower*. Cooper recalled how the Malaysian roommate she was assigned on a summer study abroad trip to South Korea was disappointed to learn that all Black women were not "sassy like Harriette and Laura Winslow," the characters on the roommate's favorite U.S. television sitcom, *Family Matters*. The roommate expressed disappointment when Cooper stated, "We're not all like that."[18] Cooper did not have the language for it then, but later she would come to realize that Black womanhood had been essentialized around the world.

Black women professionals cannot escape the controlling Mammy image, either. Citing the work of Rhetaugh Dumas, Collins connects these epistemological frames to social structures and outcomes. Collins writes, "Black women executives are hampered by being treated as mammies and penalized if they do not appear warm and nurturing."[19] Evans unveils a similar pattern in the experiences of the Black flight crew she details in *Cabin Pressure*. In these contexts, the Black woman is expected to nurture everyone else but be nurtured by no one. If she is not nurturing, she is punished for that. Too often, in order to bridge the divide, the weight is borne on the backs of Black women who are forced to engage in the emotional labor required to contradict the controlling images society has of them. It is crippling. This micro, meso, macro link is critically important. It should aptly be viewed as a continuum with the organizational (meso) level in the middle. It is the ever-present but largely invisible tether. Sociologist Victor Ray argues that organizations can be vehicles for racializing people, the spaces and places they inhabit, and the distribution of knowledge.[20] This results in racialized organizations fully primed to perpetuate inequality through a built-in racialized distribution of the organization's resources. I argue that respect is one of those seldom-disclosed resources. Controlling images must be actively resisted.

Christopher Doob operationalizes color-blind racism as "whites' assertion that they are living in a world where racial privilege no longer exists … [while] their behavior supports racialized structures and practices."[21] Jennifer Mueller's 2017 article "Producing Colorblindness" offers insight into the epistemologies (i.e., ways of knowing) that prevent some Whites from recognizing their role in continuing racial oppression. Mueller analyzes "105 papers produced between 2008 and 2011 by White undergraduates at a large, public university in the southern U.S."[22] Building on Mills's epistemology of "white ignorance," Mueller unveils ways the students attempted to use color-blind frames to discount the significance of race in the continuing structuring of opportunities.[23] She uncovered how this process required active (if not deliberate) agency on the part of the students.[24] Mueller's typology exposes a type of White racial cognition that gets advanced as racial ignorance or naivete. This ignorance or naivete then gets packaged as forgivable or a form of White sympathy-seeking victimhood that maintains and even supports racist practice.

Color-blind racism has been the primary theoretical lens used by scholars who want to study the contemporary connection between White racial attitudes and continuing inequality. In "Reproducing Colorblindness," Mueller connected social structure (the patterns, organization, and structure of society that exist outside the individual) to the rhetoric her students employed. This discovery led her to the conclusion that the students were constantly creating new White logics to justify continuing inequality. The students' mental maneuvers exempted them (and their kin) from either social responsibility for inequality or a moral obligation to change it. The process Mueller identified happened through deployment of an epistemology of ignorance that allowed them to avoid seeing, acknowledging, or knowing, any structural causes for continuing inequality.

Mueller's four White epistemologies of ignorance include: 1) evasion, 2) mystification of practical solutions, 3) tautological ignorance, and 4) willful color-blindness. She classifies these as offensive and defensive tactical maneuvers. Evasion uses many techniques, including avoiding direct conversations about race. Students' evasion is framed as either a purported desire not to be rude or because the student possesses a "non-confrontational" personality type. Students in Mueller's study did not want to talk about such matters. Blacks, however, have no choice but to live through and with such unpleasantness. The second tactic, mystification of practical solutions, includes ideas like "[it is] impossible to 'change a mindset . . . so unconsciously ingrained' in so many people's lives."[25] Therefore, if it is impossible to change deeply held opinions, why try? Students in Mueller's study indicated such actions would be futile, and so they would be on a fool's errand to try. This evokes the image of Sisyphus, doomed to push a boulder up a hill, fall short, and then be forced to start again, over and over. Mueller defined the third epistemology of White ignorance, tautological ignorance, as maneuvers "that produce racially conscious logic, but embed morally laden assumptions of whites' sincere, passive ignorance." These efforts represent an inward battle. Mueller writes, "Logical maneuvering is often geared toward rescuing white virtue, as most whites require some degree of psychic ignorance to perform and enjoy the spoils of domination." Students used the fourth maneuver, willful use of color-blind logics, as a tool to downplay the influence of racial privilege on their family's success. One student said, "[My family] dabbled in slavery until 1864." Evasion is an offensive maneuver; Mueller classifies the others as defensive.[26] All of these tactics produce (or reproduce) racial ignorance.

As the Dr. King quote at the beginning of this chapter entreats, Mueller encourages the kind of introspection that makes ignorance hard and perhaps even uncomfortable. Her work dispels the idea that individual White racism results largely from ignorance about facts. I argue that these insights extend to the macro level too. Mueller's students actively used societally ingrained White logics and deployed learned cognitive processes to advance their own racist interests. They learned this in their networks. The intent of this "racist interest" may not have been the oppression of all non-White bodies, but, even if it was solely to maintain a status quo with them on top, it has the effect of advantaging Whites and continuing the oppression of non-Whites. Toward this end, Mueller concludes that Whites have continuing material interests in White supremacy. As Angela Davis stated and Ibram X. Kendi popularized, "It is not enough to not be a racist. You must be anti-racist."[27]

White Victimhood and Conscientious Stupidity

White ignorance gives rise to White victims. These "victims" may quickly denounce their actions and beg for forgiveness, or they might feign a lack of knowledge of the harm that their actions have caused. A third technique goes something like "I am sorry that you felt that way" or "I am sorry that you took it that way." This is usually followed by an assertion of no ill intent. In most cases, the assertion of "White victimhood" is concomitant with a rejection of attempts to label the person as racist. Bonilla-Silva and Zuberi's work demonstrates that exposure to the existence of structural racism leads Whites to charge that they are being personally accused of being racists.[28] Then they staunchly resist this label and in so doing seek to discount both systemic and individual-level racism. Some assert inconsistencies like "That was a racist act, but I am not a racist." As a result, we have what Blaut and later Bonilla-Silva call "racism without racists." Bonilla-Silva's body of work exposes the falsity of this popular notion (of racism without racists) and shows that there *are* racists and that color-blind denial has been one of their most effective devices.

We live in a social world, and none of us lives in a vacuum. The reflexive rejection of the label "racist" indicates a failure to look in the mirror, but it also suggests the realization that bad actors are in fact people who often have to pay the consequences for their bad deeds. And few are willing to pay the full price. Most succeed in avoiding the consequences by engaging in offensive and defensive maneuvers such as the ones Mueller outlines. Some, but all too few, squarely look at their actions, own them, apologize sincerely, and make amends.

I'm So Sorry

Allison Ettel, now known by many as "Permit Patty," told CNN News she was sorry for calling 911 on a girl selling water outside of her building. On the call, Ettel can be heard telling the 911 operator that the child was "illegally selling water without a permit."[29] After the video went viral, Ettel did several media interviews in which she offered a series of non sequitur apologies. "I should never have confronted her," she told CNN; Ettel continued, "and I am embarrassed ... it was taken out of context... [I feel] manipulated. People don't understand."[30] She went on to explain that the girl was screaming loudly, and it was disturbing her work, so she simply went to politely ask the girl to be quiet. "I tried to be polite," Ettel told *Today*, "but I was stern. I said, 'Please. I'm trying to work. You're screaming. You're yelling... Can you please keep it down?'"[31] Ettel's statements reduce an eight-year-old girl to the stereotypical "angry Black woman." The stereotype paints the angry Black woman as loud and unwilling to listen to reason. By contrast, Ettel paints herself as the victim.[32] Some apology! Ettel also claims the public street as her own to regulate.

Amy Cooper, the woman who threatened to make a false police report alleging that Christian Cooper assaulted her, also apologized for her actions. In comments to CNN, Cooper said, "I'm not a racist. I did not mean to harm that man in any way."[33] These comments were made after the video of her actions had been widely shared and around the time her employer's investigation resulted in her termination. Criticism spread. People suggested the apology, which began with the words, "I am not a racist," was more about attempting to repair Ms. Cooper's reputation than an apology to Christian Cooper. Ms. Cooper hired a public relations firm and released the following statement, a second apology:

> I want to apologize to Chris Cooper for my actions when I encountered him in Central Park yesterday. I reacted emotionally and made false assumptions about his intentions when, in fact, I was the one who was acting inappropriately by not having my dog on a leash. When Chris began offering treats to my dog and confronted me in an area where there was no one else nearby and said, "You're not going to like what I'm going to do next," I assumed we were being threatened when all he had intended to do was record our encounter on his phone. He had every right to request that I leash my dog in an area where it was required. I am well aware of the pain that misassumptions and insensitive statements about race cause and would never have imagined that I would be involved in the type of incident that occurred with Chris. I hope that a few mortifying seconds in a lifetime of forty years will not define me in his eyes and that he will accept my sincere apology.[34]

Amy Cooper's second apology was also problematic. She took the liberty of calling Christian Cooper "Chris." This assumed a familiarity they did not have, and it hearkened back to a time when Whites routinely failed to call Blacks by courtesy titles. Amy Cooper's second apology also suggested that she and Christian Cooper were alone in the park, but that is not true. Christian Cooper's sister, Melody, was with him, and she was not hidden. Melody Cooper is the one who recorded the infamous video, so her presence was well known to Amy Cooper too. Finally, Amy Cooper suggested that her mistake was a momentary lapse of judgment lasting "a few mortifying seconds." However, now it is well-known that, when the 911 dispatcher called Amy Cooper back, she claimed that Christian Cooper had tried to assault her.[35] A few seconds can define any life. People in New York City, a place haunted by the memory and ghosts of those who survived 911, should know and feel this more acutely than others. Anyone who missed a train and was not at work when the towers came down knows this. Anyone sitting in a jail or prison serving time for a foolish decision made in a split second knows this. Why should Amy Cooper be exempted from this reality or its consequences? In an attempt to seal her victimhood, Amy Cooper told CNN that, since the video posting, her "entire life" had been destroyed.[36] The only thing sincere about Amy Cooper's apology appears to be her sincere attempt to escape public scrutiny for her own racist actions.

Anthony Brennan III is a 60-year-old White man. Less than a week after George Floyd was killed, Brennan was out cycling in his Maryland community and grew angry when he saw three White young adults posting fliers in support of Black Lives Matter and advocating protests against police brutality. The fliers read, "A man was lynched by the police. What are you going to do about it?" Brennan got off his cycle, snatched fliers from one of the young people, intimidated another, and physically assaulted a third. Brennan offered another version of the false "I am so sorry" apology. After being charged, Brennan suggested that there were underlying matters people did not know about, which prompted his response.[37] His statement read, "I am sick with remorse for the pain and fear I caused the victims on the trail, and online. I am cooperating fully with authorities. I am committed to making amends by addressing, through counseling, the underlying issues that led to my abhorrent behavior."[38] The implication is these underlying issues somehow explain and/or justify his behavior. The effect is to position himself as a victim and discount his own responsibility for the trauma and fear his "abhorrent behavior" caused. After all, the public performance of his violent behavior says that if White youth are not safe in speaking up against racism, Black people know that *they* are certainly not safe in doing so.

"I am sorry" is not always an insincere statement. Some people express regret for their acts of anti-Black racism with an "I'm sorry" that seems sincere. New Orleans Saints quarterback Drew Brees is popular with fans and with his teammates, so when Brees (briefly discussed in chapter 9) took an insensitive and ill-informed position about why some NFL and other players take a knee during the playing of the national anthem, some, including some of his own teammates, expressed hurt and outrage. To his credit, Brees apologized, but he followed that apology with a period of reflection. Then he penned a follow-up response regarding what he had learned from his discussions with others that caused him to now believe his earlier statements were objectionable. The statement read, in part, "I would like to apologize to my friends, teammates, the City of New Orleans, the black community, NFL community and anyone I hurt with my comments yesterday. In speaking with some of you, it breaks my heart to know *the pain I have caused*. In an attempt to talk about respect, unity, and solidarity centered around the American flag and the national anthem, I made comments that were insensitive and completely missed the mark on the issues we are facing right now as a country. . . . [My comments] lacked awareness and any kind of compassion or empathy." Brees posted his response on Instagram, where it could be viewed by his more than 1.7 million followers. Whether Brees wrote the statement himself or hired someone to do so, the lack of equivocation and willingness to accept personal responsibility for his actions present throughout the entire statement—"I made comments," "I have caused [pain]," "this is where I stand," "I stand with the black community," "issues we are facing as a country," et cetera—strike the chord of sincerity.[39] Brees's second apology was not perfect, nor was it devoid of attempts to back away from responsibility, but missing the mark may be more a reflection of the journey the football player is on (but has not yet completed) than insincerity.

School is a microcosm of society, and, like it or not, racism is endemic in our society. One bad apple can spoil the whole bunch, so whether or not school officials believe attitudes, behaviors, or beliefs are only espoused by a few, they have responsibility to investigate further. That is what happened in 2019 when racial unrest came to a boil at Owatonna High School in Minnesota soon after a White student posted a racial slur on Snapchat. The resulting investigation led to difficult conversations about race and a realization that the post was not a one-off or just the action of one bad apple. Instead, school officials realized that the small Black student population in the school faced a daily deluge of racial attacks and invalidations. These incidents contributed to the Black students' general feelings of marginalization and isolation.[40]

Some people say "I'm sorry" and sort of mean it. On April 15, 2018, two young Black men were arrested for sitting in a Starbucks on Spruce Street in the Rittenhouse Square section of Philadelphia.[41] The two men did not order anything. They were waiting for a business associate to join them. One of the young men asked for the code to go to the bathroom. Things quickly escalated then. A Starbucks employee refused to grant the code and demanded they leave. She called the police reportedly because the two were sitting in Starbucks without buying something. Police escorted the pair out in handcuffs. By now, the White man they were there to meet had arrived, but even his vouching for them could not protect them from arrest. Like a number of the accounts retold in this book, calling the police on Black people for engaging in routine activities draws on a history of social control and is an overt attempt to weaponize the police against Black people. Approximately six weeks later, amid public outcry and boycotts, Starbucks apologized. The company announced that all of its approximately 8,000 stores would be closed for a day for its employees to attend mandatory bias training.[42]

Approximately two years later, Starbucks was back in the news for a race-related incident. After widespread protests of the Minneapolis police killing of George Floyd, Starbucks issued a public statement of support for the Black Lives Matter movement. On June 4, 2020, an official Starbucks tweet read, "Black Lives Matter. We are committed to being a part of the change." Soon thereafter, however, employees received an email prohibiting them from wearing Black Lives Matter paraphernalia, including pins, at work. After public backlash to this apparent hypocrisy, Starbucks reversed its prohibition against Black Lives Matter attire worn by employees.[43]

Throughout this chapter, I have tried to encourage readers to take a long look in the mirror. If that look is clear sighted, some will no doubt find that they have issued the next kind of apology: I'm sorry, but I really don't mean it. At former Dallas police officer Amber Guyger's trial for the murder of Botham Jean (discussed in chapter 8), Guyger and her defense team asserted continuing claims that she shot Jean because she believed he was an intruder in her apartment and meant her harm. Guyger showed very little emotion at the trial as she presented an account of her victimhood. After prosecutorial objections, sustained by the judge, broke the flow of this account, Guyger's lip began to quiver. In her defense attorney's next move, he pulled out the weapon Guyger had used to kill Jean, showed it to Guyger, and said, "So you pulled out your weapon, and you fired. Why did you fire?" As if on cue, Guyger turned away from the gun, shook her head, dropped her eyes, and she began to sob. Her next words were inaudible. Then she said, "I was scared. I was scared this person was in my apartment, and he was going to kill me, and I'm so sorry. I'm sorry." When the judge asked Guyger to repeat her answer for the benefit of the court stenographer, she pulled herself together and said, "I was scared whoever was inside of *my* apartment was going to kill me, and I have to live with that every single day that I hurt. . ."[44] Guyger did not finish the sentence. The prosecutor objected on grounds that the answer was unresponsive.

Guyger's reduction of her act of taking a 26-year-old man's life to a personal hurt she would carry "every single day" offers insight that her apology is void. She did not speak of the denial her actions created for Jean. There was no mention of how her actions robbed Jean of the opportunity to grow, perhaps marry, have children, and reach his full potential. There is no mention of pain, grief, and anguish her actions brought on Jean's family and friends. Her apology is riddled with hypocrisy and White victimhood. Any pain that she might feel is of her own causing. It is based on her own failings of judgment. Guyger's feelings pale in comparison to the pain the friends and loved ones of Botham Jean carry every day. Like several others, Guyger is sorry she was questioned and ultimately prosecuted and sorrier still that she will face consequences.

The denial of Black humanity runs throughout these non-apologies. They recognize White pain and discomfort and dismiss Black pain through inference that Blacks are subpersons and therefore unable to feel pain, or they invoke stereotypes (born out of ideologies used to justify slavery and rationalize the cruel treatment of Black bodies) to suggest that Blacks have the superhuman ability to endure pain. Whites, however, are fragile.[45] White victimhood (often in the cry of "reverse discrimination") is a frequent trope. It is especially effective when White women use it and level it against Black men. Melody Cooper said she decided to post the video of her brother's account with Amy Cooper in order to show a watching world how the "weaponization of white women's tears" gets used against Black men (and women). This is White women's superpower.

The weaponization of tears is but one aspect of the superpower White women wield. Historical representations of virtuous White womanhood are tied up in concepts of piety and virtue, and this White womanhood is seen by many as being inherently fragile. Robin DiAngelo's *White Fragility: Why It's So Hard for White People to Talk about Racism* evidences the prescient nature of White insensitivity to racial matters.[46] DiAngelo also establishes that White men are even more likely than White women to exhibit distress and inability to tolerate even the least amount of racial distress. One response to this White male fragility can be found in the rise of federal executive orders (issued under Trump) to prevent use of government funds for training about important issues contributing to social inequity. The racial discomfort Whites feel in addressing or learning about matters of racial inequity produces the oft-used "I am the victim now" public outcry.

Whites learn to wield their victimhood early and often. A White teenage woman and her boyfriend, both seniors at a high school about 45 miles outside of Atlanta, shocked the nation when they posted a video on TikTok concocting a "recipe for N——s."[47] The two teens wrote various words and phrases on slips of paper. These included "Black," "don't have a dad," "eat watermelon & fried chicken," "rob people," and "go to jail." A cup sat on top of each paper. One by one, the two placed the appropriate word or phrase in the sink and then poured water from the cup into the sink, symbolizing that the ingredient went into their recipe. As they lifted the cup where the words "rob people" are written underneath, one of the teens could be heard saying "specifically Whites" and the other responding "yeah, they do that." Next, they focused on a piece of paper that had the words "make good choices" on it, but when they picked up that cup, it was empty, so they did not use it in their recipe. School officials quickly condemned the teens' video posting, and they were expelled.

Once identified, the students began receiving threatening calls, and the female student purportedly posted this apology on Instagram, "I want to apologize for the abhorrent video I posted. I know in my heart how wrong it was. My BF is racist and he slowly normalized his racism on me. Still I should never have let him. I believe Blacks are human too, made in the image of Christ. I have disappointed God and I want to apologize. *Please don't contact my college. It's my future and one mistake should not ruin a life.*"[48] The post was deflective, not reflective, and motivated by personal gain. Her last words do not reflect on the gravity of her actions or recognize the irony that Black lives are ruined every day by the perils of racism. Her words "one mistake should not ruin a life" are blind to the fact that the criminal justice system relegates a disproportionate number of Black and brown people to permanent second-class status all for "one mistake." Or that innocent Black and brown people are disproportionately targeted by the justice system and then incentivized to plead guilty for crimes they have not committed. They fail to recognize that anti-blackness is pervasive and Black men, women, boys, and girls are subjected to microaggressions on an almost daily basis. The female student also placed all of the responsibility on her boyfriend and thereby maintained her own purity and victimhood status. These students will likely live with the consequences of their deeds for many years to come. That may not be fair, but it is a consequence totally of their own making.

The school board's response to this was decisive. It quickly investigated and then suspended the students, but, in placing the blame solely on the teens, the school district missed an important opportunity to address the wider culture that bred the attitudes the two students felt brazen and protected enough to share. The teen who widely shared the TikTok video said she did so because she wanted people to know how racist the "kids" at her school were. This suggests s a systemic issue, not an individual one.

Not surprisingly, there is a gendered pattern to the responses. Females are more likely to use some version of the "I am so sorry response," but it is also important to know that while one reaction might be dominant, other responses are often deployed as well. "I am so sorry" can very quickly slip into White victimhood. In such cases, even the actual victims of the racist act often seem conflicted and come to the ready defense of the perpetrator. We can see this in Christian Cooper's comments about Amy Cooper. In an interview with CNN, Christian Cooper expressed regret that Amy Cooper had lost her job, and he encouraged people to stop threatening her. He went on to say, "I think her apology is sincere.... I'm not sure that in that apology she recognizes that while she may not be or consider herself a racist, that particular act was definitely racist . . . granted, it was a stressful situation, a sudden situation—you know, maybe a moment of spectacularly poor judgment. But she went there and had this racist act that she did."[49] She went "there." "There" is the ready place Wells identified over 100 years ago. It is the claim of White female victimhood at the hand of Black male perpetrators that is almost certain to bring an armed response. Christian Cooper suggested that Amy Cooper reflect on her actions—in the past, present, and future—and then decide whether she is indeed a racist.

As discussed earlier, former Dallas police officer Guyger also attempted to paint herself as a victim. At trial, she stated, "No police officer would ever want to hurt an innocent person." Then Guyger said, "I feel like a terrible person. I hate it. I hate that I have to live with this every single day of my life. And I ask God for forgiveness."[50] Guyger's language choice in saying "no police officer would ever want to hurt an innocent person" insinuates a false narrative that she was acting in line with her duties—very stressful duties as a public servant—and that Jean was engaged in behavior that had rightly brought him under her reasonable suspicion. But perhaps her most unenlightened and selfish statement was "I hate that I have to live with this," which was oblivious to the fact that the point of the trial was that Botham Jean did not get to live at all, having been killed by Guyger in his own home. The purported "bad choices" of individuals like Michael Brown, George Floyd, and Sandra Bland all resulted in death sentences, and without a charging instrument or the benefit of a judge and jury. However, the bad choices of Whites who kill Blacks are treated quite differently.

Sincere Ignorance and Conscientious Stupidity Are One

Sincere ignorance and conscientious stupidity are two sides of the same coin. They are distinct, but they are one. There is a complicity and duplicity inherent in conscientious stupidity. Consider the adage "ignorance is bliss." Now consider the adage "when you know better, you do better." Remaining ignorant is a choice. It is a willful election. Perhaps actress and activist Cicely Tyson said it best. In an interview with Oprah Winfrey published after her death, Tyson said, "Your guilt lies in your innocence. You can't live in this society . . . and not know what's going on with a race of people."[51] Some choose to remain ignorant because full knowledge would place them in either a legal or moral, ethical position to make a change, a change that requires the expenditure of some form of capital—social, economic, cultural, or symbolic. Martin Luther King Jr. said, "Men convinced themselves that a system [slavery] that was so economically profitable must be morally justifiable. They formulated elaborate theories of racial superiority. Their rationalizations clothed obvious wrongs in the beautiful garments of righteousness."[52]

Conclusion

True understanding is something that requires pursuit. As Woodson noted in *The Mis-Education of the Negro*, "The mere imparting of information is not education. Above all things, the effort must result in making a man think and do for himself."[53] In many of the encounters discussed in this chapter, the White "bad actor" used some form of ignorance—of the harm of their actions or of their actual intentions—as an excuse, but in an era when information is readily available, ignorance is a choice. The charge here is the same one that appears in the biblical proverb: "Search me, O God, and know my heart: try me and know my thoughts; And see if there be any wicked way in me, and lead me in the way everlasting."[54] It is simply not enough to do what you think is right to do. In order to avoid the pitfalls of conscientious stupidity and sincere ignorance, a person must search out this ideal. Without the search, the best an individual can hope for is to the stay the same. But there are other options too. One could atrophy. I hope the readers of this book will choose to grow in wisdom and in stature. As Muhammad Ali once said, "The man who views the world at 50 the same as he did at 20 has wasted 30 years of his life."[55] Too many people have lost their lives. No life should be wasted.

"Whiteness is a powerful embodied form of being in the world," writes George Yancy. In his book, *Black Bodies, White Gazes*, Yancy relays an account from a White Jewish mother of an interracial child. The mother expressed disbelief and disdain that the police stopped her Black son's Black male friend and pulled the latter over in front of her home. Police made the stop on suspicion the car he was driving was stolen. The White Jewish mother tried to intervene, but "her son responded angrily reminding her that being stopped by police and questioned because he is driving a nice-looking car is something that happens to him all the time." Yancy continues, "Her state of disbelief [at the daily indignities her interracial son faces] as she later realizes, 'signifies the vast space of white blindness to the dailiness of racism . . . Ambushed by her whiteness . . . she realized that her subject position is productive of a form of ignorance.'"[56]

CHAPTER 11

Policy Matters

> The philosophers have only interpreted the world,
> in various ways; the point, however, is to change it.
>
> —KARL MARX

This is one of the shortest chapters in the book. At first, I lamented that, and I looked for ways to make it longer. In the end, I realized that I was bearing a burden that was not of my creation. I thought about all the ways I had spoken truth to power in chapter 9 to share with readers the toll "the weight" takes, and I decided that I was not going to willingly take that burden upon myself. Racism is a problem White people created, and White people will need to acknowledge it to solve it. Only then can we as a society work collaboratively on solutions. Eggers and O'Leary, the authors of *If We Can Put a Man on the Moon: Getting Big Things Done in Government*, similarly caution that "getting things done isn't merely a systems problem. It isn't merely a policy problem. It's a human problem as well."[1] Although they speak specifically to challenges in implementing public policy objectives in government, the point still resonates: no lasting change occurs unless people change. Despite this certitude, I will offer a few brief insights and suggest a few policy recommendations that speak to the potential for this current moment of racial unrest to bring about lasting change in society. But as Barbara Tomlinson and George Lipsitz caution in *Insubordinate Spaces*, the needed change may require forming new democratic processes.[2]

This chapter asks: How will we create new democratic processes that foster positive social change? And how will we as a society respond to violence? Inherent in this second question is the question of how we can stop or prevent violence.

We need to consider prevention on a number of levels, including before violence occurs, immediately after it occurs, and over the long term (Rob Nixon's concept of slow violence). Our response to violence—especially racial violence—has been too patchwork. It is as if we were children wishing for a panacea, but there is no panacea. With that in mind, no recommendation herein should be treated as some type of silver bullet. Eggers and O'Leary write, "Though understanding the systems . . . is critical to successful implementation, we also need to understand the people rolling the boulder up the hill, particularly how their behaviors are shaped by the culture in which they toil."[3]

The gripping, compelling influence of culture must never be forgotten or ignored, especially when trying to implement social policy. It is the micro link, and, as I identified in the tenets of BOP, there is a symbiotic macro and micro connection to racism: It is sustained on a micro level, but it operates on a macro level. It is also sustained on a macro level, and it operates on micro level. Therefore, it is necessary to address the issues at both a systems level and an individual level. In keeping with the focus of this book, the policy recommendations I advance bear this in common: They call for a recognition that no one in society is out of place. They encourage policy makers to consider impacts from the bottom to the top (and everyone in between) and not to discount the voices of people of color. Our policy-making processes must provide safeguards and checks to ensure that they do not perpetuate disparities in society or dismiss structural forces. The first step toward eradicating systemic and anti-Black racism from U.S. society is to acknowledge its continuing existence and how it is being maintained. The recommendations offer ways for policy makers to see and correct the marginalization of many Black and otherwise non-conforming bodies that has historically occurred through implicit and explicit assumptions that White perspectives, experiences, and logics are the only experience (or the only experience that matters) in the world. The second objective of the recommendations is to force a recognition that, in many respects, diversity is not lacking, inclusivity is.

Many companies and other groups in society say they are against anti-Black racism. They may even put out official statements to that effect. Some go a step further and devote some programming to the issue or give money to support a more mainstream Black organization, and then they wash their hands. What I am encouraging is the sustained maintenance of a kind of accountability scorecard that interrogates not what institutions say they believe but what they do. Inside such a system, the objective of the scorecard is not perfection but continuous improvement. This cannot be done while maintaining the status quo. We need to increase diversity at the top of organizations, and we need to listen to and respect the knowledge, expertise, and insights of Black people, Indigenous people, and other people of color with respect to their embodied life experiences. Systemic changes are needed to create more equal opportunities for everyone. All the policy recommendations I offer should be read with that in mind.

Corporations, government agencies, and other institutions are used to keeping data that allow them to make projections and forecasts. They use tools to assess where they fell short or exceeded goals and then generate a story about not only what happened but why it happened. When these entities fall short, they generate a plan for how to address it.

Policy Recommendation 1

Daily microaggressions inflict real harm, and the perpetrators should incur real and clear consequences. The sanction need not be grave, but failure to address the injurious nature of microaggressions suggests that they are acceptable or even just. Without the threat of repercussion for them, the microaggressions and wounding will likely continue. This was the case with the students in Jena, Louisiana (the Jena Six), discussed in chapter 9. Animosity between the Black and White students grew after the school failed to meaningfully sanction the White students who hung threatening nooses from a prominent tree on campus. Even the language the school chose—calling the nooses "ropes"—denied history and downgraded the severity of the incident. This subtle language choice helped legitimate the soft response and punishment.

The nooses were placed there for the express purpose of announcing to the entire Black community—students at the high school, their parents, and the larger society—that despite the school administrators' declaration that students could sit wherever they wanted, the area under the tree remained White space. The clear message was that the individual racist acts of the students were actually supported (and perhaps even encouraged) by the community. Instead of punishment, the White actors who initiated the conflict had their hands slapped, and the Black students who later retaliated were charged as adults and threatened with decades-long sentences. The actual harm the White students inflicted should have been properly acknowledged and punished. There should have been an open dialogue on the matter. Part of that dialogue should have included acknowledgment and discussion of the continuing individual and group attitudes about where groups belong through an assertion about the exclusivity of certain spaces. All the resulting incidents might have been avoided if some such action had been taken.

There may be general reticence to adopt a policy that requires clear consequences for acts of racial hostility, especially because bad actors often feign ignorance of the offensive nature of their behavior. However, if organizations offer clear guidelines about what kinds of behavior constitute infractions, punishing the behavior becomes more palatable. There are behavioral expectations for students. Every school has them. These expectations entail standards of conduct, and policies outline how to respond when these standards are not met. The act of placing a noose from a tree, especially in the context described in chapter 9, could certainly be punishable under a number of common school discipline policies on bullying, disorderly conduct, taunting, and threat or intimidation.[4]

In *Biased: Uncovering the Hidden Prejudice That Shapes What We See, Think, and Do*, psychologist Jennifer Eberhardt discusses how the app Nextdoor handled complaints that bias was fueling their crime posts.[5] Nextdoor describes itself as "the neighborhood hub for trusted connections and the exchange of helpful information, goods, and services." It asserts, "We believe that that by bringing neighbors together, we can cultivate a kinder world where everyone has a neighborhood they can rely on."[6] Despite this altruistic aim, early users reported problems with racial profiling on the platform. Shawn Dromgoole outlined a similar experience. Neighborhood crime posts were dominated by reports of "suspicious activity" involving little more than the report of a Black person—usually a man—in the area. It created a lot of incivility on the site, and Nextdoor searched for ways to change things. They approached Eberhardt and other scholars.

Based on the scholars' recommendations, Nextdoor decided on a three-pronged approach to the problem. First, the scholars suggested that Nextdoor slow down people's decision-making process. This would offer some protection from allowing bias to influence individuals' personal decision making. They added a checklist in the "crime and safety" tab of the app that would do just that. Users now must fill out the checklist before they can post purported "suspicious activity."[7] The checklist includes questions that direct the would-be poster to concentrate on what it is about a person's behavior that makes him or her suspicious, not traits like a person's race. This focus on behavior represents a cognitive shift. The criterion for suspicious activity cannot just be social category (e.g., Black man). The second recommendation Nextdoor implemented was requiring posters to give enough detail to isolate a specific individual. In this way, every person in a certain social category cannot be subject to suspicion. Finally, the app provided a definition of racial profiling and expressly prohibited it. These steps allowed Nextdoor to curb racial profiling on the site by over 75%.[8] Naming something, defining it, and stating that the activity was prohibited had direct benefits for Nextdoor. I believe it can have benefits for others as well.

Policy Recommendation 2

Calls for social justice are growing louder and louder. In the midst of such a moment, it is easy for even well-meaning people to move too quickly. To be certain, change is overdue and must happen. Before implementing a policy, it is important to understand whether the policy disparately impacts any group. To ascertain this prior to implementation, I recommend considering the policy through an intersectional lens. To illustrate the importance of this, I discuss the CROWN Act.

The CROWN Act was first proposed in the California legislature to prevent discrimination against Black hairstyles in the workplace and school. California became the first state to ban discrimination based on natural hairstyles. These include dreadlocks, braids, cornrows, twists, and Afros—styles worn predominantly by African Americans. The California law made it illegal to target people based on hairstyles often associated with race. But across the nation there are many school and workplace dress codes in place that deem certain ethnic or non-Eurocentric hairstyles "unprofessional." Some schools have punished students whose hair does not comply with Eurocentric standards of beauty and acceptability. While rules should be followed, disparate impact (i.e., practices and policies that adversely affect one group of people in a protected class more than another) should be guarded against.

We need to seriously consider ways to provide this protection in public and private contexts; otherwise the pattern first effectuated in the Supreme Court's invalidation of the Civil Rights Act of 1875 will continue. Soon after the end of Reconstruction, the court declared the 1875 law unconstitutional. The court opined that because the Fourteenth Amendment outlawed discrimination by state governments, there was no authority for it to be used to regulate private businesses. Discriminatory private actions were deemed beyond the reach or protection of the law. It is time for a movement toward genuine social equality. Today holds the promise of a new Reconstruction and actualization of the promise of America.

Policy Recommendation 3

We should work to create a culture in which continuous improvement is desired and expected, and we should create processes allowing this to happen. There is an educational tool called GIFT (Group Instructional Feedback Technique).[9] It allows instructors to receive confidential information from their students on how they can improve the quality of a course. A facilitator encourages feedback from the students, and this helps the students to feel heard. All responses are listed, and students arrive at a consensus about what the instructor is doing that contributes positively to their learning. Specific suggestions are included for improving learning. The consensus model allows students to come to an accord on what is most salient. It also allows the instructor to receive a manageable list of suggestions for improvement that he or she might implement. I encourage the use of a similar model. Such an approach has numerous benefits. It encourages a system of two-directional listening. This continuous improvement loop also counters color-blind racism, the frame that perpetuates racism by focusing on how "things are so much better now than they used to be."

Policy Recommendation 4

Some may be familiar with the phrase "No harm, no foul." But just because harm may not be seen or talked about does not mean it does not exist. People suffer in silence, and it is difficult for them to get the assistance they need. Marginalized groups are more likely to be in this position.

It is important to get rid of the mentality that judges lack of harm by lack of tears. Let us again examine the case of Travis Miller Sr. If we look at Miller's comments in interviews days after the incident, he talked about the trauma he suffered and continues to suffer. We see his controlled effort not to break down in front of his tormentors, and later we hear the toll that it has exacted on him. Oumou Kanoute was also dismissed by people who said that she had not been harmed—after all, she did not appear distraught. Often we do not see what is obvious to others, and people certainly do not see what they do not look for or expect. My fourth policy recommendation as a way to improve disparities with respect to outcomes is to focus on providing opportunities for the standpoint of others to be heard. This could occur though formal exercises as a regular part of ongoing training or informal means to anonymously collect and consider all voices. Another approach could involve strategic partnerships and collaboration with other groups, agencies, and individuals to ensure representation of all voices. The input of the whole community must be reflected.

I again turn to the example of instant replays in sporting events. It amazes me that from one angle things might look one way, but from another angle, from a different perspective, they appear altogether differently. In contested matters, officials consult all perspectives before they make a final determination. I think a great deal can be learned from this. Sometimes decisions have to be made in a split second. Still, I am also struck by the fact that it is often a sequence of earlier events that forces police or other state actors into a situation in which they are called upon to make a split-second decision. As Nextdoor discovered, there is benefit to forcing people to go through a reasoned analysis. It is critical to ask people at all levels of an organization to consider the situation from a perspective other than their own and to provide opportunities to discuss the same. James Baldwin said, "I imagine that one of the reasons people cling to their hate so stubbornly is because they sense, once hate is gone, they will be forced to deal with pain."[10] Instead, too many people have been content to inflict pain. It is time for a reckoning.

Recommendation 5

In a culture that sometimes acknowledges racism but often fails to acknowledge the existence of racists, one of the most revolutionary things that institutions can do is to acknowledge that racism is endemic in society. If racism is endemic in society, remnants of it likely exist in our organizations, and people carry it in the door. The other recommendations rely on this realization. No industry is immune from it, nor is any section of the country.

Cody Renard Richard is a Black man who has worked as a stage manager on Broadway, a purported liberal bastion in U.S. society, for decades. Richard told CNN News,

> Racism is in every art form.... I have to echo the cries of America right now, Black lives matter, and if these ... things continue to happen in our workplaces and everyday life, then that statement doesn't ring true. Saying we have to start from the bottom and hold people accountable, we have to start calling people out and having these uncomfortable conversations.... It's time to own up to what you're saying ... and ... move through the world with ... more ... consciousness.[11]

Consciousness that racism exists and is performed by individual racist actors and through systemic practices embedded in institutions will make it easier to name, discuss, and eradicate. But people (at the micro level) and organizations (at the macro level) have to mean it when they say it. It cannot be like when Starbucks embraced Black Lives Matter with one public statement but then acted otherwise with a private directive to employees.

Policy Recommendation 6

Stop checking the box. Too many organizations approach things like bias training as a necessary item on a to-do list that must be performed and then can be checked off. This is another form of the panacea approach. Training is not a cure for eradicating a racist society. My sixth recommendation is to acknowledge that training does not change hearts but to commit to training anyway. Incorporating ongoing and mandatory implicit-bias testing can help people recognize their blind spots. It can also remove the ready excuse that people did not know about or mean to engage in offensive behavior. Chapter 10 included a discussion of how change begins in the individual and called for people to take a look in the mirror. Implicit-bias training is such an examination. Reflexive assertions like "I am not a racist" will not make the world a better place, and they certainly will not keep Black people safe. Instead, people need to be willing to consider thinking "I am a racist (or I might be a racist) and now this is what I am willing to do about it."

In a report published by the RAND Corporation, researchers Anita Chandra and others discuss ways that stress, trauma, and adverse experiences like racism can affect the health of individuals and their communities. Their policy recommendations include providing a framework for responding to community stress when (not if) it happens. The authors boldly assert that "[placing] well-being at the center of policy making is a new and promising approach at the local and national level."[12] If we truly want equity, it is an approach we must take.

Policy Recommendation 7

Inequality in America has been racialized since before the founding of the United States. We should commit to disaggregating data (i.e., to break data down in order to see the subcategories and better understand how all subgroups are affected) and thereby unearth the multiple stories behind the data. Once those patterns are discernible, we need to commit to doing something about it. The incident at Smith College discussed in chapter 7 escalated because a caller first misgendered Oumou Kanoute and then continued to insist that the student looked out of place and thereby suspicious. The independent investigation that followed found that race did not play a factor in the call. However, despite Smith College's claims to racial diversity, during the regular school year only about 160 out of the school's 2,500 students identify as Black. In the summer, the percentage of Black students must be discernibly less. It is only reasonable to assume that the student's race and cultural presentation of self (short natural hairstyle and a baseball cap) influenced the caller's perception. The college's claims that almost one-quarter of its student population identifies as a racial or ethnic minority are true, but it does not paint a complete picture of the presence and embodied experience of Black students on the campus.

Conclusion

Public policy should be an exercise of writing across time. A famous line conveyed in popular culture dates from NASA's Apollo expeditions to the moon. It is said that on day three in space, Astronaut Jack Swigert communicated, "Houston, we have a problem." In actuality, Swigert said, "Okay, Houston. We've had a problem here."[13] In either case, the problem was significant. The United States has had a problem with racism, and the United States has a problem with racism. Public policy approaches must recognize both. They should be aimed at dismantling institutional practices that work to disadvantage groups, and they should do this by enforcing fair hiring and fair housing laws, addressing environmental racism, desegregating schools, promoting affirmative action, and addressing predatory policing and the impact of fines, fees, and other practices that act as a surtax on Black life.

CHAPTER 12

Tell "the Story"

Lest We Forget

> I come to you and say, our destiny is calling—one without
> hate, oppression, and violence—and it is our turn to answer.
>
> —ROBERT BATTLE

In *The New Jim Crow* Michelle Alexander quotes an 1853 speech by Frederick Douglass. Speaking on behalf of delegates of the National Colored Convention, Douglass said:

> A heavy and cruel hand has been laid upon us. As a people, we feel ourselves to be not only deeply injured, but grossly misunderstood. Our white countrymen do not know us. They are strangers to our character, ignorant of our capacity, oblivious to our history and progress, and are misinformed as to the principles and ideas that control and guide us, as a people. The great mass of American citizens estimates us as being a characterless and purposeless people; and hence *we hold up our heads*, if at all, against the withering influence of a nation's scorn and contempt.[1]

Douglass's words still resonate today. This chapter makes the continuing declaration that we—a proud, beautiful Black people—will hold up our heads. The chapter affirms Black creativity, resilience, strength, and pride and argues that these attributes are the unintended by-products of our struggle and when properly wielded help people of color resist and fight racist paradigms. Sociologist Erving Goffman would call it the blessing in the burden, but make no mistake: this is a burden that must be lifted, and we will fight until our last breath toward that end.

Black Agency

Agency cannot be fully comprehended without understanding the structural forces that act to curtail it. Structures are those factors of influence (such as race, religion, gender, social class, ethnicity, ability, and customs) that confine or limit an agent and his or her decisions. Storytelling is an important agentic act. Nikole Hannah-Jones, architect of the *New York Times Magazine's* 1619 Project, said it best: "[It is] not just the power of storytelling but the power of being able to tell your own story and not allowing someone else to frame the world but to do that framing for yourself."[2] Hannah-Jones not only did that for herself, she did it for countless other Black Americans who came before, those present now, and for those to come. The 1619 Project has been termed a "historical analysis of how slavery shaped American political, social, and economic institutions." Some leading historians have challenged the project, but Hannah-Jones and others have stood fast and continued to tell the story of an oppressed people from the point of view of those oppressed people. Together with the Pulitzer Center, the *Times* "has produced educational materials based on the 1619 Project . . . intended to enhance traditional curricula."[3]

In a country built in part on the principle of freedom of speech, not all speech is treated equally.[4] Over the last 10 years, there have been a number of attacks on brilliant Black intellectuals. Some of them are not known to me. Some are dear friends. In each case, it has been an attempt to silence them and counter and diminish their will to speak truth to power. The most egregious recent case was the University of North Carolina (UNC) trustees' early and consistent refusal to act on tenure consideration for Hannah-Jones, who had been appointed to the Knight Chair in Race and Investigative Journalism at UNC's Hussman School of Journalism and Media.[5] Despite stellar credentials and the support of faculty, students, and administration, a significant number of trustees and large donors rebuffed Hannah-Jones and her work, and others were noticeably silent. After a public battle in which students of color at UNC were among Hannah-Jones's staunchest supporters, the board approved Hannah-Jones's tenure in a 9-to-4 vote.[6] But Hannah-Jones declined. Instead, she will be the inaugural Knight Chair in Race and Journalism at Howard University, a historically Black college in Washington, D.C., and alma mater of Vice President Kamala Harris (among other notable graduates).[7] The fact that the UNC trustees ultimately voted in favor of Hannah-Jones's tenure is insignificant, especially because it ignores that an important objective of the refusal was accomplished. Hannah-Jones is a Pulitzer Prize winner and MacArthur Foundation "genius" grantee. Susan King, dean and John Thomas Kerr Distinguished Professor at the Hussman School of Journalism, said, "Nikole

Hannah-Jones isn't just a great journalist—she's a once-in-a-generation journalist."[8] Hannah-Jones's credentials are beyond reproach, and the trustees' failure to vote on her tenure application until responding to pressure was not only an assault on academic freedom but also an assault on her very will, dignity, and humanity. It was a tragedy, and that is where the message lies. According to the National Center for Education Statistics, Blacks comprise fewer than 6% of college professors nationwide.[9] Citing a 2013 Teachers Insurance and Annuity Association of America report, an article in *Inside Higher Ed* reported that Black women made up only "2.8 percent of the tenured faculty in the U.S. universities in the data set."[10] Amid growing attacks on critical race theory and theorists led by conservative members of Congress, governors, and others, the rebuff of Hannah-Jones told other scholars and activists: "You'd better be quiet and get in line. Your credentials likely cannot touch Hannah-Jones's, so you know that *you* are not safe. Do not speak up. Do not speak out. We may let you keep your job—as long as you say what we tell you to say. And do not say certain things." According to *Carolina Alumni Review*, "Tenure approval process started in summer 2020."[11] During much of the time afterward, the trustees "took no action on the Hussman school's bid for her to receive a tenured professorship." No other Knight Chair had been subject to such treatment. The rebuff was a rejection of Hannah-Jones and her ideological views as expressed through endeavors like the 1619 Project. The UNC trustees' initial failure to give Hannah-Jones tenure was pushback against her ideas and amounted to an assertion that "you, Black woman, do not get to interpret history, only we do, and when you try, we will reject your ideas, and we will reject you." This is how whiteness acts as a possessive investment in rightness.

The silencing and rejecting of Black perspectives and expressions extends beyond academe. Consider television host Laura Ingraham's doubletalk on the issue of whether athletes should speak out about social and political matters. Ingraham suggested that Drew Brees had a right to his opinion but that LeBron James should just "shut up and dribble."[12] But we will not shut up. The remaining pages of this book are devoted to a retelling of our history and affirmative declarations of what Black people have done and accomplished as a people and what we will do, even if all we have is faith. I have a new faith that a change is gonna come. I hope that many of the readers of this book will be part of the change.

We must support reforms for the criminal justice system. We must end predatory lending. We must protect voting rights. We must increase public school funding and make it independent from property taxes. These will lead to a more equitable society. Systemic problems require systemic solutions, and we are all part of the system. It also means that those who argue that they did not own slaves still must acknowledge that they have benefited from the wages of whiteness. In the words of Martin Luther King Jr., "For too long the depth of racism in American life has been underestimated. The surgery to extract it is necessarily complex and detailed. As a beginning it is important to X-ray our history and reveal the full extent of the disease."[13]

We Will!

We will sing

In his 1899 poem "Sympathy" Paul Laurence Dunbar declared, "I know why the caged bird sings!"[14] The bird—beating its wing "till its blood is red on the cruel bars" and singing but "not a carol of joy or glee"—represents Black people. Maya Angelou continued the metaphor in titling her 1969 autobiography *I Know Why the Caged Bird Sings*.[15] Like our ancestors, we will continue to sing. We will sing Sojourner Truth's declaration, "Ain't I a Woman?" We will not forget Billie Holiday's haunting "Strange Fruit" and remind listeners about the heinous realities of lynching. We will get ready with the Impressions for the change Sam Cooke declared was gonna come. We will sing to our children, as Nina Simone sang to us, that they are young, gifted, and Black, and together with our children all across the African diaspora, we will join with James Brown to sing: "Say it loud—I'm Black, and I'm proud." We will teach our girl children and our boy children Aretha's anthemic call to "give me my propers" and demand "R-E-S-P-E-C-T," and when the world does not give it to them we will teach them to rise up unafraid, as Andra Day sings and discover the fighter inside them, so that, as Common and John Legend sing, the glory will be ours whenever it comes.

From the hulls of slave ships to the fields we had to steal away from, music has kept and inspired Black people, and Black people have used that music to lift ourselves and the world. So despite the realities of anti-blackness and racism, we will sing, and, to paraphrase James Baldwin, with every note we will vomit up all the filth we have been taught about ourselves and half-believed, and we will walk on the earth as though we have a right to be here.[16] Because we do. We built this world.

We will speak truth to power

Ida B. Wells-Barnett's biographer, Paula Giddings, provides great insight into the crusader's life and times as well as her motivations. Giddings reminds the reader that one of the first choices of free people after the Civil War entailed the opportunity to get married. We also learn that at the end of the Civil War, 90% of African Americans were illiterate, perhaps not surprisingly. It had been illegal to educate enslaved people. Now that they were free, many craved an education. Young Ida

Wells went to school. Young Ida believed it was her job to learn, even when that meant reading by a dim light at home. Her mother also saw the value of education, and she went to school with Ida. Her mother wanted to learn how to read the Bible. Later, Ida would become a teacher. It was one of the ways she knew she could support her minor siblings after the death of their parents. When he was alive, her father would ask her to read the newspaper to him. He was very interested in race matters. In those mainstream White papers, Blacks became scapegoats for White problems. Ida Wells's story has been told elsewhere in this book, but it bears noting that Wells determined that if newspapers could be used to spread lies, she could use them to speak truth.

Like Wells before us and all the Black journalists, novelists, songwriters and playwrights since, we will call out racism (and all its cousins) when we see it, as we see it. And in so doing we will silence the plausibility of claims of ignorance, lack of ill intent, and naivete and create counter-frames that legitimate the perceptions, feelings, rationalizations, analyses, conclusions, and insights of oppressed people.

We will learn from our mistakes

Bayard Rustin was the architect for the March on Washington and many of the other advances of the civil rights movement at the middle of the 20th century, but few people know about his contributions. As a gay Black man, he was relegated to the background, and for a long time historians and others forgot, overlooked, or omitted his contributions. I knew his name, but I was ashamed when I came to realize how many names of other Black crusaders in the LGBTQ community (and Black LGBTQ victims of violence) I did not know.

Rosa Parks was an American hero, and she should be celebrated, but there are countless other Black women heroes who should be studied and celebrated. Nine months before Parks was famously arrested in Montgomery, Alabama, 15-year-old Claudette Colvin was arrested there for a similar reason—refusing to give up her bus seat to a White woman. No movement could be mobilized around Colvin, though, because as a pregnant, unmarried teen, she did not fit the image commensurate with the prevailing politics of Black middle-class respectability. Recently I found myself shackled by the same politics of Black middle-class respectability. When Rayshard Brooks was killed at the hands of police outside a Wendy's in Atlanta, I quickly determined that he was no George Floyd. I stopped short of saying that he deserved his fate (for hitting the officer, taking another officer's taser, fleeing the scene, and then pointing and firing the taser at the officer). I did not say it, but I thought it. Then I saw video of an interview Rayshard Brooks did with an agency trying to assist felons. Brooks described his encounters with the criminal justice system—a system that by now none can deny is disproportionately harsher on African Americans—and I realized that when Brooks encountered the officers, he was fighting for his life. He had a deadly fear of ensnarement again in the criminal justice system. Despite the declaration "I know why the caged bird sings" made by Paul Laurence Dunbar in "Sympathy" and echoed by Maya Angelou in her autobiography of the same name, I realized *not all caged birds sing*. For some, like Sandra Bland, being caged is death. Then I realized that even among Blacks in America, not all Black lives are regarded with the same value. I recognize that this is taking on the slave master's mentality—enslaved people who were good (docile and hardworking) had value, and those who were bad (rebellious and questioning) did not. I remembered the refrain that "all lives won't matter until all Black lives matter," and it hit me: I needed to look in the mirror and make sure that I valued all Black lives. I challenge the reader to do the same. We will learn from our mistakes. We must.

We will never lose our humanity

Despite being classified as subhuman, property, and a host of other derogatory things, we will never lose our humanity. This again hearkens back to the Dunbar poem "Sympathy." Our existence in this country as chattel property and then as second-class citizens means that we know the pain the caged bird feels. It is a kind of pain that robs you of energy. It is an undeserved, debasing, and debilitating pain. Because of our acute and intimate knowledge of this plight, we retain a measure of sympathy for others. To lose that sympathy is to lose or give away part of our humanity, and we refuse to let the oppressor take one more thing from us.

Christian Cooper, the man birding in the Ramble section of New York's Central Park, "expressed regret for the extent of the retribution" against Amy Cooper, the woman who threatened to call the police on him. An interview with Mr. Cooper gives some insight into his character. He said, "I am pretty adamant about not being a participant [in] my own dehumanization."[17] For Christian Cooper, to glory in Amy Cooper's pain would be to give away part of his humanity. The brother of Botham Jean, the man killed in his own home by a police officer who said she thought she was in her own apartment and feared Jean was a perpetrator, hugged his brother's killer and told her he forgave her.[18] The mother of Jonathan Ferrell, who was shot multiple times by a police officer, said, "He [the officer] took my son from me, but I can only stand here and tell you that I believe God is the one listening to me right now and God would want me to forgive. If I don't forgive, it will be on me forever."[19] The family of victims of the 2015 Charleston Church Massacre did the same.[20] I am also reminded of Patrick Hutchinson, a Black Lives Matter protester in the UK who bent down and picked up a counter-protester who was being beaten. At risk of harm to himself, Hutchinson carried the man to safety.[21] We will never lose our humanity.

We will never lose our rage

Even when we forgive, we will never forget. As Nikole Hannah-Jones said at the 2017 Power of Storytelling Conference in Bucharest, "What drives me is rage."[22] It is a righteous rage fueled by a desire to get people to see what they have been blind to. Anti-Black racism is so ingrained in society that it is rendered almost invisible. Hannah-Jones reminds us that there are some things people choose not to see. Part of the root of Black rage is knowing the depth of our humanity and the mercy (unmerited favor) we have afforded White folks. So while they choose blindness, we clothe ourselves with righteous rage that fuels righteous action.

We will continue to testify, sometimes without saying a word

Words are not always necessary, and sometimes they are less eloquent than our silence or our actions. Words also fail to convince unrepentant hearts, and they drain the speaker of energy. So in wisdom we will continue to testify, sometimes without saying a word. In *Crushing: God Turns Pressure into Power*, Bishop T. D. Jakes writes, "Blood continues to exonerate individuals who were wrongfully incarcerated. . . . It acts as a testifying agent to actions others have not witnessed. . . . Then blood becomes a witness to the past by its existence in the present."[23] We will support the work of the Innocence Project and other efforts to free wrongly incarcerated persons. We will also work for the abolition of prisons and support the work of organizations like Critical Resistance (which seeks to build an international movement to end the Prison Industrial Complex), Free-Dem Foundations (founded by three formerly incarcerated men, seeking to help build community cohesion and self-sufficiency in the neighborhoods where they were raised), and the Elsinore Bennu Think Tank for Restorative Justice (which develops strategies to heal communities broken by criminal and state-sponsored violence).

One of the most powerful images of the last several years is a photo of a young Black woman at a Black Lives Matter protest in Whitefish, Montana. Samantha Francine looks into the eyes of her tormentor. He is male and White and appears old enough to be her father. His fists are clenched, and he is raging, but Samantha Francine, unflinching and unbowed, looks directly into the man's angry eyes and at once asserts her humanity and her refusal to be silenced. Two weeks after the police murder of George Floyd in Minneapolis and with the Covid-19 pandemic spreading, the unmasked man came within inches of Francine's face. He yelled and swore, with spittle almost certainly expelled from his mouth, yet she would not be moved a millimeter. In an interview with CBS News, Francine said she never once thought of backing down. She told CBS's Vladimir Duthiers, "I wish I didn't have to be in that photo. I wish that the world was different, but since I am in that photo, I want to own it, and I want to live it."[24]

Sometimes you are silent, and at other times you must speak. Cody Renard Richard spent decades as a stage manager on Broadway. In that time, he endured numerous microaggressions. After the George Floyd protests, Richard felt it was time to speak up. Broadway was closed, and he had rare time to reflect. He told CNN that there is a time to be quiet, and there is a time to speak. So we will speak—in our silences and through elocution—knowing that our silence is invited by the oppressor and that our speaking up might result in pushback. Knowing this, we still will not back down.

We will laugh

After comedian Jay Pharoah was stopped by police and told to spread out on the dirty ground, an officer climbed atop him and put his knee into Pharoah's neck.[25] When Pharoah described the incident to *CBS This Morning* cohost Gayle King, he said, "I just felt disgusting—people are driving past looking at me like I'm an animal, I'm a criminal—I did something—but I'm an innocent bystander."[26] Pharoah told King that he had talked with fellow comedian Steve Harvey about the encounter, and Harvey had told Pharoah that he (Pharoah) had just gotten his first "being Black in America sandwich."[27] It was biting social commentary. King commented, "Yeah, and it [the sandwich] doesn't taste good." They shared a moment of amusement, and the laughter acted as catharsis. Anger is another viable choice, and another is to cry, but, as James Baldwin indicates, to cry in the face of oppression carries an inherent danger: you might never stop.

Solange Knowles described being humiliated by a public TSA patting down of her Afro-style hair at a checkpoint in Miami, Florida, purportedly a search for explosives. After expressing her outrage on social media, Knowles decided to play a game. On a social media account she posted: "Discrim-FRO-nation . . . My hair is not a storage drawer . . . Let's play a little game called: What did TSA find in Solange's Fro?" The singer received a number of humorous responses. The resultant laughter eased her tension (and rage at the humiliation she suffered based on application of a racially discriminatory policy) before the long flight. The British *Daily Mail* reported, "The TSA defended hair pat-downs, stating that 'additional screening may be required for clothing, headware [*sic*] or hair where prohibited items could be hidden.'"[28] Since then, the policy has been revised.

Whether in short form (see Niecy Nash's video *To the Next BBQ Becky: Don't Call 911. Call 1-844-WYT-FEAR*) or long form (read D. L. Hughley and Doug Moe's *How Not to Get Shot and Other Advice from White People*, which *Black En-*

terprise magazine called "hilarious, yet soul shaking"), we will continue to see and expose the absurdity in White supremacy.

Laughter has other benefits too. Jackie "Moms" Mabley was born in the 1890s and she died in 1975. Her Biography.com profile states, "She experienced a horrifying traumatic childhood. Her firefighter father was killed in an explosion when she was 11 and her mother was later hit and killed by a truck on Christmas Day. And by the beginning of her teens, she had been raped twice."[29] This Black woman was known as "the funniest lady in the world." She took on an easily accessible "mom" persona and offered everyday wisdom, served with a little raunch on the side, and biting commentary on society. She inspired some of the most successful female comedians of the modern era, including Whoopi Goldberg, who directed the 2013 documentary *Moms Mabley: I Got Somethin' to Tell You.*[30] Mabley turned the pain of her multiple oppressions into a form of resistance that was personally healing, affirming for her, and inspirational to others. A host of Black comedians have laughed us to life. Their standup comedy stands up to oppression. Redd Foxx, Dick Gregory, Richard Pryor, Whoopi Goldberg, Dave Chappelle, Jonathan Slocum, and too many others to name have all provoked society, inspired us, and let us know we are not alone. We will continue to laugh, and, because we laugh, we will live.

We will be first-class citizens

Whether it is the fight for economic justice, the fight for equality in educational opportunity and funding, the fight for police and criminal justice reform, the fight for immigration reform, or the fight for voting rights—including the restoration of voting rights of felons, we will fight to be what Fannie Lou Hamer called "first-class citizens," and we will exercise that right. We owe it to those who fought, bled, and died for us.

Black resistance and the reclaiming of space—social and geographic—operate as often-ignored contemporary responses to racism. For hundreds of years, there have been varied forms of Black resistance—from the many slave rebellions to today's activist movements such as Black Lives Matter. When a White woman tried to tell a group of Black Oaklanders how they should use the park space, the group responded with weekly, large, family-reunion-style cookouts that effectively claimed the whole space for their exclusive use and enjoyment. This is one of the many forms of resistance that people of color have engaged in throughout our history in America.

Freedom is a hallmark of American democracy, yet in many ways racism (or the fear of being subjected to racist acts) influences African Americans' willingness to move to and through certain spaces. Slavery, Black Codes, Jim Crow laws, and other tools have been used to instill fear in people of color and keep them in their place—a position of subservience to Whites. I am encouraged by works like Barbara Tomlinson and George Lipsitz's *Insubordinate Spaces* and Rebecca Louise Carter's *Prayers for the People*.[31] These books recognize that place is a form of power. Tomlinson and Lipsitz argue that there is manifest power in what they call places of possibility (like the arts, education, and social movements) to bring about new forms of democratic social change.[32] Carter finds such a place of possibility in Black communities, specifically post-Katrina New Orleans.[33] We will keep claiming space in schools, sports, recreation, housing, and elsewhere. Wherever decisions are made, we will be there. It is part of first-class citizenship.

A subset of claiming space is the idea of *reclaiming* space. Carter describes the activities of a local antiviolence movement in New Orleans. Religious leaders are active participants, and so are the mothers of young people lost to violence. These grieving mothers hold birthday parties for their deceased children on the sites of their loss or other important public places. They reclaim space. According to Carter, their acts of reclamation allow the women to "grieve well." Carter writes, "Grieve well and you grow stronger."[34] The reclaimed sites transform places of violence into places of protest, memory, and commemoration. We will reclaim space.

We will fight until all Black lives matter

We will not be content with the liberation of only some Black people from the shackles of oppression, and we will fight until *all* Black people—male, female, young, old, LGBTQ, and a host of other intersectional identities—are free from discrimination and negative or disparate outcomes. Ella Baker said, "Freedom is a constant struggle." BOP is attentive to intersectional identities. We will fight because all lives won't matter until all Black lives matter, and, in declaring the value of our intersectional lives, we will affirm the lives and struggles of others and join in their fight.

We will define ourselves

In her agenda-raising book *Black Feminist Thought*, Patricia Hill Collins makes an important declaration about self-definition and active resistance against being defined by the controlling images in the world. Self-definition, Collins cautions, is essential to survival. Self-definition represents "the journey from internalized oppression to the 'free mind.'" Self-definition is liberating because it rejects both the definitions of others and the peril of internalization, which often leads to self-harm. Black culture, including music, dress, hair, literature, and Black epistemologies are a way to affirm our worth. As our ancestors before us, we will free our minds. And self-definition, Collins writes, fosters action.[35]

We will breathe

Even if it is with our last breath, we will change the world. In the church tradition in which I was raised and unabashedly embrace today, we say you have to lay your burdens down and leave them there. George Floyd can only rest in power if we pick up his burden. We become ministering angels on the earth. In essence, we become the mama that George Floyd cried out for that day. Rest in power, George Floyd. Rest in power.

We will reclaim our bodies and find spaces and moments of joy

Black people find joy in community. While we work for the worldwide beloved community, we will never ignore or dismantle the Black community, which has offered us such spaces and moments of great joy. This book largely examines practices of virulent racial entrenchment manifested in post-Obama expressions of anti-blackness as seen in discursive, legal, interactional, and extralegal contexts. In *Hunger: A Memoir of (My) Body*, Roxanne Gay writes, "Every body has a story and a history." She asserts, "I am determined to be more than my body ... what my body has endured."[36]

In addition to community, spaces and moments of joy can be found in pushing past boundaries to where the Black body is uninhibited and Black individuals are free to express themselves as they like. UCLA gymnast Nia Dennis uses her body to pay tribute to Black culture. Watching her is like seeing poetry in motion. She moves across the floor with dignity, grace, confidence, and beauty to the beat of music—Beyoncé, Kendrick Lamar, 2Pac, Missy Elliott, Soulja Boy, and Megan Thee Stallion. With each motion, Dennis both dissents against and redefines the politics of respectability surrounding women's performances. In an episode of the television show *Any Day Now*, a drama featuring flashbacks of scenes from segregated Birmingham, Alabama, during the 1960s, young Rene touts, "Aunt Kiki says colored people are free and uninhibited. She says moving your whole body is a celebration [of that]."[37] We will regulate our bodies as we see fit.

Even in contemporary U.S. society, there are boundless examples of institutional and individual examples of Whites trying to exert control over Black bodies. In 2018, Dallas Cowboys football team owner Jerry Jones stood in solidarity with President Trump and insisted his players stand with "toes on the line" during the playing of the national anthem. Jones's order reflected a slaveholder mentality. When Georgia's Kelly Loeffler, a part owner of the WNBA Atlanta Dream, was in the midst of a reelection campaign for her U.S. Senate seat and spoke out against the WNBA's support of the Black Lives Matter movement, the largely minority Atlanta Dream team members responded. They adorned their bodies with Warnock for Senate T-shirts (Raphael Warnock was Loeffler's opponent in the race), posed for photos, and then posted these images for the world to see. Then they went out into the community and campaigned for Warnock. Additionally, they urged the league to remove Loeffler from its board and encouraged her to sell her interest in the Atlanta Dream. Warnock won the Senate race. Black bodies tell a story, but it is not simply a story of oppression. So, as we celebrate our beautiful, talented, Black community of overcomers and believers, we will continue to proudly hail Black excellence in all its forms and to push back against those who say "Why does it have to always be about being Black?" It is more than about our bodies. It is about our community—our proud, Black community of bodies.

Conclusion

I want to say a few parting words about myself. My identities have been central to my examination in this book, especially my race and gender. I am a race scholar. I claim that title as much by virtue of the fact that I have a PhD in sociology and write, teach, and do research on contemporary race relations as I do by virtue of my 55 years of lived experience. My father has been deceased for over 20 years now, but I still remember his words encouraging me to pursue higher education. He said, "Baby girl, there's two ways to make it in this world: common sense or an education." Then he looked at me with all the love a father should have for his child, and he continued, "You gon' need an education." One thing I am certain my father would agree with is that you do not need fancy degrees or titles to realize that anti-Black racism is as brazen now as it has been at almost any point in U.S. history.

My father was right about a lot of things. But, while he loved me, he was not a Black woman. Surviving in a world that values neither your blackness nor your gender requires an *uncommon* common sense, and that is an education you cannot get in school. Only life teaches you this. Thriving in this world, in this skin, and with these identities makes some people angry. Perhaps that is why I was not surprised when former Louisiana governor Bobby Jindal wrote, "[Kamala Harris's] family is an immigrant success story. So why does she prefer to play victim?"[38] Similarly, I was not surprised to hear one commentator express rage that throughout her vice presidential debate (with Republican candidate Mike Pence) Senator Harris did not use "appropriate" courtesy titles when speaking about the then-current president. That charge reminded of a story Isabel Wilkerson relays in her book *Caste: The Origins of Our Discontents*. Wilkerson introduces the reader to Miss. She writes, "Her name is Miss. It is only Miss. It is Miss for a reason."[39] Growing up in Alabama, Miss's father witnessed his mother and grandmother constantly being disrespected by Whites that refused to show them even basic courtesies. Miss's father decided to outwit them all, and he pledged to name his firstborn girl Miss. This subversive act of naming would force White society to say her name and put some respect on it. He wanted to make sure his daughter was afforded the title his mother and grandmother had been unfairly denied. The irony inherent in the charge levied against Kamala Harris, now Vice President Harris, seemed to be lost on her accuser. It was not lost on me. He seemed upset about a purported 90 minutes of disrespect. I wondered where his outrage was for the 450-plus years of subjugation—in its various forms—that Black women have suffered. I do not in any way wish to suggest that either the effect or intent of Senator Harris's language choice (in not using honorifics) was disrespect. In fact, at the start of her vice presidential debate she told the moderator to feel free to call her "Kamala," and she constantly referred to her running mate as "Joe." But these are things my multiple identities allow me to see. Today America has its first female vice president, and she is a woman of color. But we should not be so naive as to think that means racial and gender discrimination has subsided.

Author, scholar, and critic Joan Morgan asserts, "Black women can see the forest and the trees."[40] Other groups have this kind of vision too, but it is keener in Black women. Our multiple disadvantages sharpen our focus and heighten our understanding of the workings of various facets of society. Black women permeate every walk of American life—from the highest spots to the lowest. We are, at once, hypervisible and invisible, and the latter allows us to see without being seen and understand without being understood. That is our lament and our joy. As basketball coach Doc Rivers noted, "It's amazing why we [Blacks] keep loving this country, and this country does not love us back."[41] But Black women, who are subjected to racism in society and sexism in our homes, community and the larger society, know that there is not only a thin line between love and hate, they also often coexist. We love the promise of this country, and we hate that that promise, the promise of Reconstruction, is yet unfulfilled.

I cannot dance. I mean, not to save my life. I have the proverbial two left feet. In my youth, I heard many people say that White people could not dance, but cable television and then social media imploded that fiction for me. However, I have come to wonder if it was a metaphorical dance that was being discussed. To keep our sanity, some Black folks learn to do this two-step dance of deference and strength. Many Whites do not. The night of the vice presidential debate, Kamala Harris danced beautifully.

Despite claims to the contrary, racialized ideologies that demonize Black life and culture pervade the United States. These views suggest and assert that Black bodies in certain neighborhoods, schools, organizations, and positions are out of place. Kamala Harris's run for the White House is a tale of Black dignity and self-definition. To paraphrase former Supreme Court justice Ruth Bader Ginsburg, it is a bold declaration that Black women belong in all places where decisions are being made. There will be no blackout. Black people belong in all places where decisions are being made, and to quote Ella Baker, "We who believe in freedom cannot rest until it comes." Selah.

NOTES

INTRODUCTION

1. Ernest Allen Jr., "Ever Feeling One's Twoness: 'Double Ideals' and 'Double Consciousness' in *The Souls of Black Folk*," *Contributions in Black Studies* 9/10 (1992): 55–69. In *Souls*, Du Bois calls double consciousness "a peculiar sensation . . . this sense of always looking at one's self through the eyes of others, of measuring one's soul by the tape of a world that looks on in amused contempt and pity. One ever feels his twoness—an American, a Negro; two souls, two thoughts, two unreconciled strivings; two warring ideals in one dark body, whose dogged strength alone keeps it from being torn asunder." Later in *Souls*, Du Bois writes, "The Negro is a sort of seventh son, born with a veil, and gifted with second-sight in this American world,—a world which yields him no true self-consciousness, but only lets him see himself through the revelation of the other world." W. E. B. Du Bois, *The Souls of Black Folk* (1903; repr., New York: Oxford University Press, 2008), 8. Allen makes the point that double-consciousness and twoness are related but distinct: "The sole, positive attribute associated with African American duality [inherent in double-consciousness] was to be culled from the 'gift of second sight.'" Allen, "Ever Feeling One's Twoness," 65.

2. Audre Lorde, "The Master's Tools Will Never Dismantle the Master's House," in *This Bridge Called My Back: Writings by Radical Women of Color*, ed. Cherríe Moraga and Gloria Anzaldúa (New York: Kitchen Table, Women of Color Press, 1983), 98–101.

3. I am struck by Simone Browne's insights on this dance revealed in *Dark Matters: On the Surveillance of Blackness*. Browne discusses what she calls "performances of freedom and suggestions of alternatives to ways of living under routinized surveillance." See Simone Browne, *Dark Matters: On the Surveillance of Blackness* (Durham, N.C.: Duke University Press, 2015), 8.

4. Ibid., 5.

5. Megan M. Wood, "Dark Matters: On the Surveillance of Blackness," *Surveillance and Society* 14, no. 2 (2016): 286–288.

6. Lisa Bloom, *Suspicion Nation: The Inside Story of the Trayvon Martin Injustice and Why We Continue to Repeat It* (Berkeley, Calif.: Counterpoint, 2015).

7. Barbara Harris Combs, "Black (and Brown) Bodies out of Place: Towards a Theoretical Understanding of Systematic Voter Suppression in the United States," *Critical Sociology* 42, nos. 4–5 (2016): 535–549.

8. The growth of voter identification laws began en masse after the first election of Barack Obama to the highest position in the land was accomplished through the support of a coalition of minority voters, including White women.

9. While the term "Black bodies" is somewhat problematic, I remain committed to this characterization because it serves the twofold purposes of allowing the discussion to focus on intersectional Black identity, and it allows other non-Black subjugated bodies to see ways the theory might be useful for interrogating their experiences in society.

10. In *Black Reconstruction in America*, Du Bois discusses the psychological wage of whiteness. This psychological wage is only able to be realized through the devaluation of Black existence; this is especially the case for poorer Whites. See W. E. B. Du Bois, *Black Reconstruction in America*, ed. Henry Louis Gates Jr. (New York: Oxford University Press, 2014); and Khalil Gibran Muhammad, *The Condemnation of Blackness: Race, Crime, and the Making of Modern Urban America* (Cambridge, Mass.: Harvard University Press, 2010).

11. This book concentrates on the embodied experiences of Blacks in the United States; however, as Charles Mills notes, it is important to understand that White supremacy is a global phenomenon.

12. A further stratification occurs among Black bodies that privileges male Black bodies.

13. Richard Wormser and Bill Jersey, *The Rise and Fall of Jim Crow* (New York: St. Martin's Press. 2003); C. Vann Woodward, *The Strange Career of Jim Crow* (New York: Oxford University Press, 2001).

14. Michael Klarman, *From Jim Crow to Civil Rights: The Supreme Court and the Struggle for Racial Equality* (1994; repr., New York: Oxford University Press, 2006), 5–6, argues that judges tend to read their own values into the Constitution, some to a lesser extent than others. According to Klarman, such reading occurs in the pull between political and legal axes.

15. Gary Orfield and Erica Frankenberg, with Jongyeon Ee and John Kuscera, "Brown at 60: Great Progress, a Long Retreat and an Uncertain Future," Civil Rights Project / Proyecto Derechos Civiles, May 15, 2014, https://civilrightsproject.ucla.edu/research/k-12-education/integration-and-diversity/brown-at-60-great-progress-a-long-retreat-and-an-uncertain-future.

16. The spaces include neighborhoods that are deemed Black or White, respectively, but can also be found in other aspects of life, including career choices, recreational activities, and religious or other cultural expressions.

17. Violence will be defined more fully in chapter 3. However, I want to make clear that due to the legacy of slavery, the disproportionate violence to which Black bodies are subjected includes the violence of hunger, food insecurity, being educated in substandard schools, and living next to hazards.

18. Mickey Guyton, "What Are You Gonna Tell Her?," on *Bridges* (UMG Recordings, 2020).

CHAPTER 1. Testify

1. Frederick Douglass, letter to Ida B. Wells, in Ida B. Wells-Barnett, *The Red Record* (Frankfurt: Outlook Verlag, [1895] 2018), preface, accessible via Project Gutenberg, https://www.gutenberg.org/files/14977/14977-h/14977-h.htm.

2. Amanda Gorman, "The Hill We Climb," recited at the presidential inauguration of Joe Biden, January 21, 2021.

3. Howard Winant, *The World Is a Ghetto: Race and Democracy since World War II* (New York: Basic Books, 2001). Winant says racism should be understood by its consequences and not the intent or beliefs of actors.

4. Howard Winant, "Durban, Globalization, and the World after 9/11: Toward a New Politics," *Poverty and Race* (Poverty & Race Research Action Council), January/February 2002, 21, https://www.prrac.org/durban-globalization-and-the-world-after-9-11-toward-a-new-politics.

5. Michael Omi and Howard Winant, *Racial Formation in the United States*, 3rd ed. (New York: Routledge, 2015), 110.

6. Bryan S. Turner, *The Body and Society: Explorations in Social Theory*, 3rd (Thousand Oaks, Calif.: Sage Publications, 2008). When I speak about bodies, I am not talking about flesh or fleshy things; however, this idea is useful as a vehicle for understanding how some bodies are thought of and treated as less than human. Human beings are capable of reason, and they are entitled to humanity and dignity. My focus on bodies considers the body less as a fleshy thing and more as a site on which violence is enacted, but I also consider the ways in which individuals and groups have resisted that bondage and asserted control over their own bodies.

7. Biopolitics is a kind of politics of the body. It is a form of government in which populations are regulated through biopower—a type of political power that governs all aspects of human life. The study of anatomy and disease was an important aspect of the emergence of biopower. In this, we see people being judged by their deviation from a norm regarding their health and anatomy. Anatomo-politics gave way to biopolitics. See Vanessa Lemm and Miguel Vatter, eds., *The Government of life: Foucault, Biopolitics, and Neoliberalism* (New York: Fordham University Press, 2014).

8. For Foucault, the norms that anatomo-politics birthed gave way to a new kind of constraint that was largely free of coercion. The norms in society became associated with a kind of truthfulness or reality that masquerades as knowledge. By this I mean that the beliefs of those in power are represented as the truth. All bodies were judged in terms of their relation to the norm. When bodies do not conform to the normative standards they are presumed deviant. In a health context, people who deviated from the healthy norms of society would be viewed as deserving of death. A parallel exists today when out-of-place Black bodies are deemed deserving of the punishment they receive (up to and including death).

9. Some racial enclosures are less totalitarian and rigid than others, but they are all constraining.

10. Bryan S. Turner, *Regulating Bodies: Essays in Medical Sociology* (New York: Routledge, 1992), 12–13.

11. Harvey Young, *Embodying Black Experience: Stillness, Critical Memory and the Black Body* (Ann Arbor: University of Michigan Press, 2010), 99.

12. George Yancy, *Black Bodies, White Gazes: The Continuing Significance of Race*, 2nd ed. (Lanham, Md.: Rowman & Littlefield, 2016), xxx.

13. Osagie Obasogie, *Blinded by Sight: Seeing Race through the Eyes of the Blind* (Stanford: Stanford University Press, 2013), 3.

14. Ibid., 54, 174. Parents and guardians might refuse to let a child play with someone of another race. Friends also indicated disapproval of racial mixing. Obasogie found some blind people would specifically seek out information about a person's race. This information mattered to them.

15. Michel Foucault, *Discipline and Punish* (New York: Vintage Books, 1995), 136.

16. Hortense J. Spillers, *Black, White and in Color: Essays on American Literature and Culture* (Chicago: University of Chicago Press, 2003), 206.

17. Glenn E. Bracey II and Wendy Leo Moore, "'Race Tests': Racial Boundary Maintenance in White Evangelical Churches," *Sociological Inquiry* 87 (2017), https://doi.org/10.1111/soin .12174, 282, 285.

18. Loïc Wacquant, "'A Black City within the White': Revisiting America's Dark Ghetto," *Renaissance* 2, no.1 (1998): 141–151.

19. *Being Black in Corporate America: An Intersectional Exploration* (Coqual, 2019).

20. "Racial Bias in the Workplace," *CBS This Morning*, February 11, 2021, https://www.cbs .com/shows/cbs_this_morning/video/vg5XF1PIRlkOUtc4UMicXQBPKZZLTtJz /linkedin-and-cbs-this-morning-on-challenges-black-professionals-face-in-the-workplace.

21. My definition of White supremacy is consistent with one offered by the Anti-Defamation League (ADL). The ADL argues that White supremacy is larger than racism or bigotry. It includes beliefs about the genetic, mental, and cultural superiority of Whites; the desirability of separation of the races; and the dominance of Whites. As such, I view the MAGA (Make America Great Again) movement as a White supremacist order.

22. Brandi Thompson Summers, *Black in Place: The Spatial Aesthetics of Race in a Post-Chocolate City* (Chapel Hill: University of North Carolina Press, 2019).

23. Summers's book tells a story of the political economy and how, for the singular purpose of capital gain, communities have been displaced. This displacement has been accomplished by parties being dispossessed of their land and through misappropriation of their culture. In Summers's text, gentrification is the tool used to accomplish this end.

24. Summers, *Black in Place*, 3–4.

25. Merriam-Webster.com Dictionary, s.v. "testify," accessed June 27, 2020, https://www .merriam-webster.com/dictionary/testify.

26. On September 15, 1883, Ida B. Wells boarded a train traveling from Memphis, Tennessee, to her teaching appointment in nearby Woodstock. After Wells seated herself in the rear car (with White men and women), she was told to move to the forward car. The forward car contained Black and White passengers, and, unlike the rear car, smoking and drinking were allowed there. Wells would not move, and several White men (including a railroad employee) tried to forcibly remove her. Wells bit one of the men, and she exited the train on her own volition. Wells then filed a suit against the railroad. An 1882 statute required that trains provide equal accommodations for its non-White passengers. Wells's suit argued that the railroad violated this law. Wells won in the lower court, but in April 1885 the Tennessee Supreme Court

reversed that decision and found in favor of the railroad. See "Ida B. Wells Case," Digital Public Library of America, http://dp.la/item/8fdc4cecc932be68b7af2180ed2468d8.

27. Barnett, *Red Record*. Wells explores and debunks the reasons given for what Frederick Douglass termed "Southern barbarism" against Blacks. In this book I attempt to do the same.

28. Ibid.

29. Ibid., chap. 1, "The Case Stated."

30. Ida B. Wells, *Southern Horrors: Lynch Law in All Its Phases* (Project Gutenberg, 1892 [2005]), preface, https://www.gutenberg.org/files/14975/14975-h/14975-h.htm.

31. Quoted in Dean Myers, *Now Is Your Time! The African American Struggle for Freedom* (New York: Amistad, 1991), 210.

32. Ida B. Wells-Barnett, *Lynch Law in Georgia* (Chicago: [1899]), https://www.loc.gov /item/91898209.

33. Paula Giddings, *Ida: A Sword among Lions: Ida B. Wells and the Campaign against Lynching* (New York: Amistad, 2009), 346–347.

34. Large groups of Whites gathered to witness some lynchings, evidencing that the activity was widely and sometimes enthusiastically supported by large numbers of Whites. See Amy Louise Wood, *Lynching and Spectacle: Witnessing Racial Violence in America, 1890–1940* (Chapel Hill: University of North Carolina Press, 2009).

35. In its unanimous decision in *Brown v. Board of Education*, 347 U.S. 483 (1954), the U.S. Supreme Court opined that segregation in the public schools had a detrimental effect on African American children. The decision stated, "Whatever may have been the extent of psychological knowledge at the time of *Plessy v. Ferguson*, this finding is amply supported by modern authority." See 347 U.S. at 494. Then, at footnote 11, the court cited the work of social scientist K. B. Clark, "Effect of Prejudice and Discrimination on Personality Development," paper presented at the Mid-century White House Conference on Children and Youth, 1950; Gunnar Myrdal, *An American Dilemma: The Negro Problem and Modern Democracy* (New York: Harper, 1944); and others for this proposition.

36. *Brown v. Board of Education of Topeka*, 347 U.S. 483 (1954).

37. Scott Brewer, "Scientific Expert Testimony and Intellectual Due Process," *Yale Law Journal* 107 (1998), 1553; Stephen B. Presser, review of Douglas Gerber, *To Secure These Rights: The Declaration of Independence and Constitutional Interpretation*, 1995, *Constitutional Commentary* 14, no. 1 (1977): 229–230, 229. This note does not address the subsequent controversy regarding the validity of the Clarks' findings. I only use it to support the power of social scientific findings to influence culture, law, and thereby society. For a contrary reading, see Anjay Mody, "Brown Footnote Eleven in Historical Context: Social Science and the Supreme Court's Quest for Legitimacy," *Stanford Law Review* 54, no. 4 (2002): 793.

38. Dylan Thomas, "Do Not Go Gentle into that Good Night," in *Country Sleep and Other Poems* (London: J. M. Dent, 1951).

39. Michael J. Klarman, "How *Brown* Changed Race Relations: The Backlash Thesis," *Journal of American History* 81, no. 1 (1994): 81–118. At pages 101–118, Klarman emphasizes *Brown's* role in crystallizing Southern Whites' desire to maintain educational and social segregation and the beginnings of the Massive Resistance Movement. Massive Resistance was a campaign of new state laws to thwart desegregation. The Southern Manifesto (formally titled the "Decla-

ration of Constitutional Principles") also comes out of this period. Approximately 100 federal legislators from both houses signed the document alleging the *Brown* decision was a violation of states' rights. In many communities, whole school systems shut down rather than integrate.

40. Michael J. Klarman, *From Jim Crow to Civil Rights: The Supreme Court and the Struggle for Racial Equality* (New York: Oxford University Press, 2004).

41. In a February 10, 1966, convocation address to Illinois Wesleyan University, Martin Luther King Jr. discussed the idea that you cannot legislate morality. King said, "While it may be true that morality cannot be legislated, behavior can be regulated. It may be true that a law cannot change the heart, but it can restrain the heartless." "Dr. Martin Luther King, Jr. Speech at Illinois Wesleyan University," Illinois Wesleyan University, https://www.iwu.edu/mlk/.

42. Chester Pierce, "Psychiatric Problems of the Black Minority," In *American Handbook of Psychiatry*, ed. Arieti Silvano (New York: Basic Books, 1974), 512–523.

43. Zora Neale Hurston, *Dust Tracks on a Road: An Autobiography* (New York: Harper Perennial, 1996), 176.

44. Etienne G. Krug, Linda L. Dahlberg, James A. Mercy, Anthony B. Zwi, and Rafael Lozano, *World Report on Violence and Health* (Geneva: World Health Organization, 2002), https://www.refworld.org/docid/54aa8f744.html.

45. Chris Samuel, "Symbolic Violence and Collective Identity: Pierre Bourdieu and the Ethics of Resistance," *Social Movement Studies* 12, no. 4 (2013): 397–413.

46. Johan Galtung, "Violence, Peace, and Peace Research," *Journal of Peace Research* 6, no. 3 (1969): 167–191.

47. Seema R. Patrikar, "Study in Domestic Violence against Women in India: Determinants and Consequences," PhD thesis, Gokhale Institute of Politics and Economics, 2014, chapter 1, 21, https://dspace.gipe.ac.in/xmlui/handle/10973/34588.

48. Erving Goffman, *Frame Analysis* (New York: Harper & Row, 1974).

49. Ibid., 64. Emphasis added.

50. David T. Wellman, *Portraits of White Racism*, 2nd ed. (New York: Cambridge University Press, 1993), xi.

51. Sociologist Victor Ray has developed a theory of racialized organizations. Ray suggests organizations can be thought of as meso-level racial structures. See Victor Ray, "A Theory of Racialized Organizations," *American Sociological Review* 84, no. 1 (2019): 26–53.

52. L. A. Bell, C. R. Castaneda, and X. Zuniga, "Racism: Introduction," 59–66, in *Readings for Diversity and Social Justice* 4th ed., edited by Maurianne Adams et al. (New York: Routledge, 2018), 66.

53. Eviatar Zerubavel, *Social Mindscapes: An Invitation to Cognitive Sociology* (Cambridge, Mass.: Harvard University Press, 1999).

54. Eviatar Zerubavel, "Lumping and Splitting: Notes on Social Classification," *Sociological Forum* 11, no. 3 (1996): 421–33.

55. Ibid., 39.

56. See Barbara Harris Combs, "Black (and Brown) Bodies out of Place: Towards a Theoretical Understanding of Systematic Voter Suppression in the United States," *Critical Sociology*, 42, nos. 4–5 (2016): 535–49; Barbara Harris Combs, "No Rest for the Weary: The Weight of Race, Gender, and Place inside and outside a Southern Classroom," *Sociology of Race and Ethnicity*

3, no. 4 (2017): 491–505; Barbara Harris Combs, "Everyday Racism Is Still Racism: The Role of Place in Theorizing Continuing Racism in Modern U.S. Society," *Phylon* 55, nos. 1–2 (2018): 38–59; Thomas F. Gieryn, "A Space for Place in Sociology," *Annual Review of Sociology* 26 (2000): 463–496; Eduardo Bonilla-Silva, "More than Prejudice: Restatement, Reflections, and New Directions in Critical Race Theory," *Sociology of Race and Ethnicity* 1, no. 1 (2015): 75–89; Barbara Harris Combs, "A Jim Crow State of Mind: The Racialization of Space in the McKinney, Texas Pool Party Incident," *American Behavioral Scientist* 65, no. 8 (2021): 1027–1048.

57. Nirmal Puwar, *Space Invaders: Race, Gender, and Bodies out of Place* (Oxford, England: Berg, 2004).

58. Nirmal Puwar, "The Racialised Somatic Norm and the Senior Civil Service," *Sociology* 35, no. 3 (August 2001): 651. Puwar is describing the British senior service system.

59. See Charles Mills, *The Racial Contract* (Ithaca: Cornell University Press, 1997); Carole Pateman, *The Sexual Contract* (Stanford: Stanford University Press, 1988).

60. Mills, *Racial Contract*, 53.

61. Cheryl Harris, "Whiteness as Property," *Harvard Law Review* 106, no. 8 (1993): 1709–1791.

62. Sherene Razack, ed., *Race, Space, and the Law: Unmapping a White Settler Society* (Toronto: Between the Lines, 2002), 15.

63. Combs, "Black (and Brown) Bodies Out of Place."

64. Puwar, *Space Invaders*, 8.

65. Susan Hanson, "Gender and Mobility: New Approaches for Informing Sustainability," *Gender, Place and Culture: A Journal of Feminist Geography* 17, no. 1 (2010) 5–23.

66. See Devon W. Carbado and Cheryl I. Harris, "Intersectionality at 30: Mapping the Margins of Anti-Essentialism, Intersectionality, and Dominance Theory," *Harvard Law Review* 132, no. 8 (2019): 2193–2239 for an overview of insights since Kimberlé Crenshaw introduced the term "intersectionality" in "Demarginalizing the Intersection of Race and Sex: A Black Feminist Critique of Antidiscrimination Doctrine, Feminist Theory and Antiracist Politics," *University of Chicago Legal Forum* 1989, no. 1:139–167. At page 140, Crenshaw writes, "Because the intersectional experience is greater than the sum of racism and sexism, any analysis that does not take intersectionality into account cannot sufficiently address the particular manner in which Black women are subordinated."

67. Richard Delgado and Jean Stefancic, *Critical Race Theory: An Introduction* (New York: New York University Press, 2012). The first tenet of critical race theory is that racism is not aberrant; instead, it is the ordinary, everyday experience of people of color.

68. On February 23, 2020, an unarmed 25-year-old Black man named Ahmaud Arbery was jogging through a predominantly White middle-class neighborhood in Brunswick, Georgia. During his run, Mr. Arbery stopped by the site of a house under construction. He went in and looked around. Video surveillance shows he did not take anything. Two residents of the neighborhood (a father and son, respectively named Gregory and Travis McMichael) witnessed Arbery running. The father later said he believed Arbery had been burglarizing the neighborhood and called for his son to get his weapon; then the two pursued Arbery. A third resident, Roddie Bryan, is also said to have assisted in the chase. After the McMichaels and Bryan cornered Arbery, a fight ensued over the weapon. Arbery was shot several times and died of his

wounds. It took 74 days for the McMichaels to be charged with his death. It took even longer for Bryan to be charged. On March 13, 2020, a 25-year-old black woman named Breonna Taylor was shot and killed by police as she slept in her Louisville, Kentucky, apartment. Police entered the home at night under a no-knock warrant. Taylor's boyfriend, who was licensed to carry a firearm, shot at the intruders. Police fired 20 rounds; eight hit Taylor. The main subject of the police investigation did not reside at Taylor's address, but police believed he was connected to Taylor.

69. The spring and summer of 2020 were a period of protracted racial unrest in the United States. Just a week before the Travis Miller incident, the father and son accused of falsely imprisoning and killing Ahmaud Arbery were finally arrested. The weeks after the Miller incident were also fraught. A white woman in Central Park, incensed because a Black man birding in the protected Ramble area there rebuked her for being in violation of the rules by not having her dog on a leash, used her white privilege to threaten to weaponize the police against him because of the rebuke. The woman called police and falsely accused the Black man of assaulting her. Later in the week, George Floyd was killed by police in Minneapolis. Floyd was killed during an encounter in which one officer restrained him by pressing his knee into the prostrate man's neck and holding it there for over nine minutes. Other officers participated in the restraint. The encounter was recorded. Throughout the exchange, Floyd repeatedly cried, "I can't breathe." Despite this, the Travis Miller incident was my ignition point.

70. Mariel Padilla, "Black Deliveryman Says He Was Blocked and Interrogated by White Driver," *New York Times* May 17, 2020.

71. The incident occurred in Ashford Hills subdivision in Edmond, Oklahoma. According to the US Census (Population Estimates 2019, V2019), Edmond, Oklahoma, is 80.2% White alone (75.4% if you do not count those who identify as Hispanic White), 5.3% Black, 2.0% American Indian, 3.4% Asian, 7.7% "two or more race," 0.0% Native Hawaiian or other Pacific Islander, and 6.6% Hispanic or Latino. "QuickFacts: Edmond city, Oklahoma," United States Census Bureau, https://www.census.gov/quickfacts/edmondcityoklahoma.

72. A full-length video of the encounter was posted on YouTube. See All Urban Central, "Black Delivery Driver Starts Crying after Being Held against Will by White Homeowners in Gated Comm," May 14, 2020, https://www.youtube.com/watch?v=8mw5HQ2hufc.

73. Miller said, "I have had things like this happen when I was in Jersey. Normally I would handle myself better. Right now I just need to calm down."

74. All Urban Central, "Black Delivery Driver Starts Crying."

75. Ibid.

76. "'I Literally Cried for Hours After': Delivery Driver Speaks with News 4 after Being Blocked In while on the Job in NE OKC Neighborhood," Oklahoma News 4, May 14, 2020, https://kfor.com/news/local/i-literally-cried-for-hours-after-delivery-driver-speaks-with-news-4-after-being-blocked-in-while-on-the-job-in-ne-okc-neighborhood.

77. An enslaved person accused of any crime committed against a white person was doomed because no testimony could be made by a slave against a white person. Therefore, the enslaved individual's side of the story could never be told in a court of law. Enslaved persons were excluded from juries as well. After "freedom," Blacks continued to be excluded from juries

through most of the modern civil rights movement. Today attacks on voting rights continue to disenfranchise countless African Americans.

78. Michel Foucault, *The Order of Things: An Archaeology of the Human Sciences* (New York: Routledge, 2002).

79. Lindsey Bever and Robert Costa, "9 Dead in Shooting at Historic Charleston African American Church: Police Chief Calls It Hate Crime," *Washington Post*, June 17, 2015.

80. Maya Angelou, *Phenomenal Woman: Four Poems Celebrating Women* (New York: Random House, 1994).

81. Rob Rapley, *Reconstruction: America after the Civil War* (Arlington, Va.: PBS, 2019), video.

82. John Stauffer, Zoe Trodd, and Celeste-Marie Bernier, *Picturing Frederick Douglass: An Illustrated Biography of the Nineteenth Century's Most Photographed American* (New York: Liveright, 2015).

83. Abigail Cain, "How Frederick Douglass Harnessed the Power of Portraiture to Reframe Blackness in America," *Artsy*, February 2, 2017, https://www.artsy.net/article/artsy-editorial-frederick-douglass-photographed-american-19th-century.

84. Shawn Michelle Smith, *Photography on the Color Line: W. E. B. Du Bois, Race, and Visual Culture* (Durham, N.C.: Duke University Press, 2004). Smith has written further about these images in *American Archives: Gender, Race, and Class in Visual Culture* (Princeton University Press, 1999) and in "Looking at One's Self through the Eyes of Others: W. E. B. Du Bois's Photographs for the 1900 Paris Exposition," *African American Review* 34, no. 4 (Winter 2000): 581–599.

85. This quote from Shawn Michelle Smith appears at the Library of Congress site that houses the Paris Exhibition. See "African American Photographs Assembled for 1900 Paris Exposition," https://www.loc.gov/pictures/collection/anedub/dubois.html.

86. Giddings, *Ida*.

87. Ida B. Wells, *Crusade for Justice: The Autobiography of Ida B. Wells*, 2nd ed. (Chicago: University of Chicago Press, 2020), 57.

88. Sandra Gunning, *Race, Rape, and Lynching: The Red Record of American Literature, 1890–1912* (New York: Oxford University Press, 1996), 4.

89. Brenda Wall, *The Rodney King Rebellion: A Psychopolitical Analysis of Racial Despair and Hope* (Chicago: University of Chicago Press, 1992).

90. David Montgomery, "Sandra Bland, It Turns Out, Filmed Traffic Stop Confrontation Herself," *New York Times*, May 7, 2019.

91. Mills, *Racial Contract*, 11.

92. Baldwin in Raoul Peck, *I Am Not Your Negro* (N.p.: Velvet Film, 2016).

93. This book specifically considers the experience of people of African descent in America, but because I consider a long historical record, I sometimes use different terms, including "Black," "African American," and "enslaved persons" to provide more clarity for the period under examination. I am mindful that some reject the term "African American." I use it largely to reflect the insights reflected in Du Bois's conceptualization of double consciousness.

94. Goffman, *Frame Analysis* (New York: Harper & Row, 1974).

95. Joe R. Feagin, *The White Racial Frame: Centuries of Racial Framing and Counter-Framing* (New York: Routledge, 2013); "nature of the problem": Patrikar, "Study in Domestic Violence Against Women in India," chapter 1, 21.

96. Eduardo Bonilla-Silva, *Racism without Racists: Color-Blind Racism and the Persistence of Racial Inequality in America*, 5th ed. (Lanham, Md.: Rowman & Littlefield, 2018), 33.

97. Bracey and Moore, "Race Tests," 284–285.

98. Shannon Sullivan, *Revealing Whiteness: The Unconscious Habits of Racial Privilege* (Bloomington: Indiana University Press, 2006), 10.

99. Martin Luther King Jr., *Strength to Love* (1963; repr., Minneapolis: Fortress Press, 2010), 39.

100. Karl Marx, "Theses on Feuerbach," 1845, thesis 11, Marxists Internet Archive, https://www.marxists.org/archive/marx/works/1845/theses/index.htm.

101. Toni Morrison, "Toni Morrison Talks with Michel Martin about *Mercy*," *All Things Considered*, December 10, 2008.

102. Deborah Jacobs, a law enforcement expert and former executive director of the New Jersey chapter of the American Civil Liberties Union, turned the notion of a few bad apples on its head. In describing the pattern of abuse and torture that former Chicago police chief John Burge and his subordinates used to illicit false confessions from hundreds of Black men, Jacobs stated, "Patterns tell you that you have a bad orchard, not just a bad apple." Quoted in Sarah Macaraeg and Yana Kunichoff, "Nothing Happens to the Police: Forced Confessions Go Unpunished in Chicago," *Guardian*, January 28, 2016.

CHAPTER 2. This I Believe

1. Lewis R. Gordon, *Bad Faith and Anti-Black Racism* (New York: Humanity Books, 1995), ix.

2. Emile Durkheim, *The Rules of Sociological Method*, 8th ed. (Chicago: University of Chicago Press, 1938). First published in French in 1895.

3. Aída Hurtado, "Theory in the Flesh: Toward an Endarkened Epistemology," *Qualitative Studies in Education* 16:2 (2003): 219.

4. Stuart Hall, "Encoding/Decoding," in *Culture, Media, Language* (London: Hutchinson, 1980), 128–138.

5. Patricia Hill Collins, "Learning from the Outsider Within: The Sociological Significance of Black Feminist Thought," *Social Problems* 33, no. 6 (1986): s14–s32. See also Patricia Hill Collins, *Black Feminist Thought: Knowledge, Consciousness, and the Politics of Empowerment* (New York: Routledge, 2000).

6. See Cherríe Moraga and Gloria Anzaldúa, "Entering the Lives of Others: Theory in the Flesh," in *This Bridge Called My Back: Writings by Radical Women of Color*, 2nd ed., (New York: Kitchen Table: Women of Color Press, 1983), https://www.colorado.edu/wgst/sites/default/files/attached-files/this_bridge_pdf.pdf.

7. Ibid., 23.

8. Tamara Beauboeuf-Lafontant, *Behind the Mask of the Strong Black Woman: Voice and Embodiment of a Costly Performance* (Philadelphia: Temple University Press, 2009).

9. Moraga and Anzaldúa, "Entering the Lives of Others," 23.

10. Lewis Gordon, *Bad Faith and Antiblack Racism* (Amherst, N.Y.: Humanity Books, 1995).

11. Danielle Sered, "Young Men of Color and the Other Side of Harm," *Vera Report*, December 2014, https://www.vera.org/publications/young-men-of-color-and-the-other-side-of-harm-addressing-disparities-in-our-responses-to-violence.

12. Steven W. Thrasher, "Police Hunt and Kill Black People like Philando Castile. There's No Justice," *Guardian*, June 19, 2017.

13. Paul Zollo, "Keedron Bryant Sings, 'I Just Want to Live,' Written by his Mother," *American Songwriter*, accessed June 1, 2020, https://americansongwriter.com/keedron-bryant-sings-i-just-want-to-live-written-by-his-mother.

14. Stacey Patton, "In America, Black Children Don't Get to Be Children," *Washington Post*, November 26, 2014; Monique W. Morris, *Pushout: The Criminalization of Black Girls in Schools* (New York: The New Press, 2016).

15. Phillip Atiba Goff et al., "The Essence of Innocence: Consequences of Dehumanizing Black Children," *Journal of Personality and Social Psychology* 106, no. 4 (2014): 526–545, https://www.apa.org/pubs/journals/releases/psp-a0035663.pdf.

16. Kareem Abdul-Jabbar, "Don't Understand the Protests? What You're Seeing Is People Pushed to the Edge," *Los Angeles Times*, May 30, 2020.

17. Katherine McKittrick, *Demonic Grounds: Black Women and the Cartographies of Struggle* (Minneapolis: University of Minnesota Press, 2006), xii.

18. "Interpersonal racism" is the term used to describe acts of racism between one person and another. The focus tends to be on how one person is treating another instead of the related systemic issues that might prompt the treatment. Overwhelmingly, this is how people are taught to see racism. People want to believe that racism is the exception and that we live in an equal society. This facilitates the idea that racism as something that is being performed by bad people who are doing something contrary to the norm. In many ways, the terms "systemic racism" and "structural racism" are synonymous, and I use the terms interchangeably, but "structural racism" tends to be used more to address the historical, cultural, and social psychological aspects of our racialized society. To address anti-black systemic racism, we need to look at the systems that are creating a playing field that is not level. Institutional racism includes the structures, policies, and practices (formal and informal) that reinforce racist standards in a workplace or organization. Examples of institutional racism include discriminatory hiring or disciplinary practices, the silence or exclusion of certain voices at various levels of the organization, and a work culture that privileges a White point of view. Internalized racism is conscious or unconscious acceptance of the racist attitudes held by the dominant society about your group. As such, it is a form of internalized oppression. Here the oppressed adopt many of the white supremacist-based beliefs about the inferiority of the group. "Implicit bias" refers to individuals' unconscious attitudes and beliefs. Individuals tend to process information based on unconscious ideologies they have ingrained. Then, based on these learned associations, people act on their biases. These actions contribute to negative treatment of others and negative outcomes for the disfavored group.

19. Donna Bivens, "What Is Internalized Racism," in *Flipping the Script: White Privilege and Community Building*, by Maggie Potapchuk et al. (Silver Springs, Md.: MP Associates; Conshohocken, Pa.: Center for Assessment and Policy Development, 2005), 44.

20. Alejandro de la Fuente and Ariela Gross, *Becoming Free, Becoming Black: Race, Freedom*

and the Law in Cuba, Virginia, and Louisiana (Cambridge, England: Cambridge University Press, 2020), 83.

21. For a time, only White male property owners could vote. Then in Article I Section 4, of the Constitution, the matter of who could vote was left to the states to determine.

22. Martin Luther King Jr., *Why We Can't Wait* (1964; repr., New York: Signet, 2001), 119.

23. Jacob Passy, "How 'Redlining' Still Hurts Home Values," *MarketWatch*, May 5, 2018, https://www.marketwatch.com/story/how-redlining-still-hurts-home-values-2018-04-26.

24. Anne Schindler, "Jacksonville Couple Sees Home Appraisal Jump 40 Percent," *First Coast News* (Jacksonville, FL), August 25, 2020.

25. "Complaint Alleges Discrimination in Woman's Home Appraisals," AP News (Associated Press), May 19, 2021, https://apnews.com/article/race-and-ethnicity-0884c92233ccdb0519 9efc15f7655c7a.

26. Debra Kamin, "Black Homeowners Face Discrimination in Appraisals," *New York Times*, August 25, 2020.

27. Alejandra Borunda, "Racist Housing Policies Have Created Some Oppressively Hot Neighborhoods," *National Geographic*, September 2, 2020, https://www.nationalgeographic .com/science/article/racist-housing-policies-created-some-oppressively-hot-neighborhoods. Borunda cites Jeremy S. Hoffman, Vivek Shandas, and Nicholas Pendleton, "The Effects of Historical Housing Policies on Resident Exposure to Intra-Urban Heat: A Study of 108 U.S. Urban Areas," *Climate* 8, no. 1 (2020): 12, https://doi.org/10.3390/cli8010012.

28. See *Color of Money: Home Mortgage Lending Practices Discriminate Against Blacks* (Atlanta Journal and Atlanta Constitution, 1988), reprint of a four-part series published, May 1–4, 1988, www.powerreporting.com/color/color_of_money.pdf.

29. Mary Van Beusekom, "COVID May Cut U.S. Life Expectancy, Especially in Blacks, Latinos," CIDRAP News (Center for Infectious Disease Research and Policy), January 15, 2021.

30. Michael Geruso, "Black-White Disparities in Life Expectancy: How Much Can the Standard SES Variables Explain," *Demography* 49, no. 2 (May 2012): 553–574.

31. Kriston McIntosh et al., "Examining the Black-White Wealth Gap," Brookings Institution, February 27, 2020, https://www.brookings.edu/blog/up-front/2020/02/27/examining -the-black-white-wealth-gap.

32. Princeton Student Climate Initiative, "Racial Disparities and Climate Change," August 15, 2020, https://psci.princeton.edu/tips/2020/8/15/racial-disparities-and-climate-change.

33. "Racial Disparities and Climate Change," Princeton Student Climate Initiative, August 15, 2020, https://psci.princeton.edu/tips/2020/8/15/racial-disparities-and-climate-change.

34. Qian Di et al., "Air Pollution and Mortality in the Medicare Population," New England Journal of Medicine 376 (2017): 2513–2522, https://www.nejm.org/doi/full/10.1056 /nejmoa1702747.

35. Nina Martin and Renee Montagne, "Nothing Protects Black Women from Dying in Pregnancy and Childbirth," *ProPublica*, December 7, 2017, https://www.propublica.org /article/nothing-protects-black-women-from-dying-in-pregnancy-and-childbirth.

36. Sofia Carratala and Connor Maxwell, "Health Disparities by Race and Ethnicity," Center for American Progress, May 7, 2020, https://www.americanprogress.org/issues/race/reports /2020/05/07/484742/health-disparities-race-ethnicity.

37. Yi-Fu Tuan, *Space and Place: The Perspective of Experience*, 5th ed. (Minneapolis: University of Minnesota Press, 2001), 3.

38. McKittrick, *Demonic Grounds*.

39. Racialized place-based attitudes also facilitate a will to be free and to resist such oppression. The efforts of the oppressed to be free or exert their free will are often met with more violence.

40. Jamie Peck and Adam Tickell, "Neoliberalizing Space," *Antipode: A Radical Journal of Geography* 34, no. 3 (December 2002): 380–404.

41. Vittorio Bufacchi, "Two Concepts of Violence," *Political Studies Review* 3, no. 2 (2005): 193–204.

42. Ibid., 196.

43. Rob Nixon, *Slow Violence and the Environmentalism of the Poor* (Cambridge, Mass.: Harvard University Press, 2011), 2.

44. President Trump formed a 1776 Commission with, among other goals, the purpose of discounting teachings that suggested slavery has shaped the American experience. The commission rejected teaching that the legacy of slavery continues to shape outcomes today.

45. See George Lipsitz's theorization of the "white spatial imaginary." In *How Racism Takes Place* (Philadelphia: Temple University Press, 2011), Lipsitz outlines how hazards and anything noisome are concentrated somewhere else (i.e., outside the white spatial imaginary, which is pure, clean, and homogeneous).

46. Gabriel Abend, "The Meaning of 'Theory,'" *Sociological Theory* 26, no. 2 (June 2008): 173–99.

47. Ibid., 177–178.

48. Gloria Anzaldúa, *Making Face, Making Soul / Haciendo Caras: Creative and Critical Perspectives by Feminists of Color* (San Francisco: Aunt Lute Press, 1990).

49. In earlier writings, I labeled these basic assumptions tenets.

50. Critical race theory is a framework advanced by legal scholars including Derrick Bell and Kimberlé Crenshaw that offers an analytical lens grounded in the proposition that racism is endemic in U.S. society. See Richard Delgado and Jean Stefancic, *Critical Race Theory: An Introduction* (New York: New York University Press, 2012).

51. Daniel G. Solórzano and Tara J. Yosso, "Critical Race Methodology: Counter-Storytelling as an Analytical Framework for Education Research," *Qualitative Inquiry* 8: (2002) 23–44.

52. David Scott, *Conscripts of Modernity: The Tragedy of Colonial Enlightenment* (Durham, N.C.: Duke University Press, 2004), 7.

53. In addition to critical race theory, BOP theory builds on Puwar's concept of "space invaders," Feagin's systemic racism and white racial frame, and Bonilla-Silva's structural racism. Each of these theories offers perceptive insights useful for understanding racial oppression, but, because racism is dynamic, sometimes new theories are necessary to expose it.

54. Nadia E. Brown, "Negotiating the Insider/Outsider Status: Black Feminist Ethnography and Legislative Studies," *Journal of Feminist Scholarship*, 3, no. 3 (2018): 19.

55. James M. Blaut, "The Theory of Cultural Racism," *Antipode: A Radical Journal of Geography*, 24, no. 4 (1992): 289.

56. George Lipsitz, "'Swing Low, Sweet Cadillac': White Supremacy, Antiblack Racism and the New Historicism," *American Literary History* 7, no. 4 (1995): 701.

57. "National Security Advisor: 'I Don't Think There's Systemic Racism' in U.S. Police Forces," CNN, May 31, 2020.

58. Jon Meacham, *The Soul of America: The Battle for Our Better Angels* (New York: Random House, 2018), 15.

59. PRRI, 2013 "American Values Survey." https://www.prri.org/research/poll-race-religion -politics-americans-social-networks.

60. Eduardo Bonilla-Silva, *Racism without Racists: Color-Blind Racism and the Persistence of Racial Inequality in America*, 5th ed.(Lanham, Md.: Rowman & Littlefield, 2018), 156.

61. Ibid., 11.

62. Stuart Elliott, "Vitriol Online for Cheerios Ad with Interracial Family." *New York Times*, May 31, 2013.

63. Stuart Elliott, "An American Family Returns to the Table," *New York Times*, January 28, 2014.

64. In the wake of the growing civil protests against racism in 2020, I have noticed a decided upward tick in the number of romantic interracial couple and friend relationships featured in commercial advertising. This pattern also exists with respect to the representation of other marginalized groups in commercials.

65. Deena Prichep, "A Campus More Colorful than Reality: Beware that College Brochure," *NPR*, December 29, 2013, https://www.npr.org/2013/12/29/257765543/a-campus-more -colorful-than-reality-beware-that-college-brochure.

66. See Edward T. Hall, *The Silent Language* (Garden City, N.Y.: Doubleday, 1959). Hall suggested that there are four types of distances that people keep. Intimate space is about 0 to 18 inches of distance while personal space is approximately 18 inches to 4 feet. Social distance is 4 to 10 feet, and public distance is over 10 feet.

67. See "The King Philosophy—Nonviolence 365," King Center, https://thekingcenter.org /king-philosophy.

68. W. E. B. Du Bois, *Black Reconstruction in America 1860–1880* (New York: Atheneum, 1935); David Roediger, *The Wages of Whiteness: Race and the Making of the American Working Class*, new ed. (New York: Verso, 2007), 12, 13.

69. Mills, *Racial Contact*, 37. Mills argues that the social contract is itself a racial contract and that consent to the racial order is both explicit and tacit. For Mills, White supremacy is the unnamed system that has ruled the world. He calls this system "global white supremacy" because White supremacy is both global and local.

70. Roediger, *Wages of Whiteness*, 137.

71. Ibid., xxi.

72. George Lipsitz, *The Possessive Investment in Whiteness: How White People Profit from Identity Politics*, 20th anniversary ed. (Philadelphia: Temple University Press, 2018), 22.

73. Larry Davis, *Why Are They Angry with Us? Essays on Race* (Chicago: Lyceum Books, 2016), 110.

74. The ecological framework recognizes that with respect to interpersonal violence, no one single factor can explain risk of victimization. Instead, risk of being victimized by interpersonal

violence is based on an interplay of factors at four levels—individual, interpersonal, commu-
nal/community, and societal.

75. Quoted in Scott Jaschik, "The Justices' Questions on Affirmative Action," *Inside Higher
Education*, December 10, 2015, https://www.insidehighered.com/news/2015/12/10/supreme
-court-justices-question-lawyers-key-affirmative-action-case. Brackets and last ellipses in original.

76. Biological notions of race have existed since the 18th century. One of the earliest was
espoused by Carl Linnaeus in his book *The System of Nature*. The book classified humankind
into subgroups and assigned character traits to each group based on the culture and place or
origin. Linnaeus assigned the most favorable attributes to his group "Europeans." Criminology,
which began as a subdiscipline of sociology, also pushed a biological understanding of criminal
nature. After World War II, which was waged to support and advocate eugenics, the United
Nations Educational, Scientific and Cultural Organization (UNESCO) denounced scientific
racism. This denunciation appeared in its 1950 antiracism statement "The Race Question."
The ideas did not go away. There have been numerous revivals of ideas based on these racist
principles. Some of the most notable have been by Nicholas Wade, a science writer for the *New
York Times*, in his book *A Troublesome Inheritance: Genes, Race, and Human History* (New
York: Penguin Press, 2014), and political scientists Charles Murray and Richard Herrnstein, in
their book *The Bell Curve* (Free Press, 1994). Both books were best sellers. Approximately 40
leading geneticists from around the world wrote a letter to the *New York Times Book Review*
and roundly criticized Wade's book. They accused the author of misappropriating and misrepresenting their research to support false arguments about differences among human societies.
While not the main premise of the book, Murray and Herrnstein argued that poor people,
especially poor Black people, are inherently less intelligent than Whites or Asians. The authors'
pseudoscience argued that differences in a host of social outcomes observed across groups are
rooted in genetics.

77. Beckie Supiano, "A Closer Look at the Comment from Justice Scalia that Sparked Outrage," *Chronicle of Higher Education*, December 9, 2015. https://www.chronicle.com/article
/A-Closer-Look-at-a-Comment/234551.

78. See *Fisher v. University of Texas at Austin*, 579 U.S.__(2016).

79. Abby Jackson, "People Are Tweeting a Modified Beyoncé Lyric to Mock," *Business
Insider*, June 27, 2016, https://www.businessinsider.com/what-becky-with-the-bad-grades
-means-2016-6.

80. See Jia Tolentino, "All the Greedy Young Abigail Fishers and Me," *Jezebel*, June 28, 2016.
Tolentino outlines the role Abigail Fisher's class privilege played in her belief that she was entitled to admission at UT Austin. The author highlights Fisher's insistence that she had worked
hard to "earn" it. Tolentino discusses how Texas parents, largely Whites with the economic
means to do so, could shop school districts. They could pay to live in the best school districts,
and they could also pay for tutors and other support to "help" their children craft compelling
essays to get into the colleges of their choice. Tolentino wrote, "The top 7 percent (formerly
10 percent) at all Texas high schools get admitted to UT's flagship campus automatically.
This means that a second-rate student at a first-rate school—a.k.a. an Abigail Fisher, does not
automatically get in. This means that a portion of white kids don't get the educational success
those property taxes were supposed to pay for. " See also Nikole Hannah-Jones, "What Abigail

Fisher's Affirmative Action Case Was Really About," *ProPublica*, June 23, 2016. Hannah-Jones opines that the case was really a battle in the war "to fight race-based policies everywhere."

81. Quoted in Robert Dallek, *Lyndon B. Johnson: Portrait of a President*, (Oxford University Press, 2004), 371.

82. Big Bill Broonzy, "Black, Brown, and White," Track 1. *Black, Brown and White* (Evidence, 1995).

83. Rita Laura Segato, "Territory, Sovereignty, and Crimes of the Second State: The Writing on the Body of Murdered Women," in *Terrorizing Women: Feminicide in the Américas*, by Rosa-Linda Fregoso and Cynthia Bejarano (Durham, N.C.: Duke University Press, 2010), 70–92.

84. By "social imaginary of gender" I mean an expectation (i.e., imagination) about how gender should be performed. Gender, and the assignment of attributes based on gender, becomes a way of organizing society. These hierarchies place men at the top. See also Charles Taylor, *Modern Social Imaginaries* (Durham, N.C.: Duke University Press, 2004), 23. Taylor defines social imaginary as "a common understanding that makes possible common practices and a widely shared sense of legitimacy."

85. The number of unsolved murders of women in Ciudad Juárez is likely much larger than hundreds. There are also hundreds of missing women.

86. Segato, "Territory, Sovereignty, and Crimes of the Second State," 75, 86.

87. Lynn Boswell, *Admissions on Trial: Seven Decades of Race in Higher Education* (Austin, Tex.: KLRU-TV, 2015).

88. Barbara Harris Combs, "Black (and Brown) Bodies out of Place: Towards a Theoretical Understanding of Systematic Voter Suppression in the United States," *Critical Sociology*, 42, nos. 4–5 (2016): 539.

89. Anders Walker, "Legislating Virtue: How Segregationists Disguised Racial Discrimination as Moral Reform Following Brown v. Board of Education," *Duke Law Journal* 47 (1997): 423.

90. Eduardo Bonilla-Silva, "The Structure of Racism in Color-Blind, 'Post-racial' America," *American Behavioral Scientist* 59, no. 11 (2015): 1358–1376; Bonilla-Silva, *Racism without Racists*.

91. Audre Lorde, *Sister Outsider: Essays and Speeches* (Berkeley, Calif.: Crossing Press, 1984), 114, 120.

92. A term coined by sociologist Patricia Hill Collins, "matrix of domination" refers to the four interrelated domains along which power is organized in society. According to Collins, the four domains are structural (used to organize oppression in society), hegemonic (used to justify the practices in society), disciplinary (used to manage oppression through the practices in society), and interpersonal (used by individuals to uphold the subordination of others). "Matrix of domination" refers to the overlapping vectors of oppression to which an individuals are subject based on the statuses they occupy. Collins clarifies that these overlapping oppressions have multiplicative, not additive, effect. See Collins, "Towards a Politics of Empowerment," chap. 12 in *Black Feminist Thought*.

93. See Joe R. Feagin, *The White Racial Frame: Centuries of Racial Framing and Counterframing*, 2nd ed. (New York: Routledge, 2013), 126. Feagin writes, "[The] view of white virtue overrides the actual reality of racist performances." Pro-White attitudes and beliefs are at the center of the White racial frame. From this center, Whites posit that they are not only virtuous but also the most virtuous.

94. Koritha Mitchell, "Keep Claiming Space!," *CLA Journal* (College Language Association) 58, no. 3/4 (2015): 229. Emphasis in original.

95. Tukufu Zuberi and Eduardo Bonilla-Silva, eds., *White Logic, White Methods* (Lanham, Md.: Rowman & Littlefield, 2008).

96. Johan Galtung, "Cultural Violence," *Journal of Peace Research* 27, no. 3 (August 1990): 291.

97. Malcolm Jenkins interview with Trevor Noah, *The Daily Show with Trevor Noah*, June 22, 2020, http://www.cc.com/video-clips/eg3aq9/the-daily-show-with-trevor-noah-malcolm-jenkins-listen-up-media-working-to-end-systemic-racism-the-power-of-white-allyship.

CHAPTER 3. The Pushback

1. Aldon Morris, "W. E. B. Du Bois at the Center: From Science, Civil Rights Movement, to Black Live Matter," 2016 James Weldon Johnson Distinguished Lecture, Emory University, Atlanta, April 14, 2016.

2. See Aldon Morris, *The Scholar Denied: W. E. B. Du Bois and the Birth of Modern Sociology* (Berkeley: University of California Press, 2017). Founded in 1865, Atlanta University was the nation's first institution to grant graduate degrees to African Americans. In 1869, Clark College, also in Atlanta, was founded. Clark College became the nation's first four-year liberal arts institution for African Americans. In 1988, the institutions merged to form Clark Atlanta University, where I now teach.

3. Saidiya Hartman, *Scenes of Subjection: Terror, Slavery, and Self-Making in Nineteenth-Century America* (Oxford University Press, 1997).

4. See Kai Wright interview with author and Ida B. Wells biographer Paula Giddings, Greene Space at WNYC and WQXR, "I've Done My Work: Ida B. Wells and The Women Pushing Back Today," United States of Anxiety: Gender and Power podcast, October 16, 2018, https://www.youtube.com/watch?v=Da8-Jz7-oCo.

5. Bell hooks, quoted in Laura Barcella, *Fight Like a Girl: 50 Feminists Who Changed the World*, illustrated ed. (San Francisco: Zest Books, 2016), 132; Judith Butler, "Endangerer/ Endangering: Schematic Racism and White Paranoia," in *Reading Rodney King, Reading Urban Uprising*, edited by Robert Gooding-Williams, 15–16 (New York: Routledge, 1993).

6. A Black feminist ideology must be attentive to a number of variables. According to Deborah King, "A black woman's survival depends on her ability to use all the economic, social, and cultural resources available to her from both the larger society and within her community." Deborah K. King, "Multiple Jeopardy, Multiple Consciousness: The Context of a Black Feminist Ideology," *Signs* 14, no. 1 (1988): 49. See also Patricia Hill Collins, *Fighting Words: Black Women and the Search for Justice* (Minneapolis: University of Minnesota Press, 1998). Collins discusses the important role of history in transforming Black women's thought into theory.

7. Steven W. Thrasher, "Police Hunt and Kill Black People Like Philando Castile. There's No Justice," *Guardian*, June 19, 2017.

8. An article in the *New York Times* suggests that in the span of a 13-year period, police pulled Castile over on 49 separate occasions, "often for minor traffic infractions." See Sharon LaFraniere and Mitch Smith, "Philando Castile Was Pulled Over 49 Times in 13 Years, Often for Minor Infractions," *New York Times*, July 16, 2016. The AP Wire reports 52 stops during the same period.

9. Mary Douglas, *Purity and Danger: Analysis of Concepts of Pollution and Taboo* (New York: Routledge, 1966), 45.

10. George and Louise Jefferson were the characters in the sitcom *The Jeffersons*, which aired from 1975 to 1985. The Jeffersons were a hardworking Black family who became prosperous after the success of their dry cleaning business. This success allowed them to "move on up" from Queens to a "deluxe [Manhattan] apartment in the sky." Their former neighbors, Archie and Edith Bunker, remained in Queens.

11. Elizabeth Gillespie McRae, *Mothers of Massive Resistance: White Women and The Politics of Mass* (Oxford University Press, 2018).

12. Slavery was the principal cause of the political dispute that resulted in several states seceding from the Union and the waging of the Civil War. The Lost Cause ideology, however, reframed that history and argued that the Civil War was waged over states' rights. A propaganda campaign began with the aim of misrepresenting what the Civil War was about and to paint the White South in more favorable terms. This campaign suggested that the South was moral and just in the fight for states' rights. It suggested that while White southerners lost the war, they were not wrong. They were merely outnumbered. The successful Lost Cause campaign had other elements too. It argued that enslaved persons were well taken care of and had favorable working conditions, were happy under servitude; and loved and were loyal to their masters. Films and writings (fiction and nonfiction) were created in support of these beliefs. Then those representations of the era were presented as fact and packaged as history. Finally, the Lost Cause campaign insisted that masses of enslaved persons willingly came to the aid and defense of the southern way and fought for the Confederacy to maintain that way of life and painted southerners as deeply religious people fighting for a just cause. These ideas were infused in textbooks and consumed by generations to come. In light of this campaign, all across the nation fallen Confederates were painted as valiant heroes who should be celebrated. The celebration was said to be a veneration of heritage, not hate. Soon the southern landscape and beyond was replete with Confederate iconography. This project was led by women, especially those who had lost loved ones in the war. While it is rare for the losing side of a war to have monuments, Monument Avenue in Richmond, Virginia, the Confederate capital, is one example of this visual landscape. It is replete with statues of Confederate war heroes. The issue of how to memorialize the Confederate dead continues to divide the nation. It is part of the unresolved agenda of the war. While civil wars usually end with the losers facing consequences, some as severe as death, at the end of the American Civil War that did not happen. As early as 1863, President Lincoln began to outline a 10% plan that would return the southern states to the Union and provide a general pardon to all southerners except high-ranking Confederate officials. Lincoln did not want the lion's share of southerners to face repercussions. After Lincoln's April 15, 1865, assassination, President Andrew Johnson continued this laissez-faire policy, so, though the Confederates were traitors to the nation, they just went home. The spring and summer 2020 protests against police violence and killings prompted the removal of a number of Confederate statues. They also raised questions about the inconsistency of condemning athletes and others who exercise their First Amendment right to free speech by kneeling during the playing of the national anthem and calling those who do so un-American yet embracing those who were actual traitors to the country.

13. *Reimagining American History Education* (N.p.: Woodrow Wilson Foundation, 2019), https://woodrow.org/wp-content/uploads/2019/05/WW-American-History-Report.pdf.

14. Michel Foucault, *Power/Knowledge: Selected Interviews and Other Writings, 1972–1977*, ed. C. Gordon (Brighton: Harvester Press, 1980), 146, 149.

15. Harold Garfinkel, "Conditions of Successful Degradation Ceremonies," *American Journal of Sociology* 61, no. 5: (1956) 420–424.

16. In contemporary memory, consider acts such as leaving Michael Brown's body on Canfield Drive for four hours and highly public stops, searches, and frisks. These are aimed not only at direct victims but bystanders who are told: "This could be you; you cannot do anything to prevent it." These are performative acts, not just utilitarian ones.

17. Africans were enslaved in Mexico, Canada, and the Caribbean.

18. Today this area is known as Fort Monroe in Hampton, Virginia.

19. James Horn, *1619: Jamestown and the Forging of American Democracy* (New York: Basic Books, 2018), 2, 87.

20. The slave codes were actually written for living beings considered property. There were no codes for a chair's behavior or a chicken's behavior because they were a different kind of property.

21. "Slave Codes," ushistory.org, accessed Friday, June 05, 2020, http://www.ushistory.org/us/6f.asp.

22. The condition of African Americans as property is reinforced by the Supreme Court 1857 decision in *Dred Scott v. Sandford* (60 U.S. 393), where the court declared that the rights of slaveowners were constitutionally protected by the Fifth Amendment because slaves were categorized as property.

23. Edmund S. Morgan, *The Labor Problem at Jamestown, 1607–1618* (New York: Oxford University Press, 1971). It is said that John Smith told the colonists to "work or starve." Archaeologist William Kelso has challenged the broad perception of the settlers as lazy and suggests that a drought may have been the true cause of the period known as "the starving time" (1609–1610) See Marilyn Johnson, "New Jamestown Discovery" *Smithsonian Magazine* (July 28, 2015) https://www.smithsonianmag.com/smithsonian-institution/new-archaeological-research-jamestown-reveals-identities-four-prominent-settlers-discovery-180956028. However, early sources support Morgan's assertion. See, for example, Ralph Hamor, *A True Discourse of the Present Estate of Virginia* (London: John Beale for W. Welby, 1615), 26, in which starving colonists ("bitten with hunger and pennury") are said to have been found "bowling in the streetes" instead of working.

24. Morgan, *Labor Problem at Jamestown*.

25. William Waller Hening, ed., *The Statutes at Large; Being a Collection of All the Laws of Virginia from the First Session of the Legislature, in the Year 1619* (New York: R. & W. & G. Bartow, 1823), 1:254–255.

26. William Waller Hening, The *Statues at Large: Being a Collection of All of the Laws of Virginia* (Richmond, Va.: Samuel Pleasants, 1809–23), 2:170, 260, 266, 270.

27. One could be punished for harming the property of another. Therefore, the tort offense was framed as that of causing harm to the slave owner (through a type of tortious interference with property) and not the slave.

28. According to the Digital History website, "Until the mid-1660s, the number of white indentured servants was sufficient to meet the labor needs of Virginia and Maryland. Then, in the mid-1660s, the supply of white servants fell sharply." See "Virginia Slave Laws," accessed August 21, 2021, http://www.digitalhistory.uh.edu/disp_textbook.cfm?smtID=3&psid=71.

29. The doctrine seemed to ignore the possibility of a child being born from the union of White woman and Black man. This was unfathomable.

30. Sally E. Hadden, *Slave Patrols: Law and Violence in Virginia and the Carolinas* (Cambridge, Mass.: Harvard University Press, 2001), 4. See also Tony Platt, "Crime and Punishment in the United States: Immediate and Long-Term Reforms from a Marxist Perspective," *Crime and Social Justice* 18 (Winter 1982): 38–45.

31. Bertram Wyatt-Brown, *Southern Honor: Ethics and Behavior in the Old South* (Oxford: Oxford University Press, 1983); Eugene D. Genovese, *Roll, Jordan, Roll: The World the Slaveholders Made* (New York: Random House, 1976).

32. Hadden, *Slave Patrols*, 102.

33. This allowed the territory to collect revenue on the sale of slaves through the market.

34. Leslie Harris, *In the Shadow of Slavery: African Americans in New York City, 1626–1863* (Chicago: University of Chicago Press, 2003), 38. Some were spared and returned to slavery.

35. Robert Hunter, "Colonial New York's Governor Reports on the 1712 Slave Revolt," SHEC (Social History for Every Classroom), accessed June 6, 2020, https://herb.ashp.cuny.edu/items/show/690.

36. Brian Gilmer, "On the 300th Anniversary of a Slave Revolt," *Progressive*, April 6, 2012, https://progressive.org/op-eds/300th-anniversary-slave-revolt-need-learn-lessons.

37. Peter C. Hoffer, *Cry Liberty: The Great Stono River Slave Rebellion of 1739* (New York: Oxford University Press, 2010), 122–125. Hoffer argues that the slaves believed they were owed these wages and accidently killed the owner and another person there.

38. Mark E. Smith, ed., *Stono: Documenting and Interpreting a Southern Slave Revolt* (Columbia: University of South Carolina Press, 2005).

39. Herbert Aptheker, *American Negro Slave Revolts*, 5th ed. (New York: International Publishers, 1983), 187–189.

40. Ibid.

41. Some of the regulations were in effect before the Negro Act but were not strictly enforced. After the Stono uprising, such activities were strictly prohibited and policed for compliance.

42. Ibid., 64.

43. Achille Mbembe, *Critique of Black Reason*, trans. Laurent Dubois (Durham, N.C.: Duke University Press, 2019).

44. Gerald Horne, *The Counter-Revolution of 1776* (New York: New York University Press, 2014), 85.

45. See James Oliver Horton. *Slavery and the Making of America* (New York: Oxford University Press. 2005); David Brion Davis, *Inhuman Bondage: The Rise and Fall of Slavery in the New World* (New York: Oxford University Press, 2006); and Ira Berlin, *Many Thousands Gone: The First Two Centuries of Slavery in North America* (Cambridge, Mass.: Harvard University Press, 1998).

46. U.S. Constitution, Article I, Section 2.

47. Congressional "act[s] respecting fugitives from justice and persons escaping from the service of their masters" were enabled by Article 4, Section 2, Clause 3, of the Constitution, which contained the fugitive slave clause. The Emancipation Proclamation freed enslaved persons in the Confederate States then in rebellion. It did not free all enslaved persons.

48. Alejandro de la Fuente and Ariela Gross, *Becoming Free, Becoming Black: Race, Freedom and the Law in Cuba, Virginia, and Louisiana* (Cambridge, England: Cambridge University Press, 2020), 83.

49. Alejandro de la Fuente and Ariela Gross, "The 'Inconvenience' of Black Freedom: Manumission, 1500s–1700s," chap. 2 in *Becoming Black, Becoming Free,* 39–78.

50. Ibid.

51. In this case, any children born while a woman was free would remain free.

52. De la Fuente and Gross, *Becoming Black, Becoming Free,* 202–222. Some Blacks possessed phenotype traits that allowed them to pass as White in the society. States like Virginia developed racial purity laws, which allowed the state to further police the boundaries of whiteness and deny the benefits of whiteness to those citizens who might be able to pass. States did this through birth certificate records and other vital statistics that they kept. These official documents were passports that opened up other privileges such as access to education, voting, certain jobs, and the ability to marry citizens. "Not a Negro" certificates were official court declarations that an individual (perhaps someone who came from another state or had phenotype traits that were on the border of placing them under suspicion of being Black) was not a member of the disfavored Negro race. These certificates protected a person against the kind of discrimination visited upon Blacks.

53. David Walker, *Appeal to the Colored Citizens of the World* (Boston: David Walker, 1829), available online (as *Walker's Appeal, in Four Articles*) at Documenting the American South, 2001, https://docsouth.unc.edu/nc/walker/walker.html. In a number of southern states, mere possession or distribution of the book was punishable by death. *Appeal* encouraged slaves to fight for their freedom by revolting against their masters. Walker's father was an enslaved person; however, his mother was free, so under the laws that said a child's status followed that of the mother, he was free. Ironically, those laws were in place largely to prevent the children born of White men's relations with enslaved women from changing their caste status in society. Walker's abolitionist talk and writings angered Whites, especially in the South. His life was in constant threat, but Walker refused to flee to Canada. He died a mysterious death in Boston in 1830.

54. The figures for "Free Colored and Slave Population" in Ohio for 1830, the nearest census year, were 9,568 free residents and 6 enslaved persons. *Negro Population in the United States, 1790–1915* (1918; repr., New York: Arno, 1968), 57. A rounded figure of 10,000 persons is not unreasonable considering that minority populations were easily undercounted at this time.

55. Nikki Taylor, *Frontiers of Freedom: Cincinnati's Black Community, 1802–1868* (Athens: Ohio University Press, 2005), 51.

56. Ibid., 26, 51, 54, 133.

57. Ibid., 26.

58. Morals laws and attacks will be discussed in greater detail in discussion of the Moynihan Report in chapter 6.

59. According to Taylor, the actual concerns were less altruistic. Middle-class Whites did

not want Blacks in the area, and working-class Whites, mostly Irish, were concerned about job competition from Blacks.

60. Taylor, *Frontiers of Freedom*, 58.

61. George Lipsitz, "The Racialization of Space and the Spatialization of Race: Theorizing the Hidden Architecture of Landscape," *Landscape Journal* 26, no. 1 (2007): 13. http://www .jstor.org/stable/43323751.

62. Taylor, *Frontiers of Freedom*, 121.

63. Douglas R. Egerton, "Averting a Crisis: The Proslavery Critique of the American Colonization Society," *Civil War History* 43, no. 2 (June 1997): 142–156.

64. Edward Cavanagh and Lorenzo Veracini, eds., *The Routledge Handbook of the History of Settler Colonialism* (Milton Park, England: Taylor & Francis, 2016), 217.

65. A number of Princeton University graduates were instrumental in the formation of ACS. According to the Princeton & Slavery website, "Colonization was more of an intellectual movement for moderately antislavery whites than a practical option for free blacks." One of the ACS founders, Charles Fenton Mercer (Princeton Class of 1797), "worried that former slaves would be a drain on public resources and a threat to the prevailing social order . . . was deeply concerned that free blacks would initiate a race war . . . [and] contended that white racism would prevent blacks from ever being able to achieve upward mobility in the United States." Craig Hollander, "Princeton and the Colonization Movement," Princeton and Slavery, https:// slavery.princeton.edu/stories/princeton-and-the-colonization-movement. See also Douglas R. Egerton, "'Its Origin Is Not a Little Curious': A New Look at the American Colonization Society," *Journal of the Early Republic*, 5, no. 4 (Winter 1985: 463–480.

66. Eric Burin, *Slavery and the Peculiar Solution: A History of the American Colonization Society* (Gainesville: University of Florida Press, 2008).

67. Enslaved people in Haiti won their freedom through a violent revolt against French colonial rule. Walker and several of his fellow abolitionists openly celebrated the Haitian revolt by parading in the streets in solidarity with them. In *Appeal*, Walker encouraged Blacks in America to similarly revolt.

68. According to Patrick H. Breen, *The Land Shall Be Deluged in Blood: A New History of the Nat Turner Revolt* (New York: Oxford University Press, 2016), 98, 231, approximately 120 blacks were killed, but in an appendix Breen notes this number may be closer to 200.

69. "Thoughts for All Time," National Park Service, Frederick Douglass National Historic Site, District of Columbia, accessed August 20, 2021, https://www.nps.gov/frdo/learn/history culture/thoughts-for-all-time.htm.

70. Nancy Krieger, "Shades of Difference: Theoretical Underpinnings of the Medical Controversy on Black/White Differences in the United States, 1830–1870," *International Journal of Health Services* 17, no. 2 (1987): 259–278. Krieger writes that "based upon a handful of vital statistics and insanity rates derived from the 1840 Census," Senator John C. Calhoun asserted that there were higher levels of insane and idiots among Blacks. If such numbers were elevated, I ask readers to consider the violent beatings, rapes, subsistent diets, harsh living conditions, and hard labor to which Blacks were subjected and whether these conditions are more likely causes for the same.

71. Albert Deutsch, "The First U.S. Census of the Insane (1840) and Its Use as Pro-Slavery Propaganda," *Bulletin of the History of Medicine* 15, no. 5 (1944): 473.

72. This notion survived slavery and has been used to justify actions like Black Codes and resistance to school desegregation. It is an early iteration of the ideas in Anders Walker's 1997 *Duke Law Journal* article, "Legislating Virtue: How Segregationists Disguised Racial Discrimination at Moral Reform." Walker exposes how this operates. He describes how the *Brown* decision prompted southerners to reframe their opposition to social integration of Blacks (which would be prohibited under the law) and instead couch it as a legally permissible morality campaign. The aim was not only to subvert integration but also to maintain White supremacy. Despite the court's order, southern Whites mounted a successful massive resistance campaign against the social integration of Blacks in society. See Anders Walker, "Legislating Virtue: How Segregationists Disguised Racial Discrimination as Moral Reform Following *Brown v. Board of Education*," *Duke Law Journal* 47 (1997): 399–424.

73. De la Fuente and Gross, *Becoming Black, Becoming Free*.

74. Ruth Quinn, "Harriet Tubman: Nurse, Spy, Scout", U.S. Army, May 27, 2014, https://www.army.mil/article/126731/harriet_tubman_nurse_spy_scout. Tubman would free over 700 additional slaves in the Combahee Ferry Raid during her work as a scout for the Union army. See Sarah H. Bradford, *Scenes in the Life of Harriet Tubman*, electronic ed. (Auburn, N.Y.: W. J. Moses, Printer, 1869), 86, available at Documenting the American South, 2000, https://docsouth.unc.edu/neh/bradford/bradford.html. At the end of the war, the Union failed to compensate Tubman. See Bradford, *Scenes in the Life*, 38. Bradford also recorded that Tubman was forced to return to Canada via a baggage car and treated quite poorly. She writes, "The last time Harriet was returning from the war, with her pass as hospital nurse, she bought a half-fare ticket, as she was told she must do; and missing the other train, she got into an emigrant train on the Amboy Railroad. When the conductor looked at her ticket, he said, 'Come, hustle out of here! We don't carry niggers for half-fare.' Harriet explained to him that she was in the employ of Government, and was entitled to transportation as the soldiers were. But the conductor took her forcibly by the arm, and said, 'I'll make you tired of trying to stay here.' She resisted, and being very strong, she could probably have got the better of the conductor, had he not called three men to his assistance. The car was filled with emigrants, and no one seemed to take her part. The only word, she heard, accompanied with fearful oaths, were, 'Pitch the nagur out!' They nearly wrenched her arm off, and at length threw her, with all their strength, into a baggage-car. She supposed her arm was broken, and in intense suffering she came on to New York" (46).

75. Paul Finkelman, *Dred Scott v. Sandford: A Brief History with Documents*, 2nd ed. (Boston: Bedford/St. Martin's Press, 2016).

76. *Dred Scott v. John F. A. Sandford*, 60 U.S. 393 (1857). See also "The Dred Scott Decision," Digital History, accessed August 21, 2021, https://www.digitalhistory.uh.edu/disp_textbook.cfm?smtID=3&psid=293.

77. "Dred Scott Decision." Emphasis added.

78. Beverly Greene Bond and Susan Eva O'Donovan, eds., *Remembering the Memphis Massacre: An American Story* (Athens: University of Georgia Press, 2020).

79. John Strausbaugh, *City of Sedition: The History of New York City during the Civil War* (New York: Twelve, 2016). See also Harris, *In the Shadow of Slavery*, 279–288.

80. John Strausbaugh, "White Riot: Why the New York Draft Riots of 1863 Matter Today," *Observer*, July 11, 2016, https://observer.com/2016/07/white-riot-why-the-new-york-draft-riots-of-1863-matter-today.

81. Strausbaugh, *City of Sedition*, 221–222, 261–266. Lincoln's conscription law subjected all males 20 to 35 and all unmarried males 35 to 45 to potential military duty. The men would be entered into a lottery. Ironically, since the law only applied to citizens, African Americans were exempt from it.

82. Harris, *In the Shadow of Slavery*.

83. No children were killed in the fire, but they were left homeless and their condition rendered more precarious.

84. "New York Draft Riots," History.com, October 27, 2009, updated August 21, 2018, https://www.history.com/topics/american-civil-war/draft-riots.

85. Stewart E. Tolnay and E. M. Beck, A Festival of Violence: An Analysis of Southern Lynchings, 1882–1930 (Urbana: University of Illinois Press, 1995), 260.

86. Amy Kate Bailey and Karen Snedker, "Practicing What They Preach? Lynching and Religion in the American South, 1890–1929," *American Journal of Sociology*, 117, no. 3 (2011).

87. Some argue that Nathan Bedford Forrest and his troops committed the atrocities at Fort Pillow as a direct response to Lincoln's Emancipation Proclamation and the Union decision to arm Black men in the fight against the Confederacy.

88. See Congress of the Confederate States of America, Statutes at Large, 1st Cong., 3rd sess., May 1, 1863, "[No. 5]—Joint Resolution on the Subject of Retaliation."

89. Three escaped slaves made their way to Fort Monroe in Hampton, Virginia, and sought refuge there. A request was made for their return. Union major general Benjamin Butler refused to send the fugitives back. To justify this, he classified them as property, more specifically contraband of war. As contraband of war, the rules of engagement said they did not have to be returned.

90. Chandra Manning, *Troubled Refuge: Struggling for Freedom in the Civil War* (New York: Vintage Books, 2017), 174.

91. Manning notes that in some camps women outnumbered men. This came with its own set of issues and injustices. Ibid., 16.

92. Manning puts the count at "hundreds of thousands." Ibid., 37.

93. Ibid., 55, 32.

94. Jon Meacham, *The Soul of America: The Battle for Our Better Angels* (New York: Random House, 2018), 58.

95. Mbembe, *Critique of Black Reason*, 127.

96. Douglas Blackmon, *Slavery by Another Name: The Re-enslavement of Black Americans from the Civil War to World War II* (New York: Anchor Books, 2009). This is not to suggest that slavery was by any means a good or desirable state. Rather, it references the fact that under the system of slavery, enslaved persons were at least valued as property, so owners had some interest in providing slaves a base level of care. By contrast, under the convict leasing system, bodies had little value. The convict leasing system was so rigged as to always supply fresh convict lessees.

97. Ibid.

98. Ruth Wilson Gilmore, *Golden Gulag: Prisons, Surplus, Crisis, and Opposition in Globalizing California* (Berkeley: University of California Press, 2007), 12.

99. George Lipsitz, "'In an Avalanche Every Snowflake Pleads Not Guilty': The Collateral

Consequences of Mass Incarceration and Impediments to Women's Fair Housing Rights," *UCLA Law Review* 59 (2012) 1789.

100. *The Present-Day Ku Klux Klan Movement: Report by the Committee on Un-American Activities, House of Representatives, Ninetieth Congress, First Session* (Washington, D.C.: U.S. Government Printing Office, 1967).

101. The Compromise of 1877, which handed the presidency to Rutherford B. Hayes in exchange for the removal of Union troops from the South, ended Reconstruction.

102. W. E. B. Du Bois, *Black Reconstruction in America* (New York: Free Press, 1988), 30.

103. Quoted in W. E. B. Du Bois, "Reconstruction and Its Benefits," *American Historical Review* 15, no. 4 (1910): 794–795. Ta-Nahesi Coates echoed that refrain in the title of *We Were Eight Years in Power*, his 2017 book of essays about President Obama's presidency.

104. Lorraine Boissoneault, "The Deadliest Massacre in Reconstruction-Era Louisiana Happened 150 Years Ago," *Smithsonian*, September 28, 2018, https://www.smithsonianmag.com /history/story-deadliest-massacre-reconstruction-era-louisiana-180970420.

105. Herbert Shapiro, *White Violence and Black Response: From Reconstruction to Montgomery* (Amherst: University of Massachusetts Press, 1988), 12.

106. The Meridian (Mississippi) Race Riot began on March 8, 1871, and took place over three days. A White Republican judge and about 30 Black people were murdered at the hands of a mob of White Klansmen. Some accounts record different numbers. Quoting a statement from William Kellogg, then Louisiana governor, the *Facing History and Facing Ourselves* website records that on June 1874, in Coushatta Parish in Louisiana, a paramilitary group known as the White League murdered six white Republicans and approximately 20 Black freedmen. "White League Massacre at Coushatta," Facing History and Ourselves, accessed September 24, 2021, https://www.facinghistory.org/reconstruction-era/white-league-massacre -coushatta-1874. On July 8, 1876, in Hamburg, South Carolina, a series of civil disturbances were planned and administered by White Democrats against Black Republicans. Black militiamen in Hamburg were surrounded and attacked; seven were killed. The attacks served multiple objectives, but an important one was to roll back Black gains. There was also the Easter Sunday Colfax Massacre in Colfax, Louisiana, where armed White militiamen killed between 60 and 120 Black men.

107. In his first presidential debate of the 2020 season, Donald Trump called on the Proud Boys, a far-right organization that promotes violence, to protect the integrity of the ballot. I (and others) translate this as a call to keep Black and brown bodies away from the polls through violent intimidation or worse.

108. Ida B. Wells, *Crusade for Justice: The Autobiography of Ida B. Wells*, 2nd ed. (Chicago: University of Chicago Press, 2020), 42–48.

109. Paula Giddings, *Ida: A Sword among Lions: Ida B. Wells and the Campaign against Lynching* (New York: Amistad, 2009).

110. Hilary Mc Laughlin-Stonham, "The Rise of White Supremacy," chap. 3 in *From Slavery to Civil Rights: On the Streetcars of New Orleans 1830s–Present* (Liverpool: Liverpool University Press, 2020).

111. Steve Luxenberg, *Separate: The Story of Plessy v. Ferguson, and America's Journey from Slavery to Segregation* (New York: W. W. Norton, 2019).

112. Plessy had seven-eighths White heritage and looked White.

113. Brook Thomas, *Plessy v. Ferguson: A Brief History with Documents* (Boston: Bedford Books, 1997).

114. The Louisiana statute Plessy challenged used the phrase "equal but separate accommodations" to describe the facilities that would be provided for each race. This language was a direct attempt to circumvent the protections guaranteed to the emancipated population under the Equal Protection Clause of the Fourteenth Amendment.

115. This is a reference to the *Slaughterhouse Cases of 1873* (83 U.S. 36, 1873), in which the Supreme Court ruled that states' rights were distinct from federal rights; the Slaughterhouse Court held that the Constitution could only legally uphold federal civil rights and not those granted by individual states.

116. In 1904, Mississippi became the second state to require mandatory segregation on its streetcars. In 1905, several jurisdictions in the bordering state of Tennessee followed suit, but African Americans boycotted the streetcars because of their segregation policies.

117. Wells indicated that the Supreme Court's ruling in the *Civil Rights Cases of 1883* had established the principle on which *Plessy* was based. In 1883, the Supreme Court invalidated the Civil Rights Act of 1875, which had outlawed discrimination by private actors (businesses). In the 1883 cases, the Supreme Court said Congress had no authority to regulate private actions even if they might be discriminatory. Further, in the 1876 case of *United States v. Cruikshank* (92 U.S. 542) the court held that despite the adoption of the Fourteenth Amendment, the Bill of Rights (i.e., the first ten amendments to the Constitution) did not apply to individuals or state government.

118. The NAACP notes that of the thousands lynched from 1882 to 1968, 75% were Black, and, among the Whites who were lynched, many suffered this fate either because they expressed anti-lynching views or tried to help Blacks. "History of Lynching in America," NAACP, https://naacp.org/find-resources/history-explained/history-lynching-america.

119. Sherillyn Ifill, *On the Courthouse Lawn: Confronting the Legacy of Lynching in the Twenty-First Century*, tenth anniversary ed. (Boston: Beacon Press, 2018).

120. *Lynching in America: Confronting the Legacy of Racial Terror*, 3rd ed. (N.p.: Equal Justice Initiative, 2017), https://lynchinginamerica.eji.org/report.

121. *New York Sun*, February 2, 1893, in *The Burden of Race: A Documentary History of Negro-White Relations in America*, by Gilbert Osofsky (New York: Harper and Row, 1967), 181–184.

122. Christopher Waldrep, *Lynching in America: A History in Documents* (New York: New York University Press, 2006).

123. W. E. B. Du Bois, *The Souls of Black Folk* (1903; repr., New York: Oxford University Press, 2008).

124. Walter C. Rucker and James N. Upton, eds. *Encyclopedia of American Race Riots* (Hartford, Conn.: Greenwood, 2007).

125. In 1872, Currier and Ives created a lithograph depicting the first African American members of Congress. Henry Louis Gates notes what a historic moment this was. "When Frederick Douglass saw the portrait . . . he said, 'At last, the black man is represented as something other than a monkey.'" "The Black Congressmen of Reconstruction: Death of Representation,"

Mobituaries Podcast, season 2, episode 3, https://www.mobituaries.com/the-podcast/the-black-congressmen-of-reconstruction-death-of-representation. *The Crisis*, the official magazine of the NAACP, was originally *The Crisis: A Record of the Darker Races*. In its early years, Du Bois had a great deal of control over the magazine. Besides articles and opinion pieces, it prominently featured art, and it would go on to play a role in the Harlem Renaissance. In a 1926 speech, "The Negro in Art: How Shall He Be Portrayed," which was later adopted into an article, Du Bois said, "All art is propaganda." He continued: "I stand in utter shamelessness and say that whatever art I have for writing has been used always for propaganda for gaining the right of black folk to love and enjoy. I do not care a damn for any art that is not used for propaganda." See W. E. B. Du Bois, "Criteria of Negro Art," *The Crisis* 32 (1926): 295. Works in *The Crisis* were carefully selected to achieve that end.

126. The Harlem Renaissance was a period of Black cultural and intellectual revival that began in the early 1900s (others date its origin later) and extended to the 1930s. Alain Locke's collection of fiction, poetry, and essays titled *The New Negro* is one of the major works of the period. The "New Negro" possessed a confidence, assertiveness, and pride that the plantation-raised or born "Old Negro" did not, which allowed him or her to outspokenly advocate for the rights of Black folks. Unlike the "Old Negro," the "New Negro" did not accept indignities and largely refused to submit to the practices and performance of Jim Crow racial segregation.

127. Burns said he would not fight Johnson for less than $30,000. He was paid that and guaranteed a portion of any funds made through showing the fight in movie theaters. Johnson was only paid $5,000. The amount of $30,000 in 1908 is equivalent to over $4.2 million today.

128. Geoffrey Ward, *Unforgivable Blackness: The Rise and Fall of Jack Johnson* (New York: Vintage Books, 2006).

129. Ken Burns, *Unforgivable Blackness: The Rise and Fall of Jack Johnson* (Alexandria, Va.: PBS Home Video, 2005).

130. Barak Y. Orbach, "The Johnson-Jeffries Fight 100 Years Thence: The Johnson-Jeffries Fight and Censorship of Black Supremacy," *New York University Journal of Law and Liberty* 5 (2010): 270–346, quote on 273. Temperature forecast cited in Dale W. Laackman, *Selling Hate: Marketing the Ku Klux Klan* (Athens: University of Georgia Press, 2020), audio edition.

131. Ward, *Unforgiveable Blackness*, 59–60.

132. Harvey Young, *Embodying Black Experience: Stillness, Critical Memory and the Black Body* (Ann Arbor: University of Michigan Press, 2010), 99.

133. Tom Stanton, *Hank Aaron and the Home Run that Changed America* (New York: William Morrow, 2004).

134. "Woodrow Wilson and Race in America," *American Experience*, PBS, accessed August 21, 2021, https://www.pbs.org/wgbh/americanexperience/features/wilson-and-race-relations.

135. Everything old is new again. During the 2020 election cycle and amid the backdrop of a global pandemic, the Office of the Postmaster General was again used to deploy attacks on Black gains in the form of challenges to timely delivery of mail in ballots and complicity in unfounded allegations of widespread voter fraud.

136. All applicants for federal jobs were required to provide a photograph as part of their application packet. The photographs were used to screen out non-White applicants.

137. John Milton Cooper, *Woodrow Wilson: A Biography* (New York: Vintage Books, 2011), 11.

138. Cameron McWhirter, *Red Summer: The Summer of 1919 and the Awakening of Black America* (New York: Henry Holt, 2011).

139. David Krugler, *1919: The Year of Racial Violence: How African Americans Fought Back* (New York: Cambridge University Press, 2015).

140. Claude McKay, "If We Must Die," BlackPast.org, accessed August 21, 2021, https://www.blackpast.org/african-american-history/primary-documents-african-american-history/if-we-must-die-1919.

141. Brendan Wolfe, "Racial Integrity Laws (1924–1930)," in *Encyclopedia of Virginia*, accessed August 21, 2021, https://encyclopediavirginia.org/entries/racial-integrity-laws-1924-1930.

142. The law stood for 43 years, until it was overturned by the Supreme Court decision in *Loving v. Virginia*, 388 U.S. 1 (1967).

143. See Peggy Pascoe, *What Comes Naturally: Miscegenation Law and the Making of Race in America* (New York: Oxford University Press, 2009). Pascoe argues that laws against race mixing had an added and intentional negative effect on Black spouses who were prohibited by law from inheriting property. This practice contributed to continuing inequality today and the persistent Black-White wealth gap. It was and is a form of economic violence and a blatant attempt at social control. It says, "Stay with your own kind or suffer the economic consequences."

144. In January 1923, the Rosewood Massacre occurred in Levy County, Florida. The town of Rosewood was destroyed. The Blacks of Rosewood fought back, but ultimately all the Black residents of the town were driven out. The White townspeople called on KKK reinforcements to help accomplish the Black expulsion. It started because several White men lynched a Black Rosewood resident because of unsupported accusations from a White woman.

145. Alicia Lee and Sarah Sidner, "99 Years Ago Today America Was Shaken by One of Its Deadliest Acts of Racial Violence," CNN, June 1, 2020.

146. Candacy A. Taylor, *Overground Railroad: The Green Book and the Roots of Black Travel in America* (New York: Abrams Press, 2019).

147. *The Negro Motorist Green Book: 1948*,1, New York Public Library Digital Collections, accessed June 7, 2020, https://digitalcollections.nypl.org/items/6fa574f0-893f-0132-1035-58d385a7bbd0.

148. Isabel Wilkerson, *The Warmth of Other Suns: The Epic Story of America's Great Migration* (New York: Vintage, 2011), 580–581.

149. Ibid., 375.

150. Arnold Hirsch, *Making the Second Ghetto: Race and Housing in Chicago, 1940–1960* (Chicago: University of Chicago Press, 1998), 171–212; Thomas Sugrue, *The Origins of the Urban Crisis: Race and Inequality in Postwar Detroit* (Princeton: Princeton University Press, 1996).

151. The Civil Rights Act of 1964 is very similar to the law the court invalidated. But the Fourteenth Amendment Equal Protection Clause has still never been interpreted to bar private discrimination. Congress does have the power to regulate interstate commerce through the Commerce Clause.

152. 347 U.S. 483 (1954).

153. 349 U.S. 294 (1955).

154. See Walker, "Legislating Virtue," 404n23. The title "Black Monday" refers to Monday, May 17, 1954, the day that the Supreme Court decision in the first *Brown* case was announced.

155. Ibid., 399.

156. Ibid., 65n3, 63–64.

157. A conspiracy theory emerged during this period, and the violence of Red Summer and protests were blamed on the Bolsheviks. The government alleged the violence was the plot of Black militants associated with communism.

158. James Jackson Kilpatrick, *The Southern Case for School Segregation* (New York: Crowell-Culver Press, 1962). Kilpatrick had a nationally syndicated newspaper column called "A Conservative View," which ran for 30 years. He was also a frequent correspondent on *60 Minutes*.

159. Cited in Walker, "Legislating Virtue," 407.

160. Ibid., 410–411. States set up obstacles to getting marriage licenses that would have a disproportionate impact on Blacks. They might limit the hours of operation or require that the clerk be petitioned at home. A 1958 Georgia voter registration law was also tied to morals. Under the 1958 voter registration act, a person was required to either read and interpret a section of the Constitution or show they were of good moral character. Being unmarried or having a child out of wedlock disqualified a person from good moral character. Ibid., 417.

161. Ibid., 420. Walker shows how numbers of "illegitimate" Black children were inflated by making it harder for Blacks to get marriage licenses and birth records than it was for Whites.

162. Stephanie R. Rolph, *Resisting Equality: The Citizens' Council, 1954–1989*, Kindle ed. (Baton Rouge: Louisiana State University Press, 2018).

163. Ben Goldberger, ed., *100 Photographs: The Most Influential Images of All Time* (New York: Time Books, 2015).

164. Fred D. Gray, *Bus Ride to Justice* (Montgomery, Ala.: Black Belt Press, 1995), 69.

165. *Browder v. Gayle*, 142 F. Supp. 707 (1956).

166. *Gayle v. Browder* 352 U.S. 903 (1956).

167. Joseph Crespino, *Strom Thurmond's America* (New York: Hill & Wang, 2013), 101–103. This was a "Declaration of Constitutional Principles" written by southern members of Congress and signed by approximately one-fifth of the members of Congress. All signatories were members of the former Confederate States. South Carolina senator Strom Thurmond prepared the first draft of the manifesto (soon after the first *Brown* decision).

168. Chana Kai Lee, *For Freedom's Sake: The Life of Fannie Lou Hamer* (Champaign: University of Illinois Press, 2000).

169. Combs, *From Selma to Montgomery: The Long March to Freedom (New York: Routledge, 2013)*.

170. John Lewis, "Turning Points," *Washington Post*, December 26, 1999.

171. Ibid.

172. Combs, *From Selma to Montgomery*.

173. George Lipsitz, *How Racism Takes Place* (Philadelphia: Temple University Press, 2011), 25–50, describes the "white spatial imaginary" (i.e., desired white aesthetic or imagined social space). The "black spatial imaginary" is described in ibid., 51–72.

174. Ibid., 31.

175. Janell Ross, "A Rundown of Just How Badly the Fair Housing Act Has Failed," *Washington Post*, July 10, 2015.

176. Joseph William Singer, "Trump Administration Withdraws Obama Era Rules on 'Affirmatively Furthering Fair Housing' (AFFH)," Harvard University, https://scholar.harvard.edu/jsinger/blog/trump-administration-withdraws-obama-era-rules-%E2%80%9Caffirmatively-furthering-fair-housing%E2%80%9D.

177. "Trump Administration Civil and Human Rights Rollbacks," Leadership Conference on Civil and Human Rights, accessed August 21, 2021, https://civilrights.org/trump-rollbacks.

178. Lipsitz, *How Racism Takes Place*.

179. For a more complete listing of the Trump administration's attacks on civil rights, see "Trump Administration Civil and Human Rights Rollbacks."

180. "Watch: Yolanda Adams Sings 'Hallelujah' at National Covid Remembrance," *PBS NewsHour*, January 20, 2021. https://www.pbs.org/newshour/politics/watch-yolanda-adams-sings-hallelujah-at-national-covid-remembrance.

181. Quoted in Michael Crowley and Jennifer Schuessler, "Trump's 1776 Commission Critiques Liberalism in Report Derided by Historians," *New York Times*, January 18, 2021.

182. Ibid.

183. Ibid.

184. Eduardo Bonilla-Silva, *Racism without Racists: Color-Blind Racism and the Persistence of Racial Inequality in America*, 5th ed. (Lanham, Md.: Rowman & Littlefield, 2018).

185. Kareem Abdul-Jabbar, "Don't Understand the Protests? What You're Seeing Is People Pushed to the Edge," *Los Angeles Times*, May 30, 2020.

186. Koritha Mitchell, "Identifying White Mediocrity and Know-Your-Place Aggression: A Form of Self-Care," *African American Review* 51, no. 4 (Winter 2018): 253.

CHAPTER 4. The Historical Fear Factor

1. Arash Javanbakht and Linda Saab, "What Happens in the Brain When We Feel Fear," *Smithsonian*, https://www.smithsonianmag.com/science-nature/what-happens-brain-feel-fear-180966992.

2. According to the American Institute of Stress, this is an acute stress response that can be triggered by real or imaginary perceived threats.

3. Kristen, Day, "Being Feared: Masculinity and Race in Public Space," *Environment and Planning A: Economy and Space* 38, no. 3 (March 2006): 569–586.

4. Alejandro de la Fuente and Ariela Gross, *Becoming Free, Becoming Black: Race, Freedom and the Law in Cuba, Virginia, and Louisiana* (Cambridge, England: Cambridge University Press, 2020).

5. Kevin Kruse, "The Politics of Race and Public Space: Desegregation, Privatization and the Tax Revolt in Atlanta," *Journal of Urban History* 31, no. 5 (2005): 610–633.

6. Ibid., 611.

7. Corey Robin, *Fear: The History of a Political Idea* (New York: Oxford University Press, 2004).

8. Paul G. Bain et al., "Collective Futures: How Projections about the Future of Society Are

Related to Actions and Attitudes Supporting Social Change," *Personality and Social Psychology Bulletin* 39, no. 4 (April 2013): 524. https://doi.org/10.1177/0146167213478200.

9. This is where gains by one group only come at the expense of losses by another group. The net gain is zero. Many Whites fear gains by Blacks will come at their expense. Put simply, they believe Black gains can only come about through White losses.

10. Michael Norton and Samuel Sommers, "Whites See Racism as Zero-Sum Game That They Are Now Losing," *Perspectives on Psychological Science* 6, no. 3 (2011): 215–218.

11. Jon Meacham, *Soul of America: In Search of Our Better Angels* (New York: Random House, 2019), 47.

12. Ibid., 119, 110.

13. Ibid., 111–132.

14. Quoted in ibid., 144.

15. Michael Rogin, *Ronald Reagan the Movie and Other Episodes of Political Demonology* (Berkeley: University of California Press, 1988), 68.

16. The so-called political radicals largely consisted of Blacks fighting back against rising nationwide police-sanctioned White supremacist terror attacks against the African American community.

17. Rogin, *Ronald Reagan the Movie and Other Episodes*, 69.

18. Chapter 3 established that certain Black bodies may be more at risk of particular types of violence. For example, Black and male identity is more likely to be subjected to physical and political violence (through the disenfranchisement that some felons are subject to). A Black and female identity is at greater risk for economic violence (through the lower wages paid to Black females) and emotional and certain types of physical violence. Arguably, the most vulnerable population is Black, transgender youth. This book cannot do service to a discussion of these matters, but it would be in error not to mention them. See Trace Strangio, "Deadly Violence against Transgender People Is on the Rise. The Government Isn't Helping," ACLU, August 21, 2018, https://www.aclu.org/blog/lgbt-rights/criminal-justice-reform-lgbt-people /deadly-violence-against-transgender-people-rise.

19. Micki McElya, *Clinging to Mammy: The Faithful Slave in Twentieth-Century America* (Cambridge, Mass.: Harvard University Press, 2007).

20. Jan Nederveen Pieterse, *White on Black: Images of Africa and Blacks in Western Popular Culture* (New Haven, Conn.: Yale University Press, 1992).

21. Kenneth W. Goings, *Mammy and Uncle Mose: Black Collectibles and American Stereotyping* (Bloomington: Indiana University Press, 1994).

22. Patricia Ann Turner, *Ceramic Uncles and Celluloid Mammies: Black Images and Their Influence on Culture* (Charlottesville: University of Virginia Press, 1994).

23. David Pilgrim, *Understanding Jim Crow: Using Racist Memorabilia to Teach Tolerance and Promote Social Justice* (Oakland: PM Press, 2015), 17. Pilgrim writes, "These antiblack depictions were routinely manifested in or on material objects: ashtrays, drinking glasses, banks, games, fishing lures, detergent boxes, and other everyday items" (5). These objects both reflected and shaped attitudes toward African Americans. Pilgrim's collection of racist memorabilia became the initial foundation for the Jim Crow Museum for Racist Memorabilia at Ferris State University. Pilgrim is founder and director of the museum.

24. Chauncey Alcorn, "Aunt Jemima Finally Has a New Name," *CNN Business*, February 9, 2021, https://www.cnn.com/2021/02/09/business/aunt-jemima-new-name/index.html.

25. Mary Douglas, *Natural Symbols: Exploration in Criminology* (London: Cressett Press, 1970), xiii.

26. Even in the blaxploitation film era, which seemed to elevate Blacks, films still featured stereotypical depictions of hypersexual Black men and women. See Lawrence Novotny, *Blaxploitation: Films of the 1970s: Blackness and Genre* (London: Routledge, 2007), 54–55.

27. Ronald Jackson II, *Scripting the Black Masculine Body: Identity, Discourse and Racial Politics in Popular Media* (Albany: State University of New York, 2006), 13.

28. Lawrence W. Levine, *Black Culture and Black Consciousness*, 30th anniversary ed. (Oxford University Press, 2007).

29. Patrick McGilligan, *Oscar Micheaux: The Great and Only: The Life of America's First Black Filmmaker* (New York: Harper Perennial, 2008).

30. Cedric J. Robinson, *Forgeries of Memory and Meaning: Blacks and the Regimes of Race in American Theater and Film* (Chapel Hill: University of North Carolina Press, 2007), 128, xvii, 137–139, 141.

31. The 1927 Supreme Court decision in *Buck v. Bell* (274 U.S. 200 (1927) would increase the vulnerability of people society labeled as "feeble-minded" or "imbeciles." Fear of this category of people resulted in institutionalization and sterilization.

32. Donald Bogle, *Toms, Coons, Mulattoes, Mammies, and Bucks: An Interpretive History of Blacks in American Films* (New York: Continuum, 2001).

33. Wells extensively discusses the Black Buck stereotype and its use as a psychological projection in her work on lynching.

34. Bogle, *Toms, Coons, Mulattoes, Mammies, and Bucks*, 4–6, 8, 7.

35. Ibid., 14.

36. Historically narrow definitions of beauty operate to maintain White supremacy. For example, the Miss America pageant began in 1921. By 1930s, the official rulebook for the pageant said only women of the White race could compete. Even after Bess Meyerson, the first (and only) Jewish American Miss America was crowned in 1945, Blacks were still not able to compete. As far back as 1923, African Americans were allowed to appear in musical numbers on the stage of the pageant. They were usually cast as slaves. Whiteness could expand, but Black was still disfavored.

37. Bogle, *Toms*, 9.

38. Ida B. Wells, *Southern Horrors: Lynch Law in All Its Phases* (Project Gutenberg, 1892 [2005]), https://www.gutenberg.org/files/14975/14975-h/14975-h.htm .

39. Jonathan Katz, "Shooting an Unarmed Black Man Was Self-Defense, Officer's Lawyer Tells Charlotte Jury," *New York Times*, August 18, 2015.

40. Rtmadmincd, "Police Release 911 Tape in Fatal Shooting," *Chicago Defender*, September 18, 2013, https://chicagodefender.com/police-release-911-tape-in-fatal-police-shooting. Bowdlerization (asterisks) in original. The *Chicago Defender* is an African American newspaper founded in 1905.

41. Alex Johnson, "Officer in Jonathan Ferrell Killing: 'He Kept Trying to Get My Gun,'" August 12, 2015, NBC News, https://www.nbcnews.com/news/us-news/officer-jonathan-ferrell-killing-he-kept-trying-get-my-gun-n409491.

42. Kim Severson, "Asking for Help, then Killed by an Officer's Barrage," *New York Times*, September 16, 2013.

43. Cleve R. Wootson Jr. and Michael Gordon, "City of Charlotte Reaches Settlement with Officer Randall Kerrick," *Charlotte Observer*, October 8, 2015.

44. Ibid.

45. George T. Winston, "The Relations of the Whites to the Negroes," *Annals of the American Academy of Political and Social Science* 18 (1901): 108–109.

46. Willie Horton, a Black man, was a convicted felon who raped a White woman (and bound her boyfriend) while he was on a weekend furlough program. The case gained national recognition when George Bush used it in advertisements in his successful presidential campaign against his opponent Governor Michael Dukakis of Massachusetts. The furlough program was established by the state of Massachusetts, and Bush used it to argue that Dukakis was not sufficiently tough on crime. The case reinforced race-based fears about Black men's propensity to rape White women.

47. Associated Press, "White North Carolina Cop Panicked before Shooting Black Man after Car Crash: Prosecutor," *New York Daily News*, August 4, 2015.

48. Jonathan Katz, "Shooting Unarmed Black Man was Self-Defense, Officer's Lawyer Tells Charlotte Jury," *New York Times*, August 18, 2015.

49. Christine Hauser, "Video Is Released from 2013 North Carolina Police Shooting," *New York Times*, August 6, 2015.

50. M. L. Nestel, "Exclusive: Mother Whose Panicked 911 Call Led to Police Shooting Death," *Daily Mail*, September 23, 2013.

51. Ibid.

52. Hauser, "Video Is Released from 2013 North Carolina Police Shooting." Of the ten shots that hit Ferrell, eight were fired while he was collapsed on the ground.

53. Charles Mills, *The Racial Contract* (Ithaca: Cornell University Press, 1997), 60.

54. Wilson did not go to trial. The grand jury did not indict him, despite the popular belief that prosecutors can get a grand jury to "indict a ham sandwich."

55. Excerpts are taken from Josh Sanburn, "All the Ways Darren Wilson Described Being Afraid of Michael Brown," *Time*, November 25, 2014, https://time.com/3605346/darren-wilson-michael-brown-demon.

56. Additionally, consider the spectacle of families at the border being separated. These images flooded media outlets. Some people even gathered at the border to watch the "spectacle," and many others regularly consumed this violence on television and remained unmoved to act.

57. Sanburn, "All the Ways Darren Wilson." Emphasis added.

58. Ibid.

59. Brent Staples, "Black Men and Public Space," *Harper's Magazine*, December 1986, 19–20; W. Kamau Bell, "Happy Birthday! Have Some Racism from Elmwood Café!," blog post, January 28, 2015, http://www.wkamaubell.com/blog/2015/01/happy-birthday-have-some-racism-from-elmwood-cafe.

60. Marcus Hunter and Zandria F. Robinson, *Chocolate Cities: The Black Map of American Life* (Berkeley: University of California Press, 2018).

61. Elise Solé, "'Gas Station Gail': Store Manager Calls Police on Parents and Children Buying Drinks: 'It's Like a Riot out Here,'" *Yahoo!Life*, October 17, 2018, https://www.yahoo.com

/lifestyle/gas-station-gail-store-manager-calls-police-parents-children-buying-drinks-like
-riot-201315580.html.

62. Reginald Andrade, "I Was Reported to Police as an 'Agitated Black Male'—for Simply
Walking to Work," ACLU, October 10, 2018, https://www.aclu.org/blog/racial-justice/race
-and-criminal-justice/i-was-reported-police-agitated-black-male-simply.

63. Cleve R. Wootson Jr., "Bahama Breeze Manager Fired after Calling the Police on Black
Sorority Members," *Washington Post,* June 26, 2018.

64. Bill Hutchinson, "Hobby Lobby Employees Called Cops on Black Customer Who
Apparently Looked like a Crime Suspect," *ABC News*, May 17, 2018, https://abcnews.go.com
/US/hobby-lobby-employees-called-cops-customer-apparently-looked/story?id=55230358.

65. "Black Airbnb Guests Say They Were Racially Profiled," CNN, May 12, 2018, https://
www.youtube.com/watch?v=JWhhGA-XeXw.

66. Dakin Andone, "Woman Says She Called Police When Black Airbnb Guests Didn't
Wave at Her," May 11, 2018, https://www.cnn.com/2018/05/10/us/airbnb-black-rialto
-california-trnd/index.html.

67. Associated Press, "Airbnb Owner Blames Her Black Guests' 'Lack of Good Nature' as
Reason for Her Neighbor Calling the Police," *Los Angeles Sentinel*, May 10, 2020.

68. Andone, "Woman Says She Called Police."

69. "Hear Neighbor Explain Why She Called 911 on Black Airbnb Guests," CNN, May 12,
2018, https://www.youtube.com/watch?v=JWhhGA-XeXw.

70. Amber Jamieson, "A White Woman Called the Police on Bob Marley's Granddaughter
for Not Smiling at Her," *BuzzFeed News*, May 10, 2018, https://www.buzzfeednews.com/article
/amberjamieson/black-artists-airbnb-white-woman-police-cops.

71. Ibid.

72. The precise length of time is disputed.

73. CNN, "Hear Neighbor Explain Why She Called."

74. Ibid.

CHAPTER 5. Presumed Criminal

1. Charles Blow, "The Killing of Ahmaud Arbery," May 6, 2020, *New York Times*.

2. George Yancy, *Black Bodies, White Gazes: The Continuing Significance of Race*, 2nd ed.
(Lanham, Md.: Rowman & Littlefield, 2016), 220.

3. D. L. Hughley and Doug Moe, *How Not to Get Shot and Other Advice from White People*
(New York: Harper Collins, 2018), audiobook.

4. Haven Orrechio-Egresitz, "Gregory McMichael, Who Is Charged in the Killing of
Ahmaud Arbery, Worked for Years in DA Jackie Johnson's Office without Required Gun
Training," *Insider*, May 13, 2020, https://www.insider.com/gregory-mcmichael-worked-for
-years-without-deadly-force-training-2020-5.

5. Free Blacks had their movement and access to public transportation constrained as well.

6. Philomena Essed, *Understanding Everyday Racism: An Interdisciplinary Theory* (Newbury
Park, Calif.: Sage, 1991).

7. Phillip Atiba Goff et al., *The Science of Justice: Race, Arrests, and Police Use of Force* (Los
Angeles: Center for Policing Equity, 2016), 15, https://policingequity.org/images/pdfs-doc

/CPE_SoJ_Race-Arrests-UoF_2016-07-08-1130.pdf. The Center for Policing Equity is a national nonprofit organization whose aim is to eliminate bias in policing. They seek to do this by measuring bias and partnering with law enforcement agencies to eradicate it.

8. Bart Landry, *The New Black Middle Class and the Twenty-First Century* (New Brunswick, N.J.: Rutgers University Press, 2018), 213.

9. Susan Svrluga, "U-VA Student Bloodied in Arrest Reaches Settlement with the State," *Washington Post*, June 21, 2018.

10. [Jason Johnson], "OpEd: Martese Johnson and The Rhetorical Talisman: 'I Go to UVA,'" NBC, March 20, 2015, https://www.nbcnews.com/news/nbcblk/essay-i-go-uva-you-f-ing -racists-martese-johnson-n327241.

11. Svrluga, "U-VA Student Bloodied in Arrest."

12. Martese Johnson, "Martese Johnson, The U.Va. Student Assaulted by Officers Last Spring, Speaks Out," *Vanity Fair*, October 14, 2015, https://www.vanityfair.com/news /2015/10/martese-johnson-the-uva-student-assaulted-by-officers-last-spring-speaks-out.

13. [Jason Johnson], "OpEd: Martese Johnson and The Rhetorical Talisman."

14. Sonia K. Kang et al., "Whitened Résumés: Race and Self-Presentation in the Labor Market," *Administrative Science Quarterly* 61, no. 3 (September 2016): 469–502.

15. Andre M. Perry, "Black Workers Are Being Left Behind by Full Employment," Brookings Institution, June 26, 2019, https://www.brookings.edu/blog/the-avenue/2019/06/26 /black-workers-are-being-left-behind-by-full-employment; Valerie Wilson, "Black Unemployment Is at Least Twice as High as White Unemployment at the National Level and in 14 States and the District of Columbia," Economic Policy Institute, April 4, 2019, https://www.epi.org /publication/valerie-figures-state-unemployment-by-race.

16. Jhacova Williams and Valerie Wilson, "Black Workers Endure Persistent Racial Disparities in Employment Outcomes," Economic Policy Institute, August 27, 2019, https://www.epi .org/publication/labor-day-2019-racial-disparities-in-employment.

17. John Boles, *Thomas Jefferson: Architect of American Liberty* (New York: Basic Books, 2017), 84–85.

18. Jon Meacham, *Thomas Jefferson: The Art of Power* (New York: Random House, 2012), 55, xxvi. Boles states that Jefferson fathered five children with Hemings. Boles, *Thomas Jefferson*, 1.

19. Thomas Jefferson, "Extract from Thomas Jefferson's *Notes on the State of Virginia*," Monticello, accessed June 20, 2020, http://tjrs.monticello.org/letter/1314. Emphasis added. First elision appears in source.

20. Boles, *Thomas Jefferson*, 4.

21. Thomas Jefferson, "Extract from Thomas Jefferson's *Notes on the State of Virginia*."

22. Craig Steven Wilder, *Ebony and Ivy: Race, Slavery and the Troubled History of America's Universities* (New York: Bloomsbury Press, 2013), 137.

23. Nancy MacLean, *Democracy in Chains: The Deep History of the Radical Rights Stealth Plan for America* (New York: Penguin Books, 2017).

24. Soon after Buchanan's death, MacLean gained access to his archives. She unearthed copious correspondence between the economist and billionaire Charles Koch. MacLean also gained insight into the ways Buchanan trained his students to push back against the *Brown* decision and attack race mixing without the use of overt racial language. Instead, he encouraged them to attack *Brown* through the veneer of economic and political precepts. This rev-

elation is consistent with the argument in BOP tenet 7 that suggests, when invoked through discourse, that those who attempt to push Black bodies back into a position of relative subservience to Whites use seemingly race-neutral language that is laden with race-based ideas. While overt racialized language is not employed, the new language stands as a proxy for race.

25. Marshall Steinbaum, "The Book that Explains Charlottesville," *Boston Review*, August 14, 2017, http://bostonreview.net/class-inequality/marshall-steinbaum-book-explains-charlottesville.

26. "University of Virginia," in "*U.S. News* Best Colleges," https://www.usnews.com/best-colleges/uva-6968.

27. Matt Kelly, "UVA'S Civil War Story Is Not All Confederate," *UVA Today,* September 20, 2018, https://news.virginia.edu/content/uvas-civil-war-story-not-all-confederate.

28. Jon Meacham, *The Soul of America: The Battle for Our Better Angels* (New York: Random House, 2018), 278.

29. Rosie Gray, "Trump Defends White-Nationalist Protesters: 'Some Very Fine People on Both Sides,'" *Atlantic*, August 15, 2017, https://www.theatlantic.com/politics/archive/2017/08/trump-defends-white-nationalist-protesters-some-very-fine-people-on-both-sides/537012.

30. James S. Robbins, "Trump's Charlottesville Comments Twisted by Joe Biden and the Media," *USA Today*.

31. Ibid.

32. Quoted in Meacham, *Soul of America*, 5.

33. Readers can imagine more colorful language that might be used to convey this idea.

34. "Virginia Man Calls Cops after Being Fouled in Basketball Game, Witnesses Say," Fox 5 Washington DC, https://www.youtube.com/watch?v=a-lwC4lc9jo.

35. David Williams, "Woman Says Supermarket Called Police on Her While She Was Helping a Homeless Man," *Houston Style Magazine*, August 2, 2018, http://stylemagazine.com/news/2018/aug/02/woman-says-supermarket-called-police-her-while-she.

36. Ibid.

37. Jerry Iannelli, "Here's a List of South Florida Wells Fargo Locations that Keep Getting Sued for Racism," *Miami New Times,* November 18, 2018https://www.miaminewtimes.com/news/south-florida-wells-fargos-keep-getting-sued-for-racism-10917703

38. Tanya Chen and Remy Smidt, "Here's What Happened after Viral Video Captured a Dollar General Manager Calling the Police on a Woman Trying to Use Coupons," *Buzz Feed*, July 27, 2018. https://www.buzzfeednews.com/article/tanyachen/dollar-general-manager-police-black-woman-coupons.

39. In an effort not to further victimize the child, I choose not to name him in this discussion. I do this with many of the young victims, but generally I name the adult perpetrators.

40. Jeffrey C. Mays and Sean Piccoli, "A White Woman, Teresa Klein, Called the Police on a Black Child She Falsely Said Groped Her," *New York Times*, October 12, 2018.

41. Enjoli Francis and Bill Hutchinson, "I Don't Forgive This Woman, and She Needs Help," *ABC News*, October 16, 2018, https://abcnews.go.com/US/white-woman-apologizes-alleging-black-child-assaulted-york/story?id=58505763.

42. Rana Novini and Michelle J. Kim, "Fallout Continues in Brooklyn," *NBC News 4*, October 15, 2018, https://www.nbcnewyork.com/news/local/cornerstore-caroline-fallout-brooklyn

-outrage-over-viral-video-of-white-woman-calling-911-on-black-boy-claiming-he-groped-her
/1711354.

43. Ibid. See also Mays and Piccoli, "White Woman, Teresa Klein, Called the Police."

44. Cleve R. Wootson Jr., "It Took This Black Man Years to Open His Lemonade Stand. Then Someone Thought He Was Robbing It," *Washington Post*, July 23, 2018.

45. Drew Costley, "Black Owner of SF Lemonade Stand Has Police Called on Him While Trying to Open His Business," *San Francisco Chronicle*, July 22, 2018.

46. "Cops Called on Black Man Opening His Business," CNN, July 23, 2018, https://www .cnn.com/videos/us/2018/07/23/san-francisco-black-man-lemonade-business-police-called -sot-vpx.cnn.

47. "Police Officer Resigns," CNN, May 17, 2019, https://fox2now.com/news/police-officer -resigns-with-a-settlement-after-wrongly-pulling-gun-on-black-man-picking-up-trash.

48. John Spina, "Black Man Detained for Picking Up Trash outside Boulder Home Not Surprised by New Police Data," *Denver Post*, May 2, 2019.

49. Maria Perez, "Neighbors Called Police on 11-Year-Old Black Boy Delivering Newspapers, Mother Claims," *Newsweek*, July 11, 2018, https://www.newsweek.com/police-called -black-boy-delivering-newspapers-mother-claims-1019401.

50. Black women are subject to this too.

51. See Patricia Williams, *Alchemy of Race and Rights Diary of a Law Professor* (Cambridge, Mass.: Harvard University Press, 1991). Williams recounts her experience of being denied entry to a Benetton boutique in New York City. She uses this as an entree to tell a broader story about race and exclusion.

52. Eli Blumenthal, "Nordstrom Rack Apologizes for Accusing 3 Black Teens Shopping for Prom of Theft," *USA Today*, May 8, 2018.

53. Julia Jacobo and Erica Y King "'Profiling Is Real': Former Obama Staffer Mistaken as Burglar While Moving into New York City Apartment," *ABC News*, May 2, 2018, https:// abcnews.go.com/Politics/profiling-real-obama-staffer-mistaken-burglar-moving-york/story?id =54877597.

54. Crystal Hill, "Black Former Obama Aide Was Moving into His NYC Apartment. The Police were Called," *Miami Herald*, May 1, 2018.

55. Ibid.

56. Ibid.

57. Anthropologist David Kertzer describes a perp walk as "a ritual degradation that publicly signals . . . change in status from an ordinary citizen." Quoted in John Tierney, "The Big City: Even Perps May Prefer Walk of Fame." *New York Times* March 1, 1999.

58. Erik A. Garrett, "The Rhetoric of Antiblack Racism: Lewis R. Gordon's Radical Phenomenology of Embodiment," *Atlantic Journal of Communication* 19, no. 1 (2011) 13.

59. Rana Novini and Michelle J. Kim, "Fallout Continues in Brooklyn over 'Cornerstore Caroline' as Community Rallies," *NBC News*, October 16, 2018, https://www.google.com /amp/s/www.nbcnewyork.com/news/local/cornerstore-caroline-fallout-brooklyn-outrage -over-viral-video-of-white-woman-calling-911-on-black-boy-claiming-he-groped-her/1711354 /%3famp.

60. Landry, *New Black Middle Class*, 213.

61. Phillip A. Goff et al., "The Essence of Innocence: Consequences of Dehumanizing Black Children," *Journal of Personality and Social Psychology* 106, no. 4 (2014): 526–545.

CHAPTER 6. Massah Has Spoken

1. Donesha Aldridge, "911 Calls in Ahmaud Arbery Case | 'He's Running Down the Street,'" *11 Alive News*, https://www.11alive.com/article/news/crime/911-calls-ahmaud-arbery/85 -4819d3d9-6133-40de-b3a9-f8fa3f889574. Brackets in original. Admittedly, it can be argued that McMichael was shouting at his son or Roddie Bryan (in the other vehicle); however, later comments by Bryan's attorney make it clear that McMichael repeatedly yelled at Arbery and ordered him to stop running.

2. Sarah Dorn, "Man Who Leaked Ahmaud Arbery Video Says He Was Trying to Stop a Riot," *New York Post*, May 9, 2020.

3. James M. Blaut, "The Theory of Cultural Racism," *Antipode: A Radical Journal of Geography*, 24, no. 4 (1992): 290.

4. Eduardo Bonilla-Silva and Tukufu Zuberi, eds., *White Logic, White Methods: Racism and Methodology* (Rowman & Littlefield, 2008). The authors and contributors to this volume argue for an overhaul of social science methodologies and move to a more inclusive, multicultural approach.

5. Here I suggest that in employment, government, law, and other such institutional contexts racial and ethnic minorities might assume midlevel management roles or higher, but the policies and practices they enact often support White supremacy or are at the behest of White overseers (or both).

6. David Montgomery, "How Miriam Carey's U-turn at a White House Checkpoint Led to Her Death," *Washington Post*, November 26, 2014.

7. Accounts vary as to the precise number of shots fired.

8. Montgomery, "How Miriam Carey's U-turn at a White House Checkpoint."

9. Tom Dart, "Former Texas Officer Who Fatally Shot Unarmed Woman Found Not Guilty," *Guardian*, April 7, 2016.

10. Chris Sadeghi, "Fired Deputy Daniel Willis Found Not Guilty of Murder," KXAN News, April 7, 2016, https://www.kxan.com/news/fired-deputy-daniel-willis-found-not-guilty -of-murder.

11. "Yanez Audio Squad 151," July 6, 2016, traffic stop transcript, Ramsey County, Minnesota, https://www.ramseycounty.us/sites/default/files/County%20Attorney/Exhibit%201a%20 -%20Traffic%20Stop%20Transcript.pdf

12. Madison Park, "The 62-Second Encounter between Philando Castile and the Officer Who Killed Him," *CNN*, May 30, 2017, https://www.cnn.com/2017/05/30/us/philando -castile-shooting-officer-trial-timeline.

13. Mitch Smith, "Minnesota Officer Acquitted in Killing of Philando Castile," *New York Times*, June 16, 2017.

14. Blaut, "Theory of Cultural Racism," 290.

15. Daniel Geary, *Beyond Civil Rights: The Moynihan Report and Its Legacy* (Philadelphia: University of Pennsylvania Press, 2015), 1–11, 80–91

16. Ibid.

17. Daniel Patrick Moynihan, *The Negro Family: The Case for National Action* (Washington, D.C.: Office of Planning and Research, U.S. Department of Labor, 1965), https://web.stanford.edu/~mrosenfe/Moynihan's%20The%20Negro%20Family.pdf. Emphasis added.

18. Quoted in Thomas Byrne Edsall and Mary D. Edsall, *Chain Reaction: The Impact of Race, Rights, and Taxes on American Politics* (New York: W. W. Norton, 1992), 54.

19. Ibid.

20. Geary, *Beyond Civil Rights*, 8, 73.

21. Anders Walker, "Legislating Virtue: How Segregationists Disguised Racial Discrimination as Moral Reform Following Brown v. Board of Education," *Duke Law Journal* 47 (1997): 423.

22. Dorothy Roberts, *Killing the Black Body: Race, Reproduction and the Meaning of Liberty*, 2nd Vintage ed. (New York: Vintage Books, 2017), 8.

23. Joyce A. Ladner, *The Death of White Sociology* (New York: Random House, 1973).

24. Akasha Gloria Hull, Patricia Bell-Scott, and Barbara Smith, eds., *All the Women Are White, All the Blacks Are Men, but Some of Us Are Brave: Black Women's Studies* (Old Westbury, N.Y.: Feminist Press, 1982).

25. Moynihan, *Negro Family*, 35.

26. Stanley Fish, *There's No Such Thing as Free Speech . . . and It's a Good Thing, Too* (New York: Oxford University Press, 1994), 89, 91.

27. Geary, *Beyond Civil Rights*, 172–205.

28. Premilla Nadasen, "From Widow to 'Welfare Queen': Welfare and the Politics of Race," *Black Women, Gender + Families* 1, no. 2 (Fall 2007): 52–77.

29. Geary, *Beyond Civil Rights*, 207.

30. The AFDC program had been in effect from 1935 to 1996. Its dismantling was in part based on a political belief that the program incentivized women having children and not working.

31. Welfare programs had long been under attack. A 1969 paper by American psychologist Arthur Jensen claimed IQ was largely a product of genetics. His paper was used by some to oppose Head Start and other social welfare programs.

32. Obama's speech to Morehouse graduates and his My Brother's Keeper initiative embraced the assumptions of the Moynihan Report. See Kimberlé Crenshaw's critique of My Brother's Keeper in "The Girls Obama Forgot," *New York Times*, July 29, 2014.

33. Ladner, *Death of White Sociology*.

34. Earl Wright II and Thomas C. Calhoun, "Jim Crow Sociology: Toward an Understanding of the Origin and Principles of Black Sociology via the Atlanta Sociological Laboratory," *Sociological Focus* 39, no. 1 (2006): 1.

35. Geary, *Beyond Civil Rights*, 7–8.

36. Rick Neale, "Dunn Jury Hears from Former Fiancée, Juror Dismissed," *Floridatoday.com*, September 27, 2014, https://www.floridatoday.com/story/news/local/2014/09/27/dunn-jury-hears-former-fiancee/16352219.

37. Derek Kinner, "Michael Dunn Verdict: Florida Man Found Guilty on Attempted Murder in Loud Music Trial," *Huffington Post*, February 14, 2014.

38. "Timeline for Michael Dunn Murder Case in the Death of Jordan Davis," *Florida Times Union*, February 4, 2014.

39. Kinner, "Michael Dunn Verdict." Emphasis added.

40. Ibid.

41. Lisa Bloom, *Suspicion Nation: The Inside Story of the Trayvon Martin Injustice and Why We Continue to Repeat It* (Berkeley, Calif.: Counterpoint, 2015).

42. Michael Brendan Dougherty, "NBC: We're Sorry We Edited the Trayvon Tape to Make George Zimmerman Sound Racist," *Business Insider*, April 4, 2012, https://www.business insider.com/nbc-apologizes-to-george-zimmerman-for-editing-a-911-call-to-make-him-sound -really-racist-2012-4.

43. "The George Zimmerman Trial: Critical Phone Calls," Call #1, University of Missouri-Kansas City Law School, http://law2.umkc.edu/faculty/PROJECTS/FTRIALS /zimmerman1/zimcalls.html.

44. Mark S. Brodin, "The Murder of Black Males in a World of Non-Accountability: The Surreal Trial of George Zimmerman for the Killing of Trayvon Martin," *Howard Law Journal* 59, no. 3 (2016): 765–785; William M. Welch, "Police: Trayvon Martin Shooting 'Avoidable'; Large Cache of Evidence Released in Zimmerman Case," *USA Today*, May 18, 2012.

45. Koritha Mitchell, "Keep Claiming Space!," *CLA Journal* (College Language Association) 58, no. 3/4 (2015): 232.

46. Bloom, *Suspicion Nation*; Brodin, "The Murder of Black Boys," 775, 777.

47. Bloom, *Suspicion Nation*.

48. Sean Collins, "The Killing of Ahmaud Arbery, an Unarmed Black Jogger in Georgia, Explained," *Vox*, June 24, 2020, https://www.vox.com/identities/2020/5/6/21249202/ahmaud -arbery-jogger-killed-in-georgia-video-shooting-grand-jury.

49. Jeremy Bentham, *The Theory of Legislation*, trans. Richard Hildreth (New York: Harcourt, Brace, 1931), 111–113.

50. Cheryl I. Harris, "Whiteness as Property," *Harvard Law Review* 106, no. 8 (June 1993): 1707–1791.

51. Ibid.

52. Public Release Incident Report for G20-11303, Glynn County (Georgia) Police Department, accessed May 7, 2020, https://int.nyt.com/data/documenthelper/6915-arbery-shooting /b52fa09cdc974b970b79/optimized/full.pdf. Emphasis added.

53. Ibid.

54. Michael Brice-Saddler and Cleve R. Wootson Jr., "Georgia Attorney General Assigns Fourth Prosecutor in Killing of Ahmaud Arbery," *Washington Post*, May 11, 2020.

55. Mariel Concepción, "Comedian Michael 'Kramer' Richards Goes into Racial Tirade, Banned from Laugh Factory," *Vibe*, November 20, 2006. https://web.archive.org/web /20061208090628/http://www.vibe.com/news/news_headlines/2006/11/comedian_michael _kramer_richards_goes_into_racial_tirade. Asterisks in original.

56. George Yancy, *Black Bodies, White Gazes: The Continuing Significance of Race*, 2nd ed. (Lanham, Md.: Rowman & Littlefield, 2016), 232.

57. Michael Hatt, "Race Ritual and Responsibility: Performativity and the Southern Lynch-

ing," in *Performing the Body, Performing the Text*, edited by Amelia Jones, Andrew Stephenson Nfa, and Andrew Stephenson (New York: Routledge, 1999), 77. Emphasis added.

58. See Concepción, "Comedian Michael 'Kramer' Richards Goes into Racial Tirade." According to *Vibe* magazine, "The next day, Richards asked if he could return to the comedy club to publicly apologize to the audience, and even requested some of the prior day's patrons be invited, but instead he did his normal routine and did not apologize."

CHAPTER 7. *You* Don't Belong *Here*!

1. Kevin Draper, "A Disparaging Video Prompts Explosive Fallout within ESPN," *New York Times*, July 4, 2021. Emphasis added.

2. Nichols asserted that the position was contractually hers. Ibid.

3. George Barnhill to Captain Tom Jump, Glynn County Police Department, *New York Times*, https://int.nyt.com/data/documenthelper/6916-george-barnhill-letter-to-glyn /b52fa09cdc974b970b79/optimized/full.pdf#page=1.

4. Nirmal Puwar, *Space Invaders: Race, Gender, and Bodies out of Place* (Oxford, England: Berg, 2004).

5. Barbara Harris Combs, "A Jim Crow State of Mind: The Racialization of Space in the McKinney, Texas Pool Party Incident," *American Behavioral Scientist* 65, no. 8 (July 2021): 1029.

6. Koritha Mitchell, "Keep Claiming Space,!" *CLA Journal* (College Language Association) 58, no. 3/4 (2015): 229.

7. In her discussion of the killings, anthropologist Rita Laura Segato makes a distinction between utilitarian violence and performative violence. Segato suggests that all violence has a performative or expressive dimension. See Rita Laura Segato, *La escritura, en el cuerpo de las mujeres asesinadas en Ciudad Juárez* (Buenos Aires: Tinta Limón, 2013), 88. Translated via Google translator.

8. Michael Hatt, "Race Ritual and Responsibility: Performativity and the Southern Lynching," in *Performing the Body, Performing the Text*, ed. Amelia Jones, Andrew Stephenson Nfa, and Andrew Stephenson (New York: Routledge, 1999), 77.

9. Frontier defense is a military concept that involves policing and protecting an area from a perceived threat. In the United States it has a long history of excusing and justifying Indigenous dispossession and territorial conquest—aggressive actions masquerading as defensive ones.

10. Jennifer Lash, "For Members of Congress Traditional Lapel Pin Serves as More than Just a Form of Identification," *Roll Call*, January 20, 2005.

11. *CBS This Morning*, June 1, 2020.

12. Scott Jaschik, "The Admissions Tour that Went Horribly Wrong," *Inside Higher Ed*, May 7, 2018, https://www.insidehighered.com/admissions/article/2018/05/07/colorado-state -investigates-why-native-american-students-admissions.

13. Carma Hassan, Steve Almasy and Nick Valencia, "Texas A&M Investigating Reports of Racial Slurs toward High School Visitors," CNN, February 12, 2016, https://www.cnn.com /2016/02/12/us/texas-am-racial-incident/index.html.

14. There have been a number of notable partnerships between Blacks and White allies that have not entailed the savior complex, which is laced with White supremacist ideology in its inference that Blacks do not possess the intellect or drive to redeem themselves and that redemption is only possible with their assistance.

15. For a similar idea, see Walter Mignolo, *The Darker Side of Western Modernity: Global Futures, Decolonial Options* (Durham, N.C.: Duke University Press, 2011), 87. Mignolo says that in the European Enlightenment, people living in the Global South were seen as backward and viewed as living at the level of Europeans from a much earlier time in history. As a result, they viewed them as both rationally and ontologically deficient.

16. Barbara Harris Combs, "Black (and Brown) Bodies out of Place: Towards a Theoretical Understanding of Systematic Voter Suppression in the United States," *Critical Sociology*, 42, 535–549.

17. "Investigative Report of July 31, 2018 Incident," Sanghavi Law Office, October 28, 2018, Smith College, https://www.smith.edu/sites/default/files/media/Documents/President/investigative-report.pdf.

18. Ibid.

19. Elaine Chun and Joe R. Feagin, *Rethinking Diversity Frameworks in Higher Education* (New York: Routledge, 2019), 134.

20. Colleen Flaherty, "1 Police Call, Lasting Damage to Smith," *Inside Higher Ed*, April 15, 2021, https://www.insidehighered.com/news/2021/04/15/one-police-call-lasting-damage-smith.

21. Nicholas De Genova, "The Incorrigible Subject: The Autonomy of Migration and the U.S. Immigration Stalemate," *Journal of Latin American Geography* 16: 1 (2017): 24.

22. "All I Did Was Be Black," CBS, August 2, 2018, https://www.youtube.com/watch?v=dwEU7IviUqM.

23. Chun and Feagin, *Rethinking Diversity Frameworks in Higher Education*, 134–135.

24. "Framing Questions on Intersectionality," U.S. Human Rights Network, Rutgers Center for Women's Global Leadership, accessed August 26, 2021, https://ushrnetwork.org/uploads/Resources/framing_questions_on_intersectionality_1.pdf.

25. I remind the reader that BOP theory assumes that intersectionality will be built into the analysis.

26. Quoted in Chun and Feagin, *Rethinking Diversity Frameworks in Higher Education*, 134.

27. Bell hooks, "Preface to the first edition," in *Feminist Theory: From Margin to Center*, 3rd ed. (New York: Routledge, 2014), xvii–xviii.

28. Patricia Hill Collins, "Learning from the Outsider Within: The Sociological Significance of Black Feminist Thought," *Social Problems* 33, no. 6 (1986): S14.

29. "Data about Smith," Smith College, https://www.smith.edu/about-smith/institutional-research-smith-data. In 2020, families earning less than $60,000 would be Pell-eligible; families earning less than $30,000 a year were eligible for the full amount.

30. "Common Data Set 2019–2020," Smith College, https://web.archive.org/web/20200710192919/https://www.smith.edu/sites/default/files/media/Smith%20College_Common%20Data%20Set%202019-2020_Complete_0.pdf.

31. hooks, *Feminist Theory*.

32. Louwanda Evans and Wendy Leo Moore, "Impossible Burdens: White Institutions, Emotional Labor, and Micro-Resistance," *Social Problems* 62, no. 3 (August 2015): 446, 452.

33. Anne Warfield Rawls and Waverly Duck, *Tacit Racism* (Chicago: University of Chicago Press, 2020); Sara Bullard, ed., *The Ku Klux Klan: A History of Racism and Violence*, 4th ed. (Darby, Pa.: Diane, 1996).

34. The four central frames of color-blind racism are abstract liberalism, naturalization, cultural racism, and minimization of racism.

35. Eduardo Bonilla-Silva, *Racism without Racists: Color-Blind Racism and the Persistence of Racial Inequality in America*, 5th ed. (Lanham, Md.: Rowman & Littlefield, 2018).

36. Caroline Criado-Perez, *Invisible Women: Data Bias in a World Designed for Men* (New York: Harry N. Abrams, 2019), xiii.

37. Pat Eaton-Robb, "Police Called on Black Student Sleeping in Her Yale Dorm," *AP News*, May 9, 2018. https://apnews.com/1bc77114e0024b5b97c891d48209eae7/Police-called-on-black-student-sleeping-in-her-Yale-dorm.

38. Mihir Zaveri, "Doubletree in Portland Fires 2 Employees after Kicking Out Black Man Who Made Call from Lobby," *New York Times*, December 28, 2018.

39. Frantz Fanon, *Black Skin, White Masks*, rev. ed. (New York: Grove Press, 2008), 80.

40. Maureen Dowd, "Bite Your Tongue," *New York Times*, July 25, 2009.

41. Quoted in "Missed Opportunities, Shared Responsibilities," *Harvard Magazine*, July 1, 2010, https://harvardmagazine.com/2010/07/report-on-cambridge-police-sgt-crowley-professor-gates; full report: *Missed Opportunities, Shared Responsibilities: Final Report of the Cambridge Review Committee* (Cambridge, Mass.: City of Cambridge, 2010), 3–4. https://www.cambridgema.gov/cpd/Publications/2010/06/cambridgereviewcommittee/cambridgereviewcommitteefinalreport.

42. Dred Scott v. Sandford, 60 U.S. 393 (1856), 407.

43. W. E. B. Du Bois, *The Souls of Black Folk* (repr.; New York: Oxford University Press, 2008).

44. Elizabeth Hordge-Freeman and Gladys L. Mitchell-Walthour, "Introduction: In Pursuit of Du Bois's 'Second-Sight' through Diasporic Dialogues," in *Race and the Politics of Knowledge Production: Diaspora and Black Transnational Scholarship in the United States and Brazil* (New York: Palgrave Macmillan, 2016),1.

45. Situated knowledge: Donna Haraway, "Situated Knowledges: The Science Question in Feminism and the Privilege of Partial Perspective," *Feminist Studies*, 14, no. 3 (Autumn, 1988): 575–599. Standpoint theory: Dorothy Smith, "Women's Perspective as a Radical Critique of Sociology," in *The Feminist Standpoint Theory Reader*, ed. Sandra Harding (New York: Routledge, 2004), 21–34. Insider-outsider status: Patricia Hill Collins, "Learning from the Outsider Within: The Sociological Significance of Black Feminist Thought," *Social Problems* 33, no. 6 (1986): S14–32; Collins, *Black Feminist Thought*.

46. Donna Haraway, "Situated Knowledges," 583.

47. Ibid., 586. Emphasis added.

48. Charles Hale, *Engaging Contradictions: Theory, Politics, and Methods of Activist Scholarship* (Berkeley: University of California Press, 2008), 1–31.

49. Bell hooks, *From Margin to Center*, vii.

50. Ibid.

CHAPTER 8. It's All White Space

1. Donesha Aldridge, "911 Calls in Ahmaud Arbery Case | 'He's Running Down the Street,'" *11 Alive News*, https://www.11alive.com/article/news/crime/911-calls-ahmaud-arbery/85 -4819d3d9-6133-40de-b3a9-f8fa3f889574.

2. Cheryl Harris, "Whiteness as Property," *Harvard Law Review* 106, no. 8 (1993): 1729.

3. Ibid., 1714.

4. Shannon Sullivan, *Revealing Whiteness: The Unconscious Habits of Racial Privilege* (Indiana University Press, 2006), 10.

5. Shannon Sullivan, *Good White People: The Problem with Middle-Class White Anti-Racism* (SUNY Press, 2014), 20. Sullivan suggests that Whites often do this with good intentions.

6. Harold Garfinkel, "Conditions of Successful Degradation Ceremonies," *American Journal of Sociology* 61, no. 5: (1956) 420–424.

7. Kyle Arnold, "A Texas Doctor Says American Airlines Nearly Kicked Her Off a Flight for an 'Inappropriate' Romper,'" *Dallas News*, July 9, 2019.

8. Neil Vigdor, "Woman Required to Cover Up on American Airlines Flight Says Race Was a Factor," *New York Times*, July 10, 2019.

9. Lee Moran, "Serena Williams' Fierce French Open Outfit Is Fit for a 'Goddess,'" *Huffington Post*, May 28, 2019, https://www.huffpost.com/entry/serena-williams-french-open-outfit_n _5cece883e4b00356fc26d677.

10. Associated Press, "Serena Williams Hits Out Again at Drug Testing 'Discrimination,'" *ESPN*, July 25, 2018, https://www.espn.com/tennis/story/_/id/24189408/serena-williams-hits -again-drug-testing-discrimination.

11. For example, in *Police Department of the City of Chicago v. Mosely*, 408 U.S. 92, 101–102 (1972), the court held that the regulation of speech based on the content or subject matter should be subject to strict scrutiny and must be narrowly tailored to serve a substantial governmental interest.

12. Simone Browne, "'What Did TSA Find in Solange's Fro?': Security Theater at the Airport," chap. 4 in *Dark Matters: On the Surveillance of Blackness* (Durham, N.C.: Duke University Press, 2015).

13. Janelle Griffith, "Black Cheerleader Kicked Off Team over Her Natural Hair, Mom Says," NBC NEWS, December 18, 2019, https://www.nbcnews.com/news/nbcblk/black -cheerleader-kicked-team-over-her-natural-hair-mom-says-n1104181.

14. Julia Jacobs and Dan Levin, "Black Girl Sent Home from School over Hair Extensions," *New York Times*, August 21, 2018.

15. Natalie Dreier, "Senior Told to Cut Dreadlocks or Can't Walk at Commencement," Fox 23 News, January 22, 2020.

16. All of the cases below overlap with the historical fear-factor frame, the presumed criminal frame, and *You* Don't Belong *Here*!, but they are discussed here because they typify the concept of White ontological expansion.

17. Nicole Rojas, "Black Man Records White Woman Calling 911 after Accusing Him of Breaking into His Own Car," *Newsweek*, August 17, 2018, https://www.newsweek.com/woman -calls-police-video-black-man-breaking-own-car-milwaukee-reporachel-1078717.

18. Kimberly Veklerov, "Black Firefighter on Inspection Duty in Oakland Gets Videotaped, Reported to Police," *San Francisco Chronicle*, June 24, 2018.

19. Narjas Zatat, "BBQ Becky's 911 Tapes Released in Full and They're Shocking," *Indy 100*, September 4, 2018.

20. Ibid.

21. Jeff Wilste, *Contested Waters: A Social History of Swimming Pools in America* (Chapel Hill: University of North Carolina Press, 2010), 78–86, 125–153, quote from page 5. In 1949, when Fairground Park in Missouri was integrated, a police officer used his body to shield a Black patron who was being kicked and beaten by White rioters. After the riot, the pool was ordered segregated again. See also "Racial History of American Swimming Pools," *The Bryant Park Project*, NPR, May 6, 2008; Jennifer Ritterhouse, *Growing up Jim Crow: How Black and White Southern Children Learned Race* (Durham: University of North Carolina Press, 2006); Joseph Crespino, *Strom Thurmond's America* (New York: Hill & Wang, 2013); Rashad Shabazz, *Spatializing Blackness: Architectures of Confinement and Black Masculinity in Chicago* (Urbana: University of Illinois Press, 2015); Lillian Smith, *Killers of the Dream* (New York: W. W. Norton, 1949).

22. Barbara Harris Combs, "A Jim Crow State of Mind: The Racialization of Space in the McKinney, Texas Pool Party Incident," *American Behavioral Scientist* 65, no. 8 (2021): 1027–1048.

23. Jack Bass and W. Scott Poole, *The Palmetto State: The Making of Modern South Carolina* (Columbia: University of South Carolina Press, 2009), 104.

24. Wilste, *Contested Waters*.

25. "Racial History of American Swimming Pools."

26. Sarah Mervosh, "A Black Man Wore Socks in the Pool. After Calling the Police on Him, a Manager Got Fired," *New York Times*, July 9, 2018.

27. Justin Carissimo, "Woman Fired for Calling Police on Black Man Wearing Socks in Pool," CBS News, July 10, 2018, https://www.cbsnews.com/news/erica-walker-memphis -woman-fired-calling-police-black-man-wearing-socks-pool-2018-07-09.

28. Tanya Eiserer, "Full Transcript of Amber Guyger's 911 Call after Shooting Botham Jean," *5 Newsonline.com*, April 19, 2019, https://www.5newsonline.com/article/news/crime/full -transcript-of-amber-guygers-911-call-after-shooting-botham-jean/269-28fb11e1-5cf7-4c33 -b868-ac6978a60afb.

29. Audio link in Larry Collins et al., "Amber Guyger Takes Stand on 5th Day of Testimony," *NBCDFW.com*, September 23, 2019, https://www.nbcdfw.com/news/local/watch-live-amber -guyger-murder-trial-day-5/241802.

30. In some interviews, Guyger suggested the door was partially ajar.

31. WFAA, "Full Video: Amy Guyger's Testimony," September 28, 2019, https://www.youtube .com/watch?v=J7IgyPh8UkQ. Emphasis added.

32. Ibid. Emphasis added.

33. Ibid.

34. Erik Ortiz, "Texts between Amber Guyger, Dallas Police Partner Revealed at Murder Trial," NBCNews.com, September 24, 2019.

35. In August 2020, Guyger appealed her sentence. Her attorneys asserted that there was insufficient evidence to convict her for murder.

36. Ray Sanchez and Ashley Killough, "Former Dallas Police Officer Amber Guyger Asks Appeals Court to Throw Out Murder Conviction for Killing Botham Jean," CNN, April 27, 2021, https://www.cnn.com/2021/04/27/us/amber-guyger-appeal-botham-jean-murder/index.html.

37. David R. Roediger, *Working toward Whiteness: How America's Immigrants Became White: The Strange Journey from Ellis Island to the Suburbs* (New York: Basic Books, 2006).

CHAPTER 9. The Weight

1. "Harlem," in Langston Hughes, *The Collected Poems of Langston Hughes* (New York: Knopf/Random House, 1994), 426.

2. Toni Morrison talk at Portland State University, 1975.

3. The b-word itself is derogatory term most often used to describe women. When applied through an intersectional (as modified by the word Black before it), its weight and the force of the insult is meant to be amplified. You are not just a b-word. You are a Black b-word. While women are on the bottom of the hierarchy, Black women are the lowest rung in the hierarchy.

4. Laura Green, "Negative Racial Stereotypes and Their Attitudes toward African-Americans," Jim Crow Museum of Racist Memorabilia, https://www.ferris.edu/htmls/news/jimcrow/links/essays/vcu.htm.

5. Mark Peffley, Jon Hurwitz, and Paul M. Sniderman, "Racial Stereotypes and Whites' Political Views of Blacks in the Context of Welfare and Crime," *American Journal of Political Science* 41 (1997): 31.

6. Elijah Anderson, "The White Space," *Sociology of Race and Ethnicity* 1, no. 1 (2015): 13.

7. Etienne G. Krug et al., eds., *World Report on Violence and Health* (Geneva: World Health Organization, 2002), 9.

8. Anthony B. Zwi, Richard Garfield, and Alessandro Loretti, "Collective Violence," in ibid., 213–239.

9. Johan Galtung, "Cultural Violence," *Journal of Peace Research* 27, no. 3 (August 1990): 291–305.

10. Kirk A. Johnson et al., *Microaggressions at the University of Mississippi A Report from the UM Race Diary Project* (University of Mississippi, 2018), ii. https://socanth.wp2.olemiss.edu/wp-content/uploads/sites/154/2018/10/Microaggressions-report-10-9-18.pdf.

11. Ibid., iii. In a later published version of the findings from this study, the authors use the typology set forth by psychologist Derald Sue, *Microaggressions in Everyday Life: Race, Gender, and Sexual Orientation* (Hoboken, N.J.: John Wiley & Sons, 2010). Like Sue, the authors classify microaggressions as "microinsults, microassaults, and microinvalidations" in order to classify findings in their study of the racial diaries of over 1,300 students attending a large southern college. See Kirk A. Johnson et al., "Mapping Microaggressions on a Southern University Campus: Where Are the Safe Spaces for Vulnerable Students?," *Social Problems* 68, no. 1 (2021).

12. Simone Browne, *Dark Matters: On the Surveillance of Blackness* (Durham, N.C.: Duke University Press, 2015).

13. Patricia Hill Collins, *Fighting Words: Black Women and the Search for Justice* (Minneapolis, Minnesota: University of Minnesota Press, 1998), 75.

14. Collins, *Fighting Words*, argues that writing across time is an effort at contextualizing history.

15. Browne, *Dark Matters*, 6.

16. James McBride, *Deacon King Kong* (New York: Penguin, 2020), 212.

17. Frantz Fanon, *Black Skin, White Masks*, rev. ed. (New York: Grove Press, 2008), 71.

18. Scholars including Eric Foner and W. E. B. Du Bois have provided accurate refutations of the Dunning school.

19. Quoted in Bruce Watson, *Freedom Summer: The Savage Season That Made Mississippi Burn and Made America a Democracy* (New York: Viking, 2010), 48.

20. Barbara Harris Combs and Jodi Skipper, "'It's Open Season on Negroes': Teaching the Past, Present, and Future of the Black Freedom Struggle," *Southern Quarterly* 52, no. 1 (2014): 135, https://www.muse.jhu.edu/article/567255.

21. This was my second year of teaching at the institution. My family remained in Georgia throughout my first year and fourth year at UM.

22. James Loewen, *Sundown Towns: A Hidden Dimension of American Racism* (New York: New Press, 2005).

23. Ironically, the groups that include the people who work the hardest for the lowest rewards are often derided as "lazy" by those who exploit them.

24. Thomas Shapiro, *The Hidden Cost of Being African American* (New York: Oxford University Press, 2005).

25. Emily Badger, "Whites Have Huge Wealth Edge over Blacks (but Don't Know It)," *New York Times*, September 18, 2017.

26. Michael W. Kraus, Julian M. Rucker and Jennifer A. Richeson, "Americans Misperceive Racial Economic Equality," PNAS 114, no. 39 (2017), 10324–10331.

27. NAACP Criminal Justice Fact Sheet, accessed August 29, 2021, https:://www.naacp.org /criminal-justice-fact-sheet.

28. Len Engel et al., "Racial Disparities and Covid-19," National Commission on Covid-19 and Criminal Justice, November 2020, https://build.neoninspire.com/counciloncj/wp -content/uploads/sites/96/2021/07/Racial-Disparities-and-COVID-19-Report.pdf.

29. William Darity Jr. "Stratification Economics: The Role of Intergroup Inequality," *Journal of Economics and Finance* 29, no. 2 (2005): 144–145.

30. Paula Giddings, "The Life and Work of Ida B. Wells," interview with Kai Wright on *The United States of Anxiety* podcast, WNYC Studios, May 8, 2020, https://www.wnycstudios.org /podcasts/anxiety/episodes/life-and-work-ida-b-wells.

31. Susie Steinbach, *Understanding the Victorians*, 2nd ed. (New York: Routledge, 2016).

32. Ibid., 133.

33. The 19th-century "cult of true womanhood" or cult of domesticity emerged from the ideology of domestic spheres. The cult of true womanhood suggested that a true woman possessed the virtues of piety, purity, submissiveness, and domesticity.

34. Steinbach, *Understanding the Victorians*, 125.

35. Giddings, "Life and Work of Ida B. Wells."

36. James Baldwin, "Black English: A Dishonest Argument", 1980, quoted in Raoul Peck, *I Am Not Your Negro* (N.p.: Velvet Film, 2016).

37. When I speak of enduring racism, I mean one of a host of possible responses. I do not limit this to just standing there and taking the attacks leveled against you, but I also do not mean to denigrate the person who responds without flinching or a counter-attack. I am amazed by the quiet, steely strength of Elizabeth Eckford, who entered Central High School in Little Rock, Arkansas, all alone amid the jeers of protesters, and of Samantha Francine, the young black woman at a Black Lives Matter protest in Montana who stared into the eyes of a hate-filled white counter-protester. See Rita Omokha, "Protester Says Her Calm Captured in This Viral Photo Was Inspired by Advice from Her Father," *Women's Health Magazine*, June 10, 2020, https://www.womenshealthmag.com/life/a32818419/viral-protest-photo-whitefish-mt -samantha-francine.

38. David Montgomery, "The Death of Sandra Bland: Is There Anything Left to Investigate?," *New York Times*, May 8, 2019.

39. Jon Meacham, *The Soul of America: The Battle for Our Better Angels* (New York: Random House, 2018), 222.

40. Taylor Branch, *Parting the Waters: America in the King Years, 1954–63* (New York: Simon & Schuster, 1989), 881.

41. "That Act Was Unmistakably Racist," CBS News, June 9, 2020, https://www.cbsnews .com/news/amy-cooper-christian-cooper-speaks-out-that-act-was-unmistakably-racist.

42. Sarah Maslin Nir, "White Woman Is Fired after Calling Police on Black Man in Central Park," *New York Times*, May 26, 2020.

43. Brakkton Booker, "White Woman Is Fired after Calling Police on Black Man," *Morning Edition*, NPR, May 26, 2020, https://www.npr.org/2020/05/26/862230724/white-woman -who-called-police-on-black-bird-watcher-in-central-park-placed-on-le.

44. "I Can't Breathe," CBS News, June 9, 2020, https://www.cbsnews.com/news/amy -cooper-christian-cooper-speaks-out-that-act-was-unmistakably-racist.

45. Michel Martin, "Fear of Black Men: How Society Sees Black Men and How They See Themselves," *Morning Edition*, NPR, March 31, 2015, https://www.npr.org/2015/03/31 /396415737/societys-fear-of-black-men-and-its-consequences.

46. Chelsea Prince, "Atlanta Private School Suspends Students after Video Shows Mock Lynching in Bathroom," *Atlanta Journal-Constitution*, March 6, 2020; "Atlanta Students Suspended after Staging Mock Lynching," BET, https://www.bet.com/news/national/2020/03 /06/atlanta-students-mock-lynching.html.

47. "Photo of 4 Black Students, Gorilla and 'Monkey See, Monkey Do' Label Spark Controversy," January 9, 2020, CBS News, https://www.cbsnews.com/news/photo-4-black-students -gorilla-monkey-see-monkey-do-label-spark-controversy.

48. Angelina Velasquez and Jamie Kennedy, "Principal Expresses Outrage over Racist Photo in Student Yearbook," *CBS46.com*, https://www.cbs46.com/news/principal-expresses-outrage -over-racist-photo-in-student-yearbook/article_fd2e7abe-ab76-11ea-9564-8b17a3e59e32.html. According to the article, "The photo shopped [*sic*] image . . . depicts a student standing with

the Civil Rights leader as he holds a binder that reads, 'Official N-Word Pass.' Assigned to 'student name.' Given by black speech n—a."

49. Maureen Downey, "Collins Hill High School Decides to Recall Yearbook with Racial Slur in Photo," *Atlanta Journal Constitution*, June 11, 2020.

50. William Smith describes racial battle fatigue as psychophysiological symptoms (like anxiety, stress, anger, and depression) people of color may experience as they navigate living and/or working in hostile White spaces.

51. Wade Goodwyn, "Beating Charges Split La. Town along Racial Lines," *All Things Considered*, NPR, July 30, 2007, https://www.npr.org/templates/story/story.php?storyId=12353776.

52. Ibid.

53. Mychal Bell was convicted by an all-White jury. There was a large public outcry over prosecution of the boys. Bell was originally tried and convicted as an adult, but that conviction was overturned when an appellate court ruled that he should have been tried as a juvenile. Bell faced retrial as a juvenile. Days before the retrial was to begin, Bell accepted a plea deal. He pleaded guilty to second-degree battery (a misdemeanor) and was sentenced to 18 months. Amy Waldman, "The Truth about Jena," *Atlantic*, January/February 2008), https://www.theatlantic.com/magazine/archive/2008/01/the-truth-about-jena/306580. Charges were also reduced against the other five defendants. The defendants pleaded no contest and were fined. See "5 defendants Plead No Contest in 'Jena Six' Case," CNN, June 26, 2009, https://www.cnn.com/2009/CRIME/06/26/louisiana.jena.6.

54. "The Situation Room," CNN, May 31, 2020, transcript, http://transcripts.cnn.com/TRANSCRIPTS/2005/31/sitroom.02.html.

55. W. E. B. Du Bois, *The Souls of Black Folk* (repr.; New York: Oxford University Press, 2008),xiii.

56. Jennifer Jeanne Patterson, "The 'Minnesota Paradox': A State Grapples with Stark Racial Disparities." *U.S. News & World Report*, June 4, 2020, https://www.usnews.com/news/national-news/articles/2020-06-04/george-floyds-death-exposes-the-minnesota-paradox.

57. James M. Blaut, "The Theory of Cultural Racism," *Antipode: A Radical Journal of Geography*, 24, no. 4 (1992).

58. Rashawn Ray, "Fraternity Life in Predominantly White Universities in the U.S.: Saliency of Race," in *Race and Ethnicity in Secret and Exclusive Social Orders: Blood and Shadow*, ed. Matthew Hughey (New York: Routledge, 2015), 87.

59. Scott Jaschik, "Names, Symbols, and Race," *Inside Higher Education*, August 4, 2014, https://www.insidehighered.com/news/2014/08/04/u-mississippi-tries-new-approach-its-history-race-and-faces-criticism.

60. Jake New, "Deadliest and Most Racist?," *Inside Higher Ed*, March 10, 2015, https://www.insidehighered.com/news/2015/03/10/several-sigma-alpha-epsilon-chapters-accused-racism-recent-years.

61. Alvin Tillery, "Is the #BlackLivesMatter Movement Winning?," September 16, 2019, comments at James Weldon Johnson Institute, Emory University.

62. Emma Garcia, "Schools Are Still Segregated and Black Children Are Paying Price," Economic Policy Institute, February 12, 2020, https://www.epi.org/publication/schools-are-still-segregated-and-black-children-are-paying-a-price; Alana Semuels, "Segregation Has Gotten

Worse, Not Better, and It's Fueling the Wealth Gap between Black and White Americans, *Time*, June 19, 2020, https://time.com/5855900/segregation-wealth-gap; Christian Smith and Michael O. Emerson, *Divided by Faith: Evangelical Religion and the Problem of Race in America* (Oxford University Pres, 2001).

63. For discussion of employment segregation by race and gender, see Beth Mintz and Daniel H. Krymkowski, "The Intersection of Race/Ethnicity and Gender in Occupational Segregation: Changes over Time in the Contemporary United States," *International Journal of Sociology* 40, no. 4 (2010): 31–58; Kim A. Weeden, "Occupational Segregation," *Pathways: A Magazine on Poverty, Inequality, and Social Policy*, special issue 2019, https://inequality .stanford.edu/sites/default/files/Pathways_SOTU_2019.pdf.

64. These spaces include neighborhoods that are deemed "Black neighborhoods" or "White neighborhoods," but balkanization can also be found in the likes of career choices and recreational activities.

65. Martin, "Fear of Black Men," https://www.npr.org/transcripts/396415737.

66. Soon after the Trayvon Martin incident, Congressman Bobby Rush was escorted off the floor of Congress for donning a hoodie and thus being seen as breaking the rules of decorum. Leo Cunningham knows that as a Black man he is seen as a threat. I argue that the performative act of escorting Rush off the floor is meant to tell Blacks everywhere that if it could happen to Rush in the hallowed halls of Congress, it could happen to you too. You are only safe if you stay in line, abiding by lines drawn by those in power, lines that are constantly shifting. See Corey Boles, "Rep. Bobby Rush Is Scolded for Wearing a 'Hoodie' on House Floor," *Wall Street Journal*.

67. Martin, "Fear of Black Men."

68. Ibid.

69. Eldridge Cleaver, *Soul on Ice* (New York: Dell, 1967), 117.

70. Ashley Southall, "Police Officer Who Manhandled Tennis Star James Blake Avoids Trial," *New York Times*, May 14, 2017.

71. Tribune Media Wire, "NFL Player Michael Bennett Says He Was Targeted by Police for 'Simply Being a Black Man,'" WREG, September 6, 2017, https://www.wreg.com/news/nfl -player-michael-bennett-says-he-was-targeted-by-police-for-simply-being-a-black-man.

72. "Drew Brees' Teammate Malcolm Jenkins among Many Stars to Speak Out against Quarterback's Controversial Comments," ESPN, June 3, 2020, https://www.espn.com/nfl /story/_/id/29263512/drew-brees-teammate-malcolm-jenkins-many-stars-speak -quarterback-controversial-comments.

73. Maura Hohman, "Nashville Community Rallies around Black Man Who Said He Was Scared to Walk Alone," *Today*, June 1, 2020, https://www.today.com/news/nashville -community-rallies-around-black-man-who-said-he-was-t182833.

74. Ibid.

75. Will Thorne, "Jay Pharoah Says LAPD Drew Guns on Him While Walking, Kneeled on His Neck," *Variety*, June 12, 2020, https://variety.com/2020/tv/news/jay-pharoah-jogging -lapd-kneeling-on-his-neck-1234633312.

76. For what amounts to a version of the "the talk"—what Black parents must tell their children about, see WFYI, "10 Rules of Survival if Stopped by the Police," PBS Black Culture Con-

nection, https://www.pbs.org/black-culture/connect/talk-back/10_rules_of_survival_if
_stopped_by_police. On Black males' "outsize risk" of being killed by police, see Ryan Gabrielson, Eric Sagara and Ryann Grochowski Jones, "Deadly Force in Black and White," *ProPublica*, October 10, 2014, https://www.propublica.org/article/deadly-force-in-black-and-white.

77. Rachel Siegel, "Golf Course That Called the Police on Black Women Loses Business, Faces Call for State Investigation," *Washington Post*, April 27, 2018.

78. "Harlem," in Langston Hughes, *The Collected Poems of Langston Hughes* (New York: Knopf/Random House, 1994), 426.

79. Audre Lorde, "A Litany for Survival," in *The Collected Poems of Audre Lorde* (New York: W. W. Norton, 2000), 24.

80. Aris Folley, "Maxine Waters Responds to Mailed Bombs: 'I Ain't Scared,'" *The Hill*, October 25, 2018, https://thehill.com/homenews/house/413085-maxine-waters-responds-to
-bomb-threats-i-aint-scared

81. Kate Davis and David Heilbroner, directors, *Say Her Name: The Life and Death of Sandra Bland* (HBO, 2018).

82. Vittorio Bufacchi, "Two Concepts of Violence," *Political Studies Review* 3, no. 2 (2005): 193–204.

83. Cedric Thornton, "George Floyd's 6-Year-Old Daughter Says Her 'Daddy Changed the World,'" *Black Enterprise*, June 5, 2020, https://www.blackenterprise.com/george-floyds
-6-year-old-daughter-says-her-daddy-changed-the-world.

84. Andie Judson, "Mothers, Children Block Off Sacramento Streets in Peaceful March for George Floyd," *ABC News 10*, June 7, 2020, https://www.abc10.com/article/news/local
/sacramento/sacramento-george-floyd-protest/103-e31dfc7f-8a3d-4fb0–9f1f-89664b5229b7.

85. Erick Levenson and Aaron Cooper, "Derek Chauvin's Trial in Death of George Floyd Begins with Showing Jurors Video of His Final Moments," CNN, March 30, 2021; "Derek Chauvin Sentenced to 22½ Years for Murder of George Floyd," *Richmond Free Press*, July 1, 2021.

86. Yaron Steinbuch, "Darnella Frazier Wasn't Looking to Be Hero by Filming George Floyd Video: Lawyer," *New York Post*, June 12, 2020.

87. Rebecca Carter, *Prayers for the People: Homicide and Humanity in the Crescent City* (Chicago: University of Chicago Press, 2019).

88. Peyton Yager, "'I Literally Cried for Hours After': Delivery Driver Speaks with News 4 after Being Blocked In while on the Job in NE OKC Neighborhood," KFRO, May 14, 2020, https://kfor.com/news/local/i-literally-cried-for-hours-after-delivery-driver-speaks-with-news
-4-after-being-blocked-in-while-on-the-job-in-ne-okc-neighborhood.

89. Quoted in Peck, *I Am Not Your Negro*.

90. Saidiya Hartman, *Scenes of Subjection: Terror, Slavery, and Self-Making in Nineteenth-Century America* (New York: Oxford University Press, 1997).

91. Louwanda Evans, *Cabin Pressure: African American Pilots, Flight Attendants, and Emotional Labor* (Lanham, Md.: Rowman & Littlefield, 2013), 110.

92. Ibid., 95, 98.

93. Ibid., 60, 95.

94. Ibid., 108.

95. "Social Determinants of Health," Office of Disease Prevention and Health Promotion, August 30, 2021, https://www.healthypeople.gov/2020/topics-objectives/topic/social -determinants-of-health

96. Joe Feagin, "The Continuing Significance of Race: Antiblack Discrimination in Public Places," *American Sociological Review* 56, no. 1 (1991): 103.

97. W. Kamau Bell, "Happy Birthday! Have Some Racism from Elmwood Café!," blog post, January 28, 2015, http://www.wkamaubell.com/blog/2015/01/happy-birthday-have-some -racism-from-elmwood-café.

98. Kareem Abdul Jabbar, "Don't You Understand the Protests?," *Los Angeles Times*, May 30, 2020.

CHAPTER 10. Sincere Ignorance and Conscientious Stupidity

1. Martin Luther King Jr., *Strength to Love* (repr.; Minneapolis: Fortress Press, 2010), 153.

2. Jean-Jacques Rousseau, *The Major Political Writings of Jean-Jacques Rousseau: The Two Discourses and the Social Contract*, trans. and ed. John T. Scott (Chicago: University of Chicago Press, 2014.)

3. Charles Mills, *The Racial Contract* (Ithaca: Cornell University Press, 1997), 131.

4. Carter G. Woodson, "How We Drifted Away from the Truth," chap. 3 in *The Mis-Education of the Negro* (Trenton, N.J.: Africa World Press, 1933).

5. Mills, *The Racial Contract*, 18–19.

6. Mills, *Racial Contract*, 56.

7. Reiland Rabaka, *W. E. B. Du Bois and the Problems of the Twenty-First Century: An Essay on Africana Critical Theory* (Lanham, Md.: Lexington Books, 2008), 63.

8. Tim Grierson, "'I Am Not Your Negro': How a New Doc Turns James Baldwin into a Prophet," *Rolling Stone*, February 3, 2017, https://www.rollingstone.com/movies/movie -features/i-am-not-your-negro-how-a-new-doc-turns-james-baldwin-into-a-prophet-117114, quoting from film *I Am Not Your Negro*. Emphasis in original.

9. In September 2020, President Trump issued an executive order instructing federal agencies and contractors that receive federal grants to end racial sensitivity training that addresses topics such as White privilege, systemic racism, intersectionality, and critical race theory.

10. James Baldwin, *The Fire Next Time* (New York: Vintage, 1992), 342.

11. Ali Meghji, "Activating Controlling Images in the Racialized Interaction Order: Black Middle Class Interactions and the Creativity of Racist Action," *Symbolic Interaction* 42, no. 2 (2019): 229–249.

12. Ibid., 229,

13. Mark Dolliver, "U.S. Time Spent with Media 2019: Digital Time Keeps Rising as Growth Subsides for Total Time Spent," *EMarketer*, May 30, 2019, https://www.emarketer.com /content/us-time-spent-with-media-2019.

14. Patricia Hill Collins developed the term "controlling images" to explain how media images reinforce racist beliefs and stereotypes, particularly of Black women.

15. Cheryl T. Gilkes, "From Slavery to Social Welfare: Racism and the Control of Black

Women," in *Class, Race and Sex: The Dynamics of Control*, ed. Amy Swerdlow and Hanna Lessinger (Boston: G. K. Hall, 1983), 294.

16. Trudier Harris, *From Mammies to Militants: Domestics in Black American Literature* (Philadelphia: Temple University Press, 1982), 4; Patricia Hill Collins, *Black Feminist Thought: Knowledge, Consciousness, and the Politics of Empowerment* (New York: Routledge, 2000).

17. Gilkes, "From Slavery to Social Welfare," 294.

18. Brittney Cooper, *Eloquent Rage: A Black Feminist Discovers Her Superpower* (New York: Picador, 2018), 2.

19. Collins, *Black Feminist Thought*, 73.

20. Victor Ray, "A Theory of Racialized Organizations," *American Sociological Review* 84, no. 1 (2019): 26–53.

21. Christopher B. Doob, *Social Inequality and Social Stratification in U.S. Society* (Upper Saddle River, N.J.: Pearson, 2013), 273. Because White logic and ideology are hegemonic, colorblind logics pervade society and are held by Whites and non-Whites alike.

22. Jennifer C. Mueller, "Producing Colorblindness: Everyday Mechanisms of White Ignorance," *Social Problems* 64, no. 2 (2017): 223.

23. Mills, *The Racial Contract*, and Charles W. Mills, "White Ignorance," in *Race and Epistemologies of Ignorance*, ed. S. Sullivan and N. Tuana (Albany: State University of New York Press, 2007), 13–38.

24. Mueller, "Producing Colorblindness."

25. Ibid., 231.

26. Ibid., 225, 231, 229, 227.

27. Ibram X. Kendi, *How to Be an Anti-Racist* (New York: One World, 2019), builds on Davis's insights.

28. Eduardo Bonilla-Silva and Tukufu Zuberi, "Introduction: Toward a Definition of White Logic and White Methods" in *White Logic, White Methods: Racism and Methodology* (Lanham, Md.: Rowman & Littlefield, 2008), 3–30.

29. According to an interview on the *Today* show, the young girl was selling water in front of her own residence. See "Woman Who Called Police on Black Girl Selling Water to Go to Disneyland Comes under Fire," *Today*, June 25, 2018, https://www.youtube.com/watch?v=KqARrnQdcQM.

30. CNN, "Woman in 'Permit Patty' Video Speaks Out: I Feel Manipulated," https://www.youtube.com/watch?v=lyJOYzof9R4

31. Ibid.

32. It was June 25, 2018, and the young girl wanted to help her out-of-work mother and perhaps raise enough to go to Disney. Amid the intense public scrutiny of her actions, Ettel later resigned from her job as CEO of a company. It is important to note that the temporary scrutiny Ettel faced is the type of daily scrutiny people of color, especially Black people, undergo.

33. Amir Vera and Laura Ly, "White Woman Who Called Police on a Black Man Birdwatching in Central Park Has Been Fired," CNN, May 26, 2020, https://www.cnn.com/2020/05/26/us/central-park-video-dog-video-african-american-trnd/index.html.

34. Amy Cooper, "Statement from Amy Cooper on Central Park Incident," Cision, May 26, 2020, https://www.prnewswire.com/news-releases/statement-from-amy-cooper-on-central -park-incident-301065492.html.

35. Troy Closson, "Amy Cooper Falsely Accused Black Bird-Watcher in 2nd 911 Conversation," *New York Times*, October 14, 2020.

36. Amir Vera and Laura Ly, "White Woman Who Called Police."

37. Jasmine Aguilera, "Cyclist Who Allegedly Assaulted a Group of Teens Posting Protest Flyers in a Viral Video Has Been Arrested," *Time*, June 6, 2020, https://time.com/5849480 /bicyclist-viral-video-teens-maryland-arrested.

38. Suzanne Pollak, "Arrested Bicyclist: 'I Am Sick with Remorse,'" MyMCMedia.org, https://www.mymcmedia.org/arrested-bicyclist-i-am-sick-with-remorse.

39. Patrik Walker, "Drew Brees Twice Apologizes Following Backlash for Comments about Kneeling during National Anthem," CBSsports.com, June 5, 2020, https://www.cbssports.com /nfl/news/drew-brees-twice-apologizes-following-backlash-for-comments-about-kneeling -during-national-anthem. Emphasis added.

40. John Eligon, "How Black Students Challenged the Racism at Their High School," *New York Times*, June 8, 2019.

41. Errin Haines Whack, "Two Black Men Arrested at Starbucks Get an Apology from Police," AP News, April 202, 2018, https://apnews.com/45547c3ae5324b679e982c4847ee1378 /2-black-men-arrested-at-Starbucks-get-an-apology-from-police.

42. Anna Orso, "One Year Later: A Timeline of Controversy and Progress since the Starbucks Arrests Seen 'Round the World,'" *Inquirer*, April 12, 2019. https://www.inquirer.com /news/starbucks-incident-philadelphia-racial-bias-one-year-anniversary-stutter-dilworth-park -homeless-tables-20190412.html.

43. Heather Murphy, "Starbucks Will Allow Employees to Wear Black Lives Matter Apparel," *New York Times*, June 12, 2020.

44. WFAA, "Full Video: Amber Guyger's Testimony," YouTube, September 28, 2019, https://www.youtube.com/watch?v=J7IgyPh8UkQ. Emphasis added. Quotes are from the video. Due to objections raised and sustained by the judge, some of this language is stricken from the record and will not appear in court transcripts.

45. Robin DiAngelo, *White Fragility: Why It's So Hard for White People to Talk about Racism* (Boston: Beacon Press, 2018).

46. Ibid.

47. Tanya A. Christian, "Georgia High Schoolers Won't Graduate after Posting Racist 'Cooking' Video," *Essence*, November 4, 2020.

48. Ashleigh Atwell, "White Teens Who Created Racist Black People Recipe Video Claim Going Viral Ruined Their 'Entire' Lives, Beg For Sympathy," *Atlanta Blackstar*, April 22, 2020, https://atlantablackstar.com/2020/04/22/white-teens-who-created-racist-black-people -recipe-video-claim-going-viral-ruined-their-entire-lives-beg-for-sympathy; Emma Guinness, "Racist TikTok Video Reportedly Gets High School Student's College Offer Rescinded," Vt.co, April 20, 2020, https://vt.co/news/racist-tiktok-video-reportedly-gets-high-school-students -college-offer-rescinded.

49. Christina Maxouris, "Christian Cooper Is Asking People to Stop Making Death Threats

Against the Woman Who Called the Cops on Him," CNN, May 27, 2020, https://www.cnn
.com/2020/05/27/us/amy-cooper-central-park-call-police-trnd/index.html.

50. Shaun Rabb, Alex Boyer and Tracy Delatte, "Amber Guyger Takes the Stand: I'm So
Sorry," Fox 2 Detroit News, September 27, 2019, https://www.fox2detroit.com/news/amber
-guyger-takes-the-stand-im-so-sorry

51. Cicely Tyson on *OWN Spotlight*, February 6, 2021, season 1, episode 101.

52. King, *Strength to Love*, 37.

53. Carter G. Woodson, *Mis-Education of the Negro*, 4.

54. Psalm 139:23–24 KJV.

55. Muhammad Ali, comments to UPI wire service, London, 1974.

56. Yancy, *Black Bodies, White Gazes*, 221, 220.

CHAPTER 11. Policy Matters

1. William Eggers and John O'Leary, "The Sisyphus Trap: The Rock, the Hill, and You:
How the Interplay between Systems and People in Government Generates Results," chap. 5 in
If We Can Put a Man on the Moon . . . : Getting Big Things Done in Government (Cambridge,
Mass.: Harvard Business School, 1992).

2. Barbara Tomlinson and George Lipsitz, *Insubordinate Spaces: Improvisation and the
Accompaniment for Social Justice* (Philadelphia: Temple University Press, 2019).

3. Ibid.

4. It will also be important to make sure that such policies are evenly used and distributed so
that Whites' inability to deal with allegations of racial animus is not used as a means to attack
and punish those who might call out their racist behaviors, attitudes, and beliefs.

5. Jennifer Eberhardt, *Biased: Uncovering the Hidden Prejudice That Shapes What We See,
Think, and Do* (New York: Viking, 2019), 182–186.

6. Nextdoor, Version 5.211.6, Apple App Store, accessed July 3, 2020, https://apps.apple.com
/us/app/nextdoor/id640360962?amp%3Bmt=8&ls=1.

7. "Prevent Racial Profiling," Nextdoor Help Center, accessed September 26, 2021, https://
help.nextdoor.com/s/article/Prevent-racial-profiling?language=en_US.

8. Eberhardt, *Biased*, 186.

9. Cynthia J. Finelli et al., "Utilizing Instructional Consultations to Enhance the Teaching Performance of Engineering Faculty," *Journal of Engineering Education* 97, no. 4 (2008)
397–411.

10. James Baldwin, *Notes of a Native Son* (Boston: Beacon Press, 1955), 101.

11. CNN Newsroom Transcripts, June 5, 2020, http://edition.cnn.com/TRANSCRIPTS
/2006/05/cnr.12.html.

12. Anita Chandra et al., *Toward an Initial Conceptual Framework to Assess Community
Allostatic Load: Early Themes from Literature Review and Community Analyses on the Role of
Cumulative Community Stress* (Santa Monica, Calif.: RAND, 2018), 14, https://www.rand.org
/pubs/research_reports/RR2559.html.

13. NASA, "50 Years Ago: 'Houston, We've Had a Problem,'" NASA History, April 13, 2020,
https://www.nasa.gov/feature/50-years-ago-houston-we-ve-had-a-problem.

CHAPTER 12. Tell "the Story"

1. Quoted in Michelle Alexander, *The New Jim Crow: Mass Incarceration in the Age of Color-blindness* (New York: New Press, 2012), 140. Emphasis added.

2. Kari Howard, "Nikole Hannah-Jones on Reporting about Racial Inequality: 'What Drives Me Is Rage,'" *Nieman News* (Nieman Foundation), October 26, 2017, https://nieman.harvard.edu/stories/nikole-hannah-jones-on-reporting-about-racial-inequality-what-drives-me-is-rage.

3. Adam Serwer, "The Fight over the 1619 Project Is Not about the Facts," *Atlantic*, December 23, 2019, https://www.theatlantic.com/ideas/archive/2019/12/historians-clash-1619-project/604093.

4. Stanley Fish, *There's No Such Thing as Free Speech . . . and It's a Good Thing, Too* (New York: Oxford University Press, 1994.

5. Katie Robertson, "Nikole Hannah-Jones Denied Tenure at University of North Carolina," *New York Times*, May 19, 2021.

6. Ian Gordon, "Nikole Hannah-Jones Finally Has Been Granted Tenure. But the Damage Is Already Done," *MoJo Wire* (*Mother Jones*), June 30, 2021, https://www.motherjones.com/mojo-wire/2021/06/nikole-hannah-jones-unc-chapel-hill-tenure-hussman-1619-project.

7. Laura Wamsley, "After Tenure Controversy, Nikole Hannah-Jones Will Join Howard Faculty Instead of UNC," NPR, July 6, 2021.

8. Gordon, "Nikole Hannah-Jones Finally Has Been Granted Tenure."

9. See Ivy Scott and Jack Lyons, "Black Women Are Largely Shut out of Coveted Tenure-Track Positions at Mass. Colleges and Universities," *Boston Globe,* July 1, 2021, citing national statistics on Black faculty.

10. Zawadi Rucks-Ahidiana, "The Systemic Scarcity of Tenured Black Women," *Inside Higher Ed*, July 16, 2021, https://www.insidehighered.com/advice/2021/07/16/black-women-face-many-obstacles-their-efforts-win-tenure-opinion.

11. "Noted Journalist Got Knight Chair, Did Not Get Tenure," *Carolina Alumni Review*, May 20, 2021, https://alumni.unc.edu/news/noted-journalist-got-knight-chair-did-not-get-tenure.

12. Shawn Langlois, "Fox News Host Laura Ingraham Famously Told LeBron James to 'Shut up and Dribble'—So What's Her Take on Drew Brees?," *MarketWatch*, June 5, 2020.

13. Martin Luther King Jr., *Why We Can't Wait* (1964; repr., New York: Signet, 2001), 109.

14. Paul Laurence Dunbar, "Sympathy," from *The Complete Poems of Paul Laurence Dunbar* (New York: Dodd, Mead, 2004).

15. Maya Angelou, *I Know Why the Caged Bird Sings* (1969; repr., New York: Chelsea House, 2019).

16. James Baldwin, *The Price of the Ticket: Collected Nonfiction, 1948–1985* (London: Joseph, 1985), 227.

17. Sarah Maslin Nir, "White Woman Is Fired after Calling Police on Black Man in Central Park," *New York Times*, May 26, 2020.

18. Katie Kindelan and Sabina Ghebremedhin via GMA, "Botham Jean's Brother on Courtroom Hug with Amber Guyger: 'She Still Deserves Love,'" ABC News, October 4, 2019,

https://abcnews.go.com/GMA/News/botham-jeans-brother-discusses-emotional-courtroom
-hug-amber/story?id=66055688.

19. Trymaine Lee, "The 911 Call that Led to Jonathan Ferrell's Death," MSNBC, September 17, 2013, http://www.msnbc.com/msnbc/the-911-call-led-jonathan-ferrells

20. Mark Berman, "I Forgive You: Relatives of Charleston Church Shooting Victims Tell Dylann Roof," *Washington Post*, June 19, 2015.

21. Ben Quinn, "Man Rescued by UK Black Lives Matter Protester Is Ex-Police Officer," *Guardian*, June 18, 2020.

22. Howard, "Nikole Hannah-Jones on Reporting about Racial Inequality."

23. T. D. Jakes, *Crushing: God Turns Pressure into Power* (New York: Faith Words, 2019), 81.

24. "Protester Stares Down Angry White Man in Powerful Image," *CBS This Morning*, June 9, 2020, https://www.cbsnews.com/video/protester-stares-down-angry-white-man-in-powerful-image.

25. "Jay Pharoah Says Police Put a 'Knee on My Neck' during Unlawful Run In," *The Talk*, CBS, June 15, 2020 https://ms-my.facebook.com/TheTalkCBS/videos/612577569375921.

26. "Jay Pharoah Tells Gayle King about Being Stopped by Police," CBS News, June 16, 2020, https://www.cbsnews.com/news/jay-pharoah-snl-tells-gayle-king-about-being-stopped-by-police-and-an-officer-kneeling-on-his-neck.

27. "Jay Pharoah Says 'Sorry' from LAPD Cops Who Forcibly Detained Him with Guns Drawn Is 'Not Enough,'" CBS News, June 17, 2020, https://www.cbsnews.com/news/jay-pharoah-lapd-detained-sorry.

28. Sadie Whitelocks, "What Did the TSA Expect to Find in Solange Knowles' Afro? Singer Tweets Her Outrage after Airport Staff Searched Her Hair," *DailyMail.com*, November 16, 2012, https://www.dailymail.co.uk/femail/article-2234199/What-did-TSA-expect-Solange-Knowles-afro-Singer-tweets-outrage-airport-staff-searched-hair.html.

29. "Moms Mabley," Biography.com, https://www.biography.com/performer/moms-mabley. Mabley was born Loretta Mary Aiken in Brevard, North Carolina. The year of her birth is not known. It is believed to be either 1894 or 1897.

30. *Moms Mabley: I Got Somethin' to Tell You* (Whoop/One Ho Productions, 2013).

31. Barbara Tomlinson and George Lipsitz, *Insubordinate Spaces: Improvisation and the Accompaniment for Social Justice* (Philadelphia: Temple University Press, 2019); Rebecca Louise Carter, *Prayers for the People: Homicide and Humanity in the Crescent City* (Chicago: University of Chicago Press, 2019).

32. Tomlinson and Lipsitz, *Insubordinate Space*, 2019.

33. Carter, *Prayers for the People*, 2019.

34. Ibid., 2.

35. Patricia Hill Collins, *Black Feminist Thought: Knowledge, Consciousness, and the Politics of Empowerment* (New York: Routledge, 2000), 123, 124.

36. Roxanne Gay, *Hunger: A Memoir of (My) Body* (New York: HarperCollins, 2016), 1.

37. *Any Day Now*, season 1, episode 15, "Blue," directed by Artie Mandelberg, aired January 5, 1999, on Lifetime.

38. Bobby Jindal, "Kamala Harris's American Example," *Wall Street Journal*, October 6, 2020.

39. Isabel Wilkerson, *Caste: The Origins of Our Discontents* (New York: Random House, 2020), 54.

40. Joan Morgan, *When Chickenheads Come Home to Roost: A Hip Hop Feminist Breaks It Down* (New York: Simon & Schuster, 2000), 52.

41. Andrew Greif, "Doc Rivers," *Los Angeles Times*, August 25, 2020.

INDEX

www.ingramcontent.com/pod-product-compliance
Lightning Source LLC
Chambersburg PA
CBHW010114270326
41929CB00023B/3348